EVELYN WAUGH

A *WRITERS AND THEIR WORK* SPECIAL

Evelyn Waugh as the Dean of Scone College in *The Scarlet Woman*, 1926.
© Harry Ransom Center, The University of Texas at Austin.

WW

EVELYN WAUGH

Ann Pasternak Slater

NORTHCOTE
BRITISH COUNCIL

This paperback edition first published in 2018 by
Liverpool University Press
4 Cambridge Street
Liverpool L69 7ZU
UK
www.liverpooluniversitypress.co.uk

on behalf of
Northcote House Publishers Ltd
Mary Tavy
Devon PL19 9PY
UK

British Library Cataloguing-in-Publication Data
A catalogue record for this book is available from the British Library

ISBN 978-0-7463-0822-6 paperback

Typeset by PDQ Typesetting, Newcastle-under-Lyme
Printed and bound by CPI Group (UK) Ltd, Croydon, CR0 4YY

Contents

Acknowledgements

It is an exciting time to be working on Waugh. In the last decade two people have brought about a change in Waugh's public status. Most recently, and with the energy, charm, and robust ebullience of his father and grandfather, Alexander Waugh conceived and achieved the massive project of producing Waugh's *Complete Works* – all forty-two volumes of them, to be published by OUP in association with Leicester University, under the leadership of David Bradshaw and Martin Stannard. They will be the definitive monument to Waugh's literary achievements and paradoxical personality. Secondly, over many years, the late John H. Wilson quietly fostered a growing, cohesive community of Waugh students and admirers. Under his guidance the Evelyn Waugh Society was transformed into a uniquely democratic scholarly forum where all Waugh aficionados, not merely or exclusively academic, found a deserved welcome. In 2003 he launched the first Evelyn Waugh Conference, at Hertford College, Oxford, on the centenary of Waugh's birth, where many of us met for the first time. We all share a profound debt of gratitude to these very different, but equally tireless pioneers.

No one working on Waugh can escape reliance on the preceding half-century's editors, scholars, and biographers who prepared the ground for this efflorescence. I have been most enlightened by the work of the founding fathers, Donat Gallagher and R. M. Davis. Richard Oram has been unstinting in his help with the Evelyn Waugh collection at the Harry Ransom Center, Texas. Chip Long and John Hirsh were scrupulous guides to Catholic questions. With characteristic critical acuity and attention to detail, Alexander Waugh, John Howard Wilson and my husband, Craig Raine, read and emended my final drafts.

Other kind friends helped in their special ways. Julian Barnes bravely let me loose on his collection of Waugh's first editions. Frances Stonor Saunders introduced me to old family friends of Waugh. Clare Asquith and Raymond Asquith invited me to read Waugh's correspondence with his godson. William Boyd's films of *Scoop* and *Sword of Honour*, and the images in Duncan McLaren's *Rhapsody for an Obsessive Love*, were inspirations of quite another, creative kind. The author and publisher are grateful to The Wylie Agency and Penguin Random House UK for their kind permission to quote from the works of Evelyn Waugh listed on pp. 315–6.

Biographical Outline

1903   28 October: Evelyn Waugh, second son to Arthur and Catherine Waugh, is born at 11 Hillfield Road, West Hampstead.

1907   First lessons from his mother, at home. Family moves to 'Underhill', 145 North End Road, Golders Green.

1909   First literary composition, 'The Curse of the Horse Race'.

1910   Attends Heath Mount Preparatory School, Hampstead.

1911   Begins his first diary, and short stories composed of succinctly titled drawings, a child's comic-strips.

1915   His brother Alec leaves Sherborne School on grounds of homosexuality. Evelyn's future place is also forfeit.

1917   In May enters Lancing College, Sussex, a traditionally High Church, minor public school. Alec's successful novel, *The Loom of Youth*, based on Sherborne, published in July.

1922   January: Enters Hertford College, Oxford, as a Scholar reading History. Contributes graphics, reviews, reports and short fiction to university magazines.

1924   Leaves Oxford with a third class degree. Begins novel, *The Temple at Thatch*. Makes silent film, *The Scarlet Woman*. Joins Heatherley's Art School, London (September).

1925   Schoolmaster at Arnold House, Llanddulas, Denbighshire (January–July). Destroys *The Temple at Thatch* on Harold Acton's criticism. Attempts suicide. Writes 'The Balance', his first notable piece of fiction. In September begins teaching at Aston Clinton, Berkshire.

1926	*P. R. B.: An Essay on the Pre-Raphaelite Brotherhood 1847–1854* is privately printed, and 'The Balance' published in a collection of short stories edited by his brother Alec.
1927	Sacked from Aston Clinton (February). Contributing to *The Daily Express*. Meets Evelyn Gardner (April). Writes *Rossetti, His Life and Works*. Takes carpentry lessons. Proposes to Evelyn Gardner (December).
1928	Begins writing *Decline and Fall*. *Rossetti* published (April). Marries Evelyn Gardner (June). *Decline and Fall* published (September).
1929	Mediterranean cruise with his wife (February–March). *Vile Bodies* begun. Marriage breaks down (July). Divorce (September).
1930	*Vile Bodies* published (January). Is received into the Roman Catholic Church (27 September). *Labels, A Mediterranean Journey* is published. Travels to Abyssinia to report the coronation of Haile Selassie for *The Times* (October–December); further travels in East and Central Africa.
1931	Returns to England (March). *Remote People*, the African travel book, is completed (August) and published (November); *Black Mischief* is begun in September.
1932	*Black Mischief* completed (June) and published (October). Sails for British Guiana (December).
1933	Travels in British Guiana and Brazil (January–May). Writes 'The Man Who Liked Dickens', deriving from his Brazilian experiences (February). Meets 'white mouse named Laura' Herbert at Herbert family home in Italy (September). Writes *Ninety-Two Days*, the Brazilian travel book (October–November).
1934	Winters in Fez, Morocco, and begins *A Handful of Dust* (January–February). *Ninety-Two Days* published (March) and *A Handful of Dust* completed (April). Expedition to Spitzbergen in the Arctic (July–August). *A Handful of Dust* published (September). Begins *Edmund Campion: Jesuit and Martyr* (September).
1935	Completes *Campion* (May). Travels to Abyssinia to report on imminent Italian invasion for *The Daily Mail* (August–December).
1936	Writes *Waugh in Abyssinia* (April–October). Pilgrimage

to Lough Derg; annulment of first marriage agreed by Rome (July); engagement to Laura Herbert. Returns to Abyssinia to report on Italian occupation (July–September). *Waugh in Abyssinia* published. *Scoop* begun (October).

1937   Marriage to Laura Herbert (17 April); honeymoon in Italy. Decides to rewrite *Scoop* (July). The couple move into Piers Court, Stinchcombe, Gloucestershire (August).

1938   Birth of daughter, Teresa (March) *Scoop* published (May). Two trips, both with Laura: to Hungary (May), and Mexico (August–October) to collect material for *Robbery Under Law: The Mexican Object-Lesson.*

1939   Completes *Robbery Under Law*; begins work on a new novel, later called *Work Suspended. Robbery Under Law* published (June). Britain and France declare war on Germany (September 3). Birth of son, Auberon (November). Joins Royal Marines (December) and abandons *Work Suspended.*

1940   Training with the Marines. Expedition to Dakar, West Africa (August–September). Transfers to Commandos in Scotland (November). Birth and death of daughter Mary (1 December).

1941   Sails for service with Commandos in Egypt (February); raid on Bardia (April). At Battle of Crete (27–31 May). Disillusioned with the war. July–August, on circuitous sea-journey home, writes *Put Out More Flags*. Rejoins Royal Marines (September).

1942   *Put Out More Flags* published. Transfers to Special Service Brigade; birth of daughter Margaret (June). *Work Suspended* published (December).

1943   Is transferred to Combined Operations HQ, London (March). Father dies (26 June). Enforced resignation from Special Service Brigade (17 July).

1944   Given leave to write *Brideshead Revisited* (January–June). Birth of daughter Harriet (May). On Allied Military Mission to Yugoslavia (from July).

1945   Returns from Yugoslavia (March). Germany surrenders. Begins *Helena* and *Brideshead Revisited* is published (May). He is demobbed and returns to Piers Court.

1946	Travels to Nuremberg for the Trials (March) and to Spain (June). Writes novella, 'Scott-King's Modern Europe', and *Wine in Peace and War*.
1947	With Laura, visits New York and Los Angeles to discuss projected film of *Brideshead Revisited* (January–March). Much taken by Forest Lawn Memorial Park; on return to England writes first draft of *The Loved One* (May–July). Birth of son James (June). Visits Scandinavia (August–September).
1948	*The Loved One* published (February). Begins lecture tour in USA (October).
1949	Returns from America (March). 'Compassion', deriving from his wartime experiences in Yugoslavia, is published (August).
1950	*Helena* finished (March). Birth of Septimus, his and Laura's last child (July). *Helena* published (September). Evelyn and Laura's last visit to America (October).
1951	Middle East tour with Christopher Sykes for *Life Magazine* (January–March). Writes *Men at Arms* (June–December).
1952	Writes *The Holy Places* (based on Middle East tour); writes his futuristic dystopia, *Love Among the Ruins*. *Men at Arms* published (September). Christmas in Goa.
1953	Illustrating *Love Among the Ruins* (January), which is published in April. Starts work on second novel of the war trilogy, currently titled *Happy Warriors*, later to become *Officers and Gentlemen* (March). Is interviewed at Piers Court by Stephen Black for the BBC's Overseas Service programme, 'Personal Call' (August), and in London for the BBC's 'Frankly Speaking' (September, and October). Depression and lethargy; rheumatism, insomnia, and over-medication.
1954	Voyage to Ceylon and mental breakdown (February), aural hallucinations probably attributable to bromide poisoning. Once recuperated, finishes *Officers and Gentlemen* (November). Death of his mother (December).
1955	Trip to Jamaica, begins and abandons *The Ordeal of Gilbert Pinfold* (January). *Officers and Gentlemen* published (May). Planning to sell Piers Court and move away from encroaching urban sprawl.

1956   Buys Combe Florey House, near Taunton, Somerset and resumes work on *Pinfold* (September). The Waughs move to their new home in December.

1957   *Pinfold* completed (January) and published (July). Wins his case against Beaverbook Newspapers (February). First plans for *Unconditional Surrender* (July). Spends several periods (also with Laura) looking after Ronald Knox, who dies in August.

1958   Travels to Rhodesia researching Knox's biography. Son Auberon is seriously wounded during military service in Cyprus; Laura flies out to be with him (June).

1959   Travels in Rhodesia (January to April). *The Life of the Right Reverend Ronald Knox* published (October).

1960   Begins work on final volume of the war trilogy, later titled *Unconditional Surrender* (April). Revised Edition of *Brideshead Revisited* published (July). *A Tourist in Africa* (drawing on the previous year's travel) is published in September.

1961   *Unconditional Surrender* finished (April) and published (October). Trip to West Indies with his daughter Margaret (November–February 1962).

1962   Begins work on his autobiography (July).

1964   Serial publication of the first, and only completed volume of his autobiography, *A Little Learning* (June–July).

1965   Is much distressed by reforms to the Roman Catholic liturgy instituted by the Second Vatican Council. *Sword of Honour*, the single-volume recension of the war trilogy, is published in September.

1966   Waugh dies at Combe Florey on Easter Day, 10 April, after attending Mass in Latin in the morning. Laura dies in 1973.

Abbreviations

Unless otherwise specified, I have referred to Waugh's first editions, published by Chapman and Hall, London. Abbreviations denoting frequently cited texts are listed below. In quotations from Waugh's texts ellipses in square brackets [...] signify my cuts; Waugh's own ellipses appear as they stand. Quotations from the Bible come from the Authorized Version (1611). Within each chapter, unattributed page numbers refer to the novel discussed in that chapter.

ALL	*A Little Learning, The First Volume of an Autobiography* (1964)
AMS	authorial manuscript (held at Harry Ransom Center, Texas)
BM	*Black Mischief* (1932)
BR	*Brideshead Revisited* (Revised Uniform Edition, 1960)
D	*The Diaries of Evelyn Waugh*, ed. Michael Davie (London: Weidenfeld & Nicolson, 1976)
DF	*Decline and Fall* (1928)
EAR	*The Essays, Articles and Reviews of Evelyn Waugh*, ed. Donat Gallagher (London: Methuen, 1983)
HD	*A Handful of Dust* (1934)
Helena	*Helena* (1950)
Holy Places	*The Holy Places* (London: Queen Anne Press, 1952)
L	*The Letters of Evelyn Waugh*, ed. Mark Amory (London: Weidenfeld & Nicolson, 1980)
Labels	*Labels, A Mediterranean Journal* (London: Duckworth, 1930)

LO	*The Loved One* (1948)
MA	*Men at Arms* (1952)
Memoranda	'Memorandum on *Brideshead*' (1947) and 'Memorandum on *Scoop*' (1957) in 'Notes on the Film Adaptations of *Brideshead Revisited* and *Scoop*' ed. Donat Gallagher, *Areté 14* (Summer 2004), 19–29.
Mitford/Waugh	*The Letters of Nancy Mitford and Evelyn Waugh*, ed. Charlotte Mosley (London: Hodder & Stoughton, 1996)
OG	*Officers and Gentlemen* (1955)
Pinfold	*The Ordeal of Gilbert Pinfold* (1957)
POMF	*Put Out More Flags* (1942)
Rossetti	*Rossetti, His Life and Works* (1928; repr. London: Duckworth, 1975)
RP	*Remote People* (Duckworth, 1931)
RUL	*Robbery Under Law: The Mexican Object Lesson* (1939)
Scoop	*Scoop: A Novel About Journalists* (1938)
SH	*Sword of Honour: A Final Version of the Novels: Men at Arms, Officers and Gentlemen, and Unconditional Surrender* (1965)
US	*Unconditional Surrender* (1961)
VB	*Vile Bodies* (1930)
WA	*Waugh in Abyssinia* (London: Longman, Green & Co, 1936)
WS	*Work Suspended* (1942)
Wu/Stitch	*Mr Wu and Mrs Stitch: The Letters of Evelyn Waugh and Diana Cooper*, ed. Artemis Cooper (London: Hodder & Stoughton, 1991)
92 Days	*Ninety-Two Days* (London: Duckworth, 1934)

OTHER WORKS CITED

Bibliography	R. M. Davis, P. A. Doyle, D. Gallagher, C. E. Linck, W. M. Bogaards: *A Bibliography of Evelyn Waugh* (New York: Whitston, 1986)

Catalogue	R. M. Davis: *A Catalogue of the Evelyn Waugh Collection* (New York: Whitston, 1981)
Critical Heritage	Martin Stannard (ed.), *Evelyn Waugh: The Critical Heritage* (London: Routledge & Kegan Paul, 1984)
Davis: *EW, Writer*	R. M. Davis, *Evelyn Waugh, Writer* (Norman, Oklahoma: Pilgrim Books, 1981)
Donaldson	Frances Donaldson: *Portrait of a Country Neighbour* (London: Weidenfeld and Nicolson, 1968)
Gallagher: *Trimmer*	D. Gallagher, '"I am Trimmer, you know" Lord Lovat in Evelyn Waugh's *Sword of Honour*', *Evelyn Waugh Newsletter and Studies* 41 (2) (2010), 2–6
Gallagher: *Disillusion*	D. Gallagher, 'Guy Crouchback's Disillusion: Crete, Beevor, and the Soviet Alliance in *Sword of Honour*', in D. Gallagher, A. Pasternak Slater and J. H. Wilson (eds.), *'A Handful of Mischief': New Essays on Evelyn Waugh* (Madison: Fairleigh Dickinson University Press, 2011), 172–219
Gallagher: *Liquidated!*	D. Gallagher, '"Liquidated!" How Lord Lovat "Kicked Waugh Out" of the Special Service Brigade and Fantasized About It Afterwards' in Donat Gallagher and Carlos Villar Flor: *In the Picture: The Facts Behind the Fiction in Evelyn Waugh's 'Sword of Honour'* (Amsterdam and New York: Rodopi, 2014), 219–52
NS Interviews	Pre-production transcript of 21 interviews for Nicholas Shakespeare's 3-part biography, *The Waugh Trilogy*, Arena, BBC 2 (1988)

Patey	D. L. Patey, *The Life of Evelyn Waugh: A Critical Biography* (Oxford: Blackwell, 1998)
Stannard I	Martin Stannard, *Evelyn Waugh: The Early Years 1903–1939* (London: Dent, 1986)
Stannard II	Martin Stannard, *Evelyn Waugh: No Abiding City 1939–1966* (London: Dent, 1992, repr. Glasgow: HarperCollins, 1993)
Stopp	F. J. Stopp, *Evelyn Waugh: Portrait of an Artist* (Chapman & Hall, 1958)
Sykes	Christopher Sykes, *Evelyn Waugh: A Biography* (London: Collins, 1975)

Introduction

The frontispiece shows the young Waugh in a still from his only surviving film, *The Scarlet Woman – An Ecclesiastical Melodrama*. Pop-eyed and irreverent, a zany in a silly wig, he's clearly having fun impersonating the (semi-fictional, gay) Dean of Scone College. Soon after, the first novel of his divine comedy opened with a disarmingly modest nudge to the reader – *Decline and Fall* 'IS MEANT TO BE FUNNY'.

Few of Waugh's later novels are quite so light-hearted. *Brideshead Revisited* specifically contradicts the claim of his youth. His conversion to Catholicism sharpened the seriousness of his subsequent work. And yet the mischievous glint in the young Waugh's eyes is still recognizable in the ageing Pinfold's beady glare. Maverick and unpredictable, he is also the most consistent of our great English comic novelists.

Of course Waugh's temperament and even his faith developed in the course of his lifetime. His novels took an undulating path towards greater depth and complexity. His self-ironizing public persona may have hardened into a grotesque. Yet his comic impulse, his moral seriousness, and his aesthetic credo remained essentially unchanged. Uniting them was his conception of the artist's craft: to transform the chaos of his own lifetime into *significant* form. At the age of 26, he put it expansively:

> If only the amateurs would get it into their heads that novel-writing is a highly skilled and laborious trade. One does not just sit behind a screen jotting down other people's conversation. One has for one's raw material every single thing one has ever seen or heard or felt, and one has to go over that vast, smouldering rubbish-heap of experience, half stifled by the fumes and dust, scraping and delving until one finds a few discarded valuables.

1

Then one has to assemble these tarnished and dented fragments, polish them, set them in order, and try to make a coherent and significant arrangement of them. It is not merely a matter of filling up a dust-bin haphazard and emptying it out again in another place. ('People Who Want to Sue Me', May 1930, *EAR* 73)

In his middle age, this most eccentric of men put the same principle more succinctly:

I have come to the conclusion that there is no such thing as normality. That is what makes story-telling such an absorbing task, the attempt to reduce to order the anarchic raw materials of life [...] The artist's only service to the disintegrated society of today is to create little independent systems of order of his own. ('Fan-Fare', April 1946, *EAR* 303–4)

Towards the end of his life Waugh's trade secret was frankly entrusted to his heroes. *The Loved One* (1948) ends with Dennis Barlow leaving Hollywood for England, exultantly laden with Waugh's own luggage – 'the artist's load, a great, shapeless chunk of experience'. *The Ordeal of Gilbert Pinfold* (1957) ends with a comparable kindling of creative fire in Pinfold's library:

As the wood crackled and a barely perceptible warmth began to spread among the chilly shelves, Mr Pinfold sat down to work for the first time since his fiftieth birthday [...] He knew what had to be done. But there was more urgent business first, a hamper to be unpacked of fresh, rich experience – perishable goods.
He [...] spread a new quire of foolscap before him and wrote in his neat, steady hand:

> *The Ordeal of Gilbert Pinfold*
> *A Conversation Piece*
> *Chapter One*
> *Portrait of the Artist in Middle-age*

(*Pinfold* 184)

Waugh's calm admission of mortality in this late novel is poignant. The experiences of a lifetime, however good, are perishable. His task was to transform living chaos into the order of imperishable art.

Waugh's artistic credo was sustained by his habitual routine of composition. Even a cursory biographical résumé demonstrates the regular traffic between life and art. His school-mastering experiences of 1925 were recast in *Decline and Fall* (1928). Amateur film-making in 1924 and journalism for *The Daily Express* in 1927 fuelled *Vile Bodies* (1930). His secondment to Abyssinia to report on the 1930 coronation of Haile Selassie for *The Times* turned into *Black Mischief* (1932). A solo trip to British Guiana in 1932 and his first wife's desertion in 1929 were brought together in his greatest novel, *A Handful of Dust* (1934). Returning to Abyssinia to report on the Italian invasion for *The Daily Mail* in 1935 prompted the journalistic satire of *Scoop* (1938).

With Waugh's second marriage to Laura Herbert in 1937 and the outbreak of war in 1939, the pattern was inevitably interrupted, and slowed down to a broader retrospective sweep. *Work Suspended*, begun in early 1939 and abandoned when war was declared, stepped back ten years to his *tendresse* for Diana Guinness in 1929, and edged towards the winter of 1934, spent in Fez writing *A Handful of Dust*. After two years of active military service, came his satiric retrospect of England's Phoney War of 1939–40 in *Put Out More Flags* (1942). Wartime privation incubated nostalgic memories of Oxford undergraduate days in the early twenties. Their glow, juxtaposed with the chill desecration of wartime Britain, dominated the opening of *Brideshead Revisited* (1945). Waugh's postwar trip to Hollywood to negotiate the abortive film of *Brideshead* in 1947 quickly turned into *The Loved One* (1948). A final retrospect of his wartime experiences from 1941 to 1945 provided raw material for the three volumes of the *Sword of Honour* trilogy (1952, 1955, 1961; trimmed and united in a single volume in 1965). This painful nine-year marathon was interrupted by a winter trip to Ceylon in 1954, when Waugh was suffering from alcoholism and chloral poisoning, directly and brilliantly transcribed in *The Ordeal of Gilbert Pinfold* (1957). Finally, the first volume of his autobiography, *A Little Learning* (1964), completed the last of many retrospective cycles by returning to his earliest years, ending with his attempted suicide while school-mastering in Wales in 1925, where *Decline and Fall* began. Like *King Lear's* Edmund, Waugh could say, 'The wheel is come full circle; I am here.'

An interesting pattern emerges from this broad overview. In *Work Suspended* the detective writer John Plant, Waugh's authorial *alter ego*, warns his publisher that he's considering a change of style. So was Waugh. The modernistic, cinematic, anarchic, satiric-phantasmagoric template, which had served him so well until *Scoop*, no longer satisfied him. He began to develop a new kind of fiction: overtly Catholic novels written in a more traditional mode, deliberately Victorian in amplitude, measured delivery, and orotundity of diction. To this group belong *Work Suspended*, *Brideshead*, the *Sword of Honour* trilogy – and *Helena*, a historical novel, published in 1950, and omitted from my chronology above because it is only obliquely related to Waugh's own life, but which also offers a covert ironic echo of the modern world at war in the power-struggles of the Roman empire. Significantly, these six novels draw on experiences lying at a temporal distance from the author's present. When life delivered an unexpected hamper of perishable goods to his door, Waugh swooped. The great, shapeless bundle of fresh experience was pecked apart and swiftly reconfigured in Waugh's inimitable earlier manner. So we have the quickly composed satiric triumphs of *Put Out More Flags*, *The Loved One*, and *Pinfold*, that interrupted and off-set the increasingly traditional achievements of his later years.

Waugh's predatory circling over his own experience is also clear from his non-fictional *oeuvre*. Details are saved and savoured. Drily noted in the diaries. Fantastically transfigured in the letters. Toyed with and tested in travel books and reportage. Picked out, polished, transformed. And delicately placed in the novels' significant order.

For the critic focusing on Waugh's art, one trouble with literary biography is that it recovers his discards: it empties out the dustbin, patiently rummages through the rubbish, and piles it up even higher elsewhere. Another distraction is that Waugh's uniquely robust, contradictory personality attracts combative responses. Anecdotes from other people's dustbins – what Waugh ruefully called 'typical Pinfolds' – and tough personal judgements of the author are added to the heap, and trivia of creative importance are lost.

Escher stairs in Wales. Parlour games and ping-pong in Addis Ababa. A face of clay. Typing errors in the Red Sea. A case of mistaken identity in Baghdad. Water dripping from an ice-swan's beak in mid-Atlantic.

All these are treasured *trouvailles* for the dustbin man; clues to Waugh's grand designs.

1

Decline and Fall
1928

Waugh said that after affecting world-weary cynicism in his last two school terms at Lancing he was 'reborn in full youth' at Oxford. Revelry and deliberate academic idleness left room for a happy, busy life in undergraduate journalism, graphic design, reviewing Union debates, plays and films, and writing profiles and short stories. In the spring term of his second year he unapologetically introduced 'Our Children's Corner' into *The Isis*: 'We are all of us young at Oxford – (who are wise?) – and do not need a psychology text-book to cause us to yearn once more for the nursery floor'. Playful and generously moralistic, it ran for a term, ending with Uncle Alfred's final valedictory advice to his nephews and nieces to 'laugh and to preserve [...] a sense of humour. You must, of course, never ridicule anything which is good, but it is better to smile good-humouredly at a wicked action than to be resentful.' In his report of the Union's Centenary debate he singled out one speech for particular praise, identifying stylistic priorities that would characterize him for a lifetime. 'Every sentence of it had an unexpected form; every epithet was unusual; every argument twisted obliquely from its usual significance or spun inside out.'[1]

His Oxford career culminated in his sitting Finals in June 1924. He had spent most of the previous vacation not revising and between whiles reading *'Alice in Wonderland*. It is an excellent book I think' (*L* 9).[2] Not a waste of time: it was to have a marked creative impact on *Vile Bodies, Black Mischief*, and *A Handful of Dust*. However, 'as I left the Examination Schools,' he wrote in his autobiography, 'I was uneasily aware that the questions had been rather inconvenient' (*ALL* 208). His answers were ranked third-class. Discomfited, he went down from Oxford, and back up to London. The next four years of his life followed a continual series of depressing jolts up and down. In the autumn of 1924 he began, full of hope, to study art, only to decide that his life-long artistic ambitions had no foundation. He was frequently drunk. One hung-over morning, in 'the most hideous fog I ever saw [...] I ran straight into a wall and found chalked on it ARE YOU WASHED IN THE BLOOD OF THE LAMB most disturbing' (D 197). In *Decline and Fall* that question swashed into the bloody visions of Blackstone Gaol's religious maniac.

By January 1925 he had run out of money, and made a pact with his father to take up a job as a schoolmaster at Arnold House, Llanddulas, the original of Llanabba Castle in *Decline and Fall*. Here Waugh, a musical moron, gave lessons on the organ (like Paul Pennyfeather), and set his sullen boys reciting grammatical definitions – 'a syllable is a single sound made by one simple effort of the voice' (later to reappear in Paul's prison reading). He went drinking with a fellow teacher, Young, the original for Captain Grimes, who was 'monotonously pederastic and talks only of the beauty of sleeping boys' (D 211).

These details, accumulating quietly in the dustbin of the *Diaries*, began to acquire a pattern. Things started propitiously. In his first, spring term at Arnold House, Waugh began a novel. Then came the hopeful news that his writer-brother Alec might find him a secretarial job with Proust's translator in Pisa. In high hopes, Waugh sent his novel's first chapters to his Oxford friend, Harold Acton. In June he heard that the job was virtually in the bag, and handed in his resignation. A series of reversals promptly followed. Acton sent back the novel with a kindly damning response: 'Too English for my exotic taste,' he wrote. 'Too much nid-nodding over port' (*ALL* 228). It sounds like a rudimentary *Brideshead*. Waugh burned it in the school boiler. At the same time the Pisa job fell through.

The extent of Waugh's depression emerges clearly from his diary. 'At the moment I can see no sort of comfort anywhere,' he wrote. 'I think that the proprietor would be quite unwilling to take me back even if I wanted to return. I can scarcely expect my poor father to give me any more money. The phrase "the end of the tether" besets me with unshakable persistence all the time'

(*D* 213). He tried to kill himself. One moonlit night he went down to the nearby beach, left a quotation from Euripides with his pile of clothes, and swam out to sea. A swarm of jellyfish turned him back. 'As earnest of my intent,' he wryly recalled, 'I had brought no towel. With some difficulty I dressed [...] Then I climbed the sharp hill that led to all the years ahead.' These were the last words of his autobiography (*ALL* 230).

That upbeat retrospect from the end of Waugh's creative life to its beginning is significantly simplified. Three years of continued vicissitudes intervened between his failed suicide and the triple triumphs of 1928 – the publication of *Rossetti, His Life and Works* (April), his marriage to Evelyn Gardner (June), and the publication of *Decline and Fall* in September. Yet the sense of abrupt oscillation, of fall transformed to rise, and rise as swiftly toppling into fall, constantly recurs in the *Diaries* of this time. Meditating on his colleague Young's confessed past, Waugh notes:

> He was expelled from Wellington, sent down from Oxford, and forced to resign his commission in the army. He has left four schools precipitately, three in the middle of term through his being taken in sodomy and one through his being drunk six nights in succession. And yet he goes on getting better and better jobs without difficulty. It was all very like Bruce and the spider.[3] (*D* 213)

A couple of days earlier we find the telling collocation: 'I debate the simple paradoxes of suicide and achievement, work out the scheme for a new book, and negotiate with the man Young to buy a revolver from him' (*D* 211). Most telling of all is the architectural oddity he encountered every day, going up and down the stairs of Arnold House, and described in almost identical words in his autobiography (222), *Diaries* (200), and *Letters* (21). 'There are three pitch pine stair cases,' he tells his mother. 'The house is on a hill with the perplexing result that one goes in at one door, climbs two stories & then on looking out of a window finds that one is on the ground floor again.'

What are 'the simple paradoxes of suicide and achievement' symbolized so neatly by Bruce's spider, Young, and the stairs of Arnold House? They are, of course, the swift rotations of Fortune's wheel, a predominantly negative image familiar to the most illiterate Elizabethan. Fortune turned her wheel and the great fell from power; in modern terms, you climb flight after flight of stairs, only to find yourself on the ground floor again. However, in Waugh's sanguine handling the emblem takes a more positive turn, and death and disaster become the natural precursors of resurrection and rebirth. Waugh plunged into the sea to die, only to rise, refreshed, and climb the hill to the years ahead. So too he celebrated his own fall in the dominant scheme of his new book, which began his rise as a writer, and which was called, of course, *Decline and Fall*.

THE BIG WHEEL

As the novel ends, Waugh ventriloquizes its message rather artlessly through Professor Silenus. Life, Silenus tells us, is like the Big Wheel at Luna Park –

> 'You pay five francs and go into a room with tiers of seats all round, and in the centre the floor is made of a great disc of polished wood that revolves quickly. At first you sit down and watch the others. They are all trying to sit in the wheel, and they keep getting flung off, and that makes them laugh, and you laugh too. It's great fun.' (*DF* 277)

It doesn't sound much like life, says Paul sadly. Oh yes it is, says Silenus – the static people of life are the observers in the ringside seats. The dynamic ones are those who keep climbing back on the wheel, only to get thrown off again. Of course there are differences of degree between the static and dynamic. As Silenus says, Paul is a static who got on the wheel by accident: by the end of the novel he's resumed his natural place at the ringside with his own kind – dim academics with names like Potts, Stubbs and Sniggs. There are others who shouldn't be on the wheel at all, who hang on giddily for a couple of revolutions, only to be flung off and disappear – life's losers like Prendergast and little Lord Tangent. Then there are those who choose to clamber back again and again – resilient survivors like Grimes, Philbrick, Doctor Fagan and Margot Metroland, who embrace every fiasco with gusto and thrive on disaster.

It is typical of Waugh's ingenuity that he should disguise the banality of his central symbol by simply turning it on its side. Fortune's wheel is a cliché. Laid flat, it turns into a modern fairground ride. In fact both images are variants on the familiar Christian cycles of birth, death and resurrection – exploited here with the irreverent optimism of Waugh's youth.

The pivotal example of this cycle is, of course, Paul Pennyfeather himself. Debagged by the drunken rioters of the Bollinger Club, he's unjustly sent down from Scone College, loses his inheritance, and is driven, like Waugh, to teaching in Wales. When Margot Beste-Chetwynde, a pupil's millionairess mother, decides to marry him, the gutter press celebrate his meteoric rise from nobody to socialite star. But just as Paul raises his glass to 'Fortune, a much-maligned lady', the police drag him off as a white slave trader. In prison he surrenders his silver cigar-piercer and bridegroom's morning suit for a baptismal bath and anonymous uniform. Paul is cathartically exhilarated by this stripping away of all he once was. His name is changed to a number, his reading matter reduced to that handbook of basic grammar ('a syllable is a single sound...'). Then Fortune, remorselessly benign, turns her wheel again. The toast is repeated as Margot rescues Paul from prison and engineers his fabricated death in a sham nursing home. Recuperating abroad, his death is constantly stressed. 'It was odd being dead' is repeated twice in a single paragraph (*DF* 206). He returns to Scone College and resumes his studious life under his original name. None of his tutors recognize him – he is the cipher he always was.

The double helix of rise and fall is the inscribed DNA of the entire novel, and the undulating sweep of Paul's life is its central example. In the manner perfected here and recurrent in the rest of Waugh's work, the novel's central design is concurrently redeployed in a number of diversifying parallels. Grimes's past history mirrors that of his original, Young.[4] He's sacked from one job after another for unmentionable crimes (indubitably homosexuality), but the system can't let an old Harrovian down. At Llanabba Castle he lands in the soup again and extricates himself by proposing to the headmaster's atrocious daughter, Flossie. In a chapter tellingly titled 'The Agony of Captain Grimes', not noticeably Christ-like, he suffers the agony in the garden before the crucifixion of marriage. At this, his lowest point, comes the offer of a fantastic job beer-tasting for the Clutterbuck brewery, his catamite pupil's family firm. The temptation is too strong. Grimes 'dies' in a fake suicide – and pops up again, with his old wooden leg and a new red wig, overseeing Margot's brothel business in South America. He resurfaces again as a convict in the penal colony at Egdon Heath and vanishes once more, leaving his hat floating on the sluggish waters of Egdon Mire. 'It seems to me it's time Grimes flitted off to another clime,' he confesses to Paul, just before his passing. He is a life force, migratory and indestructible as the swallow.

As is Philbrick. Conman and impersonator, he first appears as Llanabba Castle's butler, disappears to escape arrest for fraud, and crops up again in the coveted post of Reception Bath Cleaner at Blackstone Gaol. He's last glimpsed as 'Arnold Bennett' in a limousine. Throughout the novel he regales characters with tales of his past, all marked by delusions of grandeur and the expiation of former crimes, all tracing the Christian trajectory of *felix culpa*, the happy fault, the regenerative fall. He is a Russian prince in exile; a retired burglar, a failed novelist, a fallen ship-owner, Sir Solomon Philbrick, and, doing time in Blackstone Gaol, 'the Governor's brother: Sir Solomon Lucas-Dockery [. . .] 'Ere for arson. Burnt a castle in Wales. You can see he's a toff' (*DF* 233).

Even the much-married Margot, phoning Paul before their wedding, has a change of identity: 'I'm terribly well. I'm at home having luncheon in my bedroom and feeling, my dear, I can't tell you how virginal, really and truly completely debutante.' A miracle! Doctor Fagan, the headmaster of Llanabba Castle, also abandons his failing school to reappear as the proprietor of the shady nursing home where Paul dies to be reborn. Most telling is Fagan's exhilaration at the school's looming sports day. Despite fourteen years of repeated disasters, it repeatedly rises phoenix-like from its ashes, and Fagan looks forward 'to each new fiasco with the utmost relish.'

In sharp contrast to these self-renewing survivors are those who rashly mount the wheel to hang on briefly and giddily before being flung off forever. Prendergast is Paul's ineffectual schoolmaster colleague at Llanabba, improbably bewigged and ragged by the merciless boys. Dogged by failure, on his second turn around the wheel, he finds a brief haven as prison chaplain at Blackstone Gaol, till its resident homicidal maniac murders him. His macabre end is paralleled by little Lord Tangent, whom

Prendy accidentally shoots in the foot with the starting-gun at Llanabba Castle's ill-starred sports day. In a technique lifted from Ronald Firbank, Tangent's subsequent story is leaked in widely dispersed, casual asides.[5] Twenty pages after the accident, we hear his foot has swollen and turned black. Its amputation is casually mentioned ten pages further on. Within another fifty he is dead.

Interestingly, the manuscript of *Decline and Fall* shows Waugh only gradually worked out his schema in all its permutations. In the manuscript Tangent is initially called 'little Lord Water', later 'Lord St Simon'. His mother appears as 'Lady Coddington', later 'Codrington', later still 'Christendom'. It is only in the printed text that she becomes Lady Circumference, and her unhappy son is Tangent. A tangent is a line that touches the circumference of a circle but never crosses it. In other words, poor Tangent never gets on the Great Wheel at all.

In the manuscript the chapter describing Grimes and Flossie Fagan's wedding and his sudden demise is titled *Captain Grimes' marriage*, and Grimes's death is irreversibly real:

> But the holidays never did come for Captain Grimes. Two nights later as the Irish mail thundered through Llanabba station it took with it for some yards Captain Grimes' head which he had pillowed against the line. The station master who discovered the body found with it an envelope addressed to the Doctor... (*DF* AMS 71, rest of text as in *DF* 146)

In the printed text this passage is replaced by a suicide modelled on Waugh's own (the pile of clothes left on the seashore), and the chapter is titled *The Passing of a Public School Man*. The chapter recounting Grimes's second suicide in Egdon Mire is called *The Death of Captain Grimes* in the manuscript, but re-titled *The Passing of a Public School Man* (for the second time) in the printed text. The next chapter, recounting Paul's phoney death in the nursing home, is similarly called *The Death of Paul Pennyfeather* in the manuscript, but is corrected to *The Passing of Paul Pennyfeather* in the printed text. By their very repetition, these chapter headings punningly suggest Grimes and Paul on the Big Wheel, passing repeatedly before our eyes. Paul and Grimes are also both rewarded with chapters – nameless in the manuscript – titled *Resurrection* in the first edition. Poor Prendy, on the other hand, is consigned to his end in a chapter uncompromisingly titled *The Death of a Modern Churchman*. No resurrection for him.

The cumulative care shown in these slight adjustments is characteristic of Waugh's craft. The point about his schema is that, in Heraclitus's formulation, the way up and the way down are one and the same. Malign Fortune is benign, loss is gain, the last shall be first. Waugh, who boasted his lack of a musical ear, nevertheless had no difficulty in composing variations on his theme's 'simple paradoxes' with fiercely logical ingenuity. His most engaging variation comes with the heats raced on the eve of Llanabba Castle's sports day, where Clutterbuck wins by running one lap fewer than all the other boys and beating them to the finishing tape. The last comes first.

STYLE

Waugh, the great stylist, mirrors his structural pattern of rise and fall in its rhetorical equivalent – hyperbole tumbling into bathos. The note is firmly set on the first page, in the sustained single sentence describing the Bollinger club's annual gathering:

> For two days they had been pouring into Oxford: epileptic royalty from their villas of exile; uncouth peers from crumbling country seats; smooth young men of uncertain tastes from embassies and legations, illiterate lairds from wet granite hovels in the Highlands [...] all that was most sonorous of name and title was there for the beano.[6] (*DF* 2)

This mix of high rhetoric plummeting into anticlimax is frequently replayed. It is at its best in Waugh's parody of Pater's panegyric on the *Mona Lisa*, his elegy on the 'death' of Grimes, which we know is no death at all:

> Lord Tangent was dead; Mr Prendergast was dead; the time would even come for Paul Pennyfeather; but Grimes, Paul at last realized, was of the immortals. He was a life force. Sentenced to death in Flanders, he popped up in Wales; drowned in Wales, he emerged in South America; engulfed in the dark mystery of Egdon Mire, he would rise again somewhere at some time, shaking from his limbs the musty integuments of the tomb. Surely he had followed in the Bacchic train of distant Arcady [...] and taught the childish satyrs

the art of love? [...]Had he not, like some grease-caked Channel swimmer, breasted the waves of the Deluge? (*DF* 262, 265)[7]

Decline and Fall has the insouciant iconoclasm and cheerful irreverence of a young man's work. Grimes the inveterate pederast is sanitized as a pastoral figure teaching childish satyrs the art of love; Grimes the grease-caked Channel swimmer acquires the status of the Holy Spirit on the first day of Creation. 'Had he not moved unseen when the darkness covered the waters?' He inhabits a primal world beyond good and evil. It is his boast that he is 'singularly in harmony with the primitive promptings of humanity'. Similarly Margot allows Paul to serve the prison sentence she should have received, without apology or explanation. All she can say is, 'It's simply something that's going to happen'. Paul recognizes this natural law: though Margot is the white-slave trader, not he, it would be *'impossible'* (twice repeated, twice italicized) to imagine her in a prison cell.

Waugh, like Paul, can't help admiring the life force propelling these dynamic but essentially immoral characters. The negative side is shown most damningly in the bland indifference to justice Paul encounters in his college authorities and his guardian. It is more amusing and less acid in the hectic socializing of King's Thursday, where the education of Margot's son consists in spelling lessons and 'a lot to learn about the use of vodka' in cocktails; where the boy's two favourite books are Havelock Ellis (the latest sexologist) and *The Wind in the Willows;*[8] where the hostess goes to bed as her guests arrive, the gramophone records spin and the guests are still dancing at four in the morning.

After his marriage Waugh continued briefly to celebrate the heady world of the Bright Young Things. Then his wife left him.

2

Vile Bodies
1930

Waugh's marriage to Evelyn Gardner lasted just over a year. They met in 1927. In December Waugh proposed, and was accepted in one of those desultory telephone conversations that later become a dispiriting indicator of Adam and Nina's disengaged engagement in *Vile Bodies*. Six months later, the diary entries for the marriage are rather unpropitious:

> Evelyn and I began to go to Dulwich to see the pictures there but got bored waiting for the right bus so went instead to the vicar-general's office and bought a marriage licence [...]
>
> Evelyn and I were married at St Paul's, Portman Square, at 12 o'clock. A woman was typewriting on the altar. (22, 27 June 1928, D 294–5)

Lady Burghclere, Waugh's reluctant mother-in-law, confessed herself to be 'quite inexpressibly pained' by the match. But the couple were very much in love, as their friends later remembered. Pansy Lamb recalls She-Evelyn's 'tremendous warmth of manner... very lavish with darlings and dearests but really warm'.[1] For Harold Acton, 'she might have been his little sister. She was extremely like him, a rather boyish little girl'. The atmosphere in their Canonbury flat was 'that of a sparkling nursery: Blake's *Songs of Innocence* belonged there, and *Alice in Wonderland*'.[2]

In the early months of the marriage Waugh was seeing *Decline and Fall* through the press, and making money as a freelance journalist. In February 1929 he landed a free passage on a new Mediterranean cruiser – a trip intended to help his wife recuperate from German measles, and provide material for his first travel book, *Labels*. Unfortunately She-Evelyn fell ill with double pneumonia and the trip was abandoned in Egypt. After her recovery, they rejoined the cruise in Cairo and returned to England in May. Once settled in London, Waugh began work on *Vile Bodies*, pursuing the routine he had established with *Decline and Fall*, writing in a country retreat during the week, and coming home at weekends. But in July She-Evelyn confessed she was in love with another man. After an ostensibly reconciliatory fortnight together, she left him without warning. Her friends were as startled as her husband. As Pansy Lamb says,

> It came as an absolute bolt from the blue [...] One summer morning [...] I got this letter from Evelyn Gardner saying I think you ought to know that I have decided to leave Evelyn and go with John and she didn't give any real reasons and I didn't even know who John was. (*NS Interviews, Lady Pansy Lamb*, 75)

To his own parents, Waugh wrote with 'the sad & to me radically shocking news that Evelyn has gone to live with a man called Heygate', adding in a postscript, 'Evelyns defection was preceded by no kind of quarrel or estrangement. So far as I knew we were both serenely happy'. To Harold Acton, he wrote with more painful candour:

> My reasons for divorce are simply that I cannot live with anyone who is avowedly in love with someone else [...]
> I am escaping to Ireland for a weeks motor racing in the hope of finding an honourable grave.
> I have absolutely no plans for the future [...] Naturally I have done no work at all for two months.
> I did not know it was possible to be so miserable & live but I am told this is a common experience. (*L* 38–9)

In early August 1929, Waugh had come home to find his flat deserted. He only learned exactly what had happened the next morning, from the charlady. On 3 September he filed for divorce. She-Evelyn, to her credit, voluntarily took the unusual and demeaning step of standing as respondent, rather than petitioner. *Vile Bodies* was completed between September and October and published the following January. On 27 September 1930, Waugh was received into the Catholic Church.

*

15

It would be difficult to overestimate the permanent impact of these events on Waugh's spiritual, professional and personal life. His religious commitment stands behind all his subsequent work. Even when the novels are not overtly Catholic, the contemporary world's lack of faith is the butt of his satire. Emotionally, his wife's desertion was so shocking it was hard for him to approach it in his fiction. His later description of grief, in *Work Suspended*, carries a powerful personal resonance:

> For the civilised man [...] words form slowly like pus about his hurts; there are no clean wounds for him; first a numbness, then a long festering, then a scar ever ready to re-open. (*WS* 41)

In *Vile Bodies*, Waugh had to handle his hurts immediately. At the time he confessed that his efforts to finish it were 'infinitely difficult [...] It all seems to shrivel up & rot internally' (*L* 39). Consequently, the novel is often considered broken-backed – a comic romp that turns into a sour flop. The up-beat film adaptation, *Bright Young Things* (directed by Stephen Fry, 2003), took the last chapter's ironically titled 'Happy Ending' literally. Its soppy finale made nonsense of this, the first of Waugh's two grimmest novels. (The other is *A Handful of Dust*.)

However, it is clear that Waugh already disapproved of his times, a disapprobation which was not, originally, personally motivated. Some months before the breakup, he published an article on 'The War and the Younger Generation'. Its bleak view of his own, post-war Younger Set is central to *Vile Bodies*. Wartime rationing and ersatz food substitutes, he says, created an appetite for sham. Indulgence in education spread the rot, and the lack of an identifiable ethical discipline to resist led to moral chaos in the post-war generation:

> It is absurd to blame them if, after being nurtured on margarine and 'honey sugar', they turn instinctively to the second-rate in art and life [...]
>
> Their crude little opinions were treated with respect. Preachers in the chapel week after week entrusted the future to their hands. It is hardly surprising that they were Bolshevik at 18 and bored at 20 [...] Freedom produces sterility. There was nothing left for the younger generation to rebel against, except the widest conceptions of mere decency [...] The result in many cases is the perverse and aimless dissipation chronicled daily by the gossip-writers of the press. ('The War and the Younger Generation', April 1929, *EAR* 62)

Waugh's revulsion against the contemporary craving for sham fills *Labels*, his first travel book, based on his Mediterranean cruise with his wife, which he finished directly after *Vile Bodies*. Very early in the text he comments explicitly on his key term:

> There is a word, 'bogus' which I have heard used a great deal with various and often inconsistent implications. It seems to me that this scrap of jargon, in every gradation of meaning, every innuendo, every allusion and perversion and 'bluff' it is capable of bearing [expresses] the essence of modern Paris. (*Labels* 17)

The false, the phoney and the mendacious tout for the tourist trade all round the Mediterranean, from bogus religious dancers in Egypt to a pretentious Parisian sculpture by Cocteau, which Waugh dismissed in a stinging coinage as 'the apotheosis of bogosity' (*Labels* 20).

BOGOSITY

In the novel, Waugh's animus is primarily directed against London, not Paris. In *Vile Bodies*, 'bogus' is the Bright Young Things' buzzword, often ineptly applied. 'This word "bogus" they all use...' (as Father Rothschild notices) is delicately nudged into the reader's subliminal awareness by ten economically dispersed repetitions of Adam's 'bogus' and 'not bogus' drunken major; a *nouveau-riche* socialite ('the *most* bogus man ...rather sweet really'); bogus tickets, flags, social clubs – and (significantly) marriage. 'I do feel that marriage ought to *go on* – for quite a long time, I mean [...] otherwise it's all rather bogus, isn't it?' Actually, if not literally, it is ubiquitous: there are multiple varieties of hoax and bluff, the phoney and the fictional, lies and evasions. The novel even opens, most appropriately, with its own apotheosis of bogosity – the appearance of Mrs Melrose Ape, Revivalist evangelist, as a phoney *deus ex machina* (in Greek tragedy, a god lowered by a crane to resolve the plot). Her machine, a dusty Packard car, dangles from a crane above the hold of a Channel steamer, but Mrs Ape is resolutely earthbound, striding up the gangplank at the head of a chorus-line of despondent 'angels', their wings packed in little violin cases. Their roll-call leaps directly from Faith to Charity, Fortitude, Chastity... There is no Hope.

Chastity is sick below decks, and Creative Endeavour has lost her wings talking to a gentleman in the train.

Mrs Ape's satiric original, Aimée Semple McPherson, had appeared before an audience of ten thousand in the Royal Albert Hall in late October 1928. (A flop. She harvested a measly 40 converts and cancelled her week's booking after two nights.) Faith-healer, hot-gospeller, speaker-in-tongues, first owner of her own broadcasting company, she was – at least in America – a supremely successful self-publicist. She toured the continent in her 'Gospel Car,' a 1912 Packard, attracting three husbands, vast audiences, thousands of converts, and massive wealth. As with-it as Waugh, in one of her dramatized Sunday sermons she recreated her recent, minor flying accident as her 'Heavenly Aeroplane'. *Vanity Fair* published a set of cut-out doll's dresses in her image, unkindly adding a double-bed-with-microphone, and a collecting hat labelled 'No Coins Please' (the actual injunction at her mass services). As Waugh says of Mrs Ape, 'She was nothing if not "magnetic"'. The compliment is literal. 'She kind of draws it out of you,' a fleeced audience member on the Channel crossing admits ruefully.

In retrospect, it becomes clear that Waugh deliberately peppered the novel's very first page with a variety of shams to set his leitmotif ringing. Before the mercenary Mrs Ape even appears, we're introduced to the omniscient Father Rothschild, another dubious divine, carrying an imitation crocodile hide suitcase, stamped with someone else's initials in Gothic script, and containing a false beard. His face resembles 'plaster reproductions of the gargoyles of Notre Dame [...] tinted the colour of "Old Ivory"'.

Tourist tat, fluid identities, disguises and fancy dress are all variants on the common theme of the bogus.[3] On the choppy Channel crossing Father Rothschild's false beard is quickly paralleled by two seasick dowagers, supine in their bunks, 'rigid from wig to toe'. Simon Balcairn, failed gossip-columnist, gatecrashes Margot Metroland's party as an imposing plenipotentiary in a false beard and fake court insignia. He is rapidly unmasked, and subsequently kills himself. 'Oh Nina, *what a lot of parties*,' Adam says in the novel's most quoted passage:

(...Masked parties, Savage parties, Victorian parties. Greek parties, Wild West parties, Russian parties, Circus parties [...] parties in flats

18

and studios and houses and ships and hotels and night clubs, in windmills and swimming-baths [...] – all that succession and repetition of massed humanity...Those vile bodies...) (*VB* 132–3)

Waugh's list is almost pedantic in its historic accuracy. In July 1928 Norman Hartnell's elaborate Circus party trumped the Bath party at St George's Swimming Baths (where everyone came in bathing suits), and the Thames Boat party (where guests came as stokers). *No Matrimonial Hoofing* was stipulated at the Wild West Party of March 1929. At the Sailor Party everyone was dressed as a matelot except Raymond Mortimer, who appeared as a sponge bag. Finally, in July 1929, a society photographer snapped Waugh with his wife at a Tropical Party, uneasily kitted out in pith helmets and safari suits during the fortnight of their attempted reconciliation. Another gossip columnist's party snap had first alerted Waugh to his wife's infidelity. No wonder he turned the contemporary mania for fancy-dress parties into a sign of his time's malaise.

In the same sad fortnight, Waugh was press-ganged into another scam, the Bruno Hat hoax. Hat was a fictional German artist of sub-sub-Picassoesque abstracts, on cork bath mats with rope frames. Some were painted by Brian Howard, a Bright Young Thing in Waugh's circle. The parodic catalogue, 'Approach to Hat', was written by Waugh. The exhibition opened with Tom Mitford as Hat in a wheelchair, tinted glasses and drooping false moustache. All went well until he was bearded by Maurice Bowra in voluble German. The hoax flopped, and Howard's hopes of making his reputation as a real artist were dashed.[4]

Waugh transposes the Hat hoax directly to Adam's successful gossip column for the *Daily Excess*. First of Adam's inventions is Provna, phantasmal sculptor son of a Polish nobleman, whose works, like those of Hat, Howard and Cocteau, are bogus constructions in cork, vulcanite and steel. As in the later *Scoop*, journalism's fictions come true, and soon 'a steady output of Provnas began to travel from Warsaw to Bond Street and from Bond Street to California', where Mrs Hoop (clearly Brian Howard's adoring American mother) boasts that Provna is sculpting her son. Further fantastical fads are foisted on the gullible public. 'With sultanesque caprice,' Adam persuades his readers to dance in temperance hotels in Bloomsbury and dine in the snack bar at Sloane Square Tube Station. Adam's only failure is Waugh's mocking replay of another notorious journalistic promotion, the *Daily Mail* hat. In 1920 Lord Northcliffe, the *Mail*'s proprietor, introduced a series of 'talking-points' to expand the paper's circulation.[5] The *Mail*'s Sandringham, a high, oval-crowned hybrid half-way between topper and bowler, was invented, manufactured and promoted by the paper in vain. It didn't catch on. Nor did Adam's story about London's latest fashion, a bottle-green bowler whose very existence was immediately denied by the city hatters.

At this stage in *Vile Bodies*, Adam's bogus journalistic lies are harmlessly ingenious and Waugh's tone light-hearted. The current consensus is that Waugh's marriage broke down half-way through the composition of chapter 6. In any case he would certainly have cast backwards and forwards to sustain the motifs disseminated with such care throughout. In September 1929, he wrote to his friend, Henry Yorke (later, the pseudonymous novelist Henry Green): 'I am relying on a sort of cumulative futility for any effect it may have' (*L* 39).

SHARED MOTIFS WITH *DECLINE AND FALL*

To clarify matters for his reader, Waugh introduced two elucidatory epigraphs and, in the first edition, an *Author's Note* (later cut) prefacing the novel. The *Author's Note* makes the usual disclaimers, and clarifies chronology. He points out that the novel is set in the near future, 'when existing social trends have become more marked'; he has assumed 'a certain speeding up' for the sake of concision. This is easily evident in the novel's two month time-span, where 'last week's Prime Minister' and the leader of the Opposition, PM and MP, change places three times, and inflation converts Adam's winnings from five hundred to a thousand to a dizzying thirty-five thousand worthless pounds.

Waugh adds one further point, which has been misunderstood:

> *Vile Bodies* is in no sense a sequel to *Decline and Fall*, though many of the same characters appear in both. I think that some of the minor motives will be clearer to those who have read my first book than those who have not. (*VB* ix)

By 'minor motives' Waugh did not mean the characters' motivation (a crucial critical error) but 'motives' as his habitual plural of motif. *Vile Bodies* shares a number of motifs first set up in *Decline and Fall*, particularly the leitmotif of the Great Wheel of Luna Park, which is now recast in two forms: the racing-track visited by Waugh immediately after his wife's desertion, and the film reel deriving from his experiences making *The Scarlet Woman* and other films (now lost), after he went down from Oxford.

'FASTER! FASTER!'

In Waugh's first epigraph from *Through the Looking Glass*, Alice is urged to run *'Faster! Faster!'* by the Red Queen. She breathlessly protests that in her country you generally get to somewhere else, if you have been running very fast for a long time, as they have. The Red Queen retorts:

> *A slow sort of country! Now, here, you see, it takes all the running you can do, to keep in the same place. If you want to get somewhere else, you must run at least twice as fast as that!*[6]

The tenth chapter of *Vile Bodies* is devoted to Adam's visit to the racing-track with Agatha Runcible, and Miles Malpractice, whose boyfriend is one of the drivers. It begins with a rhetorical trope initiated in *Decline and Fall*. There, the spinning wheel of Fortune was echoed in extended paragraphs toppling from hyperbole to bathos. In *Vile Bodies* cyclic degeneration is twice replayed in prosaic terms. On arrival in the overcrowded town where the races are being held, Adam, Agatha and their friends vainly search for lodgings. They sink rapidly from the Imperial Hotel to the Station Hotel and on, 'through various gradations of Old Established Family and Commercial, plain commercial, High Class Board Residence pension terms, Working Girls' Hostel, plain Pub and Clean Beds: Gentlemen only' to the Royal George, where they have to share beds with a Mr Titchcock and are bitten by bugs. In search of food at the end of the next day, they are rejected in turn by the Imperial Hotel's Palm Court Lounge, the Café Royal, the Honest Injun Tea Shop, a working men's dining room and a fried fish shop, finally buying a bag of mixed biscuits in the Co-op.

Equally characteristically, Waugh precedes the racing-track's cyclic acceleration ending in crash by an extended verbal mosaic – snatches of technical conversation heard in the racecourse dining-room:

> '...Just cruising round at fifty [...]'
> '...Lapped at seventy-five...'
> '...Burst his gasket and blew out his cylinder heads...'
> '...Broke both arms and cracked his skull in two places...'
> '...Tailwag...'
> '...Speed-wobble...'
> '...Merc...'
> '...Mag...'
> '...crash...' (*VB* 175–6)

Adam, Agatha, and their friends are allowed entrée to the racing pits, thanks to the identifying brassards distributed by Miles's boyfriend. Angela's is marked 'Spare Driver'. When one of the drivers is injured, she is co-opted to take his place, drunk and with no idea how to drive ('goodness, how too stiff-scaring'), shoots ahead of the other competitors, careers off course, and disappears. Later she is said to have crashed into a village cross. Later still she turns up at the local railway station complaining of an enormous stone spanner in the middle of the road, and buys a ticket for London. 'So that's all right,' say her oblivious friends. No one recognizes the religious significance of the spanner in the works – the only thing that can stop the Bright Young Things in their giddy whirl.

Ten days later we catch up with Agatha in a nursing home. Her guests gather; they are warned not to excite her. Drinks circulate, the gramophone records spin, as she recalls her awful dreams, which give the necessary moral gloss:

> 'I thought we were all driving round and round in a motor race and none of us could stop, and there was an enormous audience composed entirely of gossip writers and gate crashers [...] all shouting at us at once to go faster and faster, and car after car kept crashing until I was left all alone.' (*VB* 209)

None of her friends are with her when she dies, still terrified, still struggling to drive faster and faster round the hallucinatory racetrack of her fevered imagination:

There was rarely more than a quarter of a mile of the black road to be seen at one time. It unrolled like a length of cinema film. At the edges was confusion; a fog spinning past; 'Faster, faster,' they shouted above the roar of the engine [...] Two cars had crept up, one on each side, and were closing in. 'Faster,' cried Miss Runcible, 'Faster.' [...]

They were trying to make her lie down. How could one drive properly lying down?

Another frightful corner. The car leaned over on two wheels, tugging outwards [...] The back wheels wouldn't hold the road at this speed. Skidding all over the place.

'Faster. Faster.'

The stab of a hypodermic needle.

'There's nothing to worry about, dear... nothing at all... nothing.'
(*VB* 223–4)

Agatha's 'skidding all over the place' and Waugh's image of the road unrolling like a length of film make a clear link to the penultimate chapter of *Vile Bodies*, where Colonel Blount, his daughter Nina, and Adam watch Colonel Blount's very bogus film, purportedly based on the life of John Wesley. This film derives from *The Scarlet Woman*. The captions to that silent film were Waugh's; much of it was shot in the house of Waugh's parents; Waugh's father took almost as much pleasure in it as Colonel Blount takes in *A Brand from the Burning*. As is typical of early silent film (and Waugh knew to his cost), Blount's film veers between headlong hurry and catatonic stasis. Thus it recreates both the Red Queen's injunction to go faster, and Alice's sense of no movement at all. Unlike the motor-races, it is an unalloyed comic parallel to the novel's phantasmagoric, headlong career in which everything not only goes nowhere, faster and faster, but also – particularly in Adam and Nina's stop-go on-off relationship – goes backwards as well as forwards, still ending in *nothing at all*.

The film begins unpropitiously. '*Now*,' says Colonel Blount. There is a whirring sound, and suddenly four uniformed horsemen appear on the screen, galloping backwards down the drive. The film is rewound and begun again.

'*Now*,' said the Colonel, and sure enough there appeared in small and clear letters the notice, 'THE WONDERFILM COMPANY OF GREAT BRITAIN PRESENTS'. This legend, vibrating a good deal, but without other variation, filled the screen for some time [...]

until its place was taken by 'EFFIE LA TOUCHE IN'. This announcement was displayed for practically no time at all, indeed, they had scarcely had time to read it before it was whisked away obliquely. ('Damn,' said the Colonel. *'Skidded.'*) (*VB* 235, last italics mine)

Eventually it gets going with four bewigged men in fancy costume, 'gambling feverishly', a highwayman holding up a coach, starving beggars, ladies in fancy costume dancing a minuet, all in 'breathless succession'. One of the film's peculiarities, Waugh says, was that whenever the story reached a dramatic moment, it seemed to go faster and faster. 'Villagers trotted to church as though galvanised; lovers shot in and out of windows; horses *flashed past like motorcars'* (my italics). Moments of repose, like Wesley uninterruptedly composing a sermon for four and a half minutes, seemed interminable. Even Colonel Blount sensed that a cut might be made there.

'DON'T YOU THINK, OR DON'T YOU?'

In *Vile Bodies'* cinematic world, neither aching stasis nor hectic movement get you anywhere. This futile circularity is epitomized by another leitmotif, the Younger Set's phatic filler 'do you, or do you?' 'Should they, or should they?' and, above all, *'Don't you think, or don't you?'*[7]

The Bright Young Things are incapable of coherent thought. In their vacuous and irresponsible world, the celestial hyperboles of fashionable slang are irredeemably material. 'What's London like, Fortitude?' 'Just exactly heaven. Shops and all.' ... '"Midnight Orgies at No. 10." My dear, isn't that divine?' There is no transcendence here. Aimée McPherson's celestial aeroplane is grounded. The socialites' last party is held in a so-called 'captive dirigible', an airship tethered in a field. 'Oh, for the wings of a dove', one of the novel's minor refrains, recurs in vain. Creative Endeavour's wings are lost. When Ginger and Nina finally take to the air on their honeymoon flight, Ginger looks down over the London suburbs, garbling Shakespeare ('This blessed plot, this earth, this realm, this England') while Nina is sick – just as everyone was seasick on the Channel crossing opening the novel, and a guest in the tethered airship is visibly unwell. Strung between the two poles of contemporary argot – 'how too, too sick-making' and 'angel', 'darling, how divine' – the novel swings giddily between bedazzled sham and sickening reality. There is no Hope in Mrs Ape's angel-troupe and Colonel Blount lives in what the locals call 'Doubting 'All'. It is Waugh's grim intensification of Bunyan's Doubting Castle, home of the Giant Despair in *The Pilgrim's Progress*, another favourite book of Waugh's when he was at Oxford.[8]

In *Decline and Fall* the Great Wheel of Luna Park spun round and round, and those who could hung on, and those who couldn't, watched, and only some, who didn't seem to matter much, fell off and died. *Vile Bodies* takes its title from 'The Burial of the Dead', but there are no resurrections in this godless world.[9] Characters who die, die for real, and the novel ends in an accelerando of deaths and dispersal. Flossie, the prostitute, is the first to go, hung from a chandelier in a drunken orgy at Shepheard's Hotel. Miles Malpractice, the homosexual socialite, flees the country; dim little Mary Mouse is on her way to India to become a royal concubine...'How people are *disappearing*,' poor Agatha Runcible says, just before her own death. The suicide of Simon Balcairn, the failed gossip columnist, is detailed with remorseless realism.

> He shut the door and the window and opened the door of the gas oven. Inside it was very black and dirty and smelled of meat. He spread a sheet of newspaper on the lowest tray and lay down, resting his head on it [...] There were crumbs on the floor. Then he turned on the gas. It came surprisingly with a loud roar; the wind of it stirred his hair [...] At first he held his breath. Then he thought that was silly and gave a sniff. (*VB* 113)

The delightfully facile resurrections of *Decline and Fall* are over. Now the deaths do matter: there is a painful echo of Waugh's own desperation as Simon Balcairn mutters 'Done for...End of the tether...' before he kills himself. Now, too, the wheel turns faster and faster; everything is sent skidding to the outer rim, and the novel ends in images of dispersal, disintegration, and destruction, culminating in the world war of the last chapter. In the novel's very last words, 'like a circling typhoon, the sounds of battle began to return'.

THE SECOND EPIGRAPH: REAL TEARS

Waugh's second epigraph raises an even more important question:

'If I wasn't real,' Alice said – half-laughing through her tears, it all seemed so ridiculous – 'I shouldn't be able to cry.'
'I hope you don't suppose those are real tears?' Tweedledum interrupted in a tone of great contempt.

On the day of his divorce, Waugh published an essay attacking Hardy's *Tess of the D'Urbervilles*:[10]

Compared with the inevitable tragedy and fine gloom of *Jude the Obscure*, the spiritual temper of *Tess* is like the vexation caused by a lost collar-stud [...] Heaven forbid that I blame anyone for gloom. I yield to none, as they say, in misanthropy and pessimism. The trouble about the pessimism in *Tess* is that it is bogus.

Mrs Ape's sermons arouse bogus tears, the affectation of remorse, in her maudlin audiences. Simon Balcairn cries freely ('too shy-making', Adam complains) when Margot Metroland won't invite him to her party, his career seems ruined, and suicide is his only resort. The novel is moist with unreal tears. In his essay on *Tess*, Waugh said that real tragedy arises from the dissonance between human folly and a universe that Waugh, in his reticence ignoring his private vexations, could still see positively. Agatha Runcible, smoking in the racing pits, twice tosses a lit cigarette behind her, which, 'by a beneficent attention of Providence which was quite rare in her career,' just misses falling into an open petrol tank and blowing her to blazes. In terms of Waugh's essay on *Tess*, the constitution of the universe is benign, but its denizens are irresponsible to the point of lunacy – as Adam's astronomic winnings, and the drunken Major's erratic attempts to pay them, make clear. Adam's mind-blowing incompetence in claiming his cash; Adam and Nina's naively feckless relationship; poor Agatha dying as her friends and even her nurses imperviously party around her – all these are needless, self-inflicted tragedies. They are, in the end, symptomatic of an entire generation's malaise, the 'radical instability' diagnosed by Father Rothschild which, he prophesies, will end in war.[11]

Hence the witheringly bogus penultimate chapter, in which Adam and Nina spend her wedding night at Doubting 'All, to a Christmas-card accompaniment of snow, holly, robins and apple-cheeked carol-singers. This is the novel's thirteenth chapter, just as Waugh's ominous design for his dust-jacket and the novel's frontispiece shows Agatha's skidding racing-car, prominently numbered **13**. The wedding-night is an adulterous mockery; Adam has sold Nina to Ginger to pay off his debts, and then stolen her while Ginger is called up to the war that has finally been declared. The carol-singers' refrain, '*Oh, tidings of comfort and joy, comfort and joy*', is the grimmest irony of all. Finally the novel's last and only named chapter is sardonically titled 'Happy Ending'. On 'the biggest battlefield in the history of the world,' the drunken Major finally gives Adam his thirty-five thousand pounds, now enough to buy a couple of drinks and a newspaper. And the last of Mrs Ape's angels, once a girl called Chastity, now a nameless whore, suffers the Major's embraces in the back of a stranded staff-car.

3

Black Mischief
1932

It is ironic that the objects of Waugh's harshest satire became his most devoted fans. Journalists still love *Scoop*. The Bright Young Things adored the hugely successful *Vile Bodies*, which was published in January 1930, and reached its eleventh impression by October. By then Waugh was on his way to Abyssinia, to report the coronation of Haile Selassie for *The Times*.

Waugh first heard of Abyssinia at an Irish house-party where a guest described meeting two of the Abyssinian crown princes at an embassy lunch in Cairo. Both attended in silk capes and bowler hats, which they refused to remove during the meal. They spoke no language known to the embassy interpreters (*D* 329). Research in the country-house library intensified Waugh's curiosity. 'We looked up the royal family in the *Almanack de Gotha* and traced their descent from Solomon and the Queen of Sheba,' he recalls. 'We found a history which began: "the first certain knowledge we have of Ethiopian history was when Cush the son of – ascended the throne immediately after the Deluge". [...] The real heir to the throne was hidden in the mountains, fettered with chains of solid gold.'[1] Electrified, Waugh engineered a meeting with Jack Driberg, a respectable member of the Colonial Service, known to speak eleven African languages and to have eaten human flesh twice – a clear if distant progenitor of the disreputable Basil Seal, *Black Mischief*'s anthropophagous, polyglot anti-hero. A chance encounter on a train brought Waugh the commission he needed, and within weeks he was on the long journey to Addis Ababa. *Alice in Wonderland* was still in his mind when he searched in vain for a historical parallel to life in Addis Ababa:

28

It is in *Alice* only that one finds the peculiar flavour of galvanized and translated reality, where animals carry watches in their waistcoat pockets, royalty paces the croquet lawn beside the chief executioner, and litigation ends in a flutter of playing-cards. How to recapture, how retail, the crazy enchantment of these Ethiopian days? (*RP* 29)

In the 1962 Preface to *Black Mischief* Waugh denies 'the smallest resemblance' between its hero, Seth, Emperor of Azania, and Haile Selassie. The disclaimer is perhaps less obviously mendacious than first appears, because Seth shares a recognizable innocence with Waugh's two earlier naïve victim-heroes, Paul and Adam, which is wholly unlike Haile Selassie's ruthless acumen. The Western press, and Waugh himself, tactfully refrained from commenting on the sudden death of the perfectly healthy, ruling Empress Zauditu, which conveniently cleared Selassie's way to the throne. This is only a small part of the barbarous 'black and mischievous background' that Waugh takes pains to recreate in his novel.

However, there's no denying other parodic echoes reverberating between SETH IMPERATOR IMMORTALIS, *Chief of the Chiefs of Sakuyu, Lord of Wanda and Tyrant of the Seas, Bachelor of the* [sic] *Arts of Oxford University*, and Ras Tafari, crowned Haile Selassie, Conquering Lion of the Tribe of Judah, King of Kings and Lord of Lords, Elect of God and Emperor of Ethiopia. Seth's attempts to modernize his country derive directly from Selassie's attempts to win over the League of Nations by his humane and civilized regime. Selassie's little book, *My Life and Ethiopia's Progress, 1892–1937*,[2] dictated by the illiterate Emperor during his exile in Bath in 1936–7, innocently corroborates the closeness of the parallel in retrospect. Its style is interesting. The translator speaks with relish of 'the full resources of Amharic stylistics which are apt to aid and abet a desire for almost total opacity'. In *Black Mischief's* first and penultimate chapters Waugh turns this enigmatic archaism into oblique proposals of murder ('*I fear for Seth's health and await word from your Lordship as to how best he may be relieved of what troubles him*'). Yet Selassie's tone is more transparently naïve than opaque. His Chapter 12, '*About the improvements by ordinance and proclamation, of internal administration and about the efforts to allow foreign civilisation to enter Ethiopia*', details the programme of modernization immediately preceding his coronation – the very stuff of Waugh's novel. Among 'some of the major work We now remember', the Elect of God lists the purchase of two printing presses; the invitation of foreign potentates; the import of cars and bicycles; the abolition of chain-gangs; the creation of new orders, a new flag, a new national anthem; the selective abolition of enslavement from *some* parts of the penal code; the Imperial purchase of the Bank of Abyssinia, and 'Our causing to stop the cutting off of hands and feet, which had [...] been customary for a very long time [...] Our whole people were very pleased.'

There is, in fact, a curious confluence of accurate reportage, fiction, prophecy and plagiarism in *Black Mischief*. Seth's modernizations are, initially, a near-literal replay of Selassie's. As Seth's intoxication with Progress intensifies, Waugh's hyperbolic fiction acquires prophetic authority. For instance, Seth's confused attempts to honour the two English ladies representing Britain's ineptly named Cruelty to Animals (aka the RSPCA) was later solemnly re-enacted by Selassie himself. When Waugh returned to Addis Ababa in 1936, he found an awkwardly worded flyer forbidding cruelty to animals had just been posted around town – '*Considering that cruelty and ill-treatment against tamed and utile animals are incompatible with human dignity*'... More 'humane humbug from Tafari's regime,' Waugh noted sourly.[3]

Selassie wasn't Waugh's only plagiarist. The most curious text in *Black Mischief*'s post-history is Ryszard Kapuściński's *The Emperor*, a highly acclaimed, supposedly factual account of Selassie's last days before revolution finally rubbed him out in 1975. The many unacknowledged parallels between Kapuściński's oral 'history' (1978) and Waugh's invention (1932) are remarkable indeed. One example must suffice. As the empire was tottering, Kapuściński assures us, Selassie summoned Swedish physicians to Addis Ababa to lead the Imperial court in callisthenic exercises.[4] Compare with Waugh:

> Basil hurried to the Palace to find his master in a state of high excitement.
> 'I have been reading a German book. We must draft a decree at once...Communal physical exercises. The whole population, every morning, you understand. And we must get instructors from Europe.' (*BM* 181)

BARBARITY AND MODERNISM

Waugh found the Western reports of Selassie's exotic coronation 'shocking and depressing' because they fell for the clichés captured in *Black Mischief*'s single malicious parody:

> Mr Randall typed: *His Majesty B.A....ex undergrad among the cannibals scholar emperor's desperate bid for throne...barbaric splendour...conquering hordes...ivory...elephants...east meets west...* (*BM* 84)

Waugh, on the other hand, was struck by something infinitely more complex: 'a succession of events of startling spectacular character...in a tangle of *modernism and barbarity, European, African, and American,* of definite, individual character' (*RP* 53, my italics).

Like the thrice-repeated stairs from his Welsh schoolmastering days, there is one seminal scene of absurdity from Addis Ababa that recurs in quick succession in Waugh's diary, his *Times* reports, and his subsequent travel book, *Remote People.* Returning late one night from a legation party, 'dressed in the absurd white tie and tall hat of civilisation,' Waugh paused to watch a native party squatting round the walls of a dimly-lit hut, one figure drumming, the rest singing a 'nasal, infinitely monotonous tune [...] It seemed to me typical of the whole week,' he wrote. 'On one side the primitive song of unfathomable antiquity; on the other, the preposterously dressed European, with a stockade between them' (*EAR* 118, *RP* 68–9, *D* 333).

The structure of *Black Mischief* derives from this simple collocation, and corrects it. The novel's key is not the apparent opposition between civilization and barbarism, but the entanglement of modern 'civilization' with barbarism. The gap between them is shown to be negligible. Waugh is commonly accused of racism, unjustly. Ultimately his focus is on the barbarity of the ostensibly civilized white Europeans, just as it is in Conrad's *Heart of Darkness.* In this paradoxical reversal Waugh is echoing the witty speech given by Ronald Knox at the Oxford Union's celebratory, unserious Centenary Debate in 1924, Waugh's final year at Oxford, against the motion that 'Civilisation has advanced since this Society first met'. Father Knox's comic demonstration of a contemporary return to barbarism

31

was anthropologically based: 'Vegetarianism, Teetotalism, Cremation, Painting, New Art – there is no difference between these and the customs of the merest Zulu. Barbarism may or may not be a good thing, but let us make no doubt that we are returning to it' (*The Cherwell*, 8 March 1924, 162–3). Waugh's report in *The Isis* summarized Knox's argument more obliquely.[5] Whether consciously or not, he elaborated and reaffirmed Knox's paradox in *Black Mischief*.

However, he begins by establishing a predictable antithesis between Azania's deeply primitive past and Seth's modern reforms. The novel's beginning and end are securely grounded in Azania's antediluvian prehistory, its tribal loyalties, treacheries, heroism and barbarity. This atmosphere is subtly anchored by two names: Major Joab, Seth's two-timing captain of the guard, and Boaz, the gluttonous chieftain. Both are Biblical, both significant.[6] Their characters sidle unobtrusively into the opening narrative, and emerge unmasked in the novel's cannibalistic close.

Yet the majority of the novel – its central section between these two Old Testament book-ends – deals with Waugh's 'tangle of modernism and barbarity' shared by America, Europe and Africa. East meets West, but no stockade separates the old world from the new. Waugh is careful to stabilize his mockery of modernity, conveniently rendered absurd in Seth's naïve reforms, by balancing Azanian primitivism against London's genteel savagery. Major Joab's discreet treachery when Seth is no longer in the ascendant is matched by Basil's callously casual thefts from his mother. Seth attempts to recast the menu of his native banquet in up-to-date nutritional terms ('Vitamin C: Small Roasted Sucking Porks; Vitamin D: Hot Sheep and Onions'), while in England Lord Monomark imposes equally batty fads on his weary workforce ('Two raw onions and a plate of oatmeal porridge. That's all I've taken for luncheon in the last eight months'). Basil's sordid coupling with Prudence, the daughter of Sir Samson Courteney, the British Envoy Extraordinary in Debra Dowa, is mirrored in the modish metropolitan squalor of the socialite Alastair and Sonia's ménage in London, duns at their door and copulating lapdogs fouling their bed.

According to Jack Driberg, the King of Rabbah maintained that 'in their own country Europeans eat black men, and dye red cloth with their blood'.[7] In his own way Waugh shared the king's looking-glass certainties. It may seem easy for civilized westerners to laugh at Azanian Primitive Modernism, but Azanian primitivism is outweighed by Western infantilism. The British Legation is preoccupied by bridge, whist, halma, Peggity, bagatelle, snap, and chain letters; Sir Samson knits baby clothes, and plays with an inflatable dinosaur at bath time. Their innocuous parlour game of Consequences is misinterpreted by suspicious rivals at the French Legation, creating a narrative diversion of puerile plots and fatuous consequences. Waugh's animus against the licentious irresponsibility of his ex-wife's generation is personified in Prudence's childish but far from innocent sexual games with William Bland, honorary attaché to the British Legation, and then with Basil Seal. Her casual liaisons are contrasted with Seth's military commander, the British mercenary General Connolly, whose singular devotion to his wife, the affectionate Black Bitch, is roundly deplored by the civilized standards of his white compatriots. Finally, Prudence is punished by a distasteful end, becoming the bonne-bouche of a cannibal feast.

We are fortunate that *Black Mischief*'s shocking dénouement was originally attacked in the Catholic journal, *The Tablet*. The Editor, Oldmeadow, objected above all to the sordid presentation of Prudence's afternoon assignation with Basil, and her grotesque death. The opinion of his new co-religionists was important to Waugh. Oldmeadow's review was so obtuse that he was goaded into a uniquely revealing reply:

> The story deals with the conflict of civilisation, with all its attendant and deplorable ills, and barbarism. The plan of my book throughout was to keep the darker aspects of barbarism continually and unobtrusively present, a black and mischievous background against which the civilised and semi-civilised characters performed their parts: I wished it to be like the continuous remote throbbing of those hand drums, constantly audible, never visible, which every traveller in Africa will remember as one of his most haunting impressions. (*L* 77)[8]

This is Waugh's double subject: the 'attendant and deplorable ills' of the *civilized* world, with its civilized and semi-civilized characters, and its relationship to barbarism. Barbarism is the song of unfathomable antiquity Waugh heard in Addis Ababa, whose ominous drum-beat suffuses and sustains the plan of *Black Mischief*. The detail of his method followed:

> I introduced the cannibal theme in the first chapter, and repeated it in another key in the incident of the soldiers eating their boots, thus hoping to prepare the reader for the sudden tragedy when barbarism at last emerges from the shadows and usurps the stage.

Basil and Youkoumian inflict a consignment of unwanted boots on Connolly's Azanian army, who have always fought barefoot. They stew them and make a banquet out of them.

Waugh's revelation of his favoured fictional technique – theme and virtuoso variation – is unprecedented. Indeed, it was quickly regretted. He withdrew it from publication, and never described his methods so frankly and in such detail again.

Once alerted, the reader can have no difficulty in registering *Black Mischief*'s drumbeat basso continuo, and the cannibalistic motif elusively threading through the text, from slight early references to 'the native Sakuyu, black, naked, anthropophagous', or 'the painful case of the human sacrifices at the Bishop of Popo's consecration', to the cannibal banquet at the end. Other imperceptibly significant trails consolidate the degenerative sequence. Take, for instance, the word 'grunt'. It suggests bestiality, a primitive inarticulacy whose semantic penumbra gradually modulates from the relatively innocent to the grotesque. We first hear it, twice, when the opportunist Armenian entrepreneur, Youkoumian, ignores his wife, trussed like a chicken on the floor, while he snuggles into bed with little grunts of contentment. It's repeated when the superstitious, atheistic M. Ballon settles down to sleep, protective amulet to hand. We hear it when the Azanian traditionalists object to birth control. And when Dame Mildred Porch of the RSPCA settles into the Legation car with a grunt. Poor senile Achon grunts when the weighty Imperial sword of Azania is laid on his lap. Finally the motif emerges for what it is. In the closing cannibal feast, 'black figures sprawled and grunted, alone and in couples'. And the headman, who has plied Basil with stewed Prudence, answers his question, 'Where is the white woman?' with another grunt. 'The white woman? Why, here,' he patted his distended paunch. 'You and I and the big chiefs – we have just eaten her.'

It is one of the novel's many ironies that Seth should encounter Basil, just as he is yearning for 'a representative of Progress and the New Age'. Basil is the ultimate embodiment of western barbarism. *He* is the unabashed participant in the final cannibal banquet where his habitual parasitism on womankind is consummated in the consumption of his imprudent mistress. And it is Seth, in his childish pursuit of the new, who is the avatar and acolyte of Progress in its most fatuous forms.

Waugh was, by nature and conviction, a traditionalist. For him, progress was regressive. Here he concurs with Ronald Knox. Basil convinces Seth that he can continue to feed his chieftains the raw meat of their traditional *gebbur*, if he calls it *steak tartare*. He reassures Seth that primitive nakedness is now sanitized as *Nacktkultur*. Seth boasts, 'At my stirrups run woman's suffrage, vaccination and vivisection. I am the New Age. I am the Future.' Ectogenesis and autogyros are the stuff of his dreams. But in Basil's eyes it is fortunate that Seth has taken on his kingdom's modernization at a time when bi-cameral legislature, proportional representation, an independent judiciary and the freedom of the press are 'just a few ideas that have ceased to be modern'. Seth falls instead for the attendant ills of civilization – the passing fads whose value is neatly identified by the trampled banner from his Gala of Birth-Control, which proclaims STERILITY from the gutter. The legend bleakly echoes Waugh's earlier warning in 'The War and the Younger Generation': *freedom produces sterility.*[9]

Part of Waugh's Azanian satire is obliquely aimed at the destructive speed of contemporary Soviet revolutionary reform. Stalin's first Five Year Plan (1928–32) is mockingly telescoped into Seth's One Year Plan. In the end even poor Seth begins to lose confidence in its 'permanence'. This, in its turn, dwindles into Youkoumian's 'very good champagne – I brewed it yesterday'. And that absurdity is pointedly repeated when Basil and Youkoumian later spend a day concocting cognac for the evening's fancy-dress ball. Waugh's sickened sense of unseemly haste carries over from *Vile Bodies* and *Through the Looking Glass's* 'Faster! Faster!' The White Queen tells Alice that in her country there is jam yesterday and jam tomorrow, but never jam today. For Seth, there is no tomorrow, yesterday exists only to be denied, and the Present is all. At the beginning of the novel he

35

proudly claims, 'We are Progress and the New Age [...] It is our world now because we are of the Present.' His opponent Seyid's vanquished army is a thing of the past,

> 'Dark barbarism. A cobweb in a garret; dead wood, a whisper echoing in a sunless cave. We are Light and Speed and Strength, Steel and Steam, Youth, Today and Tomorrow.' (*BM* 52)

But Seth's victory is short-lived. When Basil tries to warn him of impending revolution, he will not hear.

> 'Seth, there's a lot of talk going around. There may be trouble tomorrow.'
> 'God, have I not had trouble today and yesterday? Why should I worry about tomorrow?' (*BM* 234)

Seth's impatient reforms create a sense of time ludicrously shrunk in the wash (just as it is speeded up in *Vile Bodies*). This is intensified by the novel's unprecedented historical and geographical range. In *Decline and Fall* and *Vile Bodies* Waugh stayed in his own world and time; the novels were set in the London of the late twenties, barely venturing beyond Paul's Wales and brief trips to Marseilles and Corfu. *Black Mischief* is striking for its vastly expanded canvas, repeatedly stretching outwards in space, and backwards in time, in a sequence of brilliantly evocative panoramas. Note the drums, still muted and various, in this fine panning shot juxtaposing old and new Azania, at the close of Chapter 4:

> Vernacular hymns in the tin-roofed missions, ancient liturgy in the murky Nestorian sanctuaries; tonsure and turban, hand drums and innumerable jingling bells of debased silver. And beyond the hills on the low Wanda coast where no liners called, and the jungle stretched unbroken to the sea, other more ancient rites [...] the drums of the Wanda throbbing in sunless, forbidden places.
> Fanfare and sennet; tattoo of kettle drums; tricolour bunting strung from window to window across the Boulevard Amurath, from Levantine café to Hindu drugstore; Seth in his Citroën drove to lay the foundation stone of the Imperial Institute of Hygiene; brass band of the Imperial army raised the dust of the main street. Floreat Azania. (*BM* 150)

Black Mischief is a genuine panorama of life, in which Waugh undertakes the difficult task of creating a credible country with its own complex history and ethnography. Azania is a palimpsest of heterogeneous races, religions, and bygone power struggles. It is exemplified, for instance, by the vista from the tin roof of the *Grand Café et Hotel Restaurant de l'Empereur Seth* (originally '*Seyid*', until the name was updated after Seyid's defeat). Here observers can survey 'the several domes and spires of the Catholic, Orthodox, Armenian, Anglican, Nestorian, American Baptist and Mormon places of worship; the minarets of the mosque, the Synagogue and the flat white roof of the Hindu snake temple.' It is parodied in Prudence's much emended novel, a sub-Lawrentian effusion grandly titled *Panorama of Life*.

> *Sex*, she wrote in round, irregular characters, *is the crying out of the Soul for Completion.* Presently she crossed out '*Soul*' and substituted '*Spirit*'; then she inserted '*of man*'; changed it to '*manhood*' and substituted '*humanity*'. (*BM* 77–8)

Seth's attempts to inscribe change on Azania's tangled text are doomed to failure. Basil finds him busy mapping his new megalopolis, Seth Square at its centre, avenues named after his friends radiating outwards. As Basil turns Seth against Connolly, 'the Emperor took up his india rubber and erased Connolly's name from his metropolis. *Avenue Sir Samson Courteney* he wrote in its place.' No metropolis is built. His workmen strike when paid with his newly-printed, worthless banknotes, and Seth is left to toil on his own, vainly attempting to demolish the solid, Aberdeen granite of the Anglican Cathedral. It is like the market cross where Agatha Runcible's car crashes: a spanner in the spinning cogs of Modern Times.

Seth's reign causes a brief ripple. With his passing, Azania returns to its old ways. A new road skirts the abandoned lorry still blocking the imperial highway. New and old assimilate each other. Native Sakuyu, who made the lorry their home, repair it painstakingly with mud, grass, and flattened tins. Like the Anglican Cathedral, it can't be moved. Life in the British Legation continues as it always has done. Bretherton and Reppington drain their sundowners to the strain of Gilbert and Sullivan's *Mikado*:

> *Three little maids from school are we*
> *Pert as a schoolgirl well can be*

An unpalatable truth lurks in its complacent proprieties:

> '*Is it weakness of intellect, birdie,*' *I cried,*
> '*Or a rather tough worm in your little inside?*'

When the Editor of *The Tablet* protested at Prudence's end, stewed to a pulp with peppers and aromatic roots, Waugh coldly retorted that his criticism betrayed a defective digestion. 'It cannot matter whether she was roasted, grilled, braised or pickled, cut into sandwiches or devoured hot on toast as a savoury.' Civilized barbarism is a hard truth to swallow at the best of times. Waugh was not done with it yet.

4

A Handful of Dust
1934

Black Mischief was partly written at Madresfield Court, the home of the 7th Earl Beauchamp, and is dedicated to his two youngest daughters, Mary and Dorothy Lygon. Waugh was first invited to 'Mad' in 1931, six months after the 7th Earl was indicted for homosexuality and went into exile in Europe.

We get a strong impression of this family's recuperative effect on Waugh from his letters. After the breakup of his first marriage, he had found self-defensive refuge in the chilly persona of a man of the world. As Michael Davie, editor of the *Diaries*, points out, their tone became 'brisk, impersonal, and Tatler-ish' (*D* 307), a sardonic relay of society gossip. Friendship with the Lygons brought a welcome change. Waugh's affectionate letters to the two youngest Lygon daughters ('Blondy' and 'Poll') are exuberantly naughty and fantastical. He was clearly happy at 'Mad', composing *Black Mischief* in the day nursery in the attics, and learning to ride in the Malvern hills, in preparation for his next journey into the wilds.

The story of the Lygon family is well known to lie behind *Brideshead Revisited*, and Brideshead's stately house is routinely derived from Madresfield. Yet Madresfield first appears in Waugh's work as Hetton Abbey in *A Handful of Dust*. The local guide book baldly states of Hetton, '*This, formerly one of the notable houses of the county, was entirely rebuilt in 1864 in the Gothic style and is now devoid of interest*'. Madresfield dates back to the late twelfth century and was first improved in the Elizabethan era. From 1863–88 it, like Hetton, was perversely rebuilt. A mock-Elizabethan moated mansion, it is now a self-confessed architectural hybrid. Over 160 rooms of every conceivable style and size lie beneath two-and-a-half acres of tiles. The house has remained in the hands of the same family for twenty-eight generations.[1] Its medieval oak outer doors, so the boast went, had neither lock nor handle because the house had never been left unoccupied since its inception.

Hetton closely replicates Madresfield's architectural galli-maufry,[2] and the foibles of the 7th Earl's lifestyle. In both households champagne was decanted into a tall jug before serving. Modernizing comforts like bathrooms and effective central heating were sacrificed to the upkeep of myriad staff. Above all, behind the doom of Hetton lies the immediate tragedy of the Lygon family. In *A Handful of Dust* Tony's only child dies and Tony is lost in the jungle. Madresfield's unbroken line of descent was fractured with the ousting of the 7th Earl. His wife left Madresfield with their youngest son. All the remaining children remained loyal to their devoted, disgraced and absent father.

Madresfield's most significant architectural asset is still the family chapel, a *chef-d'oeuvre* of the Arts and Crafts movement. From 1903–23 it was painstakingly decorated with frescoes depicting the 7th Earl, his wife, and seven children, with their nanny as an angel. The colours are fresh and pure, the setting Arthurian and idealized. It is very pretty and slightly absurd – a sad tribute to the high hopes of an unspotted family line. The chapel is accurately described in *Brideshead Revisited*,[3] where it fulfils an important spiritual function. It never appears directly in *A Handful of Dust*. Yet the repeated evocation of its aesthetic is even more important. The irony of this naïvely tender family memorial embodies the novel's most important theme:

> A whole Gothic world had come to grief...there was now no armour glittering through the forest glades, no embroidered feet on the green sward: the cream and dappled unicorns had fled (*HD* 236)

This was the family Waugh joined for Christmas in 1931.

*

Black Mischief was finished in the summer of 1932, and published in the autumn. By December Waugh resumed what had by now become his creative routine, and set out on his travels again.

Darling Blondy & Poll
Well I have gone too far as usual & now I am in Brazil. Do come out & visit me. It is easy to find on account of it being the most vast of the republics of South America [...] You go up the Amazon, easily recognisable on account of its being the largest river in the world, then right at Rio Negro (easily recognised on account of being black) right again at Rio Bianco (e.r. on account of being white) and you cannot miss this village [...] (*L* 69–70)

Waugh's travels in British Guiana, by boat through the jungle, on horseback and foot over the savannah, provided material for his next travel book, *Ninety-Two Days,* and a short story, *The Man Who Liked Dickens.* For one night, Waugh had been forced to take shelter in the hut of a locally notorious religious maniac, Mr Christie. He made his escape the next morning, but the experience festered and within four weeks was fictionalized. A young man, Henty, goes abroad in the approved manner after discovering his wife's adultery, and gets lost in the jungle. The lunatic, McMaster, takes him in, cures him of fever, and keeps him prisoner. Mr Christie's religious mania is replaced by McMaster's obsession with Dickens. *Ninety-Two Days* was a short prison-sentence for Waugh. Henty is doomed to read Dickens, aloud, to a madman, for life.

The Man Who Liked Dickens is the germ of *A Handful of Dust,* and finds its proper home as the novel's penultimate chapter. Waugh needed to make only one major cut and a short insertion, some tiny adjustments and the necessary changes of name. As he later explained, after the story was published, 'the idea kept working in my mind. I wanted to discover how the prisoner got there, and eventually the thing grew into a study of other sorts of savage at home and the civilised man's helpless plight among them'.[4] To assume, as some readers do, that Waugh seized on the short story when he couldn't think of a better ending is to get the novel's genesis back to front. Furthermore, many critics find the Brazilian conclusion to a story of metropolitan adultery geographically disorientating, and *therefore* aesthetically inappropriate. Yet this grim final twist is characteristic of Waugh. Most obviously, it echoes Prudence's macabre fate ending *Black Mischief,* and, later, the heartless *envoi* for Aimée closing *The Loved One.* In each case, Waugh's deliberately remorseless moral art governs the last, unexpected turn of the screw.

41

Moreover, misplacement – the right thing in the wrong place – is the novel's keynote. There is a right time and a right place for Dickens's novels. It isn't the Amazonian jungle, day after day, week after week, year after year.

*

Initially this note is resonantly struck in baroque set-pieces like the Reverend Tendril's sermons. Originally composed for the Coldstream Guards at Jellalabad in the long-gone days of the Victorian Empire, they're now delivered with supreme inappropriateness to the villagers of Hetton:

> 'How difficult it is for us,' he began, blandly surveying his congregation, who coughed into their mufflers and chafed their chilblains inside their woollen gloves, 'to realize that this is indeed Christmas. Instead of the glowing log fire and windows tight shuttered against the drifting snow, we have only the harsh glare of an alien sun [...] Instead of the placid ox and ass of Bethlehem [...] we have for companions the ravening tiger and the exotic camel'...[5] (HD 96)

Indeed the very first words of *A Handful of Dust* establish this key. To the unattributed, crucial question, 'Was any one hurt?' comes the confusing reply:

> 'No-one I am thankful to say,' said Mrs Beaver, 'except two housemaids who lost their heads and jumped through a glass roof into the paved court. They were in no danger. The fire never reached the bedrooms I am afraid...' (HD 13)

Barely has Mrs Beaver expressed the conventional response ('No-one I am thankful to say') before we're faced with the housemaids working in the bedrooms above. They panicked, jumped and fell, down *through* a glass roof and *into* a paved court. They must have been at least two storeys up. Mrs Beaver returns us to a norm of indifferent rationality – 'They were in no danger' – which is rapidly discomposed by her next comment: 'The fire never reached the bedrooms *I am afraid...*' Her regret should be altruistic concern for the lacerated maids' unnecessary deaths. But no, it's entirely selfish, and quickly consoled: '*Luckily* [the family] had that old-fashioned sort of extinguisher that ruins *everything. One really cannot complain.*'[6] Gobbling her yoghurt, she complacently concludes: 'I must get on to them this morning before that ghoul Mrs Shutter snaps them up'. By now the situation and the sub-text are perfectly clear. Mrs Beaver is an interior decorator. In her vampiric world other peoples' disasters are her profit, bad is good, and traditional morality is turned upside down.

Hereafter, a sense of deepening disorientation is sustained throughout the novel. Princess Jenny Abdul Akbar's flat is another rococo *tour de force* of aesthetic indecorum, being

> *furnished promiscuously* and with truly Eastern disregard of the *right properties* of things; swords meant to adorn the state robes of a Moorish caid were *swung from the picture rail*; mats made for prayer were strewn on the divan; the carpet *on the floor had been* made in Bokhara *as a wall covering*. (*HD* 179, AMS 55, my italics)

All the italicized phrases are second thoughts added to and correcting the authorial manuscript. These fantastical narrative diversions encourage the critical misapprehension voiced by Malcolm Bradbury, that the novel is an amorphous triumph of 'comic anarchy'; that it is 'hardly open to direct moral interpretation'; that 'Waugh's real concern is at the level of comic tone'[7]. Not so. These moments of anarchic comedy serve a firm aesthetic rationale that is profoundly moral, as we shall see.

They are all variations on the central theme. Jenny's *promiscuous* tastes mix up the right properties of things and misplace them. Tendril's sermons were just about OK for the gallant lads at Jellalabad, not the chilblained farmers at Hetton. In the jungle, Dr Messinger confidently and erroneously accosts the uncomprehending Macushi Indians in fluent Wapishiana. In significant juxtaposition, in England at the same moment, Jock finally addresses his constituents' question on the eight-and-a-half score pig to the Minister of Agriculture – only to be told that it's a matter for the Board of Trade. Even the two poor housemaids had the right reaction (flight) in the wrong circumstances (they were in no danger on the second floor).

In each case, the right thing is in the wrong place.

This is the novel's ruling theme. Tony Last's love for Brenda is in the old tradition, 'madly feudal', as she calls it, with unconscious literalism. His life has fossilized like his bedroom, still crammed with the unbroken relics of his childhood. His weekly rituals of Sunday church, cutting flowers from the greenhouse for his house guests, embody the traditions of an outmoded world. His archaic Arcady has no place in the sexually promiscuous modern world of chromium-plated bathrooms and short-lived adulteries in service flats. Tony is the Last of a dying order, just as the Arthurian names of Hetton's bedrooms – Galahad, Guinevere, Morgan Le Fay – signal a fantasy world of idyllic romance and chivalry, but also adultery and betrayal. The novel's whole tragedy is that the love, which Hetton Abbey was meant to enshrine, is the right thing in the wrong time and place.

As Waugh continues to play on our sense of first baffled, and finally outraged propriety, the tone modulates from harmless comedy to the grim. Early on, Brenda is described affectionately rubbing against Tony's cheek like a cat. 'It was a way she had.' When she responds to John Beaver's adulterous first kiss, the mere relocation of that innocent phrase is surprisingly offensive – 'When he had kissed her, she rubbed against his cheek in the way she had.' As the novel accelerates to its first climax, the death of John Andrew, Tony and Brenda's son, these dislocations become increasingly jarring.

John Andrew's accidental death in the hunt is described with translucent clarity. Waugh's precise, factual account is deliberately artless ('Then this happened'). He scrupulously avoids melodrama or blame. 'Everyone [...] behaved with complete good sense,' he insists. But once John Andrew is dead, the leitmotif is replayed in a harsher key. Colonel Inch offers to have the huntsmen blow 'Gone to ground' at the funeral – a call properly blown over a fox retreated to its earth, not a child consigned to the dust. It is 'an atrocious suggestion', as Tony says, but it obeys the novel's strict indecorum for precisely this reason. Most shocking of all is the dreadful moment when Brenda hears of John Andrew's death. She has been worrying about John Beaver's plane flight to Paris all day, when Jock finds her:

> 'What is it, Jock? Tell me quickly. I'm scared. It's nothing awful, is it?'
> 'I'm afraid it is. There's been a very serious accident.'
> 'John?'
> 'Yes.'

'Dead?'

He nodded.

She sat down on a hard little Empire chair against the wall, perfectly still with her hands folded in her lap like a small well-brought-up child [...] She said, 'Tell me what happened [...]'

'I've been down at Hetton since the weekend.'

'Hetton?'

'Don't you remember. John was going hunting today.'

She frowned, not at once taking in what he was saying.

'John...John Andrew...I...Oh thank God ...' (HD 186–7)

Simply, devastatingly, she has the right reaction for the wrong person. The death of her maternal and marital love, and all the values that go with it, are in her mistake.

*

With the Brighton weekend supposed to facilitate Brenda's divorce, Waugh turned to a contemporary phenomenon that was well-known to be perverse. At this time, English law decreed that divorce could only be legally granted on grounds of adultery by one party. Any corresponding misconduct by the 'innocent' partner disqualified the divorce. Furthermore, a couple found to be co-operating in their divorce proceedings were guilty of collusion, also invalidating their case. Therefore the standard, simple solution was for the husband (whether the errant partner or not) to do the gentlemanly thing, as Tony does, and spend a naughty weekend with a prostitute, for his nominal adultery to be witnessed by hotel staff. In this way the polite fictions of public morality were maintained. The wife's reputation was protected as the innocent victim; the co-respondent (of either partner) was discreetly kept out of the proceedings; and the sanctity of the marriage bond was seen to be upheld by law.[8]

A. P. Herbert's *Holy Deadlock*, published in the same year as *A Handful of Dust*, methodically details every possible permutation of the legal absurdities forced on a couple attempting to divorce amicably. The novel opens with the chivalrous hero, just like Tony, on his way to Brighton with a prostitute, to act out the charade of adultery on hotel evidence. It fails. Further failures drive home Herbert's argument that English divorce law was intransigent, irrational and immoral. It promoted prostitution, enforced perjury and engendered hostility in couples seeking separation in good faith. Herbert was eventually instrumental in reforming English divorce law in 1937. Of course Waugh, as a Catholic, did not condone Herbert's scepticism about the marriage-bond. Yet he emphatically shared his derision for the vagaries of contemporary law, and supported Herbert's reforms.[9]

Waugh's treatment of Tony and Brenda's breakup intensifies the reader's sense of wide-spectrum dislocation. We have to keep our sense of normal values, and their inversion, steadily distinct. Initially it seems quite straightforward. Tony has trouble adapting to the revelation of Brenda's adultery: 'He had got into the habit of loving and trusting Brenda' (right sentiment for wrong person). Brenda, however, is a woman who readily twists reality for her own ends. Her letter to her solicitor coolly presents a selective version on the right facts – with a brazenly misplaced gloss: *'my husband* [...] *always remained in the country when my studies took me to London. I realised that he no longer cared for me.'* Her 'studies' were a pretext that took her to her lover in London; she no longer cared for her husband.

In Waugh's handling of the Brighton weekend, the legal lunacies anatomized by Herbert's rational narrative are further aggravated by the introduction of a child, whose innocent perspective betrays the adults' moral chaos. When Tony meets the prostitute, Milly, at the station, he finds to his dismay that she has her daughter in tow. Naturally Winnie wants to go to the seaside with her mother. In these extraordinary circumstances Tony is, understandably, just as eager to get rid of her. All our feelings of bewildered propriety are voiced in Winnie's utterly reasonable protests, as Tony struggles to pack her off with one of the private detectives in attendance. 'I want to go to the seaside,' she cries. 'I won't go with that man. I want to go to the seaside with my mummy.' Tony's weary acquiescence is roundly condemned by the detectives. Having Winnie there, they grumble, 'sets a nasty respectable note'. They're equally disapproving that evening, when Tony wants to drink with them, instead of committing adultery with Milly like a good boy. 'Everything in this case seemed to be happening as though with deliberate design to shock their professional feelings.'

We, too, are shocked to see the true 'right properties of things' in such profound disarray. At the time of his wife's desertion, Waugh wrote to Harold Acton, 'Everyone is talking so much nonsense on all sides of me [...] that my wits reel' (*L* 39). Attempting to convey this sense of overwhelming disorientation, Waugh reverted to the image of the lost collar stud he had used in his essay denigrating the tragedy of *Tess of the D'Urbervilles* (see p. 26), but now this disproportion is what is so profoundly wrong:

> For a month now he had lived in a world suddenly bereft of order; it was as though the whole reasonable and decent constitution of things, the sum of all he had experienced or learned to expect, were an inconspicuous, inconsiderable object mislaid somewhere on the dressing table. (*HD* 216)

'No outrageous circumstance [...] no new, mad thing' can add a jot to the all-encompassing chaos around him. The next morning, rising early, he shares a companionable breakfast with Winnie. Then, dismally recollecting his adulterous obligations, he wakes Milly. Fully clothed, dressing-gown tight about his neck, he gets into bed with her for a second breakfast to be served, and their intimacy observed. Normally people don't eat two breakfasts. It is, in some sense, wrong. Here, Tony explains to Winnie, it is 'the Law' and wrong is right. When she's a big girl, she'll understand.

As it turns out, however, Brighton's lunacies fulfil a profounder rationale. On his return to London, Tony finds that Brenda is suing him for an extortionate alimony destined to buy the mercenary but reluctant Beaver. He is finally goaded into resistance. The worm turns and the novel's inverted morality is set right at last.

> Brenda is not going to get her divorce. The evidence I provided at Brighton isn't worth anything. There happens to have been a child there all the time. She slept both nights in the room I am supposed to have occupied. If you care to bring the case I shall defend it and win. (*HD* 237)

In taking Winnie with them, Tony unwittingly did the right thing in the apparently wrong time and place.

*

At this point Waugh paused, writing to his friend, Diana

Cooper, with some satisfaction: 'What I have done is excellent. I don't think it could be better. Very gruesome. Rather like Webster in modern idiom [...] the general architecture is masterly'.[10] Then he began afresh on the Brazilian part of the story, initially designated Book II, which was to complete the novel's complex structure.

It is immediately striking that, in order to do so, Waugh later inserted a passage which precedes Tony's rebuff, quoted above – but does not appear in the original manuscript. The entire addition runs:

> [Tony] hung up the receiver and went back to the smoking-room. His mind had suddenly become clearer on many points that had puzzled him. A whole Gothic world had come to grief... there was now no armour glittering through the forest glades, no embroidered feet on the green sward; the cream and dappled unicorns had fled... (*HD* 236–7, not in AMS 70)

Significantly, this is the first time Waugh raises the motif of an idealized and lost 'Gothic world'. It derives naturally from the Arthurian names of Hetton's bedrooms and is promptly reaffirmed in the title of the next – new – chapter, *In Search of a City*. Tony departs for Brazil with Dr Messinger, in pursuit of a fabulous lost city variously known to the natives as 'the Shining, the Many Watered, the Bright Feathered, the Aromatic Jam'. For Tony, of course, it is 'a transfigured Hetton', 'Gothic in character, all vanes and pinnacles, gargoyles, battlements [...] everything luminous and translucent; a coral citadel crowning a green hilltop sown with daisies' (*HD* 160). The rest of this chapter cross-cuts Tony's increasingly disastrous journey into the jungle with the waning of Brenda and Beaver's affair in London. The next chapter economically adapts the short story, *The Man Who Liked Dickens*, now retitled *Du Côté de Chez Todd* (in accordance with the lunatic Mr Christie's change of name to Mr Todd).[11] A very brief epilogue returns us to Hetton. After Tony's presumed death in the Amazonian jungle, the house has passed into the hands of an impoverished branch of the Last family, who fund its upkeep by turning it into a silver fox farm.

Many critics find fault with this finale. Their reservations were first expressed by Waugh's friend, the novelist Henry Green, who found the ending 'so fantastic that it throws the rest out of proportion', clashing with the realism of the first half, which is 'convincing', 'a real picture of people one has met'.[12] Waugh plaintively replied that the Indians were also real people he had met. The pith of his defence followed:

> I think I agree the Todd episode is fantastic. It is a 'conceit' in the Webster manner – wishing to bring Tony to a sad end I made it an elaborate & improbable one [...] But the Amazon stuff had to be there. The scheme was a Gothic man in the hands of savages – first Mrs Beaver etc. then the real ones, finally the silver foxes at Hetton. All that quest for a city seems to me justifiable symbolism. (*L* 88)

In 'Fan-Fare', an authorial retrospect written twelve years later for his American fans, Waugh makes two more points. The first is crucial, and little understood. *A Handful of Dust*, he says, 'dealt entirely with behaviour. It was humanist and contained all I had to say about humanism'. The second confirms the novel's genesis from the short story, and reiterates its theme: it grew 'into a study of other sorts of savage at home and the civilised man's helpless plight among them' (8 April 1946, *EAR* 304, 303).

So Waugh describes his novel in three repeated, idiosyncratic terms – Websterian, Gothic, and humanist – all of which need clarification. The plays of Webster, the Jacobean dramatist, are certainly macabre, 'elaborate & improbable'. In language and staging they are 'conceited', in the Renaissance sense of being richly metaphorical. In very broad terms, it is easy to see Waugh translating this Jacobean-grotesque template into modern idiom, in which (as we'll see) the single structural conceit of dislocation will come to a head.

'Gothic' can also suggest ornate improbability in the Websterian mode, but Waugh's associations here are more eclectic. He admired and loved European Gothic architecture. He also relished the fantastical element in high Victorian mock-medievalism. It is worth noting that he deletes a sentence in his manuscript, describing Hetton Abbey as 'a huge building conceived in the late generation of the Gothic revival, when the moment had lost its fantasy & become structurally logical and stodgy' (*HD* 59; *AMS* 19), precisely because he did not want something stodgy and logical. Hetton's architectural extravaganza is scrupulously echoed in the novel's controlled architectural perversity, which is underscored in three chapters titled

'English Gothic'.[13] The Todd episode is, on Waugh's own admission, deliberately 'fantastic' in the best manner of the Gothic revival. It is structurally unexpected, *apparently* illogical, the very reverse of stodgy.

Tony, however, is also 'a Gothic man', in the sense of being out of his time, by nature affiliated to an idealized past. He is the right thing in the wrong time. In Waugh's clearer alternative gloss, he is 'the civilised man' among savages – innocent, courteous and trusting, their helpless prey.

In 'Fan-Fare' Waugh identified *A Handful of Dust*'s 'humanism' in contrast to the specifically Catholic *Brideshead*. That is, it deals with a society that has no religion. Lacking a spiritual, eschatological dimension, the novel can only deal with human 'behaviour'. There is a strong whiff of anthropological detachment inherent in this term.[14] Waugh registers the behaviour of his heathen humans as a dispassionate zoologist charts the animal kingdom.

*

This benighted 'humanist' world is indifferent to Christian faith and fidelity. The congregation at Hetton is oblivious to the irrelevance of Tendril's sermons because 'Few of the things said in church seemed to have any particular reference to themselves'. When John Andrew dies, Tony confesses that 'the last thing one wants to talk about at a time like this is religion'. And when Mr Todd asks 'Do you believe in God?' Tony replies, 'I've never really thought about it much'. It is telling that, in one of the handwritten insertions modifying the short story's typescript for the novel, Waugh prefaces Tony's reply with: 'I suppose no'. Waugh's 'no' was misread and has erroneously become the affirmative 'I suppose so' in all printed texts following the first edition's error (*HD* 328; *AMS* 100).

In the anomie of this heathen society there is godless benediction for the adulterers ('Bless you both'), and indifference for the victim ('*Hard Cheese for Tony*'). Brenda and her friends inhabit a moral void impervious to responsibility or blame. When John Andrew dies, 'everyone agreed that it was nobody's fault..."It wasn't anyone's fault," they said'. When Brenda's brother tries to insinuate that Tony is responsible for her infidelity, he's silenced by Tony's flat rejoinder, 'I haven't been thinking particularly whose fault it is'. Tony's unrecriminatory innocence is certainly more appealing, but it is merely the less culpable face of a society bereft of morality, whose lack of values Waugh refuses to endorse. It is reminiscent of the Bright Young Things in *Vile Bodies*, and their feckless response to disasters like Agatha's car crash – 'So that's all right'. There is no sequence of cause and effect. Nothing has consequences; no one has responsibilities, and no one is to blame.

Man without religion is either bestial or a child. In the novel's final chapter, the younger Lasts refer to Tony's memorial service as a 'jamboree', and their father protests, '*Jamboree*? Is nothing sacred to you children?' Throughout, Waugh stresses the childlike qualities of his characters. Brenda, sitting quietly, like a child in a room full of grown-ups, to hear with relief the death of her own child. Beaver, with his unformed handwriting and puerile dependence on 'Mumsy'. Hence, too, the novel's stress on games. These children haven't yet learned to take any human institutions seriously. Tony and Brenda's marriage is a game, diversified by more games like their silly diets. Christmas is a round of party games. Even the future is a game of palmistry, given a new twist by reading the soles of people's feet. But games don't always work out, as Mrs Rattery admits over her patience: 'It's a heart-breaking game'. All the novel's children founder at the moment when their particular prize seems just in reach – just as John Andrew dies pursuing his childish dream of riding with the hunt.

This is the point of the City. 'All that quest for a city,' Waugh protested, 'seems to me justifiable symbolism.' It embodies all that is idealistic and unreal in Tony's hopes of Hetton. It is an image of the infantile aspirations of Brenda, Beaver, and even Thérèse de Vitré, the Creole heiress Tony meets on his journey to Brazil. For each of them, in the novel's last chapters, Waugh contrives parallel glimpses of the City, already well-established as luminous, translucent, many-watered, shining, a 'radiant sanctuary'. While Tony wanders in the jungle, Brenda and Beaver see out the last party of the season. Beyond the curtained restaurant, London at dawn is transformed into a visionary mirage:

The empty streets ran with water, and the rising sun caught it as it bubbled round the hydrants; the men in their overalls swung the nozzles of their hoses and the water jetted and cascaded in a sparkle of light. (*HD* 197)

But inside the air is stuffy and Beaver is restless: Brenda's dream is about to fade. Tony's brief shipboard romance with Thérèse is presented in just the same terms. After days of foul weather come sunlight and calm, 'blue water that caught the sun in a thousand brilliant points, dazzling the eyes'. The ship itself, had Tony but known it, is another mirage of the elusive City, with its bright decks and shining portholes. Thérèse is Tony's little sister in aspiration, greedy for an Aromatic Jam no different from Hetton. She confides that she's on her way home to find a rich Catholic husband. 'It will be easy because I have no brothers or sisters and my father has one of the best houses in Trinidad,' she says. 'Our son will have the house. It will be easy,' and again, 'in Trinidad it will be quite easy'. On Tony's analogy we know already that her world of naïve expectation and childlike certainty is doomed.

In Search of a City ends with Tony's fevered vision of his butler announcing 'The City is served'. The *fata morgana* of its alabaster towers and fluttering pennants draw him on towards Todd's hut, and a life sentence reading Dickens aloud to a madman. This is truly the worst of all right things in the wrong place. Waugh himself was reading Dickens 'with avid relish' in Brazil.[15] In the first year of his marriage, Tony enjoyed reading aloud to Brenda, until she confessed it was 'torture' for her. He read happily to John Andrew on winter evenings in the nursery. In entirely different circumstances, this fate would have held no horrors for him.

*

Waugh prepares for the novel's remorselessly slow-moving climax with admirable economy. Tony's delirious hallucinations in the forest allow Waugh to bring together a phantasmagoric jumble of past miseries and present nightmares. All time is present, as Tony relives Brenda's infidelity, John Andrew's death, animal snap with Mrs Rattery, the two breakfasts in Brighton, the bribe of green mechanical mice and the flight of

Rosa and her terrified Indian guides. In the next chapter, Tony's continued hallucinations enable Waugh to replace the short story's artlessly lengthy flashback, detailing the reason for Henty's flight to Brazil, by a single economical paragraph in which Tony comes to his final realization.[16] Like Lear, he finds reason in madness:

> 'I will tell you what I have learned in the forest, where time is different. There is no City. Mrs Beaver has covered it with chromium plating and converted it into flats. Three guineas a week, each with a separate bathroom. Very suitable for base love. And Polly will be there. She and Mrs Beaver under the fallen battlements...' (*HD* 325, AMS 97)

For Tony, this is the final bitter recognition of his vain ideals. For Waugh, it is much more. Here in Brazil, *time is different* (the phrase is repeated four times in five pages), and *There is no City* resonates far beyond the novel's materialist world. It evokes the Biblical lamentation for the Fall of Jerusalem, later to recur in *Brideshead*: 'For here we have no continuing city, but we seek one to come.'[17] That is, the temporal world does not last; only heaven is eternal. But in Tony's humanist, secular world there can be no abiding City, neither earthly nor celestial, neither here nor to come. And in his living death with Mr Todd (in German *Tod* means death), there will be no time either. Todd steals Tony's watch to fob off the explorers who come looking for him. On the eve of their arrival he sets up an Indian drinking bout where Tony is drugged into a deep sleep. They are told that Tony is dead. But Tony lives on in a limbo where nothing can mark off the uniform succession of hours, days and years. In his interminable secular purgatory, there is no hope of escape, or redemption.[18]

*

This dénouement also derives from Waugh's Brazilian travels. During his days of miserable privation and exhaustion, tormented (like Tony) by every conceivable parasite, footsore and saddle-weary, he was sustained by the goal of a settlement called Boa Vista ('beautiful sight'), locally reputed to be an El Dorado of every conceivable luxury. When he finally reached it, he was bitterly disappointed, and the mock-heroic lamentation of *Ninety-Two Days* clearly prefigures the fallen battlements of Tony's Camelot:

> ...the Boa Vista of my imagination had come to grief. Gone; engulfed in an earthquake, uprooted by a tornado and tossed sky-high like chaff in the wind, scorched up with brimstone like Gomorrah, toppled over with trumpets like Jericho, ploughed like Carthage...tall Troy was down. *(92 Days* 87)

Waugh's subsequent, repeatedly thwarted attempts to leave Boa Vista, where he was stranded for weeks instead of the promised few days, create the funniest, low-key comic sequence in the book. The mundane frustrations of this enforced sojourn, merged with his single night chez Mr Christie, are transformed into the transcendental horror of Tony's doom.

Many critics feel that Tony *deserves* some kind of 'punishment', finding fault with his – and Waugh's – reactionary rejection of progress, from the virtues of *en suite* bathrooms to the convenience of open marriages. To do so is to misunderstand a satiric reticence Waugh later regretted. Our age cannot see its own face in his glass, because the values he attacks obliquely are the values our century espouses. The thoughtless, freethinking liberalism of Malcolm Bradbury, and others, blinkers them to Waugh's repudiation of a society he sees as 'humanist', godless and adulterous. For them, it is rational and sexually liberated. The blame is laid on Tony.[19] Hence, in 'Fan-Fare' Waugh pointedly denied that he was a satirist, because satire requires a moral base shared by author and readers, which Waugh felt no longer existed. Regrettably, his critics' misperceptions prove him right. So, for instance, Bradbury comments on Brenda's inadvertent response to John Andrew's death, not as a sign of her moral degradation, but as exhibiting the virtues of her adulterous relationship:

> The effect is less outrageous than delicate, calling up other than moral responses; it appeals to truthfulness, to the tenderness between Beaver and Brenda that has genuinely been established, to the boredom that Brenda has felt at Hetton and the excitement of London which has made her happy again.[20]

The moral chaos attacked by Waugh is all too evident in Bradbury's obtuseness. Are truthfulness and tenderness not moral concepts? Are truthfulness, tenderness – or *'genuine'* above all! – accurate terms for the attachment between Beaver and Brenda? Or for her lies and callousness to Tony? Is she to be excused merely because she was bored and is now happy? *Does her affair make her happy?*

In America the novel was published in a serialized form for which Waugh provided a different ending that replaced the entire Brazilian section and the epilogue.[21] Waugh's brief alternative, disdainfully titled 'By Special Request', provides a profoundly ironic, mundane conclusion robbed of any eternal dimension, as grim as the derisively titled 'Happy Ending' closing *Vile Bodies*. Tony's humdrum travels pass without comment. He returns home, and rejoins Brenda. He fails to say anything about her affair. Later she becomes pregnant. He secretly takes over her London flat for affairs of his own.

For readers with other than moral responses, for 'humanist' readers in its lowest sense, that may indeed seem a happy ending. All is well.

5

Scoop
1938

Waugh had one extraordinary experience in his Brazilian travels. On the long trek back from disappointing Boa Vista, he set out alone before dawn one day, confidently riding towards the encampment of St Ignatius. The Catholic priest there, tactful Father Mather, was the kindest of hosts. He would be pleasantly surprised by Waugh's unexpected appearance at midday.

Waugh was under the impression that he knew his way. There was the familiar line of the hills; here the creek that the map erroneously marked as a substantial river. Here, too, was a clear path through the savannah's dry scrub. The early morning was fresh and cool; the horse stepped out briskly. The day wore on; the sun grew hot; the path dwindled and disappeared. Waugh dismounted to lead his exhausted horse. He had eaten nothing the night before. He had no provisions. His native guides were hours behind him. He was thirsty, hungry, and lost. 'It was one of the low spots of the journey,' he remarks, with studied understatement. 'I had been given a medal of St Christopher before I left London. I felt that now, if ever, was the moment to invoke supernatural assistance. And it came' (*92 Days* 110).

In quick succession Waugh found water – a broad creek flowing in the wrong direction. Horse and man drank and set out again. 'And there the real miracle occurred.' He came across a Wapishiana Indian outside his solitary hut saddling an ox. He spoke English. He was setting out for Bon Success via St Ignatius. His wife gave Waugh a copious meal. Waugh was too tired to do more than collapse in the old man's hammock, and calculate the likelihood of such a collocation of coincidences. He estimated a cumulative probability of 1:54,750,000 before he even reached the end of the sequence.[1] Being no mathematician, he gave up and assigned the play of chance to a benevolent intervention by St Christopher.

At the end of *Ninety-Two Days* Waugh sums up his downbeat account as a 'direct, and I hope accurate' chronicle. 'It makes no claims to being a spiritual odyssey. Whatever changes there were – and all experience makes some change – are the writer's own property and not a marketable commodity.' His statement prompts, and forbids, further rumination by an outsider.

Waugh made no material capital out of his miraculous experience. It would be presumptuous to hazard more about his spiritual life than he does himself. Certainly great changes occurred between the composition of *A Handful of Dust* and *Scoop*.

Waugh returned from Brazil in May 1933. *Ninety-Two Days* was quickly written in the autumn. He spent the first months of 1934 in Morocco, absorbed in the composition of *A Handful of Dust*, which was completed in England by the spring. In July, at a couple of days' notice, Waugh joined a summer expedition to the Arctic, where he and his two companions nearly lost their lives in freak floods. Among Waugh's travels, this experience alone furnished nothing more than a short article, dismissively subtitled *Fiasco in the Arctic*. It had no perceptible influence on his fiction. Yet there must have been an accumulating spiritual debt of gratitude. Immediately on his return, in September 1934, he began the biography of the Elizabethan Catholic martyr, *Edmund Campion*, completing it by the next spring. A gift to celebrate the new buildings of Campion Hall in Oxford, its royalties went to the Hall. At the same time, Waugh was contributing numerous unpaid articles and reviews to the Catholic paper, *The Tablet*. None of this work was, in Waugh's view, 'a marketable commodity'. The increasing seriousness of his religious commitment is clear.

There are two other important strands in Waugh's life at this time, which are closely bound up with his growing Catholic engagement: love and divorce. After the breakup of his marriage, he had fallen in love with Teresa Jungman, a beautiful and devout Catholic socialite. She steadfastly refused anything more than friendship to Waugh, still technically a married man. The limitations of their relationship had sent Waugh to Brazil with a 'heart of lead' (*D* 356). It was she who gave him the medal of St Christopher.

When Waugh converted to Catholicism after his wife's desertion, he had assumed that both factors would debar him from remarriage and fatherhood. Although Catholic friends later advised him of the possibility of annulment, he set in train the lengthy ecclesiastical procedure only after his return from Brazil. On the eve of the preliminary court hearings in October-November 1933, the elated Waugh proposed to Teresa, 'and got raspberry. So that is that, eh. Stiff upper lip and dropped cock' (*L* 81). Waugh's *Diaries* show that he was still hopelessly in love with her during his Arctic adventure in the summer of 1934. Meanwhile the ecclesiastical courts had heard his appeal, but returned no answer.

It is telling that in this suspended period of subterranean change Waugh's diary falls silent, many letters are lost, and of the remainder many are undated. At an unidentified point during the composition of *Campion*, Waugh took 'a *great* fancy to a young lady named Laura', variously described in his letters as, first, a 'white mouse'; later 'only 18 years old, virgin, Catholic, quiet and astute', with 'a long thin nose and skin as thin as bromo' – a high-class, translucent lavatory paper (*L* 80, 92). The tender, tentative relationship grew through the months devoted to completing *Campion*, and was sustained in the four months Waugh then spent in Abyssinia as war correspondent for the *Daily Mail*. On his return in January 1936 he heard that – after two years delay – the Diocesan Court had finally found in favour of his annulment. Final ratification still had to come from Rome, but there was no reason to expect further difficulties. Waugh settled down to writing up his next travel book, *Waugh in Abyssinia* (the publishers' punning title which he abhorred). He proposed to Laura in a memorably tender, honest letter (*L* 104–5).

Six months passed. Still no news from Rome.

In the end Waugh undertook a penitential pilgrimage to Lough Derg in Ireland. After two year's silence his diary is resumed on the dawn of his return:

London, Tuesday 7 July, 1936

Holyhead midnight; sleeper and sandwich. Euston 5.30 daylight. Drove through empty streets to St James's where I found telegram 'Decision favourable. Godfrey.' (*D* 391)

Archbishop Godfrey presided over the Diocesan Court in Rome. Waugh bathed, shaved, but did not sleep. At 8 he rang Laura's home and was told that she was in church with her mother. He followed, knelt behind them; in the porch he told his news. The same morning he visited Diana Cooper whom he found in a face pack; within weeks that *trouvaille* triggered the opening scene of the future *Scoop*.[2]

Many years later he admitted to Christopher Sykes, his first biographer and friend, that the inexplicable delay in Rome 'nearly drove me mad, but I can never feel any bitterness about it. I regard it as manifestly the work of the Holy Ghost [...] If things had gone as I wanted I would never have married Laura.'[3]

*

In August 1935 Waugh had joined the company of some hundred journalists in Abyssinia, waiting for Mussolini's expected invasion after the rainy season ended. The *Daily Mail* was one of only two English papers taking the pro-Italian stance that accorded with Waugh's Catholic sympathies. The assignment was not a success. Four months' close proximity deepened Waugh's previous loathing of the press. He found journalists 'lousy competitive hysterical lying' (*L* 98). He missed the one great scoop of the war, and his own scoops all flopped. No wonder he wanted to call 'Waugh in Abyssinia' *A Disappointing War*.

The major scoop of the war concerned the involvement of an American-backed entrepreneur, Rickett – one of several proto-types for *Scoop*'s Mr Baldwin – who negotiated a vast concession of mineral rights which Haile Selassie granted to the Americans, in the terrain to be covered by the impending Italian advance. It was an ingenious act of self-defence on Selassie's part, and is transferred directly to *Scoop*, to the confusion of William Boot. Waugh was more acute than his politically infantile hero. On the journey to Djibouti, Rickett's airy name-dropping of the pack he hunted with in the Midlands had already aroused Waugh's suspicions, but not William's.[4] But when the Rickett story broke, Waugh was out of Addis Ababa following a more exciting trail of his own, involving a French spy, improbably named Count Maurice de Roquefeuil de Bousquet. Within hours of this story,

Waugh stumbled on secret information about the Abyssinian line of defence. Neither was of the least interest to the *Daily Mail*. The eyes of the world were on Rickett alone. Later, Waugh obtained advance details of the Italian Minister's departure from Addis, which he knew indicated the beginning of the Italian invasion. To outmanoeuvre his rivals, he cabled the news in Latin. No one at the *Mail* knew Latin. The message was thrown away, Waugh's scoop misfired and he was fired. *A Disappointing War* indeed.

Throughout *Waugh in Abyssinia*, the journalists' heightened expectations acquire an ironic refrain: 'How wrong we were!' Many colourful fates were predicted for Haile Selassie following the Italian invasion – suicide, assassination, death in battle, rescue by British aeroplane. In the event, he quietly took a train out of the country. 'How wrong we were!' Similar reversals recur in the press bulletins. A story was floated that an American nurse had been blown up in a bombing raid. Waugh and his colleagues wired back, 'Nurse unupblown'. That reversal becomes a feature of *Scoop*: 'ADEN UNWARWISE', 'UNPRO-CEED LAKUWARD', 'NEWS EXYOU UNRECEIVED'.

In a letter to his friend, Diana Cooper (the original of *Scoop's* Mrs Stitch), Waugh told her that the *Mail's* new war correspondent in French Somaliland 'has never set foot in Abyssinia [...]' he sits in his hotel describing an entirely imaginary campaign – 18,000 abyssinians and 500,000 sheep killed by poison gas [...] in a place he found on the map which in point of fact consists of one brackish well' (*Wu/Stitch* 56). A bitter observation, directly dramatized in *Scoop*:

> In his room in the annexe Sir Jocelyn Hitchcock [...] went to the map on the wall and took out his flag [...] hovering uncertainly over the unscaled peaks and uncharted rivers of that dark terrain, finally decided, and pinned it firmly in the spot marked as the city of Laku.
>
> [...]'Hitchcock's story has broken. He's at the Fascist head-quarters scooping the world.'
> 'Where?'
> 'Town called Laku.'
> 'But he can't be. Bannister told me there was no such place.' (*Scoop* 139, 157)

'Laku' is a cartographer's misunderstanding. In Ishmaelite it means 'I don't know'. Mendacious Sir Jocelyn is based on Sir Percival Phillips, who scooped greenhorn Waugh and broke the Rickett story. Fortunately for him, he died a year before *Scoop* was published.

In December 1935 Waugh left Abyssinia with relief. On his way home he decided to call on an acquaintance he had met in London, a diplomat's wife whose name he had forgotten, living, he thought, in Baghdad. 'I did a thing at Bagdad that only happens in nightmares,' he told Diana Cooper. In Addis he had made enquiries: 'I said who is a pretty fair haired woman married to a diplomat in Bagdad and they said that's easy we can tell you in one she is Tita Clark-Kerr. Well that sounded a likely name so I sent a telegram [...]' It said 'Would I be welcome if I came to you for the weekend Evelyn Waugh'. The reply was oddly unenthusiastic: 'Fairly. Ambassador.' Undeterred, Waugh 'arrived to find two totally strange people and my real hostess lives in Tehran.'[5] It was the first of two mistaken identities fuelling *Scoop*. The second came when Waugh returned to Abyssinia in the summer of 1936 to observe the country under Italian rule. He flew to Asmara to see Mussolini's single significant achievement, a modern Roman road penetrating the country to its northernmost interior. The town, originally built for a population of 2,000 had been swollen by an Italian workforce of 60,000, and what Waugh tactfully described as 'seven unattached white women' provided by the considerate Italian authorities. The telegram announcing the arrival of the ambiguously gendered Evelyn Waugh reduced the local Press Officer to a fever of ill-founded sexual excitement. He met every possible train and plane. 'The trousered and unshaven figure which finally greeted him must have been a hideous blow' (*WA* 246).

The *Daily Mail* had provided Waugh with his first and last typewriter. Crossing the Red Sea on his way to Addis Ababa, he learned to type: 'There is no news and if there wrew wr were funny how hard that word is to get right wr were gotvit...' (*L* 99). His inexpertise is jovially bestowed on William Boot:

> One finger was not enough; he used both hands. The keys rose together like bristles on a porcupine, jammed and were extricated; curious anagrams appeared on the paper before him [...] Still he typed. (*Scoop* 213)

All these trivial experiences shape *Scoop*, Waugh's happiest and most intricately constructed novel, which is elaborately built on a playful pattern of mistaken identities, anagrams, metathesis (switched letters, as in 'methatesis'), narrative reversals, transposition and transfiguration.

*

Scoop is strung between two major transpositions pivoting on false identities. At the beginning, William Boot, rustic author of the *Beast*'s nature column, is mistakenly sent as war correspondent to Ishmaelia, instead of his cousin, the popular socialite novelist John Boot. The novel ends with William's atrocious Uncle Theodore masquerading in William's place as guest of honour in Lord Copper's celebratory banquet. The novel's motto could be *The Boot is on the wrong foot*.

Transposition is the novel's camshaft: the plot rotates around it; the smallest stylistic cogs drive it. In Waugh's habitual manner, the pattern is introduced by an arresting cameo on the first page:

> Algernon Stitch was standing in the hall; his bowler hat was on his head; his right hand, grasping a crimson, royally emblazoned dispatch case, emerged from the left sleeve of his overcoat; his other hand burrowed petulantly in his breast pocket [...] He spoke indistinctly, for he was holding a folded copy of the morning paper between his teeth.
> 'Can't get it on,' he seemed to say. (*Scoop* 4)

This is an icon of transposition: the minister has his right arm down the left coat-sleeve. Throughout the novel, minor crossovers repeat the leitmotif. In the Megapolitan offices 'on a hundred lines reporters talked at cross-purposes'. In Ishmaelia, the lost luggage-van finally reappears with its contents intact – because 'mysteriously it had become attached to the special train; had in fact been transposed.' Mrs Stitch struggles with a crossword clue that sounds like an anagram. Try 'Hottentot', she says. Or 'Terracotta'. (Actually, it's 'detonated'). At the *Beast*'s Megalopolitan offices, William's first meeting with the foreign editor, Mr Salter, is fraught with cross-purposes and Spooneresque metatheses. Salter has been advised to win William over with heavy hospitality and light conversation on agricultural matters – swedes, parsnips, that sort of thing. Countrymen, he's reliably informed, call them 'roots'.

> There was a pause, during which Mr Salter planned a frank and disarming opening. 'How are your roots, Boot?' It came out wrong. 'How are your boots, root?' he asked.
> William, glumly awaiting some fulminating rebuke, started and said, 'I beg your pardon?'
> 'I mean brute,' said Mr Salter. (*Scoop* 33)

Further linguistic reversals litter the intricate maze. The novel opens on 'a biting-cold mid-June morning'. London newsboys are selling 'the lunch-time edition of the evening papers'. At Boot Magna, the telegram summoning William to London is delivered by 'Troutbeck, the aged boy'. At the end of the novel, Mr Salter is met at the railway station by the village idiot, picking at paint-bubbles on the fence with 'a toe-like thumb-nail'. Under the moonlight 'the warm land lay white as frost'. Each shuttlecock reversal gives the reader a little shock of surprise.

In his habitual manner, Waugh carefully clusters these tropes of transposition for maximum impact, at the beginning and end of the novel. Transposition drives the laconic directive summoning William to his first journalistic assignment: '*Mrs Stitch. Gentlemen's Lavatory*'. Diana Cooper was a dashing and intrepid driver of a tiny black car. Waugh transposes this trait, like many of her other idiosyncracies, to Mrs Stitch, who has evaded a London traffic jam via an underground public convenience. It is another bold icon of checkerboard opposites: 'At the foot of the stairs, making, for the photographer, a happy contrast to the white tiles about it, stood a little black motor car.'[6] In Ishmaelia the identity cards distributed to William and his journalist colleagues turn on another loaded switchover. They are small orange documents, originally printed for the registration of prostitutes. The space for the thumb-print has been replaced by a passport photo 'and the word "journalist" substituted in neat Ishmaelite characters' – a pointed literalization of Stanley Baldwin's memorable accusation that the press exercise 'power without responsibility – the prerogative of the harlot throughout the ages'.

Baldwin's phrase was directed against the two press barons, Lords Rothermere and Beaverbrook, of the *Daily Mail* and *Daily Express*, whose concerted press campaign failed to oust him as

Leader of the Opposition in 1929. In *Scoop* they become Lords Zinc and Copper, of the *Brute* and the *Beast* respectively. Like Baldwin, Waugh had little respect for journalists or politicians. *Scoop* is subtitled *A Novel about Journalists*, but its political situation is no less fatuous than its reporters. As Waugh explained to the novel's prospective film-script writers, 'No great pains need to be taken to make a plausible plot for the central section. The essentials are that a potentially serious situation is being treated frivolously, sensationally, and dishonestly by the assembled Press.'[7]

In opposition to the established Jackson regime, the two political parties in Ishmaelia are the rival world powers of the late 1930s. Waugh loathed them both. Ishmaelia's Marxists and Fascists are diametrically identical, indistinguishably opposed. William asks Mr Salter who is fighting whom in Ishmaelia:

> 'I think it's the Patriots and the Traitors.'
> 'Yes, but which is which?'
> 'O, I don't know *that*. *That*'s Policy, you see [...]'
> 'I gather it's between the Reds and the Blacks.'
> 'Yes, but it's not quite as easy as that. You see, they are all Negroes. And the Fascists won't be called black because of their racial pride, so they are called White after the White Russians. And the Bolshevists *want* to be called black because of *their* racial pride. So when you *say* black you mean red, and when you *mean* red you say white...'
> (*Scoop* 55)

Even Mr Salter is confused here. (He should have said, 'when you *mean* black, you say white.') The point is not just that both parties are indistinguishable, but that political propaganda makes black seem white, and vice versa – as the orators of both sides make clear. The Ishmaelite Bolshevist claims that all whites are really black: 'Who built the Pyramids? A Negro. Who invented the circulation of the blood? A Negro'. The Ishmaelian Fascist (a Negro clad in a white silk shirt) claims that all blacks are really white – 'As you will see for yourself, we are pure Aryans. In fact we were the first white colonisers of Central Africa'.[8] While the Italian Fascists were Black Shirts, the Ishmaelian Fascists are White (shirts). By the same inverted logic the Ishmaelian Bolshevists are led by a Red, black Dr Benito, the antithetical equivalent of the White black(shirt), Benito Mussolini.

In Waugh's habitual manner, this checkerboard motif, already established by Mrs Stitch's black mini in the white-tiled gents, is also maintained in linguistic miniature. A venerable Ishmaelian Minister looks like 'a Victorian worthy in negative, black face, white whiskers, black hands', and when the Reds temporarily take over Jacksonburg, 'a red flag hung black against the night sky'.

There is nothing to choose between Ishmaelia's rival parties. Both think of themselves as Patriots and the opposition as Traitors. So, in trivial miniature, we also find Pip and Pop the Bedtime Pets, in the *Beast*'s Children's Corner, next to William's nature column and a recipe for 'Waffle Scramble' – and, later their alliterating equivalent, the Popotakis Ping-Pong Parlour in Jacksonburg. Ping-pong's instant reversibility – its high-speed ricochet to and fro, getting nowhere, epitomizes the novel's elaborately inconclusive narrative structure, and the op-art flicker of its identically opposed political parties. The novel's interchangeable press magnates – Copper and Zinc, *Brute* and *Beast* – are merely further players in the same tournament. The *Beast*, Lord Copper claims, 'stands for strong mutually antagonistic governments everywhere'.[9] Patriot or Traitor, journalist or whore? There is no difference between the mendaciously aggressive, infantile worlds of Press and Politics, the Pip and Pop of *Scoop*'s fantastic world.

*

On his return to Abyssinia in 1936, Waugh confessed that 'it was fun being pro-Italian when it was an unpopular and (I thought) losing cause. I have little sympathy with these exultant Fascists now' (*L* 109). *Scoop* is not a political novel. It ironically celebrates the magical capacity of the press to conjure fantasy news into reality, as Wenlock Jakes creates a minor Balkan war by arriving at the wrong place, and describing the carnage invented, not seen, from his windows. The world's press follow, and within days real revolution breaks out. The press have a fairy-tale capacity to turn non-events into news, and, by their habitually pre-emptive reportage, to rob late but genuine news of newsworthiness. *Scoop*'s satire of journalists is, as Waugh noted early in its composition, 'light and excellent'.

'This light-hearted tale' Waugh repeats, in a later Preface to the novel, 'was the fruit of a time of general anxiety and distress but, for its author, one of peculiar happiness.' He was courting Laura, and serenely happy. The novel took an unprecedentedly long time to write, spanning as it did Waugh's engagement, house-hunting, marriage, honeymoon, and life in a new home. His diaries and letters are filled with unprecedented freshness. Days are spent 'leaf-catching with Laura'; she is his 'darling child', 'my blessed child', his white mouse nicknamed 'Whiskers'. Hardly surprising, then, that *Scoop*'s major source is Beatrix Potter's *Tale of Johnny Town-Mouse*:

> Johnny Town-Mouse was born in a cupboard. Timmie Willie was born in a garden. Timmie Willie was a little country mouse who went to town by mistake in a hamper.

Book I revolves around William Boot's apprehensive journey up to town, away from his secure country nest. John Boot, his sophisticated metropolitan cousin, is a self-evident Johnny Town-Mouse. In Book III, the role of Town-Mouse passes to Mr Salter, reluctantly forced out of frenetic, familiar London into the bucolic terrors of Boot Magna.

Waugh is both Johnny Town-Mouse and Timmie Willie. John Boot, the fashionable novelist, is pointedly reminiscent of Waugh in 1934. He is the author of eight books, like Waugh when he left for the Arctic. The first, a life of Rimbaud, is the equivalent of Waugh's first book, the biography of Rossetti. The last, dismissively titled *Waste of Time*, 'a studiously modest description of some harrowing months among the Patagonian Indians', is Waugh's studiously modest *Ninety-Two Days*. At the end of *Scoop* John Boot joins an all-female expedition to the Antarctic, the opposite of Waugh's all-male expedition to the Arctic. Waugh was pursuing Teresa; John Boot is in flight from a young lady who gives him a lucky talisman of Irish bog-oak, a ludicrous secular inversion of Teresa's miraculous medal of St Christopher.

At the beginning of *Scoop* Waugh deliberately encourages the reader's misapprehension that John is his hero. It is the first of many false trails and futile detours. Waugh wanted to leave the chilly, Tatler-ish John Boot behind him. In his letter proposing to Laura he offers her a variety of potential life-styles, from the improvident rootlessness of his past, to 'a settled patriarchal life with a large household' (*L* 110). William's absurd family at Boot Magna is a nightmare version of the rural patriarchy Waugh was to establish with Laura. His dreams were coming true.

And so the novel's stylistic markers swell from anagram, metathesis, reversal and transposition, to transformation and transfiguration. In Ishmaelia, as in real-life Abyssinia, transformative awakenings have a natural source in the long-awaited ending of the rainy season:

> Next morning William awoke in a new world.
> As he stood on his veranda calling for his boy, he slowly became aware of the transformation which had taken place overnight. The rains were over [...] the dank weeds of Frau Dressler's garden had suddenly burst into crimson flower. (*Scoop* 197)

Waugh evokes this transfigured world in transcendent terms reminiscent of his most impassioned letters to Laura: 'It was a morning of ethereal splendour – such a morning as Noah knew [...] such a morning as only the angels saw on the first day.' Such transformations are the stuff of fairy tale. And that, of course, is Waugh's second source for *Scoop*.

Beauty and the Beast haunts the novel – a fleeting distorted echo at first, in the premonitory pairing of the rival papers, the *Brute* and the *Beast*; in Salter's anagrammatic waffle scramble of boots/roots/brute; in William's schoolboy nickname ('Beastly'). It only emerges clearly, like the cannibalism closing *Black Mischief*, with William's triumphant return to London as BOOT OF THE BEAST. William is the transformed Beast – transfigured from dud cub reporter to the cynosure of Fleet Street, the very opposite of poor sacked Evelyn. Yet Waugh specifically chooses not to end his novel on this spurious high note, instructing *Scoop*'s would-be film-makers that 'Boot should return home without ambition ever to leave again'. Like Timmie Willie, William happily returns to the obscurity from which he came.

The whole novel is thus a long detour to nowhere. The maze of its narrative is characterized by U-turns, detours, and red herrings that deliberately confuse the reader and its cast. In the last pages, a vinous optimism descends. Happy endings abound, as befits a fairy tale. A happy ending for Uncle Theodore, for Mr Salter, for Kätchen; for William, back in Boot Magna, composing

Lush Places again. '...*The waggons lumber in the lane under the golden glory of harvested sheaves,* he wrote; *maternal rodents pilot their furry brood through the stubble...*'

Waugh was no sentimentalist. William's idyll is capped by Waugh's coda. 'Outside the owls hunted maternal rodents and their furry brood.' It was May 1938. Laura, maternal rodent, had given birth to their first child, and war was on its way.

6

Work Suspended
1942
(composed 1939)

Waugh and Laura settled into Piers Court, a Georgian mansion of 'startling beauty' they discovered during their house-hunting in the winter of 1936/7 (*Wu/Stitch* 62). Waugh threw himself into 'prodigies of destruction', clearing its overgrown alleys and shrubberies. He acquired an authentic Gothic balustrade for the garden, and began collecting unfashionable Victoriana for the house. 'Ran amok at village shop,' he records with satisfaction just before his wedding, later telling Diana Cooper: 'I buy a lot of ugly things. I find I like them best and they are very much cheaper' (*D* 420; *Wu/Stitch* 67). Towards the end of the war, he writes affectionately to Laura of the Yugoslavian sculptor making 'mud pies' of his head: 'It will be a preposterous possession. It is by having preposterous possessions that one can keep them at arm's length. Well I have a preposterous wife have I not?' (*L* 198).

Georgian, Gothic, Victorian, keeping things at arm's length – these preoccupations, apparently the harmless eccentricities of a nouveau country gentleman, mark a significant consolidation of Waugh's aesthetic values. From his earliest fiction he had combined a craftsman's concern for the classic demands of elegant structure with his idiosyncratic gusto for exuberant excess. Now these opposing instincts fuelled his acquired expertise in the classic architecture of rural England where he made his home, and the Victorian furnishings he bought for it – the whatnot, the umbrella stand, and the crowded, finely painted canvasses of Victorian narrative art. Newly married, with a swiftly growing family in prospect, he deliberately turned his back on the present, trying for as long as possible to keep the world of contemporary politics at arm's length.

Between 1937 and 1939 Waugh assiduously studied the habits and habitats of his country neighbours, viewing their homes with a narrow eye – 'Good early Victorian furniture, fine grounds'; 'commodious, nondescript, very cheap house' (*D* 431). He built up a fine antiquarian collection of architectural manuals and schooled himself in the gradations of the classical Orders – Tuscan, Doric, Ionic, Corinthian, Composite. His own journalism followed an equally stately progression from the first essential ('Laying Down a Wine Cellar', December 1937) to a eulogy of rural Augustan architecture and its inhabitants ('A Call to the Orders', February 1938); a survey of Victorian furniture ('The Philistine Age of English Decoration', March 1938); ending with the countryside's current demography ('The New Rustics', July 1939). Rural life in all its aspects had become 'a permanent and delicious obsession' (*EAR* 259).

In all these essays there is a perceptible change of style, clearly marked in the opening paragraph of 'A Call to the Orders':

> How profusely they are strewn over England, the monuments of our Augustan age of architecture! They stand on all sides of us, rebuking, in their measured Johnsonian diction, their degenerate posterity. ('A Call to the Orders', February 1938, *EAR*, 215)

Waugh's prose style imitates his admired architectural model. It becomes ample, antiquated, orotund, its occasional pomposity sharpening his deliberate plunges into bathetic modernity. As in this essay's next sentence, describing

> London, that noble deer bayed and brought down and torn in pieces; the city of lamentations, ruled by Lilliputians and exploited by Yahoos, whose splendid streets [...] are now fit only to serve as the promenades of pet dogs or as vast ashtrays for the stubs of a million typists.

There is a specific point to this high style. Waugh is fighting against contemporary degeneracy on multiple fronts, including what he calls, in another essay, 'the final annulment of the long-estranged marriage of popular journalism and literature' (*EAR* 232). The Augustan manner first explored in his journalism, quoted here, will become the chosen model for his popular fiction.

An Englishman's Home, Waugh's first short story after *Scoop* and one of his best, is set in the unspoilt village of Much Malcock, where Mr Metcalfe, Waugh's *alter ego,* has just settled in his retirement. The threat of developers forces the village's elite into uneasy alliance. They occupy precisely differentiated rungs on the rural ladder Waugh had spent the last year mastering – Mr Metcalfe, *arriviste* owner of Much Malcock Hall (locally known as 'the Grumps'); dowager Lady Peabody at Much Malcock House; Colonel Hodge at the Manor; the childless, arty-vegan Hornbeams at the Old Mill (a couple straight out of Richmal Crompton's *William* books).[1] The story is a little gem of social comedy, compactly narrated in Waugh's new, measured diction.

*

The joy Waugh experienced in the Catholic community is particularly perceptible in the months following his marriage. Directly after the publication of *Scoop* in May 1938, he and Laura attended the Eucharistic Congress in Budapest. They spent August to October in Mexico, where he was collecting material for his next, commissioned book – *Robbery Under Law,* an account of the state appropriation of Mexico's oilfields under the socialist President Cárdenas. Waugh wrong-foots his future detractors by describing the Mexican peasantry, engrossed in worship in the Cathedral of Guadalupe, with strong fellow-feeling and awed respect (*RUL* 234). So much for the unrepentant snob of popular caricature. In Budapest, he misses his place on the journalists' barge for the Ascension Day flotilla on the Danube, and rejoices to be lost in the bankside crowds:

> I shall always be grateful for the confusion of tongues which landed me there [...] It was just these crowds, so diverse and so unified, that formed one of the most inspiring spectacles. One longed for them to be greater, to include all one's friends and relations and acquaintances and strangers. ('Impressions of Splendour and Grace', June 1938, *EAR* 235, 237)

Hitler's annexation of Austria preceded the trip to Budapest; Chamberlain's ill-fated Munich Agreement ('Peace in our Time') coincided with Waugh's period in Mexico. His increasing solidarity with the Christian democracy of souls was sharpened by its contrast to a world 'plague-stricken by politics'.

> At Budapest differences were being forgotten and ties strengthened; a few hours distant the conflict which dates from the fall of Adam still raged uncertainly. Europe was still divided. Here all was sunshine and warmth; there the sky was dark and a cold wind stirring. Who could say how long the good hours would last? (Ibid, EAR 238)

Waugh first predicted a second world war when writing *Vile Bodies*, exactly ten years before it came to pass. Now the sense of doom is imminent. In Mexico he finds echoes of Communist Russia and Nazi Germany and foresees their consequences: 'Government is by a semi-military executive which overrides judicature and legislature; popular consent is achieved by agitation; education is a department of propaganda [...] In the drying up of civilisation, cracks appear and widen; the parched nations shrink away from one another' (*RUL* 118, 85). His derision of the indistinguishable Fascisto-Bolshevists of *Scoop*'s Ishmaelia is overshadowed by Hitler's new menace, 'crowd patriotism', and his foresight is unerring:

> In a mob people will applaud oratory and themselves shout words which individually each of them would regard as ridiculous; worse than that they will commit atrocities from which they will recoil with horror next morning. (*RUL* 264)

It is not surprising that Waugh's first impulse was to turn his back on this world, to hold it at arm's length for as long as the good hours might last. When Diana Cooper visited Piers Court in June 1939, she complained that she had to leave her radio in the car and forgo listening to the news. In late August he was 'restless' but was still 'maintaining our record as being the only family to eschew the radio throughout the crisis' (*D* 437). *Eschew* is a precise but dated locution Waugh noticeably overuses at this time (and later becomes contagious among his critics). It reflects the stance of deliberate withdrawal he attempted to maintain as war approached.

In this aloofness Waugh instinctively allies himself with two old favourites. There is a perceptible quickening of interest in his essays on Edward Lear, 'A Victorian Escapist' (May 1938), and 'Carroll and Dodgson' (October 1939 – Waugh's last collected essay before he joined the Marines). As an undergraduate

Waugh had called *Alice in Wonderland* 'an excellent book'. It had a marked influence on the structure of *Vile Bodies*. In *Remote People* Waugh found it, rather than any historical analogue, epitomized Haile Selassie's Abyssinia. It permeated Tony's hallucinations in *A Handful of Dust*.[2] Now he considers the intellectual make-up of both authors, whom he clearly finds congenial. They too exemplify his odd marriage of Augustan restraint with Victorian exuberance. Both Carroll and Lear were artists whose minds Waugh characterizes as *precise, fastidious, self-effacing, highly competent* – classic qualities which could be applied equally well to himself as an author. And Waugh, Carroll and Lear were all artists whose work was – also in Waugh's chosen terms – *anarchic, fantastic, nonsensical*, the literary equivalent of high-Victorian philistine decoration. Moreover, like Dodgson, whose creative work was 'supremely aloof from his material life', in the years between *Vile Bodies* and *A Handful of Dust* Waugh had also chosen to keep a self-protective distance between his wounded private self, and his fiction.

Waugh's essay on Lear, the *Victorian Escapist*, defends escapism as a genuine and fertile creative compulsion, rather than the term of opprobrium it became in wartime. His own ostentatious withdrawal from politics in the summer of 1939, which Diana Cooper found so shocking, was the logical end-point of his long-standing disdain for the 'preposterous distinctions of Left and Right' fiercely debated by his contemporaries throughout the thirties. The Non-Aggression Pact between Russia and Germany (23 August 1939) simplified everything, and 'brought peace to one English heart' as Waugh later wrote of his hero, Guy Crouchback. 'The enemy at last was in plain view, huge and hateful, all disguise cast off' (*MA* 5), and Waugh immediately began assiduous efforts to get called up (*D* 437). Aloof he may have been, but when the time came he was no escapist.

It is typical of Waugh's intellectual coherence that his apparently maverick detachment logically unites his political, religious, and aesthetic convictions. In 'Art from Anarchy', a review of 1937, he said:

> I do not think any artist, certainly no writer, can be a genuine Marxist, for a writer's material must be the individual soul (which is the preconception of Christendom), while the Marxist can only think

in classes and categories [...] The disillusioned Marxist becomes a Fascist; the disillusioned anarchist, a Christian. ('Art from Anarchy', September 1937, *EAR* 206)

Waugh had always been attracted to anarchic individualists, stateless buccaneers like Basil Seal and the immortal Grimes. Yet after his first wife's betrayal the disillusioned anarchist became a Catholic, and by 1939 Waugh's fiction begins to display an intensifying concern with the individual soul. Aldous Huxley, on the other hand, whom Waugh reviewed in 1937, adopts the fashionable Marxists' preference for classes and categories, confidently decreeing that 'The human mind has an invincible tendency to reduce the diverse to the identical [...] We derive a deep satisfaction from any doctrine which reduces irrational multiplicity to rational and comprehensible unity.' Huxley's views are anathema to Waugh, the conjuror of precise particulars. For Waugh,

This seems to me the reverse of the truth [...] The trees and crops and lie of the land, the nature of the soil, require a long apprenticeship before they reveal their individual characters; a row of buildings may be a mere horizon of masonry or, to the instructed, an intricate narration of history. Men and women are only types [...] until one knows them. The whole of thought and taste consists in distinguishing between similars. ('More Barren Leaves', December 1937, *EAR* 214)

All the patient studies of Waugh's rural life are audible in this credo. They fed into *Work Suspended*, begun in July 1939 and reluctantly abandoned when war was finally declared. This first-class, unfinished novel is characterized as the 'most enigmatic' of his writings.[3] Yet he called it 'my major work' in 1941, and, in 1942, as 'my best writing' at that time.[4] It is tantalizingly good. Its apparent enigmas are clarified by his current preoccupations. And it is important, even in its partial state, because it is the clear precursor of *Brideshead Revisited*.

*

The hero is John Plant, a successful detective-story writer whose father dies in the first chapter, and who falls in love with the pregnant wife of a friend in the second. Like the negligible novelist John Boot in *Scoop*, John Plant is a mocking self-caricature. Plant, like Waugh, feels he has reached a climacteric in his writing career. The puppet of Waugh's prescient irony, Plant reassures his anxious publisher that the average reader is unlikely to notice his new, merely technical experiments. Waugh's own innovations have similarly evaded notice, and yet they are clearly marked. Gone are the dazzling snatches of unattributed dialogue, cinematic cross-cutting and Modernist fragmentation characteristic of his earlier work. Gradually, too, the technique of central themes replayed in profligate and ingenious variations will be abandoned in the overtly Catholic novels to come. The transitional *Work Suspended* is already clad in a more formal, not uniformly successful Victorian mode. In *Campion* (1935) Waugh had first attempted interminable mock-Tudor sentences a paragraph long. Here they are transformed into over-elaborate extended metaphors, usually of war, to explore emotional states. For instance, shaken by his father's death, Plant observes that the civilized man has difficulty in dealing with his feelings:

> Not until they have assumed the livery of the defence can his emotions pass through the lines; sometimes they come massed in a wooden horse, sometimes as single spies, but there is always a Fifth Column among the garrison ready to receive them. Sabotage behind the lines, a blind raised and lowered at a lighted window, a wire cut, a bolt loosened, a file disordered – that is how the civilised man is undone. (*WS* 41)

This simply means that for Plant, admitting his emotions is an act of self-betrayal. He shares his creator's admiration of an art that – as Plant twice says of his own detective stories – has 'absolutely nothing of myself in it'.[5] Plant aspires to the artistic aloofness Waugh admired in Carroll.

Waugh's most important technical experiment relates to precisely this aloofness. In *Work Suspended*, for the first time, Waugh turns to first-person narrative. This allows the reader greater intimacy with the hero: we see things through his eyes. Yet Plant's story traces an emotional development closely related to Waugh's own. Paradoxically, it affords Waugh increased objectivity, because the impercipient Plant is unaware of his own emotional growth. Consequently his subjective narrative allows Waugh to be both self-distancing and critically self-revealing. This technical change is a first run for Charles

75

Ryder's unreliable narrative in *Brideshead Revisited*. Edith Sitwell was acute in recognizing the novelty of Waugh's achievement:

> 'You are doing something in this book which is entirely new. It seems the first time that a character, speaking through his own mouth, exhibits his nature so freely *without consciousness of what he is doing*.'[6]

*

The major, universally overlooked clue to this enigmatic novel's central theme is openly dropped in its first three words, the original title of chapter one: *My Father's House*. Superficially this refers to the house and studio of John Plant's father, which are bulldozed by developers at the end of the first chapter, to make way for yet another block of featureless London flats. Plant Senior, a fine outdated artist in the Pre-Raphaelite manner, was accidentally run over by a travelling salesman of women's hosiery. His ludicrous death is emblematic in secular, cultural terms (he refused to give way to the oncoming car). But the chapter's title carries a deeper resonance: it is a quotation of St John's Gospel, 14.ii: 'In my Father's House are many mansions'. There are many ways into the house of God.

John Plant, a casual atheist like his father, is unaware of this significance. He is an unappealing hero – prim, conceited, godless, emotionally barren, satisfied by impersonal weekly congress with a Berber prostitute while wintering in Fez to finish his latest novel. Initially, in spite of his father's death, he sees no reason to change his plans. It is only on his reluctant return to England that he first feels grief in his father's deserted studio, surveying his life's work. 'Sorrow, dammed and canalised, flowed fast' –

> For the civilised man [...] words form slowly like pus about his hurts; there are no clean wounds for him; first a numbness, then a long festering, then a scar ever ready to reopen. (WS 166)

I have already applied Plant's words to describe Waugh's emotional hardening after his first wife's desertion, and the painful purgation of *A Handful of Dust*, which he began while wintering, like Plant, in Fez. Waugh, too, enjoyed weekly congress with a Berber prostitute, but was considerably more affectionate about her than the chilly Plant.[7] *Work Suspended* traces the beginning of Plant's emotional softening and his surname signals the spiritual growth that is the central concern of this traditional *Bildungsroman*.

In *Work Suspended*'s second chapter Waugh's house-hunting with Laura is transferred to Plant and Lucy, the pregnant wife of his friend Roger Simmonds. Plant's blithe decision 'to arrange for the destruction of my father's house' affords him funds to buy a country home of his own. Plant is searching for what Waugh has just found, exactly matching Piers Court in nearly every detail:

> A *house*, no matter how dingy, [. . . with] a cellar, two staircases, high ceilings, a marble chimney-piece in the drawing room, room to turn a car at the front door, a coach-house and stable–yard, a walled kitchen garden, to cost not more than £3,000 in its finished state. (*WS* 174)

Plant's burgeoning love for Lucy is fostered by his search for a new home, but Lucy is not Laura. At the end of his life Waugh freely admitted to Diana Mosley that Plant's love for Lucy was partly based on his love for Diana immediately after his first wife's desertion, when Diana befriended him during her pregnancy as the wife of Bryan Guinness. 'I was infatuated with you. Not of course that I aspired to your bed,' he says, but 'yours was the first pregnancy I observed' (*L* 638, 639). It is described with memorable tenderness. Lucy's pregnancy and Plant's quickening love follow a parallel course until her baby is born and his love dies. This relationship deliberately deflects attention from the second chapter's highly-charged and understated heart – Waugh's delicate intimation of a second love in embryo between John, and Lucy's teenage cousin, Julia. Julia is an engaging, bright, outspoken schoolgirl who has long admired Plant's books and now falls frankly for the man. Plant the narrator is preoccupied by his sexless calf-love for Lucy. In Waugh's delicate handling the reader can trace the beginning of a much more genuine relationship between Plant – avuncular, amused, benevolent and supremely unaware – and the spontaneous, emotionally generous Julia. Julia is eighteen, like Laura when she first met Waugh. The pointedly specified age gap between Plant and Julia is fifteen years; between Laura and Waugh it was twelve.[8]

Julia arouses no interest in Waugh's critics. His friend, the novelist Henry Green, was unique in recognizing her appeal.[9] Her story ends with her insisting Plant should accept a farewell box of cigars before she leaves London. She stands waiting for her unsolicited reward, and is repaid by an unprecedented surge of kindness:

> I put my hands on her shoulders and gave her a single, warm kiss on the lips. She shut her eyes and sighed. 'Thank you,' she said in a small voice, and hurried out [...]
>
> Sweet Julia! I thought. It was a supremely unselfish present; something quite impersonal and unsentimental [...] something which would be gone, literally in smoke, in less than six weeks. (WS 108)

Even in its first beginnings *Work Suspended* moves towards the end fulfilled in *Brideshead Revisited*, where John Plant's Julia is reborn as *Brideshead's* Julia Flyte. More than a wisp of smoke unites the two novels and their central relationships:

> 'It's frightening,' Julia once said, 'to think how completely you have forgotten Sebastian.'
>
> 'He was the forerunner.'
>
> 'That's what you said in the storm. I've thought since, perhaps I am only a forerunner too.'
>
> 'Perhaps,' I thought, while her words hung in the air between us like a wisp of tobacco smoke – a thought to fade and vanish like smoke without a trace – 'perhaps all our loves are merely hints and symbols.' (BR 333)

At this point Ryder still speaks as an atheist who senses more than he can understand. Yet we can guess that the incompleted arc of *Work Suspended* became the overt spiritual narrative of *Brideshead*, where youthful homosexual crush and mature heterosexual passion ultimately lead to love of God. It is telling that the symbolic hint of *My Father's House* resurfaces in *Brideshead's* first projected title, *The Household of the Faith*. *Work Suspended* is surely Waugh's first attempt to fulfil his own demanding creed, as summarized in 'Art from Anarchy', that 'A writer's material must be the individual soul (which is the preconception of Christendom).'[10]

*

Many other elements link Waugh's new preoccupations to *Work Suspended*. The most important relate to his ideas about art, and the craft of writing. The first chapter is dominated by John Plant's father, stubbornly perfecting the achievements of the Victorian era, a century too late. The passion of a collector informs Waugh's amused account of Plant Senior's crowded canvasses in the manner of Frith, his posthumous portraits of guildhall worthies, his contemporary themes conveyed with the telling titles and minutely realistic domestic iconography of Victorian narrative art. In his abandoned studio Plant recognizes his father's historic importance, and laments him 'fulfilling the broken promise of the young Millais' in the 'cadences and classical allusions' of Augustan elegiac prose. 'He completed a period of English painting that [...] had never, until him, come to maturity'.[11]

However, Plant's father is not just a vehicle for Waugh to voice his critical admiration of Victorian art. He is richly comic and highly individualized. The caricature artist of *Punch* cartoons, he deliberately dresses in capes, check suits and stock ties; he is to be seen 'muttering objurgations' outside the featureless flats ousting the mansions of his London neighbourhood. John Plant fears that his father 'inhabits the borderline of insanity' but recognizes that he is 'actually a man of indestructible sanity', very like Waugh himself. He is incorrigibly contrary: anti-Semitic during the Dreyfus scandal, pro-Semitic in the Jew-baiting thirties; a 'dogmatic atheist of old-fashioned cast' who is equally capable of propounding proofs of God's existence in the days of fashionable Marxism. In him Waugh voices his own reactionary opinions against contemporary culture – Picasso, 'disjointed negresses by Gauguin', untranslatable modernists like Joyce and Stein. He is, in fact, a prophetic projection of the cartoon persona Waugh later adopted, aggressively sporting a parodic countryman's loud check suits, in deafness wielding an antiquated ear-trumpet – the hybrid don-cum-testy-colonel of his self-caricature in *The Ordeal of Gilbert Pinfold*. 'We are extinct already. I am a Dodo,' Plant Senior would say, defiantly staring at his audience; 'You, my poor son, are a petrified egg.'

Plant Senior embodies all that Waugh admired in the exuberant Victorian originals, from Ford Madox Brown to

Dodgson, Lear and Dickens, and his own embattled stance against modernity. He is balanced by his son, whose Olympian pretensions – as a detective story writer! – are risibly self-preening ('I was always a one-corpse man'). Yet, however laughably minor Plant's achievements, he apes Waugh's fine discriminations. He boasts of 'eschewing' blunt instruments and bloody corpses; 'My poisons were painless; no character of mine ever writhed or vomited.' For Plant even detective stories are 'an art which admitted of classic canons of technique and taste'. Plant also shares Waugh's taste for 'Gothic enrichments' and, like Waugh, expresses it in an architectural metaphor:

> I despised a purely functional novel as I despised contemporary architecture; the girders and struts of the plot require adornment and concealment; I relish the masked buttresses, false domes, superfluous columns, all the subterfuges of literary architecture.[12]

A relish for structural subterfuge is shared by father and son. The novel opens with John Plant's satisfied recollection of his most elegant death scene, and its 'unnoticed [...] ingenious clue'. The phrase is pointedly echoed in *The Neglected Cue*, the title of a major picture by Plant Senior that Waugh describes in detail.

Waugh's relish for the iconographical clues to be deciphered in Victorian narrative art was passed on to his children. What this means is well illustrated by his daughter Harriet's guided tour of George Smith's *Into the Cold World* (1876), her favourite from Waugh's collection.[13] You can tell that the master of a well-to-do middle-class family has just died because there's straw scattered on the street outside to deaden the noise of carriages from the sick-room. His hat is on the tallboy. The family are in mourning; the butler is sadly showing them to the door; a 'For Sale' notice is just visible. They're too poor even to take their dog with them. The flowers are wilting, the barometer is falling. One of the pictures is of a storm at sea, and the little boy is carrying his only toy, a ship 'which is a symbol of going into stormy waters [...] The picture tells you what happens when you don't have life insurance [...] Papa used to tell the story of the pictures to you. It was like a story book, really.'

In *Work Suspended*, and then again in *Brideshead*, Waugh explicitly draws on the iconographic techniques of high

Victorian narrative art, for thematic purposes. The thematic clues of, for instance, Holman Hunt's *The Awakened Conscience* (referred to in *Brideshead*) are distantly related to the humdrum clues of modern detective stories. They are translated into literary equivalents in Waugh's fiction, as in the visual cameos strategically placed at the beginnings of novels (like *Scoop*'s Algernon Stitch with his arm down the wrong coat sleeve). In *Work Suspended* the first chapter's title, *My Father's House*, is an exact equivalent of Plant Senior's indicative picture titles like *The Neglected Cue*, and *Again?*

Plant's friend, Roger Simmonds, a recent convert to socialism, is both Plants' antithesis. Benwell, John Plant's publisher, has reason to be nervous of literary experiments, because Roger has just written an unpublishable play whose characters are all car parts: 'You never saw such a thing [...] magneto and sparking plugs and camshaft all talking in verse about communism.' Roger's *Internal Combustion* is a savage *reductio ad absurdum* of Huxley's generic types, down to their very nuts and bolts. For poor Benwell it is 'not in the least funny'. For Roger it is also serious, but not for aesthetic or ideological reasons. His literary and political opportunism has won him Lucy, an idealistic socialist heiress, as his bride. He prides himself on a work he anxiously calls 'orthodox' because it has completely eliminated even the economic character-types of socialist art, and lacks human beings altogether.

Waugh's canvas, on the other hand, is crowded with individuals and richly embellished with delicate clues to unfinished threads of plot. It seems clear, for instance, from remarks cut from the reconfigured text, that the Dickensian Jellabies, Plant Senior's housekeepers, were to blackmail John Plant over his father's lucrative trade in forged old masters. F. J. Stopp, the only critic of Waugh's work whose study was written with the author's cooperation, suggests that later in the unfinished novel 'Atwater', the man who killed Plant's father, was to settle in Plant's new home, an unwelcome uninvited guest, till Plant murdered him – leaving us with the delicious prospect of the detective story writer having to hide his own act of murder.[14] Early in the novel Plant says he dislikes serialization because it injures 'the delicate fibres of a story', which never heal completely. Waugh chose to trim some of his loose threads from his second version of the text, but left sufficient signs to corroborate Stopp's conjectures. Plant also memorably describes his father's way with large canvasses:

> My father made copious and elaborate studies for his pictures and worked quickly when he came to their final stage, painting over a monochrome sketch, methodically, in fine detail, left to right across the canvas as though he were lifting the backing of a child's 'transfer'. (*WS* 39)

So it is with Waugh. We can see one brightly coloured corner. We can only guess at the whole canvas in all its ghostly, unfulfilled detail.

*

Waugh knew the value of *Work Suspended*. He published it not once or twice but three times. Chapter 1 first appeared in Cyril Connolly's *Horizon* in 1941; the complete text followed in book form in 1942, when war-time paper shortages allowed. In 1945 *Brideshead* took up its central theme and completed it. Then Waugh was free to lay it to rest. In 1948, nine years after its first composition, it was cut, reconfigured, and republished. In this version the original titles of its two chapters, *My Father's House* and *Lucy Simmonds*, were changed to two parts, *A Death* and *A Birth*. Once again, Waugh created the satisfying circularities recurrent in his work. Yet *A Death* triggers Plant's awakening, and *A Birth* is the novel's death-knell. The 1948 Postscript tells us that Lucy's baby, like Waugh's son Auberon, was born as the war began.

> And so an epoch, my epoch, came to an end [...] My father's death, the abandonment of my home, my quickening love of Lucy, my literary innovations, my house in the country – all these had seemed to presage a new life. The new life came, not by my contrivance [...] Our story, like my novel, remained unfinished – a heap of neglected foolscap at the back of a drawer. (*WS* 238–9)

7

Put Out More Flags
1942

Waugh spent the last months of 1939 after war was declared writing *Work Suspended*, digging up his carefully landscaped garden for vegetables, and preparing Piers Court for the influx of evacuees. In desperation as his attempts at getting called up failed, he opened negotiations to launch a literary magazine, to be called *Duration*. The next day, Laura went into labour, Waugh abandoned his novel to join her, and Auberon was born.[1] The same week Waugh was summoned for a successful interview with the Marines. Celebrating that evening at his club, he learned that 'my idea for a magazine had already been anticipated by the rump of the left wing under Connolly,' got drunk, and was sick in the small hours. 'The subsequent hangover removed all illusions of heroism' (D 450–1, 17–24 November 1939).

Yet Waugh did go into war with high hopes of heroism. In August his first instinct had been to enlist as a private soldier (D 438). In what Waugh nicknamed *POMF*, one of his two *alter egos*, Alastair, has the same impulse, as his wife Sonia revealingly recalls:

> I believe I know what Alastair felt all that first winter of the war. It sounds awfully unlike him, but he was a much odder character than anyone knew [...] You see he'd never done anything for the country and though we were always broke we had lots of money really and lots of fun. I believe he thought that perhaps if we hadn't had so much fun perhaps there wouldn't have been any war [...] He went into the ranks as a kind of penance or whatever it's called religious people are always supposed to do. (*POMF* 125)

Waugh joined the Marines at Chatham Barracks in December 1939. The early months of training find him 'enjoying the war top hole' under an irresistible Brigade Commander with 'teeth like a stoat, ears like a faun, eyes alight like a child playing pirates.' Waugh often sounds like a schoolboy too, fretting for 'decent raids' in London, dismayed by failure, swanking about the tiny triumphs of training, like Alastair after his first day of manoeuvres boasting to Sonia: 'I put down smoke [...] The whole advance was held up till I put down smoke.' 'Darling, you *are* clever.' In 1941 Waugh was to write regretfully of 'that adventurous spirit with which I joined at Chatham', which he had, by then, lost (*L* 157).

In the first months Laura spent happy weekends with Waugh, as Sonia does with Alastair, in near-by hotels and rented cottages.[2] On one of many soft nights together Laura, like Sonia, conceived a child. 'This was February 1940, in that strangely cosy interlude between peace and war, when there was leave every weekend and plenty to eat and drink and plenty to smoke, when France stood firm on the Maginot Line and the Finns stood firm in Finland, and every one said what a cruel winter they must be having in Germany' (*POMF* 128).

The Finns' unexpected resistance to the Russian invasion was broken by Easter. Waugh's depression at the fall of Finland was deepened by Hitler's invasion of Denmark and Norway at the beginning of April 1940. In May he records hearing a lecture given by a survivor from a battalion reduced by three-quarters, from six hundred men to a hundred and fifty, under fire in Norway (*D* 470). The unspecified engagement late in *POMF*'s *Spring* clearly suggests Norway, a northern terrain where spring has made no impact, 'deep snow in the hills, thin ice in the valleys'.

In August 1940 Waugh sailed out of *POMF*'s world to take part in a failed raid on Dakar as the London Blitz began. On returning to England, he transferred to the Commandos with renewed hopes of belligerent action, and was again disappointed. He was sent to Egypt in February 1941, participated in a failed Commando raid on Bardia in April, and finally encountered real battle in England's ignominious flight from Crete in May 1941. Waugh rapidly mined this first-hand Cretan experience for Cedric's death on the Norwegian battlefield closing *POMF*'s *Spring*.

After the fall of Crete, Waugh was shipped home by a protracted route from Egypt, via Cape Town, Trinidad, the Azores, and Iceland, a voyage lasting from mid July to early September. In the ship's library he found a complete set of his own novels, renewed his acquaintance with the fictional figures of his past, and brought them back to life in *Put Out More Flags*. His dedicatory letter to Randolph Churchill calls these familiar figures 'a race of ghosts' from the past, who 'lived on delightfully in holes and corners' till they were disturbed by the 'rough intrusion of current history.' Later, with unnecessary modesty, Waugh dismissed the novel as a 'minor work' dashed off to occupy a tedious voyage. He under-rated it because it was a throw-back to the characters and techniques of his past; a diversion from the innovations and spiritual themes he had hoped to perfect in *Work Suspended*.

The four sections of *Put Out More Flags* encompass the *Autumn, Winter, Spring*, and brief *Summer*, from the declaration of war in September 1939 to the eve of the Battle of Britain in July 1940. Yet its clearly delineated journey from frivolity to serious engagement follows Waugh's own trajectory, from early military idealism to deep disillusion prompted by the fall of Crete a year later. As a loyal patriot in wartime, Waugh could not end his novel there, and it closes instead with the covertly undermined, upbeat thrill of Peter, Basil and Alastair's enlistment with the newly-created Commandos, whose military effectiveness in Crete Waugh had just found so wanting.

*

For all its ostensibly hasty composition, *Put Out More Flags* is tightly constructed, being delicately balanced between three oppositions. The idea of contrasting dualities makes its first, camouflaged appearance among Basil's doodled titles for the wartime book he never writes: *Berlin or Cheltenham, Policy or Generalship, Policy or Professionalism*. These occluded hints later emerge more clearly in Ambrose Silk's essays for the first and only number of his magazine, *The Ivory Tower*. Silk's titles – '*Majors and Mandarins*', '*Hermit or Choirmaster*', '*Ivory Tower v. Manhattan Skyscraper*' – direct us to conflicting responses to the war in its first phase, as Waugh himself experienced them.

Paraphrased, and correctly angled, they neatly summarize the novel's structural oppositions:

The Individual v. The Mass (*'Hermit or Choirmaster'*) plays Waugh's incorrigibly singular individualists – Basil, Ambrose, Cedric and Angela Lyne – against the derided herd mentality of the left.

Escapism v. Engagement (*'Ivory Tower v. Manhattan Skyscraper'*) sets up escapists, like Parsnip and Pimpernell (Auden and Isherwood) who fled to New York, against combatant soldiers like Cedric and Alastair. Ambrose's formulation mistakenly identifies his bellicose literary polemics as opposition to the fugitives of the left, but *The Ivory Tower* is itself escapist.

The Phoney v. The Real is Waugh's all-embracing, central theme. In what is still known as the Phoney War of 1939-40, England waited for the German attack that did not come. Against this panorama Waugh presents numerous versions of false skirmishes and frivolous war-games. Finally, as the novel ends and the Battle of Britain is about to begin, phoney engagements modulate into real combat on a nameless northern battlefield, where the selfless sacrifice of Cedric, a single individual, is seen in all its tragic futility.

THE PHONEY v. THE REAL: WAR-GAMES

Put Out More Flags offers a new variation on an old theme. *Vile Bodies* was a sustained attack on bogosity. *The Loved One* will later anatomize the American cult of the sham. *POMF* pivots on the ever-widening disjunctions between the ideal, the phoney, and the real.

The novel opens methodically with three women's hopelessly idealized images of Basil Seal. For his sister, Barbara Sothill, Basil is a second Siegfried Sassoon, 'an infantry subaltern in a mud-bogged trench, standing-to at dawn'. For his mother he joins the company of Sir Philip Sidney at Zutphen, Wolfe at Quebec, Nelson at Trafalgar. For his mistress, Angela Lyne, he is a Spartan Alcibiades, combing his dark hair before the battle of

Thermopylae. Waugh's noble historic perspectives end in bathos – Basil, unshaven and hung over, 'not at his best this morning', mocking panicky Poppet Green, his 'art-tart', as the first, false air-raid warning of the war is sounded. With the 'All Clear' London's telephone lines hum to the socialites' chatter: 'They say the last war was absolute heaven'; 'We're all feeling gay and warlike. May we come to lunch?'

In Waugh's habitual manner the Phoney War's childish war-games are first caught in an iconic moment as Freddy Sothill searches for his military kit:

> His pistol, in particular, had been a trouble. He had had the whole household hunting it, saying fretfully, 'It's all very well, but I can get court-martialled for this,' until, at length, the nursery-maid found it at the back of the toy cupboard. (*POMF* 14)

Throughout the novel's first section, *Autumn*, Waugh transfers the terminology of the battlefield to civilian squabbles. Within a few lines Basil complains about people 'gunning' for him and Angela 'carrying on a campaign' about hospitals, while the publisher Mr Bentley, seconded to the Ministry of Information, 'bellicosely' fires off memoranda defending the empire furniture and classical busts he has smuggled into his dreary office. The theatre of war dwindles to a domestic playground. Malfrey, the Sothills' stately home, is threatened by invasion – not by Germans, but evacuee children from London's slums. The housekeeper is 'loyal'; the butler for the time being is 'sound', but the housemaids desert for the glamour of the munitions factory. 'They seem to think the war is an excuse for a lark.' As winter approaches and the blackouts grow earlier, Sir Joseph Mainwaring is heard pronouncing 'One takes one's gas mask to one's office but not one's club'.

The second section, *Winter*, brings the first major offensive on the Home Front, the Connolly Campaign. Basil boasts it is 'the finest piece of serious war work I've done so far'. It is the novel's funniest sequence. When the first slum children were evacuated to respectable country billets in August 1939, there was mutual astonishment at how the other half lived.[3] In a side-swipe at Cyril Connolly, Waugh embodies all the horrors of evacuee children in the Connolly trio – Doris, 'ripely pubescent' with dark pig's eyes, prodigious bust, and a gait, 'derived from the cinematograph, that was designed to be alluring'; the psycho-pathic Micky, 'her junior by a rather stiff sentence for house-breaking' and the simple, incontinent Marlene. These children are so atrocious that both Basil Seal and the reader come to share Waugh's delight in their creation. Masquerading as the local billeting officer, Basil extracts bribes from victims unwilling to host them. His threat to impose them on the arty-crafty Harkness couple, who are hoping for genteel paying guests, is turned into an elaborately extended metaphor – the lobbing of a hand-grenade:

> 'We pay eight shillings and sixpence a week', he said. That was the safety-pin; the lever flew up, the spring struck home; within the serrated metal shell the primer spat and, invisibly, flame crept up the finger's length of fuse. Count seven slowly, then throw. One, two, three, four...
> 'Eight shillings and sixpence?' said Mr Harkness. 'I'm afraid there's been some misunderstanding.'
> Five, six, *seven*. Here it comes. Bang! 'Perhaps I should have told you at once. I am the billeting officer.'
> It was magnificent. It was war. (*POMF* 112)

Earlier, Waugh defined Basil's singularity as the Nazi inside the gates, used to 'conducting his own campaigns, issuing his own ultimatums, disseminating his own propaganda [...] an obstreperous minority of one in a world of otiose civilians.' His 'system of push, appeasement, agitation, and blackmail, [...] except that it had no more distant aim than his own immediate amusement, ran parallel to Nazi diplomacy.' While Hitler in the real world invaded Norway and Denmark in the spring of 1940, in *POMF* Basil sells off the Connolly children to the repulsive Mr Todhunter, and widens his offensive to London. Here he becomes an altogether less sympathetic figure, infiltrating a bomb-toting lunatic into the War Office, annexing the sexy lance corporal Susie from the office of Colonel Plum, and betraying his friend, the homosexual Jewish aesthete Ambrose Silk, in order to occupy his mansard flat with its rich plunder of Charvet ties and crêpe de chine pyjamas.

In *POMF*'s *Winter* the phoney war of the Connolly Campaign has all the naughtiness of a Richmal Crompton *William* story,[4] and is run in tandem with the harmlessly absurd days of Alastair's early training. His tender, shuttered weekends with

Sonia, and the company's wholly fantastical tactical exercises end with Alastair's sleepy question, 'I wonder if a real battle is much like that'. The irony is not, as you might expect, that real battles are nothing like Alastair's mock-manoeuvres, but that they are just as shambolic. As Waugh wrote to Laura after Crete,

> I have been in a serious battle and have decided I abominate military life. It was tedious & futile & fatiguing. I found I was not at all frightened; only very bored & very weary [...] The thing about battle is that it is no different at all from manoeuvres with Col. Lushington on Bagshot heath – just as confused & purposeless. (L 153)

With *Spring* the novel darkens as Basil's increasingly heartless guerilla tactics are set against military actualities. Cedric Lyne's thwarted attempts to get his regiment aboard for shipment to action realistically compress a failed embarkation lasting six days in Waugh's *Diaries* (D 475–7, 19–24 August 1940). Once again the exercise – no fictional manoeuvre this time – was characterized by futility and flap: two battalions erroneously embarked on the same ship, overladen by 400 per cent of its capacity; continual shifting of stores, loading, reloading, order, counter-order, 'desperate disorder'. One of many sources for Waugh's growing disillusion with the army.

THE IVORY TOWER: ESCAPISM v. ENGAGEMENT

Running alongside the narrative threads of Basil's sham war-work and Cedric and Alastair's dispiriting reality, is the novel's third campaign – Ambrose Silk's solo confrontation of a world at war in his magazine, *The Ivory Tower*. Significantly, his defiance is linked with France. 'Well,' says Ambrose, 'I've had enough [of Parsnip, Pimpernell, and Poppet Green]. *Il faut en finir,*' adding, *'nous gagnerons parce que nous sommes les plus forts.'* This, the ill-omened catch-phrase of blind French faith in the impregnability of the Maginot Line, was first quoted in the novel's opening pages by the quintessentially, Gallically chic Angela Lyne, Cedric's wife and Basil's mistress, as her train travelled through France in the autumn of 1939. France fell in May-June 1940. The irony of Allied reliance on the fortified, futile Maginot Line would have been a painful recent memory for the novel's original readers in 1942.

In *POMF*'s insouciant world Gallic escapism is specifically associated, via these catch-phrases, with Ambrose and Angela, both inhabiting an Ivory Tower of their own making, and both occupying distinctively different, elegant top-floor flats, in Ambrose's arty Bloomsbury and Angela's modern Grosvenor Square. Here Angela plunges her head in the sand, an alcoholic recluse in a timeless limbo – curtained windows, unchanging central heating, muttering radio and decanter at her side, while below,

> layer upon layer of rich men and women came and went about their business, layer below layer down to street level; below that again, underground, the management were adapting the basement to serve as an air raid shelter.

In her drunkenness, realization comes, and she says to herself,

> 'Maginot Line – Angela Lyne – both lines of least resistance' and laughed at her joke till the tears came. (*POMF* 157, 177)

Foremost among the real-life originals for Waugh's Ivory Tower dwellers is Cyril Connolly, over-rated litterateur and editor of *Horizon*. Ambrose's magazine, *The Ivory Tower*, is both a self-ironizing reprise of Waugh's unrealized *Duration* and a satirical version of Connolly's *Horizon*. 'Ivory Tower' is a recurrent term in Connolly's work, used uncritically to identify his own escapist stance in a piece winsomely titled *Ivory Shelter*, where he wrote that 'If war is a tin can tied to the tail of civilisation, it is also an opportunity for the artist to give us nothing but his best, *and stop his ears*.'[5] *Horizon*'s issue for December 1941, soon after Waugh's return from Crete, and certainly read by him, runs a modified extract from the first part of *Work Suspended*, alongside an effete effusion by R. C. Trevelyan, on Life's *Simple Pleasures*, such as 'The Pleasures of Watching Insects', 'The Pleasures of Touch', like 'cutting the pages of a book with a long ivory paperknife'. This is the exact equivalent of the pleasures of Mandarin detachment Ambrose espouses in his cultured arguments with his friend, the publisher Mr Bentley, in the Café Royal.

In the idle early days of the Phoney War, Oriental detachment was an acceptable position, most illustriously promoted in Yeats's poem, 'Lapis Lazuli', written in July 1936. Writing with hindsight, Waugh attacks this complacency. The left-wing Auden and Isherwood, Waugh's originals for Parsnip and Pimpernell, fled to the States embarrassingly early, in January 1939. Their pre-emptive cowardice is acidly denounced by Trotskyite Julia, an uncompromising believer in a People's Total War, in Poppet's studio:

> 'What I don't see,' she said (and what this girl did not see was usually a very conspicuous embarrassment to Poppet's friends) – 'What I don't see is how these two can claim to be *Contemporary* if they run away from the biggest event in contemporary history [...] It's just sheer escapism,' she said. (*POMF* 48)

In *POMF* Waugh widens his attack on the Oriental detachment of the Ivory Tower dwellers by repeatedly associating it with bad art, sickly-sweetness and yellow, the colour of cowardice. Benson, the butler at Malfrey, is said to be 'yellow' at the Connolly kids' invasion. Poppet Green, Basil's girlfriend, is terrified by the first, false air-raid alarm of the war and her latest atrocious painting is a derivative exercise in Dali-esque surrealism — 'an overlarge, accurate but buttercup-coloured head of the Aphrodite of Melos, poised against a background of bull's eyes and barley sugar'. Among the other Ivory Tower dwellers, drunken Angela's tremulously applied make-up looks 'rather haphazard and garish, like a later Utrillo', as 'sploshy' as her unfinished portrait by Augustus John. And Ambrose's aesthetic, propounded in the Café Royal, derives from and is referred to the Café's old habitués, Wilde and Beardsley, the decadents of the 1890s, and their *Yellow Book*. Ambrose dreams of escape from the present in a soaring, bathetic vision of insuperable vulgarity, 'a heaven of flat, blank, blue-and-white clouds cross-hatched with gold leaf on their sunward edges; a vast altitude painted with shaving-soap on a panel of lapis lazuli [...where] he stood on a high, sugary pinnacle.' 'A new Tower of Babel', Waugh adds unkindly. Not even a tower of ivory.

Early in the novel, Ambrose admires Mr Bentley's pugnacious defence of his empire busts in the Ministry of Information. 'You are *brave*, Geoffrey.' Ambrose has reason to be afraid. A homosexual Jewish aesthete, he is, as he says, everything the Nazis call degenerate. As a well-known left-wing author he's afraid of what the fascists might do to him if they get into power.

As a fellow-traveller he's anxious about repercussions from the Marxist underground – 'Too ridiculous,' scoffs Mr Bentley; 'sounds like strap hangers on the Bakerloo line'. Yet as *Spring* advances, Basil's predatory circling round Ambrose becomes genuinely menacing. Fascist or Marxist is immaterial to him, so long as he can sell Ambrose as a traitor to Colonel Plum.

However, Ambrose is no coward in his aesthetic convictions. We watch his belligerence with increasing anxiety as he fires off Waugh-like opinions in *The Ivory Tower*. But Basil, here as in *Black Mischief*, is not all bad. Last and least in Waugh's dispassionate list of motivations, Basil wishes Ambrose well rather than ill. Having betrayed him as a proto-fascist, he plays out a pleasurable *Boy's Own* melodrama, pushing Ambrose into midnight flight, disguised as an Irish priest. Abandoned at Euston Station at midnight, perched on a crate of fish, Ambrose epitomizes the multitudinous refugees of war: 'black hat perched over his eyes, black overcoat wrapped close about his knees, mournful and black eyes open, staring at the blackness.' Shoddy writing deliberately destabilizes pathos, and the final touch marks the phoney tragedy. 'From the fishy freight below him water oozed [...] making a little pool, as though of tears.' As in the Carroll epigraph to *Vile Bodies*, these fishy tears are unreal. The 27,000 'enemy aliens' and other innocent suspects, who were temporarily interned during the British spy-scare in early 1940, had little to fear – in England, at least. So Waugh complicates what might otherwise be simple dichotomies and in Ambrose unites a cluster of opposing themes. The ascetic detachment of the Oriental hermit-sage and the escapism of bad art are both counterbalanced by Ambrose's stubborn individualism and his belligerent polemics in the one and only issue of *The Ivory Tower*.

In the subsequent imprisonment of Mr Rampole, Bentley's publishing partner, for his association with the publication of *The Ivory Tower*, Waugh simplifies the conflicting tones of Ambrose's painful story to rollicking, Dickensian dramatic irony. Extended premonitions of disaster loudly accompany Rampole's morning walk to work. In blind good humour he sets out to his doom:

Look well on those buds, old Rampole; you will not see the full leaf.
'I'll be back at six,' he said.
Presumptuous Rampole, who shall tell what the day will bring

forth? [...] Never again, old Rampole, never again. *(POMF* 229–30)

Once in jail for his association with Ambrose's allegedly neo-Nazi magazine, Rampole enjoys an undisturbed war reading romances by one of his authors, pseudonymous Ruth Mountdragon (alias Mrs Parker), losing himself in 'a strange world of wholly delightful, estimable people, whom he rightly supposed not to exist' – the escapist world of bad art again.

So *Spring* draws towards its close, traversing the increasingly ridiculous mock-tragedies of two runaways, Ambrose in neutral Ireland, Rampole in jug, to end in real combat, and the death of Cedric, a single, sane man-at-arms.

THE MASS v. THE INDIVIDUAL

It is telling that the characters of Ruth Mountdragon's novels are 'radically different [...] in name [...] but spiritually as undistinguishable as larches'. *Put Out More Flags* continues Waugh's attack on socialist characterization by type and social function (Roger Simmonds's spark-plugs), and composition by collective rather than individuals. In 1939 he called Auden and Isherwood's joint authorship of *Journey to a War* their 'pantomime appearance as the hind and front legs of a monster' *(EAR* 251). In *POMF* Waugh's disdain for the herd mentality of the left is illustrated by Ambrose's lunch with left-wing friends who overcrowd the restaurant, inconclusively argue over the bill, and spill onto the pavement to disagree about where they should go next. 'There were only six of them but it was too many for Ambrose.' He finds himself thinking, 'Here is the war, offering a new deal for everyone; I alone bear the weight of my singularity.' His individualist stance is Waugh's own, and on Waugh's behalf Ambrose sets up two contrasting terms, the 'conventual'[6] (as in a convent: the composite commonality, the mass) versus the 'cenobitic' (the isolated, anchoritic, individual). It is the polarity between the communal and the individual; the mass and the man; the army and the single soldier. Initially lightly introduced in the Café Royal discussions with Mr Bentley, Ambrose's terms acquire central importance at the novel's close. His lament, 'I alone bear the weight of my singularity' is first voiced by Lady Seal, consoling herself that

'It's always been Basil's *individuality* that's been wrong [...] In wartime individuality doesn't matter any more. There are just *men*, aren't there?' Her forlorn, unfulfilled hope is that Basil's 'peculiarities' will at last be 'merged into the manhood of England'.

The role of the individual in a time of national crisis was, of course, much debated. Chamberlain's broadcast, stating that war had been declared, was criticized for being 'too personal'.[7] Waugh thought 'He did it very well' – a sentiment later transferred to Lady Seal (*D* 439, *POMF* 23). In *The Idea of a Christian Society* (1939), T. S. Eliot confessed to emotions very like Waugh's (and Alastair's) – 'a feeling of humiliation, which seemed to demand an act of personal contrition, of humility, of repentance and emendation.' Yet in war, as Lady Seal says, the individual is necessarily lost in the mass – a theme prosaically set out in Eliot's 'Note on War Poetry' (1942). It can barely be called a poem, but it reflects the terms and preoccupations of the time. What role, Eliot asks, can a writer usefully fulfil in wartime? 'Not the expression of collective emotion / Imperfectly reflected in the daily papers.' Yet 'Mostly the individual / Experience is too large, or too small'. Where, then, is the point at which the 'merely individual' coincides with the 'merely typical' to create the 'universal'?

Waugh's emphatic answer would be that the 'merely typical' can never be 'universal', and the individual is not 'mere'. His portrait of England during the Phoney War unrepentantly celebrates the inconvenient individuality of all his characters, not excluding Angela, with her 'high *and wholly individual* standard of all that the Americans meant by poise'. Basil and his mildly incestuous sister, Barbara; the singularly atrocious Connolly kids; Colonel Plum; Mr Todhunter; Ambrose's colourful pseudonyms – Hucklebury Squib, Tom Barebones-Abraham – all are members of an individualized cast. They are Waugh's vitally distinct creations, the 'race of ghosts' of his Dedicatory Epistle to Randolph Churchill, living on delightfully in the holes and corners of *POMF*'s uneasy world.

Since we have grown comfortable with Waugh's gallery of harmless British eccentrics, our surprised attention is caught when he uses Ambrose's *chef-d'oeuvre* to reiterate the novel's central opposition. In the first and last number of *The Ivory*

Tower, 'Monument to a Spartan' is Ambrose's dangerously polemical elegy for his German lover. It describes Hans joining the *Hitler-Jugend*, 'finding in tribal emotion an escape from the guilt of personal love', and dying for his love of the Jewish Ambrose. Hans is killed by his Nazi comrades because 'in their gross minds they know him to represent something *personal and private* in a world where only the mob and the hunting pack had the right to live' (my italics).[8] Ambrose dubs his elegy, semi-ironically, as 'All pure Art, my dear', but his false modesty is corroborated by Waugh in terms which for him would have signalled genuine approbation. Waugh calls it 'a story a popular writer would have spun out to 150,000 words, all there, delicately and precisely, in fifty pages of *The Ivory Tower*' (and barely two pages of *POMF*).

For all Waugh's affection, by the end of the novel he withdraws sympathy for both Basil's and Ambrose's singularity. Ambrose's culpable flight to the moral miasma of neutral Ireland is subtly suggested by Waugh's ballooning sentences describing the misty, mossy amorphousness of Ambrose's retreat. Ambrose's pen rolls away irretrievably under a side-board, his writing blurs on the damp page and his story is abandoned. The novel's sharp focus turns instead to the single soldier, Cedric Lyne.

*

Cedric has his own idiosyncrasy, the ornamental grottoes he has collected every year since Angela left him. They too are a retreat from reality, like the ivory tower and the 'holes and corners' of Waugh's dedicatory letter. It is telling that on her dispiriting visit to Waugh's beleaguered household in June 1939, Diana Cooper was taken to view a local grotto, to which Waugh later returned on his own (*D* 431, 433). This was in his own escapist period when he was 'eschewing' the radio and turning his back on the crisis. Cedric, in his frail way, is another escapist individualist, who reluctantly takes up arms from patriotic duty. He acquires considerable sympathy as the novel pro-gresses, and we witness his and his son's painfully unrewarding relationship with the impenitently indifferent Angela, drinking no longer but deep in her unsatisfactory relationship with Basil.

In the novel's closing pages, in a desolate northern theatre of war, Cedric emerges from battalion headquarters, 'a shallow cave in the side of the hill' (another grotto), to survey the terrain. His fellow-companies are too widely scattered to communicate effectively. Cedric is sent out to search for the missing Loamshires. His clarity of vision derives directly from Waugh's at the fall of Crete, and, indeed, partially transcribes it, as recounted in Waugh's diary:

> I asked Capt. Mackintosh-Flood what the situation was. He said, 'I don't know & I don't care'. So I went off to look for myself, leaving my servant & the intelligence section behind.
>
> It was always exhilarating as soon as one was alone; dependent troops were a dead weight on one's spirits and usefulness. I set off along the road we had come. (D 503)[9]

Here, finally, Waugh pays his tribute to the fragile, futile heroism of the individual combatant soldier, the novel's understated ideal:

> Cedric left his servant behind at battalion headquarters. It was against the rules, but he was weary of the weight of dependent soldiery which throughout the operations encumbered him and depressed his spirits. As he walked alone he was exhilarated with the sense of being one man, one pair of legs, one pair of eyes, one brain, sent on a single intelligible task [...]; multiply him, put him in a drove and by each addition of his fellows you subtract something that is of value, make him so much less a man; this was the crazy mathematics of war [...] There's danger in numbers; divided we stand, united we fall, thought Cedric, striding happily towards the enemy. He did not know it, but he was thinking exactly what Ambrose had thought when he announced that culture must cease to be conventual and become cenobitic. (POMF 240–1)

Soon after, a stray bullet kills him.

*

In May 1940, the brief *Summer* epilogue closing *POMF*, Hitler's troops circumvented the Maginot Line, invading France via the Low Countries. The Luftwaffe hopped over its belt of elaborate fortifications. The British Expeditionary Force was retrieved from Dunkirk. On 14 June Paris fell. Four days later Churchill spoke:

The Battle of Britain is about to begin. Upon this battle depends the survival of Christian civilisation [...] If we fail, then the whole world, including the United States, will sink into the abyss of a new dark age.

We know from Waugh's late novella, *Basil Seal Rides Again*, that Freddy Sothill (Basil's brother-in-law, Barbara's husband) and Alastair died, like Cedric, in defence of Christendom. Basil lost his toes in a dubious accident[10] and, as the portly Pobble, survived to cheat again another day. Parsnip became the Professor of Dramatic Poetry at Minneapolis; Pimpernell, the Professor of Poetic Drama at its twin-city, St Paul. Indistinguishable as larches to the last.

8

Brideshead Revisited
1945

As Waugh's disillusion with the war intensified, his next step in defence of embattled Christendom logically took him to its invisible heart, the soul of the individual. In a later essay on Saint Helena, he identifies the conviction that underlies both *Brideshead Revisited,* and the subsequent war trilogy:

> What we can learn from Helena is something about the workings of God; that He wants a different thing from each of us, laborious or easy, conspicuous or quite private, but something which only we can do and for which we were created. (*Holy Places* 13)

Waugh would have liked to achieve something conspicuous as a soldier. Even his loudest detractors freely admit his bravery. He was perfectly ready and seriously expected to sacrifice his life fighting for the survival of Christianity. For him personally, the Second World War, even more than its Abyssinian overture, was 'a disappointing war'. His assignments after the fall of Crete were humdrum. In 1943 a heaven-sent accident during a practice parachute drop – literally a happy fall – brought him injury, sick-leave, and finally official permission for three months' unpaid leave in order to write *Brideshead Revisited.* His *magnum opus.* Something which only he could do.

In his letter applying for leave Waugh said his projected novel would not deal directly with the war; nor could it be pretended to have any propaganda value, but 'it may cause innocent amusement and relaxation' to its readers (*D* 557, n.1). Most readers respond innocently and pleasurably to Ryder's two love stories, for Sebastian, and his sister Julia. Contemporaries were also quick to identify the originals Waugh denied in his prefatory Author's note: 'I am not I: thou art not he or she: they are not they.' As Nancy Mitford wrote to Waugh, everyone was saying that Lord Marchmain was the Seventh Earl Beauchamp and the Flytes were his friends, the Lygon children. However, this easy identification ignores a central difference between the two families. Lord Beauchamp had to leave England because of his homosexuality; Lord Marchmain took up voluntary exile because of his adultery. Lady Marchmain's Catholicism makes divorce impossible; in Marchmain's Venetian palazzo and continental watering-places her estranged husband, a lapsed Catholic, maintains a *ménage* of quiet propriety with his mistress, Cara.

The fact that this novel hinges on divorce is of little interest to an increasingly non-religious readership for whom marital separation and remarriage carry no stigma. For Waugh, however, *Brideshead Revisited* is steeped in theology. The impending divorces at its close provide the testing climax to a novel secondarily occupied with human affairs of the heart, and primarily preoccupied by the spiritual growth of characters subject to a divine providence of which they are profoundly unaware.

Consequently *Brideshead Revisited* continues the narrative experiment begun in *Work Suspended*. Ryder is as insouciant as Edith Sitwell observed John Plant to be. He speaks through his own mouth, freely exhibiting his nature *'without consciousness of what he is doing'*. This gives the novel a peculiar and dangerous strength. The danger lies in its being misunderstood. Ryder echoes the generally accepted social assumptions of the twentieth century, and the common reader shares his rationalist, atheist, materialist, polygamous outlook. Consequently, also, the reader by Ryder's side is as much in the dark as Ryder himself. Waugh, however, lays a series of subdued motifs, which culminate in clarificatory symbols that still remain unrecognized today. The novel's trajectory leads slowly but deliberately to revelation. Baldly put, this slow growth of understanding, mutually shared by Ryder and reader, is the novel's point.

In the discussion which follows, I will attempt to lead us through the novel's narrative, isolating the motifs that are charged with Waugh's moral and theological preoccupations, offering a partial sense of their meaning without, I hope, robbing them of their revelatory charge when Waugh himself finally explains them.

PROLOGUE

There is, initially, no perceptible distinction between Waugh and his narrator-hero, Charles Ryder, who appears in *Brideshead's* Prologue exactly like Waugh, four years into his military service in 1943. A page-long extended metaphor, in the expansive manner already tested in *Work Suspended*, establishes his disillusion with the army.

> [...] in that dark hour, I was aghast to realise that something within me, long sickening, had quietly died, and felt as a husband might feel, who, in the fourth year of his marriage, suddenly knew he had no longer any desire, or tenderness, or esteem, for a once-beloved wife, no pleasure in her company, no wish to please, no curiosity about anything she might ever do or say or think [...] (*BR* 14)[1]

In the dead tone of absolute disillusion Waugh details the disorderly world of army camps long thwarted of action. Futile flaps and pointless relocations. Military discipline undermined by pettifogging trivia. The commanding officer with 'beads of moisture on the hog-bristles of his little red moustache [...] grubbing with his walking-stick like a truffling pig' in buried garbage. In the latest entrainment to an unknown destination, the CO enforces needless security. All distinguishing marks are to be removed from transport and uniforms. On the journey, sleeping troops are roused for a fictional mustard-gas attack. In savage parody, Ryder orders his men to notionally decontaminate their railway carriages with imaginary bleach. It is only as the weary men reach their final destination and begin to unload real equipment in the dark, that they 'found themselves doing something with an apparent purpose in it', and their spirits rise.

In the Revised Edition of the novel that follows, the descriptive chapter titles appear semi-parodic, in the manner of Victorian melodrama ('*Samgrass revealed*', '*Rex revealed*'). They end, however, in the climax that pointedly counters this wartime world without purpose. '*Lord Marchmain at home – death in the Chinese drawing-room – the purpose revealed*'.

The novel's purpose was originally named in a modest

'Warning' printed on the inside flap of the dust-jacket: hardly a permanent fixture.[2] In Waugh's extended Preface to the Revised Edition, six years before his death, the same point is repeated in an apparently casual parenthesis. 'Its theme – the operation of divine grace on a group of diverse but closely connected characters – was perhaps presumptuously large.' Divine grace moves in a mysterious way. Waugh imitates its workings, hiding the novel's purposes until their final revelation, while its narrative secretes incremental signs that undermine his characters' misguided aspirations.

BOOK ONE

Ryder's military Prologue is set in what Waugh later called 'a bleak period of present privation and threatening disaster – the period of soya beans and basic English'. It prompts his escape into its diametric opposite – Oxford as it *was* in Waugh's past, and *is* in the 19-year-old Charles Ryder's present of 1923, described in a style that is far from basic English. This, the most enduringly popular part of the novel, is richly nostalgic, drawing on Waugh's own delirious student days when the university was almost exclusively male. Like Waugh at dim Hertford College, Ryder begins as a thoroughly conventional undergraduate, furnishing his room with Van Gogh's *Sunflowers* and calf-bound volumes of Georgian poetry, the cultural clichés of his time. His true education begins when Sebastian, in apology for vomiting into Ryder's open window, invites him to lunch in posh Christ Church – Lobster Newberg, plovers' eggs in a nest of moss, guests from Eton – while the ostentatiously gay Anthony Blanche recites *The Waste Land* through a megaphone to the rowing hearties below. Within a term Ryder's furnishings change to expensive cigars and the skull the undergraduate Waugh had once nested in a bowl of roses, now carrying the label, *Et in Arcadia Ego*.

Poussin's two idealized pastorals with this title show classically draped shepherds reading the inscription on a tomb. It is also the title of *Brideshead*'s first, Oxford section. At first it appears simply to epitomize the Arcadian days of Charles and Sebastian's early friendship, picnicking on white wine and strawberries on a sheep-cropped knoll, smoking fat Turkish cigars, while 'the sweet scent of tobacco merged with the sweet summer scents around us' – the cigar smoke, and the love it symbolizes, that have drifted across from *Work Suspended* to inseminate its sequel.

At Brideshead Castle Ryder paints an unpeopled pastiche Poussin, 'a summer scene of white clouds and blue distances', Book I's spiritual landscape. Drinking their way through the Flyte family's neglected cellars, the young men naturally turn to pastoral images: a 'shy little wine' is a dappled gazelle in a tapestry meadow, 'like the last unicorn' – and like the lost chivalric ideal haunting Tony Last in *A Handful of Dust*. Both novels' idealized imagery derives from the chapel at Madresfield, which Waugh now transports in accurate historic detail to Brideshead Castle ('Angels in printed cotton smocks, ramblerroses, flower-spangled meadows, frisking lambs'). These recurring images sustain Book I's air of harmless pagan hedonism and primal innocence.

In his autobiography, Waugh had observed that after premature sixth-form seriousness, 'at Oxford I was reborn in full youth' (*ALL* 171). Ryder, likewise, responds to cousin Jasper's warning against his descent into dissipation by thinking: '*Descent or ascent*? It seems to me that I grew younger daily with each adult habit that I acquired' (my italics). Sebastian's teddy bear Aloysius is the talisman of their infancy; Charles and Sebastian's innocence is a finer question. In a much quoted passage Ryder concedes that though the toys of this delayed childhood 'were silk shirts and liqueurs and cigars and its naughtiness high in the catalogue of grave sins, there was something of nursery freshness about us that fell little short of the joy of innocence.' Waugh deliberately avoids openly naming a specifically sexual relationship between Ryder and Sebastian, though its suggestion harmonizes with the male love of classical Greek and Roman pastoral.[3] The nursery innocence of this intense friendship is more important than its debatable morality. Throughout *Brideshead* there is a pointed use of the word 'naughtiness' to accommodate what a less forgiving faith condemns as mortal sin. 'Naughtiness' is the mild rebuke of nursery morality Waugh repeatedly espouses. Ryder muses, 'How ungenerously in later life we disclaim the virtuous moods of our youth, living in retrospect long, summer days of unreflecting dissipation. There is no candour in a story of early manhood which leaves out of account the homesickness for nursery morality.' Up in Brideshead's cupola Nanny Hawkins embodies its indulgent understanding from the novel's Prologue to its Epilogue. Sebastian and Ryder sit on her threadbare carpet, the toy-cupboard emptied around them, while she sews: 'You're as bad one as the other, a pair of children the two of you.' As a friend of Sebastian's pleads on his behalf, in facile apology for his puking through Ryder's window, 'To understand all is to forgive all.' The cliché will acquire weight as his sad destiny is fulfilled.

Sebastian's simplicity adds weight to his epicene charm. It is he who protests against Ryder fussing over the date of Brideshead, 'What does it matter when it was built, if it is pretty?' His Catholicism has the same directness. Like Waugh in sober maturity, Sebastian in dissolute youth firmly believes in Christmas, its star and worshipping kings, *because* 'it's a lovely idea' and 'That's how I believe'. He and Julia are, by his own admission, 'half-heathen', 'semi-heathens', but they have an inherited, instinctive faith that the incredulous Ryder has never been taught.

The idyll of Charles and Sebastian's friendship is barely disturbed by their religious differences. It is severely shaken when Anthony Blanche takes Charles out to dinner, and warns him against Sebastian, that vacuous 'little bundle of charm', whom he likens to the 'in some ways nauseating picture of *"Bubbles"'.*[4] Sebastian's conversation is 'like a little sphere of soapsud [...] full of rainbow lights for a second and then – phut! – vanished, with nothing left at all, nothing'. Blanche predicts that when Charles reports this conversation to Sebastian, he will 'immediately talk about that amusing bear of his' – as he does. The fulfilled prophesy is an uncomfortable guarantee of Blanche's perspicacity. More than once in the vacations Charles is offended by Sebastian's rare, whimsically impersonal letters, the latest being written on black-coroneted late-Victorian mourning paper, *'as I am in mourning for my lost innocence'.*

Art historians trace *Bubbles* to traditional Dutch images of life's transience, symbolized in Millais' sentimental painting of the boy's bubbles, and two flower-pots flanking him, one with a flourishing plant, the other smashed. Like Sebastian's funerary notepaper, Poussin's tomb in a timeless pastoral, and Ryder's skull among the roses, the title of *Brideshead*'s Book One, *Et in Arcadia Ego*, could be glossed as a conventional reminder of death. In the same mode, the two prostitutes Sebastian and Ryder pick up at Ma Mayfield's are reductively distinguished as 'Death's Head' (for Ryder) and 'Sickly Child' (for Sebastian). Yet the predominant negative image running through the novel's first section is of *shadows*: they progressively darken the narrative, but their apparent association with death is misleading. Waugh will only provide their implicit gloss at the end of Book Two, in Cordelia's description of the Easter Week service of Tenebrae. At this stage they cast an unspecified but ominous shadow over the young men's narrative. Returning to Oxford from their first visit to Brideshead, Charles and Sebastian find 'the sun behind us as we drove, so that we seemed to be in pursuit of our own shadows'. When they meet for their second year 'We sat silent in the firelight as darkness fell' so that a caller leaves thinking the room is deserted. 'All that term and all that year Sebastian and I lived more and more in the shadows.' Sebastian's secret, solitary drinking accelerates, and he is arrested for drunken driving. 'The shadows were closing round Sebastian' and Lady Marchmain's disastrous attempts to control him are set in train. On his return from a grand tour with Samgrass, the academic toady, he vanishes into the background as Samgrass lies about their travels. '"Me?" said Sebastian from the shadows beyond the lamplight, beyond the warmth of the burning logs, beyond the family circle [...] "I don't think I was there that day, was I, Sammy?"' Sebastian fades away, 'phut! – vanished, with nothing left at all', as Blanche predicted, while Lady Marchmain reads aloud to the miserable family circle from (what else?) *The Diary of a Nobody*. At the novel's end, when Sebastian seeks haven in an African monastery as an incurable alcoholic, he simply says, 'Oh, I'm nothing.'

BOOK TWO

Waugh seems to have had difficulties with Ryder's first-person narrative in the central part of his novel. In the Revised Edition he turned the last three chapters of Book One into a short Book Two, *Brideshead Deserted*. There is a lot of material to be covered, much of it not witnessed by Ryder, problems of voice and chronology to circumvent, and important motifs to be established and explained. Above all, throughout this choppily episodic middle ground between Sebastian's Book One and Julia's Book Three, Waugh is tactfully steering his readers towards a series of instinctive moral discriminations with the insouciant Ryder at their centre.

Chapter 1 of the new Book Two continues Sebastian's decline. Instead of hunting, he sneaks off to soak in a country pub, reluctantly funded by Ryder, who leaves Brideshead in disgrace. Samgrass's lies about their continental tour are revealed. Cordelia, the novel's most reliable voice, summarizes developments with childlike moral clarity in a letter to Charles: '*Mr Samgrass has gone (good!)* [...] *Mr Mottram is very popular with Julia (bad!) and is taking Sebastian away (bad! bad!) to a German doctor.*' But Rex Mottram can pin Sebastian down no better than anyone else. After Sebastian's escape, Rex dines with Ryder, now studying art in Paris. Writing in a period of wartime privation, Waugh took some pains to describe what may now appear no more than a delicious meal. But, as Douglas Patey points out, a significant pun is suggested with the fish course.[5] Rex is gossiping about Lady Marchmain's rumoured illness:

> '[...] But Ma Marchmain won't do anything about it. I suppose it's something to do with her crack-brain religion, not to take care of the body.'
> The sole was so simple and unobtrusive that Rex failed to notice it.
> (*BR* 195)

Yet Ryder is as worldly as Rex. The reader becomes painfully aware of their shared egotism – Rex with his eye on the main chance of a lucrative marriage to Julia, Ryder only impatient to eat well, grudging Rex any attention till cognac is served ('I closed my mind to him as best I could, and gave myself to the food before me'). Rex is judged by the sign of his coarseness, his atrocious taste in brandy. For all his vaunted fine palate, disdainful Ryder is little better. The soul simply doesn't exist for either of them.

Chapter 2 baldly announces: 'It is time to speak of Julia'. The description of her first London season is curiously slushy, slithering from the winsome ('This was the creature, neither child nor woman' – twice!) and fabular ('the heroine of a fairy story turning over in her hands the magic ring'), to the arch tones of a society magazine. For the chaperones lining the ballroom walls 'one question eclipsed all others [...] who would the young princes marry? They could not hope for purer lineage or a more gracious presence than Julia's', yet her pedigree is blighted by 'the scandal of her father; that slight, inherited stain upon her brightness'.[6] Younger sons are not an option 'until some disaster *perchance* promoted them to their brothers' places'. Julia has to look elsewhere. '*No Penelope she*; she must hunt in the forest' (my italics). What is going on? Has Waugh lost his incomparable grip on the finer calibrations of style? One might argue that this instability of tone deliberately undermines the romantic narrative, but in retrospect Waugh himself was also critical of stylistic excesses he came to regret in this novel.

Admittedly there is a technical difficulty. Waugh has to use Ryder's narrative voice to recount Julia's back-history, in which he had no part; he can only repeat what she tells him later. Yet this is not Julia's voice, which, in direct speech, is convincingly colloquial. Is it parodic ballroom gossip? Can we attribute this tosh to Ryder? His self-regarding conclusion is stilted in its own way. 'All this I learned about Julia, bit by bit, as one does learn the former – as it seems at the time, the preparatory – life of a woman one loves, so that one thinks of oneself as having been part of it, directing it by *devious* ways towards oneself' (my italics).

Rex's courtship of Julia runs alongside his continued affair with Brenda Champion. Lady Marchmain struggles in vain against Julia's apostasy. In this sordid world she is a tragic figure, betrayed by Ryder, Samgrass, and Julia; mortally ill, grieving for her lost son, lapsed husband and daughter, her heart 'transfixed with the swords of her dolours' like the seven sorrows of the Virgin Mary.[7] When Lord Marchmain overrides her, permitting Rex to marry Julia, Rex opts for a Catholic wedding because 'they put on a good show'. His pragmatic conversion is laughable: the priest instructing him likens him to a 'semi-imbecile', 'an idiot child' – 'He doesn't correspond to any degree of paganism known to the missionaries.' At Bridey's bombshell that a Catholic wedding is impossible because Rex is divorced, his response is characteristic: 'I'll get an annulment. What does it cost?' As Julia later summarizes their ten years of marriage, 'He simply wasn't all there. He wasn't a complete human being at all [...] I thought he was a sort of primitive savage, but he was something absolutely modern and up-to-date that only this ghastly age could produce. A tiny bit of a man pretending he was the whole.' There is a telling difference between Rex, the modern Hollow Man who is morally 'not all there', and the half-heathen Sebastian whose disappearance into the shadows was quite another thing: there is a *via dolorosa*, a road of suffering that he, like his mother, must undertake.

Further moral discriminations are prompted by Ryder's visit to Fez, to try to bring Sebastian home before his mother dies. Anthony Blanche says Sebastian's companion Kurt, a German deserter from the Foreign Legion with secondary syphilis, looks 'like the footman in "Warning Shadows"', a melodramatic German silent film from the twenties whose title is the main point here.[8] Kurt is a physically repellent, mercenary egotist, interested only in his own well-being and the financial security Sebastian provides. He grossly mirrors the competing material-isms of Rex's high-society lust for power and Ryder's cultured self-absorption. Sebastian's relationship with Kurt is on the contrary wholly selfless. Currently Sebastian lies in a Franciscan hospital, 'withered' by alcohol, too ill to move. For the dispassionate doctor, Sebastian's illness is inevitable: 'I am here to cure people, not to protect them from vicious habits.' For the bearded, barefoot monk nursing him, it is a different story: 'He's so patient [...] so kind [...] A real Samaritan.' 'Poor simple monk [...] poor booby,' Ryder thinks, only in retrospect adding 'God forgive me!' On a later visit, the monk says Sebastian 'is so much happier today, it is like one transfigured'. 'Poor simple monk,' the worldly-wise Ryder thinks again; 'poor booby'. But the monk is no simpleton, adding: 'You know why? He has a bottle of cognac in bed with him. It is the second I have found [...] He is so naughty.' Non-judgemental nursery morality again. On Ryder's return to England, Bridey echoes the doctor, asking whether there is 'anything vicious' in Sebastian's friendship with Kurt. When Ryder replies 'No. I'm sure not';[9] nor is Sebastian insane, he's just 'found a companion he happens to like', Bridey replies,

'Then he must have his allowance as you suggest. The thing is quite clear'. Neither Bridey nor Ryder shares the doctor's view of Sebastian's 'vice', but, for Ryder, Bridey's moral clarity is a 'mad certainty' as irrational as the charity of the barefoot Franciscan. Thus Sebastian provides a touchstone encouraging the reader to discriminate between Ryder's confused values, the selfishness of Kurt and Rex, and the charity of those who actually care about him and for him.

Book Two ends with Lady Marchmain's death, and the imminent destruction of Marchmain House, to make way for London flats. Bridey commissions Charles to paint it, so launching Ryder's lucrative career as an architectural artist recording Britain's vanishing heritage. In an immensely important, pivotal scene, the fifteen-year-old Cordelia joins him while he paints. As the light fades, Ryder takes his canvas to the window, 'and lightened a shadow'. Cordelia observes sadly, of the house, 'I only came up today, and didn't realise how far the decay had gone'. Are the shadows lightened or is decay looming? Or both? Was Sebastian 'withered' or 'transfigured'? Or both? Was Ryder and Sebastian's sybaritic undergraduate life an 'ascent or descent'? Such Heraclitean paradoxes in the chance rotations of Fortune's wheel were enjoyed with impunity in the secular *Decline and Fall*. In *Brideshead* they modulate into the paradoxical consolations of Christ's Beatitudes: 'Blessed are the poor in spirit: for theirs is the kingdom of heaven. Blessed are they that mourn, for they shall be comforted. Blessed are the meek, for they shall inherit the earth [...]'[10]

Cordelia gives Waugh's only gloss on Lady Marchmain,[11] and prosaically describes the de-consecration of Brideshead chapel after her mother's Requiem Mass. The priest 'took out the altar stone and put it in his bag [...] he emptied the holy water stoup and blew out the lamp in the sanctuary and left the tabernacle open and empty, as though from now on it was always to be Good Friday'. Then, as if to the reader, she tells Ryder,

> I suppose none of this makes any sense to you, Charles, poor agnostic [...] Suddenly, there wasn't any chapel there any more, just an oddly decorated room. You've never been to Tenebrae, I suppose? [...]. Well, if you had you'd know what the Jews felt about their temple. *Quomodo sedet sola civitas* ['How doth the City sit solitary'] ... it's a beautiful chant.[12]

In a letter to his agent accompanying this instalment from the work in progress, Waugh hoped that 'the last conversation with Cordelia gave the theological clue. The whole thing is steeped in theology but I begin to agree that theologians wont recognise it' (*L* 185). Certainly most of Waugh's non-Catholic readers now are agnostic or atheist. They, like Ryder, need Cordelia's very simple gloss. The chapel's de-consecration is like the destruction of the Temple in Jerusalem, as mourned in the Lamentations of Jeremiah. The Lamentations are sung during the Easter Holy Week office of Tenebrae. Tenebrae means Shadows. *These*, not the mere shadow of death, are the *Warning Shadows* that have been growing from the novel's very first pages.

Waugh will continue to draw on the rites of Tenebrae in the rest of the novel. The reader needs to know that during Tenebrae, the evening service preceding each of the last three days of Holy Week, fifteen candles in a candelabrum used to be placed on what was known as the 'hearse'. In the course of the service, the candles were extinguished one by one, till the last candle, still burning, was hidden under the altar, so that the service ended in darkness and a great *strepitus*, a commotion made by the congregation, which re-enacted the earthquake and solar eclipse at Christ's crucifixion. Jesus was crucified at the third hour, and

> from the sixth hour there was darkness over all the land unto the ninth hour [...when Jesus...] yielded up the ghost. And behold, the veil of the temple was rent in twain from the top to the bottom; and the earth did quake, and the rocks rent. (Matthew 27.45, 50–1)

At Downside Abbey, where Waugh liked to take his Easter retreat, the *strepitus* was created by the rolling thunderclap of every monk's misericord being slammed back into place.[13] The solitary light, still burning, was replaced on the hearse to burn on through the night, prefiguring the promise of the Resurrection to come, and the congregation left in silence.

On Good Friday the doors of the tabernacle, where the Host – representing the body of Christ – is kept, are left open because there is no Host to be protected. Its void symbolizes Christ's absence from the world between His death on Good Friday, and Resurrection on Easter Sunday.

All these liturgical practices re-enact the desolation of a darkened world without Christ. In *Brideshead*'s final, third book, their connotations will encompass both imminent world war, and the increasingly errant paths of its central characters. Which is why Book Two, 'Brideshead Deserted', ends with Cordelia quoting from the Father Brown story her mother read aloud on 'the *bad* evening' when Sebastian's drinking first became apparent. Father Brown said he caught the thief 'with an unseen hook and an invisible line which is long enough to let him wander to the ends of the world and still to bring him back with a twitch upon the thread'.[14] Cordelia knows that Sebastian, Julia and her father have all left the church. 'But God won't let them go for long, you know.' They are still attached to Him by a thread, even though they think they have severed it.

As for oblivious Ryder, 'I had no patience with this convent chatter. I had felt the brush take life in my hand that afternoon; I had had my finger in the great succulent pie of creation.' No change from his dinner with Rex. His worldly hunger is unabated, and will seek further satisfaction.

BOOK THREE

Waugh marked his novel's calendar by making Book Two open with the General Strike of 1926. Now the narrative jumps ten years to the abdication crisis of December 1936. Edward VIII's decision to marry the twice-married Wallis Simpson provides the public context for Book Three's focus on socially accepted private divorces and adulteries. Ryder, like Tony Last, left for South America immediately after discovering his wife's infidelity. When he meets Celia in New York, after two years' painting in the jungle, their marriage is obviously hollow. Ryder shows no interest in the baby born after his departure. Celia christened her Caroline, after Charles, but the girl's paternity appears questionable.

Book Three's first chapter. 'Orphans of the Storm', recounts Ryder's reunion with his wife, and, on the passage back to England, his falling in love with Julia who is returning, chastened, from a failed, adulterous love affair in America. In his diary Waugh wrote, 'I feel very much the futility of describing sexual emotions without describing the sexual act; I should like to give as much detail as I have of the meals, to the two coitions – with his wife and Julia. It would be no more or less obscene than to leave them to the reader's imagination, which in this case cannot be as acute as mine' (*D* 564–5). Bound by the censorship of his time, Waugh always suggests sexual relations between his characters with scrupulous obliqueness.[15] Even though he was attacked for the sex scene in *Black Mischief*, these episodes are rare, unlubricious and always concerned with moral issues.

In *Brideshead* Charles and Celia's legitimate coition is coldly functional. A conventional hiatus marks the act. Celia says, 'Shall I put my face to bed?'

> 'No,' I said, 'not at once.'
> Then she knew what was wanted. She had neat, hygienic ways for that too, but there were both relief and triumph in her smile of welcome; later we parted and lay in our twin beds a yard or two distant, smoking. (*BR* 256)[16]

This is copulation with a blank at its heart, sterile sex in a marriage without love. Celia's hygienic ways (a euphemism for contraception) are also anathema to a Catholic like Waugh.

The union between Julia and Charles is very different. The storm lasting most of the crossing consigns Celia to her cabin, conveniently seasick, leaving Julia and Charles, both good sailors, to become intimate. The consummation of their immediate attraction is delayed till they are literally flung together on the deserted decks. This involuntary embrace is strongly sexual, the very opposite of Charles and Celia's null coition. As Waugh tells Laura, 'Sex repression is making mag.op. rather smutty' (*L* 184) – a word repeated in the novel's text:

> As we made our halting, laborious way forward, away from the flying smuts of the smoke stack, we were alternately jostled together, then strained, nearly sundered, arms and fingers interlocked as I held the rail and Julia clung to me, thrust together again, drawn apart; then, in a plunge deeper than the rest, I found myself flung across her, pressing her against the rail, warding myself off her with the arms that held her prisoner. (*BR* 287)

Julia invites Ryder to her cabin below, and they make love at last. Both versions of this union, in the First and Revised Editions (1945 and 1960), have disappointed Waugh's readers and critics, hungry for passion. Yet Waugh has just described a

111

moment of physical closeness more highly charged than actual intercourse – which none of them have noticed. Now he wants something different:

> It was no time for the sweets of luxury; they would come, in their season, with the swallow and the lime flowers. Now on the rough water *there was a formality to be observed, no more. It was as though a deed of conveyance of her narrow loins had been drawn and sealed. I was making my first entry as the freeholder of a property I would enjoy and develop at leisure.* (*BR* 287, my italics)

The passage italicized here replaces the first edition's longer version, which makes the same point less forcefully.[17] Charles takes possession of Julia – a word twice repeated in 1945. He will 'enjoy' her as a 'property'.[18] And, notwithstanding the scepticism of Waugh's antagonistic critics, this is a male-chauvinist attitude Waugh deplores. In *Work Suspended* Roger Simmonds, the Marxist opportunist, loses interest in his wife when she is pregnant, because Lucy can't perform the conjugal functions that are his by right. He looks on her as a temporarily unusable possession, and he is not commended.[19] Plant, on the other hand, is drawn to Lucy in her haven of impregnable pregnancy, losing himself in asexual adoration. Moreover, all the terms stressed in Ryder's formal sexual possession of Julia echo, most distastefully, the unprepossessing Mr Samgrass. In Book Two Sebastian calls him 'someone of mummy's' because 'he was someone of almost everyone's who *possessed* something to attract him'. He improperly welcomed Ryder to Brideshead, as though he was Ryder's host – '"You find me in solitary *possession*," he said, and indeed he seemed to *possess* the hall [. . .], to *possess* the caryatids on either side of the fireplace, to *possess* me.' Later Ryder ominously thinks of himself and Julia as having 'taken *possession*' of happiness (all italics mine).

Brideshead's many critics ignore Charles and Julia's sexually charged embrace, and unanimously condemn the apparently rebarbative formality of the actual coition. Assuming that to be Waugh's mistake, Frank Kermode, like many others, complains that the 1960 revision isn't 'much of an improvement' because 'the act of lovemaking becomes an act of formal possession, as of a house' – missing the fact that Waugh makes the same point in both versions.[20] So what is he up to?

There is more to this than a mere protest against male chauvinism. Waugh's terminology of possession ominously foreshadows Ryder's later temptation when Julia looks set to inherit the Brideshead estate. The unease reluctantly registered by Waugh's critics has been deliberately evoked and left to work unseen. But, equally deliberately, Waugh delays its decoding for many pages to come.

Waugh's friend and biographer, Christopher Sykes, remembers criticizing Julia's remark, 'where can we hide in fair weather, we orphans of the storm?' When he reminded Waugh that *Orphans of the Storm* was a trashy film from their youth, Waugh turned on him, eyes blazing. 'Why didn't you like the film?' Sykes protested that he did like it, but he was young at the time, and ignorant. 'So was I,' Waugh said. 'My object was to renew your enjoyment.' Waugh kept the reference and stubbornly introduced the film's title as his chapter heading. Sykes was baffled.[21] Here, however, as in Ryder's tawdry account of Julia's London debut, Waugh knowingly exploits the allure of popular romance, reeling in his readers towards his serious purpose. It is his twitch on the thread.

In the 'Memorandum' explaining *Brideshead* to its would-be producers in Hollywood, Waugh stated that its latter half 'shows how the Grace of God turns everything in the end to good, though not to conventional prosperity'.[22] Julia and Charles are brought together for spiritual purposes beyond their expectation or understanding. In a striking moment in Celia's cocktail party at the beginning of the Atlantic crossing, Ryder notices an uninvited guest beside the caviar-laden ice swan, gobbling caviar 'as fast as a rabbit'. The stranger surreptitiously dabs away the drip on the end of the swan's melting beak, and challenges Ryder to guess how many drops fall in a minute. This bizarre moment of gratuitous comedy resonates with curious power. It is only several chapters later that its significance will also become clear. And yet, even here, as an image of ticking inevitability, it triggers a tremor of foreboding.

However, the major symbol dominating the storm is theological, and has consequently also escaped critical attention. It draws on Ryder's first impression of Brideshead chapel in Book One, and Cordelia's account of its de-consecration ending Book Two. Ryder's original description of the chapel was disdainful: 'The sanctuary lamp and all the metal furniture were of bronze, hand-beaten to the patina of a pock-marked skin;' the oak triptych was 'carved so as to give it the peculiar property of seeming to have been moulded in Plasticine'. Now his account of the liner's luxurious furnishings is equally lofty: 'I passed through vast bronze gates on which paper-thin Assyrian animals cavorted,' past 'yards and yards of biscuit-coloured wood which no carpenter's tool had touched, wood that had been bent round corners, steamed and squeezed and polished'.

Ryder's insouciant narrative doesn't register the parallel between the trappings of the liner and the chapel. There is no evident sub-text.[23] But when the storm breaks, things become hazardous. 'The great bronze doors of the lounge had torn away from their hooks and were swinging with the roll of the ship; they paused at the completion of each half-circle, began to move slowly and finished fast with a resounding clash.' That pendulum swing is both 'irresistible' and immensely 'forbidding' – a word which must be taken literally. 'There was something forbidding in the sight of that great weight of uncontrolled metal, flapping to and fro', but Charles and Julia pass through side by side, undaunted and unscathed. Applauded by a convivial (and also adulterous) traveller, they head towards their lawless union. Naturally the excited reader shares Ryder's sense of triumph. The next day, 'The bronze doors of the lounge had been fixed', firmly wedged wide open.

They replicate the pockmarked bronze doors of the tabernacle, left open in Brideshead's de-consecrated chapel, where God no longer resides. Their resounding clash echoes the thunderclap of the misericords flung back as the last lighted candle is hidden from sight in Tenebrae, and darkness is complete.

Julia, and above all Ryder, are literally at sea, and later say so ('I was adrift in a strange sea'; 'I was all at sea.') They constantly misread the signs they sense so forcibly. Recounting her loss of faith, disastrous marriage, still-born daughter, and 'secret, vicious, disastrous escapade' that took her to America, Julia concludes, 'I suppose I shall be punished for what I've just done. Perhaps that is why you and I are here like this . . . part of a plan.' Ryder echoes her phrase, 'part of a plan', naively seeing it in terms of reward, not punishment. Just as, in Book Two, he hubristically thought of *himself* directing Julia towards himself, so now he sees their union as their just due. When Julia wistfully says of her sadness, 'It's all I've earned. You said so yesterday. My wages,' a well-versed reader will hear the Biblical echo: 'For the wages of sin is death'.[24] Ryder, poor agnostic, has no knowledge of scripture, and his acquiescence is up-beat, mercantile and materialistic: 'An I O U from life. A promise to pay on demand'. When the storm drives the other passengers to their cabins, leaving the lovers alone together, Ryder compares it to 'tact on a titanic scale'. He does not hear the ominous irony of that supercharged adjective.[25]

Ryder becomes increasingly unsympathetic as Book Three progresses. His chilly treatment of the conciliatory Celia in New York is understandable, but heartless. He deceives her without a second thought during the crossing. He refuses to return home with her when they dock, hypocritically invoking the higher claims of his art – and spends the next month with Julia. Celia is fobbed off for good when they finally meet at his private view. His resentment at her original infidelity apparently justifies any bad behaviour of his own: 'she was powerless to hurt me any more [. . .] she had given me my manumission in that brief, sly lapse of hers; my cuckold's horns made me lord of the forest'. A stale metaphor mendaciously ennobles his own adultery.

Ironically enough, the only thing redeeming Ryder is his genuine love for Julia. Celia accepts that her marriage is at an end. Ryder and Julia's affair becomes common knowledge, and their habitual presence at Brideshead is countenanced by the complaisant Rex. As Rex's guests say about the Simpson scandal, 'who cares about divorce now except a few old maids who aren't married anyway?' Yet Waugh presents 'the sweets of luxury', promised at the lovers' first coition, in luxurious terms that become increasingly suspect. Beside Brideshead's fountain Charles and Julia survey two years uninterrupted happiness as the sun sets, 'drawing long shadows across the pasture', spreading out its 'stacked merchandise of colour and scent', glorifying her 'tight little gold tunic', 'golden shoulders', the emerald ring she turns on her finger. Charles is shocked by Cordelia's plainness in comparison with Julia's 'white skin and silk and jewelled hair'. At dinner in the Painted Parlour she wears a heavily embroidered Chinese robe with a gold circle at her throat, her hands at rest among the dragons on her lap.

Vanity of vanities! In the Catholic catechism the deadly sin of lust is termed 'Luxuria'. The 'sweets of luxury' are finally baldly named for what they are when Bridey tells Julia she's living in sin with both bigamous Rex and adulterous Charles. Her intense access of remorse reminds Charles of Holman Hunt's *The Awakened Conscience*.[26]

The reference to Hunt's great painting is heavily loaded. Like the swinging doors on the liner, and Millais' *Bubbles*, it offers a pictorial analogue to the novel's sub-text in the iconographic manner of Plant Senior's pre-Raphaelite art. It depicts a young woman half-rising from the lap of her lover, as he plays the piano in a room newly-furnished for his mistress. Hunt said he wanted to present her 'recalling the memory of her childish home, and breaking away from her gilded cage with a startled, holy resolve, while her shallow companion still sings on, ignorantly intensifying her repentant purpose.' Ruskin pointed out that 'there is not a single object in all that room, common, modern, vulgar, but it becomes tragical, if rightly read'. Hunt's picture, and Ruskin's celebrated commentary, which Ryder reads to Julia but Waugh does not quote, together provide a clear gloss on Charles and Julia's relationship. Ryder is as obtuse as Hunt's shallow lover in his indulgent incomprehension of Julia's remorse. In a line later cut from Julia's long lament regretting her guilty love, she talks bitterly of cherishing her sin like an idiot child, 'bathing it, dressing it, *clipping diamonds to it*' (*BR* 316, my italics). The tragic trappings Ruskin identifies in Hunt's vulgar love-nest are upgraded to the lavish embellishments of Charles and Julia's upper-class adultery.

When the Editor of the *Tablet* complained that every detail of Prudence and Basil's affair in *Black Mischief* was sordid – bathwater dirty, Basil unshaven – Waugh ridiculed his faulty logic, saying: 'What is the inference of these carefully extracted details? That in order to preserve modesty I should have staged the illicit meeting among silk sheets, soft music, expensive perfumery and all the shoddy stock-in-trade of pornography?' (*L* 76). Now that Waugh savagely relocates his illicit lovers' meetings among the stacked merchandise of beautiful Brideshead, there are no objections from the *Tablet* – and classy adultery hooks the gullible reader.

It does not rest there. The blandishments of high-class

romance are repeatedly disrupted by Waugh's unexpected shifts of tone following Bridey's bombshell. 'All this mysterious tumult of sorrow!' Ryder exclaims, of Julia's monologue on sin. 'What had happened to us in the Painted Parlour? What shadow had fallen in the candlelight?' It sounds like the worst kind of Victorian melodrama – and is deliberate. When the lovers return to the fountain later that night, Ryder lightly compares it to the setting of a comedy. Like Hunt's shallow young man, he 'still sings on', oblivious to Julia's sharp replies:

> 'Scene: a baroque fountain in a nobleman's grounds. Act one, sunset; act two, dusk; act three, moonlight. The characters keep assembling at the fountain for no very clear reason.'
> 'Comedy?'
> 'Drama. Tragedy. Farce. What you will [. . .]'
> 'Oh, don't talk in that damned bounderish way. Why must everything be second-hand? Why must this be a play? Why must my conscience be a pre-Raphaelite picture?' (*BR* 320)

As an unbeliever, Ryder cannot share Julia's Catholic sense of sin. Her feelings of guilt are aggravated by his incredulous detachment. Holman Hunt's gloss on his picture is telling here. His frame for *The Awakening Conscience* displays the text of Proverbs 25.20: 'As he that taketh away a garment in cold weather, so is he that singeth songs to an heavy heart'. Holman Hunt said that 'These words, expressing the unintended stirring up of the deeps of pure affection by the idle sing-song of an empty mind, led me to see how *the companion of the girl's misery might himself be the unconscious utterer of a divine message*' (my italics). This is the role unwittingly played by Ryder in Julia's awakening.

THE PURPOSE REVEALED

Charles and Julia's survey of two years' happiness ends with Ryder confessing he feels 'as though all mankind, and God too, were in a conspiracy against us'. They have 'taken possession of happiness', yet how many nights can that possession last? The next chapter closes with their own fearful answer to their question. 'A few days, a few months [. . .] Then the dark.'

For Ryder, Julia's remembered sadness on shipboard now implies 'Surely I was made for some other purpose than this?' In

1938, 'when there was all that talk about going to war with Munich,' as Nanny Hawkins puts it, both public and private worlds were preoccupied by increasingly urgent purposes. Waugh's Postscript to *Work Suspended* laconically summed up his own mood at that time – a mood shared by Plant and his friends, by Julia and Ryder, by much of anxious Europe, in the summer of 1939:

> Beavers bred in captivity, inhabiting a concrete pool, will, if given the timber, fatuously go through all the motions of damming an ancestral stream. So I and my friends busied ourselves with our privacies and intimacies [...] The new life came, not by [our] contrivance.[27] (*WS* 238)

Ryder and Julia assume their sense of impending doom derives from the imminence of war, and Julia's need of a purpose finds an obvious answer. 'With the Last Trump so near,' she wants to marry Ryder and have his child. 'All I can hope to do,' she says, 'is to put my life in some sort of order in a human way, before all human order comes to an end.'

The interlocking moves begin to be set in motion; adulteries are witnessed, lawyers engaged, changes of domicile agreed, for Rex and Julia's divorce, Ryder and Celia's divorce, Julia's marriage to Ryder, Celia's to her latest immature lover, Bridey's to the widowed Mrs Muspratt. The absurd bustle of this 'game of General Post',[28] shunting husbands, wives and property to and fro, throws into sharp relief a theme that has been inconspicuously sustained from the very beginning of *Brideshead*, of futile human attempts to impose order and gain control – like beavers in captivity fatuously damming an imaginary stream. The senseless precautions against mustard gas in the novel's Prologue; Ryder Senior's out-of-date fashion tips for Charles at Oxford; Jasper's 'Grand Remonstrance', which hardens rather than deflecting Charles's love of Sebastian; Lady Marchmain's machinations to prevent Sebastian's alcoholism – all are vain. 'The heavy wheels stirred and the small wheels spun'; and the characters continue to pursue their flying, forbidden desires with undiminished appetite. Cordelia recognizes 'thwarted passion' in Charles and Julia; even Ryder catches a 'thwarted' expression in Julia's sadness; and Sebastian still ends his days an incurable alcoholic.

Only Cordelia and Bridey understand that Sebastian's suffering brings him closer to God. The novel's penultimate chapter ends with Cordelia's tender, clear-eyed account of Sebastian's current life and likely death on the fringes of a religious community near Carthage. Sadly remembering this balding, drunken derelict as 'the youth with the teddy bear under the flowering chestnuts', Ryder asks whether he suffers. Oh yes, Cordelia replies. 'One can have no idea what the suffering may be, to be maimed as he is – no dignity, no power of will. No-one is ever holy without suffering.' And Sebastian is holy; that is the one thing Ryder must understand. One day he'll be picked up dying by the monastery gate; he'll be taken in, 'and show by a mere flicker of his eyelid that he is conscious when they give him the last sacraments'. Not such a bad way of getting through one's life, she adds.

Cordelia's charity is immensely moving. She speaks of Julia not loving Sebastian 'as we do', and Ryder recognizes the implicit reproach: 'there was no past tense in Cordelia's verb "to love"'. Just before this conversation, Ryder told Julia his feeling that Sebastian was her forerunner (the thought 'that hung in the air between us like a wisp of tobacco smoke – a thought to fade and vanish like smoke without a trace'), and wondered whether 'perhaps all our loves are merely hints and symbols [...] along the weary road that others have tramped before us'. Ryder's perception of a larger love is unformed, secular and pessimistic; nor can he understand Cordelia's spiritual certainty. Thinking about their talk, he unconsciously draws on an image from the conversion of St Paul:[29]

> How often, it seemed to me, I was brought up short, like a horse in full stride suddenly refusing an obstacle, backing against the spurs, too shy even to put his nose at it and look at the thing. (BR 341)

Ryder's conscious mind resists the spirit spurring him on; in the words of the Authorised Version, *he kicks against the pricks*. His subconscious mind is more receptive, and the chapter ends with another involuntary image whose import he does not yet understand: a trapper's arctic hut, the snow piling against the door till the thaw will set in, the snows melt, and the gathering avalanche sweep the 'little, lighted place' into the ravine below. Here at last is the resonant echo answering the elusive keynote struck by the ice-swan's melting beak in mid-Atlantic – dripping, moment by moment, with the immanent inevitability of divine purpose.

*

With the novel's last chapter the game of General Post accelerates: all the participants in the chains of marriage, divorce and remarriage are in transit between domiciles and legal status when an abrupt halt is imposed by Lord Marchmain's intended return home. The relocations of property are countermanded; in the solicitors' offices deeds are returned to their strong boxes. Lord Marchmain's contradictory missives prefigure the futile flaps and counterflaps of war. His actual arrival is a painful combination of pomp and pathos. The village hangs out bunting re-painted with the Marchmain coronets. The family awaits his arrival on the steps of the great house, flanked by 'the upper servants' whose orders of precedence have been anxiously adjusted. Preceded by his gentlemen in attendance, Lord Marchmain emerges from his limousine, bowed, diminished, his nose discoloured by cold, his hands in a schoolboy's grey woollen gloves, and gathers himself to make his effortful way into the house.

Once recovered from his journey, however, Lord Marchmain takes over Ryder's gusto for the excesses of ornate late Victoriana with evident relish. He will not sleep upstairs. He wants his bedroom in the Chinese Drawing Room, with its painted hangings and Chippendale carvings. The Queen's bed must be dismantled and carried downstairs. ('The Chinese drawing room, my lord, the "Queen's bed"?' – with its four posters supporting a vast velvet canopy like the *baldachino* of St Peter's?). He demands the silver basin and ewer from 'the Cardinal's dressing room'. Having assembled the props of a comically grim, Hogarthian moral tableau, he turns slyly to Ryder. 'You might paint it, eh – and call it the *Death Bed*?' For Ryder, Marchmain's preposterous schoolboy imperatives seem like 'an awakened memory of childhood, a dream in the nursery' – 'When I'm grown up I'll sleep in the Queen's bed in the Chinese drawing-room.' Nursery naughtiness once more.

However, graver temptations follow. Lord Marchmain frets at

the prospect of Bridey inheriting Brideshead Castle with the vulgar Mrs Muspratt as his wife. She is beyond the age of childbearing. There will be no heirs. To whom should he give it instead? 'Quis?'[30] Beautiful Julia with Ryder as consort is 'much more suitable'. She dutifully demurs, 'Of course not, papa, it's Bridey's'. Ryder tells Julia 'It's monstrous for Bridey'. Lord Marchmain persists in referring to the time 'when Julia and [Charles] should be married and in possession'.

When Ryder first possessed Julia, *it was as though a deed of conveyance of her narrow loins had been drawn and sealed.* Lord Marchmain's unexpected decision to return home has reversed Bridey's expectations of taking over Brideshead Castle, and the actual 'deeds of conveyance, engrossed and ready for signing, were rolled up, tied, and put away'. Now there is every expectation that Ryder's prophetic metaphor will become material reality. His first, sexual entry via Julia's narrow loins may make him freeholder of a very large property indeed, to be enjoyed and developed at his leisure.

The prospect tempts both Charles and Julia. For Charles it is like the view gained at a turn in the avenue; like his first sight of Brideshead Castle with Sebastian; 'such a prospect perhaps as a high pinnacle of the temple afforded after the hungry days in the desert'. For insouciant Ryder the aspiration is innocuous; his rhetorical question, 'Need I reproach myself if sometimes I was taken by the vision?' expects an indulgent reply. Yet unwittingly his image echoes Satan's second temptation of Christ after his forty-day fast in the wilderness.[31]

These temptations become bound up with even graver choices, when Bridey decides it's time for his father to see a priest. Julia warns Charles that 'great Church trouble' lies ahead. Ryder's antagonism is outspoken: it's all 'tomfoolery', 'superstition and trickery'. When Bridey leads in the inoffensive Father Mackay to his father, and Lord Marchmain inflexibly dismisses him, Ryder is triumphant: 'Mumbo-jumbo is off,' he tells Julia; 'The witch-doctor has gone [...] It's great sucks to Bridey.' But he also has the grace to admit to his reader that there was 'another unexpressed, inexpressible, indecent little victory that I was furtively celebrating' – the certainty that Lord Marchmain would now disinherit Bridey in Julia's favour. As he does.

Many of Waugh's readers, being non-believers, will sympathize with Ryder's robust scepticism. He has been our errant guide throughout. Yet we may feel troubled by his impure motives; by his insensitivity to Julia's conscience; by his confident bigotry. Such uncertainties are quickly dissolved in the supremely comic discussion that follows, where no consensus can be found between all the Catholic believers – Cara, Cordelia, Julia, Bridey – on the efficacy and significance of the last sacraments. Need Lord Marchmain be actually conscious when they are delivered? Is it the holy oil or the absolution that does the trick? Can't the priest hide while the sick man dies, and validly administer the sacraments before the corpse is cold? Ryder's derision seems well founded, and at this point his earlier, casual prediction of a coming *Drama. Tragedy. Farce. What you will* seems precisely fulfilled.

Waugh lulls us, his rationalist readers, into Ryder's confidence. When Lord Marchmain is finally *in extremis*, his mistress, Cara, tries to prepare him: 'Alex, you remember the priest who came from Melstead. You were very naughty when he came to see you. You hurt his feelings very much...' We enter the death chamber with Ryder, and take up our position beside him, the doctor and nurse, while Julia and Cara kneel at the dying man's feet and Father Mackay ministers to him: 'I know you are sorry for all the sins of your life, aren't you? Make a sign, if you can. You're sorry, aren't you?' There is a world of difference between his simplicity, and Cara's inane social pressure. And we, the reasonable readers, are as taken aback as Ryder himself, when he is moved – without premeditation or faith – to kneel too, and pray for the dying man. 'O God, if there is a God, forgive him his sins, if there is such a thing as sin.' A tentative, conditional prayer, a beginning, sharpened by the love that is Ryder's salvation: 'I suddenly felt the longing for a sign, if only of courtesy, if only for the woman I loved [...] praying, I knew, for a sign [...] I prayed more simply, "God forgive him his sins" and "Please God, make him accept your forgiveness."' In a supremely powerful moment, Lord Marchmain stirs, raises his hand to his brow, and both Ryder and his sympathetic reader are involuntarily terrified:

I thought he had felt the touch of the chrism and was wiping it away. 'O God,' I prayed, 'don't let him do that.' But there was no need for fear; the hand moved slowly down to his breast, then to his

122

shoulder, and Lord Marchmain made the sign of the cross. Then I knew that the sign I had asked for was not a little thing [...] and a phrase came back to me from my childhood of the veil of the temple being rent from top to bottom. (*BR* 371)

The temple's thick veil was torn – from top to bottom, as only a divine hand could tear it – when Christ died on the cross. It is the first time Ryder recognizes his own vestigial biblical knowledge, and understands it.

That is also a sign and not a little thing.

In the previous year, a friend of Waugh's had died in very similar circumstances.[32] The climax achieved, Waugh was in a hurry to finish. 'The last dialogue poor' his diary notes, rightly, of Charles and Julia's final separation (*D* 567). Without being told, Ryder knows that Julia has chosen to reject their adulterous life together. 'I hope your heart may break; but I do understand.' For him, it is like death; the trapper's hut, that little lighted place, has been swept away. 'The avalanche was down, the hillside swept bare behind it [...] the new mound glittered and lay still in the silent valley.' He does not yet see that this is a clean sweep, a new beginning.

The epilogue seemed 'easy meat' to Waugh (*D* 567–8). Wartime brings understanding; Ryder becomes a Catholic. Brideshead is requisitioned and ruined by the army; its undamaged chapel is re-consecrated. There Ryder finds 'a small red flame – a beaten-copper lamp of deplorable design relit before the beaten-copper doors of a tabernacle [...] burning anew among the old stones'.

*

Brideshead Revisited was Waugh's most ambitious and complex novel to date. While it was an immediate and lasting popular success, its critical reception has been mixed. Its enduring appeal derives from its two love-stories and their seductive settings – one adolescent, homoerotic, and fundamentally innocent, in Oxford's idealized pastoral; the second adult, heterosexual, and adulterous, in the stacked merchandise of Brideshead Castle. Precisely these attractions were attacked by the novel's resolutely unglamourized critics. In public, Kingsley Amis dismissed it as 'a book about nobs for snobs'. Many years earlier, he had parodied the novel's high-class porn, which was, in fact, Waugh's deliberate answer to the *Tablet*'s criticism of *Black Mischief*'s sordid sex.[33] Moreover, for critics unsympathetic to Waugh's theological purpose, his apparent snobbery merely furthered an unacceptable Catholic tract.[34] Many, like George Orwell and Edmund Wilson, would have shared Henry Green's reservations: 'The end was not for me. As you can imagine my heart was in my mouth all through the deathbed scene, hoping against hope that the old man would *not* give way, that is, take the course he eventually did.'[35] For Waugh this perverse response, from a friend and respected fellow-novelist, must have painfully demonstrated both the need for what he had written, and its failure.

Criticism of Waugh commonly merges its two main objections, to his Catholicism and his snobbery, into one. The Flytes embody both. To the novel's early critics Waugh wrote a restrained reply, admitting personal snobbery, 'perhaps', in his choice of friends, and denying it both in his faith ('In England Catholicism is predominantly a religion of the poor') and the workings of his novel.[36] In fact the novel's moral hierarchy echoes Christ's Sermon on the Mount, valuing down-and-out Sebastian above up-and-coming Rex Mottram. Waugh's later *Memorandum* vainly tried to guide Hollywood's bemused filmmakers through *Brideshead*'s fine moral and psychological discriminations between characters carefully located on the spectrum from atheism to faith. This, one of the novel's main strengths, allies it with the solidity of nineteenth century fiction from which it derives.

In general the novel's critics tend to express their own ideological gripes against Waugh, rather than literary reservations. Whatever their response, Waugh could not and would not have jettisoned his central theological theme, or his regret for a historic cultural heritage threatened by war. However, as he confessed in 1960, 'the English aristocracy has maintained its identity to a degree that then seemed impossible'. Much of the novel is consequently 'a panegyric preached over an empty coffin'.[37] From the retrospect of the Revised Edition, Waugh encountered a different, irresolvable difficulty – the literary, rather than ideological weaknesses of his undertaking. In particular, he found himself 'in two minds' about Julia's monologue on sin, and Lord Marchmain's dying speech. He kept them with only slight cuts, because 'they were essentially of the mood of writing', 'an essential part of the book', even though he admitted that 'I would not now introduce them into a novel which elsewhere aims at verisimilitude'. *This* uncertainty, not his presumed snobbery, created a tonal instability in the novel which is genuinely damaging.

Waugh is the master of deadpan irony. His readers and critics are rarely sure quite how to take him. These difficulties are compounded when the style is not entirely under control. Writing in a wartime period of soya beans and basic English had an effect on Waugh's style which he soon came to deplore:

> The book is infused with a kind of gluttony, for food and wine, for the splendours of the recent past, and for rhetorical and ornamental language, which now with a full stomach I find distasteful. (*BR* Preface 9)

In *Brideshead* Waugh consciously developed the new style presaged by John Plant. He was frequently pleased by his unexpected fluency and speed of composition.[38] *Scoop* took three years to complete; *Brideshead* five months. He said he 'modified the grosser passages' in the Revised Edition, but did so less than one might expect. When are its surviving stylistic excesses a deliberate index of characters' aesthetic coarseness or moral inadequacy? When are they Waugh's own inadvertent failures of taste, explicable in terms of his eagerness to develop a new, not entirely successful style, and only excusable – if at all – as an expression of war-time privation, and thus 'an essential part of the book'?

These difficulties are intensified by Waugh's choice of Ryder as his narrator. Ryder is so deeply unaware of his own limitations that most modern readers, sharing his agnosticism, venial appetites and ambition, will take his story at his own estimation. Yet the unreliability of the hero (not necessarily the narrator) is a familiar element in the *Bildungsroman*. Waugh knew both *David Copperfield*'s first-person narrative, and the third-person interiority of Joyce's pitiless *Portrait of the Artist as a Young Man*. In both the hero changes with maturity, sometimes not for the better. Ryder's inadequacies, like John Plant's in *Work Suspended*, are deliberately planted, plotted, and marked. But the reader needs to be alert to the author's covert signs.

This is the real difficulty of the novel. Waugh's intention is *to trace the operation of divine grace on a group* [...] *of characters*, from its imperceptible beginnings to its devastating conclusion. His hero is profoundly unaware of his own role in a drama beyond his belief or comprehension. The reader is offered a series of signs so subtly introduced, so widely dispersed, that they have failed to make their mark. Yet Waugh took pains to guide his readers in a variety of ways. Most obviously, characters act as commentators. Cordelia's clear-eyed charity is transcendent and her moral perceptions are unerring. Bridey is the inconvenient voice of categorical Catholic principles. Anthony Blanche is the novel's guide in aesthetic matters, as critical of Sebastian's charm and Ryder's phoney art as Harold Acton had been of Waugh's first, incinerated novel.[39] Suggestive parallels and moral contrasts are set up between diverse characters – for instance the nursery innocence of young Sebastian and Ryder contrasts with the 'degenerate' infantilism of 'Boy' Mulcaster and his 'pert' schoolgirlish sister Celia. Arguments between the protagonists encourage readers to exercise their own judgement – from the best way to treat Sebastian's alcoholism to the effectiveness of Lord Marchmain's last rites. Single words acquire deepening resonances ('possession', 'shadows', 'deeds of conveyance', 'naughtiness'). Religious symbols, Biblical echoes, references to early film and Victorian art are all there to assist the reader.

Shortly after the war ended, Waugh was invited to visit the Nuremberg Trials as an observer. Dame Laura Knight showed him her painting

> of the prisoners in the dock with a background of corpses and burning buildings. The papers on a table had by chance taken the form of a cross and she was in doubt whether to leave them so. 'You don't think it *illustration*, do you?' she kept asking. I tried to explain that I liked 'illustration'. (*D* 646)

Waugh's novel is richly endowed with illustrative clues. Many have remained undeciphered and ignored. Of *The Sacred and Profane Memories of Captain Charles Ryder*, the sacred are neglected and the profane have popular primacy. It is telling that, even with the author's guidance, MGM rejected the proposed film of *Brideshead* because it seemed 'likely to undermine the conception of Christian marriage' – the very reverse of Waugh's intentions.

9

The Loved One (1948)

Waugh and Laura's post-war jaunt to Hollywood in 1947 was engineered, not entirely seriously, to discuss the filming of *Brideshead* with MGM's executives. Waugh's diary entry for the first 'conference' on 7 February is ominously ironic. The 'writer' (not Waugh) enters in 'local costume – a kind of woollen blazer, matelot's vest, buckled shoes. He has been in Hollywood for years and sees *Brideshead* purely as a love story. None of them see the theological implication' (D 673). Waugh gamely discovered 'something a little luxurious in talking in great detail about every implication of a book which the others are paid to know thoroughly'. But his succinct *Memorandum* summarized the novel's implications in vain, and within a month the censor rejected the project. Waugh turned with relief to his new discovery, 'a deep mine of literary gold in the cemetery of Forest Lawn' (D 675), the source of *The Loved One*. This 'beautiful tale about corpses' (L 252) was exultantly written at speed, in his old, terse style.

*

Ostensibly, MGM rejected *Brideshead* because it infringed the Motion Picture Production Code's requirements on SEX, Section II: 'The sanctity of the institution of marriage and the home shall be upheld', Subsection 1: 'Adultery, sometimes necessary plot material, must not be explicitly treated, or justified, or presented attractively'. Further explanatory sub-sub-sections forbade 'sensuous scenes' and 'more glamour and luxury than is consonant with the plot'.[1] *Brideshead* clearly broke these rules, for good reasons that MGM's executives chose not to understand. The censor, Mr Breen, dismissed it as 'a story of illicit sex and adultery without sufficient compensating moral values':

> In their confused efforts [the lovers] are suddenly stopped and turned to a new life by a special influx of God's grace [but] there does not seem to be sufficient development of the significance, the importance, and the tremendous efficacy of this grace [...] With Charles and Julia, who are guilty of double adultery, there seems to be no recognition by them that their relationship is wrong.

According to his astonishingly inattentive summary, sympathy for the lovers' 'unacceptably light attitude' might only have been permissible if due emphasis had been laid on their 'punishment, reform and repentance'. This alone, which 'does not exist in the novel', would have provided 'the proper compensating moral values required by the Code'.

In fact *Brideshead* focused on precisely the moral values ostensibly required by the Code – and *this* created problems for the Hollywood censors. The novel had received a controversial reception from Catholic critics, because it was directly focused on adultery and its growing respectability. Hollywood preferred to avoid both, while continuing to produce romantic films that glossed over infidelity and divorce without demur. Waugh observed that in Hollywood 'Every attempt is made by innuendo to pack as much lubricious material as possible into every story, while mature dramatic works intended for a *morally stable, civilised audience* have their essential structure hopelessly impaired' ('Why Hollywood is a Term of Disparagement', *EAR* 330; my italics). His general complaint tallies with his personal experience. His disappointed expectation of a 'morally stable, civilised audience' also reverts to an important declaration of literary intent, formulated a year before, in 'Fan-Fare', an essay written for his American fans when *Brideshead* was first published.

In 'Fan-Fare', Waugh answered a number of questions frequently raised by his admirers. 'Are your books meant to be satirical?' got a flat negative. Satire, he explained, 'flourishes in a stable society and presupposes homogenous moral standards' – that is, a *morally stable, civilised audience*. Satire 'is aimed at inconsistency and hypocrisy. It exposes polite cruelty and folly by exaggerating them. It seeks to produce shame.' But, he added, 'all this has no place in the Century of the Common Man where vice no longer pays lip service to virtue'. In the very sentence denying satire, Waugh ironically satirizes his society's moral void. The 'disintegrated society of today' does not even pay token lip service to virtue; it cannot recognize virtue, or vice, at all. For Waugh there is only one, aesthetic answer: 'The artist's only service [...] is to create little independent systems of order of his own' (*EAR* 304).

The Hollywood censor's blindness to Julia's remorse, Marchmain's penitence, Ryder's conversion, the entire novel's spiritual telos, merely reconfirmed Waugh's sense of contemporary moral vacuity. He claimed to find his rejection 'very funny', but it was just another illustration of the syndrome identified in 'Fan-Fare'. His Hollywood hosts, 'the great pachyderms of the film trade' were dense and invulnerable: 'one may say what one likes in perfect confidence that one is powerless to wound' (*EAR* 325). By the same token, Waugh maintained that *The Loved One* 'should not be read as a satire on morticians' (*L* 259). Satire can only be effective if the behaviour it mocks is recognizably aberrant from a social norm. And in California the aberrations so shocking to Waugh *were* the norm.

*

For Waugh, *The Loved One* contained more than satire. His preparatory essays, and later the novel, convey a strong sense of literary arousal. His intense attention to an enigma demanding solution is directly transferred to his hero. As Dennis Barlow contemplates the phenomenon of Whispering Glades, 'his interest was no longer purely technical *nor purely satiric*' (my italics).

> In that zone of insecurity in the mind where none but the artist dare trespass, the tribes were mustering. Dennis, the frontiersman, could read the signs [...] his literary sense was alert, like a hunting hound. There was something in Whispering Glades that was necessary to him, that only he could find.
> [...] There was a very long, complicated and important message [his Muse] was trying to dictate to him. (*LO* 68, 69, 90)

Waugh's initial, self-confessedly 'humdrum' ideas are disentangled in a pair of preparatory essays. 'Why Hollywood is a Term of Disparagement' registered his criticisms of Hollywood in an essay whose opening, ironic metaphor is seminal. The film community lives apart, 'like monks in a desert oasis'; their lives revolve round the few 'shrines' of its studios, two hotels, and single restaurant; they dwell in 'a continuous psalm of self-praise' (April 1947, *EAR* 325). The second essay, 'Half in Love with Easeful Death', begins by completing this metaphor of Hollywood's mock-religious status and consigning it to the dust. Archeologists a millennium hence, says Waugh, will catch cryptic twentieth-century references to 'a cult which once flourished on this forgotten strand; of the idol Oscar – sexless image of infertility – of the great Star Goddesses who were once noisily worshipped there in a Holy Wood' (October 1947, *EAR* 331).

The rest of this second essay turns to its subtitle, 'An Examination of Californian Burial Customs'. In the mine of literary gold offered by Forest Lawn Memorial Park, Waugh found 'a necropolis of the age of the pharaohs, created in the middle of the impious twentieth century'. He describes the Park's miles of underground piping invisibly watering its ever evergreen shrubs; its indestructible mock-Tudor constructions of concrete and steel embedded thirty-three feet deep in solid rock; its repro statuary, piped music, and non-sectarian chapels. In his letters Waugh boasted that he was about to dine with Forest Lawn's Founder, 'DR EATON himself'. At the entrance to Forest Lawn, Eaton's Credo is displayed beside the largest wrought iron gates in the world: 'I believe in a happy Eternal Life'. It is repeated with variations in all the segregated retreats – Babyland, Graceland, Slumberland, Vesperland, Dawn of Tomorrow. 'Be happy because they for whom you mourn are happy – far happier than ever before', 'Happy because Forest Lawn has eradicated the old customs of Death and depicts Life not Death' (*EAR* 335–6). Insistently, Waugh demands: 'What will the archaeologists of 2947 make of all this? [...] What will the professors of the future make of Forest Lawn? What do we make of it ourselves? Here is the thing, under our noses, a first-class anthropological puzzle of our own period [...] What does it mean?'

He begins with the most humdrum answers. It is a profitable business venture. It is a monument to local tradition in a country too young for traditions. In this culture of senile leisure, on 'the ultimate, sunset-shore,' Hollywood's dinosaurs, the rich retired immigrants, 'believe themselves alive, opening their scaly eyes two or three times a day to browse on salads and fruits' while 'the priests of countless preposterous cults' soothe them towards imperceptible death. The function of its sacred texts is clear:

> Forest Lawn has consciously turned its back on 'the old customs of death', the grim traditional alternatives of Heaven and Hell, and promises immediate eternal happiness for all its inmates [...] Dr Eaton is the first man to offer eternal salvation at an inclusive charge as part of his undertaking service. (*EAR* 336)

Hence California's flourishing art of embalming. The dead come 'fresh from the final beauty parlour, looking rather smaller than in life and much more dandified'. The Old World's sepulchral statuary devised images of death that are banned from Forest Lawn: not here the 'marble worms writhing in the marble adipocere'[2] of high Renaissance tomb sculpture:

> These macabre achievements were done with a simple moral purpose – to remind a highly civilised people that beauty was skin deep and pomp was mortal [...] In Forest Lawn [...] these old values are reversed. The body does not decay; it lives on, more chic in death than ever before, in its indestructible class A steel and concrete shelf; the soul goes straight from the Slumber Room to Paradise, where it enjoys an endless infancy, one of a great Caucasian nursery-party [...]
> That, I think, is the message. (*EAR* 337)

Wisely, Waugh gave Cyril Connolly *The Loved One* to publish in a single issue of *Horizon*. Connolly was supposed to prepare his sophisticated audience by an Editorial Comment in the preceding issue: in fact, his puff lazily reprinted a paragraph from Waugh's last letter, listing the ideas he had in mind.

> 1st & quite predominantly, over-excitement with the scene of Forest Lawn. 2nd the Anglo-American impasse – 'never the twain can meet', 3rd there is no such thing as an 'American'. They are all exiles uprooted, transplanted & doomed to sterility [...] 4th the European raiders who come for the spoils and if they are lucky make for home

with them. 5th Memento mori, old style, not specifically Californian. (L 265–6)

These were the disparate ideas Waugh dovetailed in *The Loved One*.

*

The central theme of *The Loved One*'s tight, logical structure can be summarized by two four-letter words – the Cult of the Sham. As often in Waugh, it is neatly symbolized early on, in this case by an item of dress. Aimée shows the curious Dennis an article of 'casket-wear': a suit complete with shirt front, cuffs, collar and bow-tie, buttoned down the front – and at the back, slit from neck to toe. It was, Waugh concludes, 'the apotheosis of the dickey'. The dickey is a sham dress-shirt front. 'Apotheosis' resonates with all the connotations of the cult, and takes us back to Mrs Ape – the 'apotheosis of bogosity' – and *Vile Bodies*.

Whispering Glades is a necropolis devoted to falsehood. Its music is canned, its art phoney, its architectural monuments specious improvements on modest British originals, from St-Peter-Without-the-Walls to the uneuphonious Wee Kirk o'Auld Lang Syne. Above all, its painted stiffs are cosmetic travesties, dandified in death, a telephone in the lifeless hand, a monocle in the unseeing eye.

The novel opens with a scene deliberately misleading the reader into thinking he is in some God-forsaken colonial outpost – two Englishmen drinking sundowners on a blistered veranda by a dry waterhole, ever-present music pulsing from the neighbouring native huts. But the waterhole was once a swimming-pool; Sir Francis Hinsley, an English knight of the old school, is being shouldered from his Hollywood sinecure by false and fruity Sir Ambrose Abercrombie. Sir Ambrose's parody of English dress consists of Eton Rambler tie, I Zingari ribbon on his boater; deerstalker and Inverness cape for the rain. Not so different from the Hollywood script 'writer' first encountered by Waugh, in 'matelot' vest and buckled shoes.

Hollywood is peopled by shams. There is the impressively named Lorenzo Medici, only 'he says it "Medissy", like that; how you said it [i.e. correctly] kinda sounds like a wop and Mr Medici is a very fine young man with a very, very fine and

133

wonderful record'...Consider, too, Baby Aaronson, the starlet who 'set a new note in personal publicity'. Initially transformed by the inventive Sir Francis into Juanita del Pablo, a scowling, black-haired Spanish anti-Fascist refugee, she was subsequently radically reconfigured into a roguish Irish red head called anything from Deirdre to Oonagh – with the loss of half her nose and all her teeth en route. In the magazine photo Guru Brahmin, Aimée's agony aunt, is a bearded, almost naked sage. In reality, he is Mr Slump, a drunken, chain-smoking hack.

The linguistic embodiment of Sham is euphemism, a stylistic trope that recurs throughout the novel. Aimée lives in 'the concrete cell which she called her apartment'. When she and Dennis swear undying love at the Heart of Bruce, she asks, innocently, 'What is a "canty day," Dennis?' and he replies, 'Something like hogmanay. I expect [...] People being sick on the pavement in Glasgow.' The funerary profession's high style is entirely euphemistic. Dennis himself, in his down-market animal mortuary, is adept, offering the owner of a dead Sealyham 'interment or incineration'. 'Pardon me?' 'Buried or burned?' Whispering Glades offers a loftier range: 'Embalment of course, and after that incineration or not', followed, according to taste, by 'inhumement, entombment, inurnment, or immurement, but many people just lately prefer insarcophagusment'.

Whispering Glades is termed 'a restricted park', because 'the Waiting Ones [...] prefer to be with their own people'. The alternative complexions discreetly offered for the deceased are 'rural, athletic, and scholarly – that is to say red, brown or white'. Making arrangements for Sir Francis Hinsley, a 'strangulated Loved One' who 'passed over with his suspenders' (by hanging himself) is not insuperably tricky. Dennis reassures the Mortuary Hostess that Sir Francis fulfils the racial requirements, but the euphemism is, as often, robustly rebutted by reality:

'Let me assure you Sir Francis was quite white.'
As he said this there came into Dennis's mind that image which lurked there, seldom out of sight for long, the sack of body suspended and the face above it with eyes red and horribly starting from their sockets, the cheeks mottled in indigo like the marbled end-papers of a ledger and the tongue swollen and protruding like an end of black sausage. (LO 58)

Euphemism, like the capable hands of Mr Joyboy, can massage away any 'special little difficulties' of this kind. It is a national skill. The New World systematically eradicates the little difficulties that give life its sharpness – just as Kaiser's Stoneless Peaches lose all their savour along with the eliminated stone, leaving a ball of damp, sweet cotton wool. Dennis drifts into reverie beside the counterfeit signatures of Kaiser's wife and aunt in their final resting place on the replica Lake Island (sic) of Innisfree,[3] 'the poeticest place in the whole darn park', as its ferryman calls it. Not for these Loved Ones the corrupting flesh and writhing worms of European funerary monuments; even deciduous trees are banned from its whispering glades. And on the Lake Island there are ever-blooming bean rows but no bees, just a piped murmur in the bee-loud glade. 'No sore fannies and plenty of poetry', as the ferryman says. In Whispering Glades, death is robbed of its sting and the biblical exclamation, 'O Death, where is thy sting? O grave, thy victory?' acquires an absurd literalism.

Waugh had been shocked by California's cult of secular success. In Hollywood he was told that 'No film of ours is ever a failure. Some are greater successes than others' (EAR 326). At Whispering Glades in The Loved One, Death is 'the greatest success story of all time'. Displayed by the park's Golden Gates, Dr Kenworthy's vision upgrades St John's Revelation. 'And behold I saw a new Heaven and a new Earth,' becomes the exclusively profane 'Behold I dreamed a dream and I saw a New Earth sacred to Happiness'. There is no Heaven here.

In his essay examining Californian burial customs, Waugh quoted from the Art Guide of Forest Lawn with Interpretations:

> The cemeteries of the world cry out man's utter hopelessness in the face of death. Their symbols are pagan and pessimistic.... Here sorrow sees no ghastly monuments, but only life and hope. (EAR 332)

On behalf of the Christian visitor, Waugh drily responded that the recurrent feature of most graveyards is still the Cross – 'a symbol in which previous generations have found more Life and Hope than in the most elaborately watered evergreen shrub'. In Whispering Glades' flower-shop Dennis overhears a Mortuary Hostess informing a Waiting One that 'the Dreamer

135

does not approve of wreaths or crosses. We just arrange the flowers in their natural beauty'. An 'arrangement' is not 'natural'. It is a denatured paradox, like Kaiser's Stoneless Peaches or the planted forests and trimmed parklands of Forest Lawn Memorial Park; or the Slumber Room attendant spraying floral tributes with scent. Yet, even though wreaths and crosses are forbidden in Whispering Glades, the Dreamer decrees that Sir Francis may be commemorated by the Cricket Club's tribute of crossed bats and wickets. 'Dr Kenworthy had himself given judgment; the trophy was essentially a reminder of life, not of death; that was the crux'. Neither *crux* nor *cross* carries Christian connotations. The new religion is a celebration of life alone, the mortality of the flesh is denied, and its plaster god is a Dreamer giving judgement.

In the culture of this pagan land, the sacred is secularized, and sanctification is bestowed on the profane. At Whispering Glades, there is a minor 'cult' of Joyboy, the significantly named senior embalmer. Aimée thinks of Guru Brahmin as her 'spiritual director'. Well sprayed with 'Jungle Venom', her sexiest scent, she goes to meet Dennis as her 'manifest destiny'. Their oath of love at the Heart of Bruce, uttered in Burns's incomprehensible dialect, has 'all the sanctity of mumbo-jumbo' – but for her, it holds 'a sacred force'.

When Waugh identified his third idea to Cyril Connolly, that the Americans are 'all exiles, uprooted, transplanted, and doomed to sterility', he added that 'The ancestral gods they abjured will get them in the end. I tried to indicate this in Aimée's last hours.' Aimée, the moribund girl friend, will become a Loved One in both its senses, and is therefore *the* 'vestal virgin' of Whispering Glades, which she calls her 'true home'. At her tranquil suicide, she is given tragic status by her comparison to Iphigenia, Alcestis and Antigone. All three were sacrificial victims of classic legend, the prey of ruthless ancestral gods. Aimée acquires classic tragic status because she alone invested faith in the fake simulacra of her adoptive country. Her faith is shattered twice over when Joyboy and Dennis court her. In their different ways both use the language of death to pursue her – Joyboy by imposing smiles on the corpses sent down for her to paint, Dennis by plagiarizing the vows of dead poets. Twice betrayed, Aimée turns to her sham shaman, and the drunken Slump advises her to take a jump from a nice high window. Defending himself to a colleague, he demands impenitently, 'Well, for Christ's sake, with a name like that?' Aimée's surname is Thanatogenos. Thanatism is 'the belief that at death the human soul ceases to exist'.[4] Without a soul, man is no more than a beast. As Cassius laments in *Othello*, 'I have lost the immortal part of myself, and what remains is bestial'.[5] That is why Aimée ends up in an animal incinerator. In California's pagan death-cult there is nothing to distinguish man from beast. Consequently, Waugh sees to it that in the Happier Hunting Ground where Dennis Barlow works, animals are also given human rites, and the words of the Burial of the Dead are impiously emended. 'Dog that is born of bitch hath but a short time to live, and is full of misery. He cometh up and is cut down like a flower.' The Happier Hunting Ground is as sacrilegious as Whispering Glades. More importantly, its heresy prepares for the cold shock of the novel's last page. Dennis arranges for Joyboy to receive an annual card in memory of 'his little pet' – *Your little Aimée is wagging her tail in heaven tonight, thinking of you.* Aimée's cadaver is slid into the animal incinerator, and Dennis settles down 'to await his loved one's final combustion'.

Aimée's death signals a larger Anglo-American tragedy than Henry James ever contemplated. There will be no resurrection for Aimée after her final combustion. By eradicating the old customs of Death, the cults of Forest Lawn and Whispering Glades celebrate a lie, the incorruptibility of the flesh. For a Catholic like Waugh, they have forfeited the soul. That is his chilling message.

10

Helena
1950

Helena is a surprising anomaly in Waugh's *oeuvre* – a semi-fictional hagiography set in the third and fourth century AD. It is defiantly subtitled 'A Novel', and has only a notional affinity to his other devotional lives of *Campion, Jesuit and Martyr* (1935), and his contemporary, *Ronald Knox* (1959).

Though the third shortest of Waugh's fictions,[1] *Helena* had the longest gestation. He had already started work on it when *Brideshead* was published in late May 1945. On 1 May his diary notes: 'The end of war is hourly expected. Mussolini obscenely murdered, continual rumours that Hitler's mind has finally gone [...] I will now get to work on St Helena.' Five days later his next entry claims, rather prematurely, 'I have done enough reading to start tomorrow on *Helena* [...] I thank God to find myself still a writer and at work on something as "uncontemporary" as I am' (*D* 627). A lot more reading was done before he published *Helena* in 1950.

The chronology of Waugh's individual works was becoming increasingly tangled. *Helena* was interrupted by the failed negotiations for *Brideshead*'s film-rights (1947), the writing of *The Loved One* (1948), the rewriting of *Work Suspended* (1949), a novella, two short stories, and numerous trips abroad. Most tellingly, in September 1945 Waugh was sidetracked from *Helena* by an appalled rereading of his school diaries, which prompted the novel-fragment, *Charles Ryder's Schooldays*. Like *Helena*, this was an escape from the horrors of a dying war, which now included the bombing of Hiroshima and Nagasaki. 'News from the outside world becomes more horrible daily – chaos and tyranny and famine and sheer wickedness throughout two thirds of Europe and all Asia [...] I have begun a novel of school life in 1919 – as untopical a theme as might be found' (*D* 636). Both novels, the completed and the aborted, were designedly 'uncontemporary', 'untopical', but *Helena*, the survivor, darkly mirrored 'many incidents in recent history'[2] in its level account of the monomaniac leaders, obscene murders and mass military betrayals of fourth century Rome.

GIBBON'S GIBBERISH

Helena corroborates Waugh's priorities when her son, Constantine, voices his ambitions in a phrase taken directly from Gibbon's *Decline and Fall of the Roman Empire*:

> 'When the historians write of me they will say that if I wish to live, I must determine to rule.'
> 'Oh, *history* [...] Keep out of history, Constantine. Stay and see what I've done, the clearing and draining and planting. That is something better than history.' (*Helena* 111–2)

Helena is Waugh's modest riposte to what he privately called Gibbon's 'great work of slander'[3]. It makes no pretensions to accurate history. Waugh's Preface warns that he often prefers the picturesque to the plausible; where the sources are silent he invents freely; he employs 'certain wilful, obvious anachronisms [...] as a literary device' (ix–x). And yet history is of central importance to this work. St Helena's legendary discovery of the True Cross was revered as material evidence of Christ's death – the historical fact on which Christianity is based, and the certain foundation of Waugh's deliberately simple faith.

In *Helena*, Waugh's gripe against Gibbon, a lapsed Catholic convert, is voiced by the early Christian Lactantius, then the historically 'greatest living prose stylist', who praises the power of art in a prophetic speculation:

> 'Suppose that in years to come, when the Church's troubles seem to be over, there should come an apostate of my own trade, a false historian, with the mind of Cicero or Tacitus and the soul of an animal,' and he nodded towards the gibbon who fretted his golden chain and chattered for fruit. 'A man like that might make it his business to write down [i.e. denigrate] the martyrs and excuse the persecutors. He might be refuted again and again but what he wrote

would remain in people's minds when the refutations were quite forgotten. That is what style does – it has the Egyptian secret of the embalmers. It is not to be despised.' (*Helena* 122–3)

Waugh does not endorse Lactantius's position as wholeheartedly as most commentators suppose. Lactantius may foresee the survival of Gibbon's high-style scepticism as the triumph of art, but his conclusion is undermined by Waugh's irony. Coming fresh from *The Loved One*, Waugh knew what he thought of embalmers (and the souls of animals). Waugh earlier warned us that, 'with all his unrivalled powers of expression,' Lactantius was 'rather vague about what to express'. The shakiness of Lactantius's position is betrayed by his opening statement in praise of art: 'You see, it is equally possible to give the right form to the wrong thing and the wrong form to the right thing...' We are back in the moral chaos of *A Handful of Dust*. Unlike Lactantius, Waugh devoted his unrivalled powers to expressing exactly what he thought. Defying Gibbon, in *Helena* he wrote what he believed to be right, in the uniquely appropriate form of his own choosing.

Hence the blurb on *Helena*'s original dust-jacket betrays Waugh's hand in its final, paradoxical, oblique put-down of Gibbon's voluminous history.

> Mr. Evelyn Waugh has worked for several years on this novel based upon St Helena's life. It should not be dismissed as trivial merely on account of its brevity, for the author has long made compression and selection his particular study and he here distils what would have occupied three or four volumes of a less industrious writer.

ANCIENT AND MODERN

Helena's first, single-sentence paragraph sets the tone of this wide-ranging, succinct narrative:

COURT MEMOIR

> Once, very long ago, before ever the flowers were named which struggled and fluttered below the rain-swept walls, there sat at an upper window a princess and a slave reading a story which even then was old: or rather, to be entirely prosaic, on the wet afternoon

of the Nones of May in the year (as it was computed later) of Our Lord 273, in the city of Colchester, Helena, red-haired, youngest daughter of Coel, Paramount Chief of the Trinovantes, gazed into the rain while her tutor read the Iliad of Homer in a Latin paraphrase. (*Helena* 1)

There, above receding vistas of the past and vividly present weather, sit the princess and slave of fairy tale. The fabled court of old King Coel is pinned to a prosaically precise, invented Roman date. The layered *millefeuilles* of literature and language are compressed within the paragraph's relaxed passage from flowers as yet unnamed to Homer's *Iliad* in a Latin paraphrase. In a single sentence, Waugh displays the skills he later attributes to Lactantius, who delighted 'in the joinery and embellishment of his sentences, in the consciousness of high rare virtue when every word had been used in its purest and most precise sense, in the kitten games of syntax and rhetoric'. Even the title of this short chapter is a little pun.

Following one of many traditions, Waugh makes Helena the daughter of Old King Cole, whose nursery-rhyme pipe and bowl and fiddlers three allow him to describe the court entertainment of a Roman visitor, Constantius. As the bards sing the king's lengthy family history from its mythic beginnings, Helena – a keen horsewoman – is dreamily absorbed in a private fantasy. She is playing horses, a childhood game that has recently acquired extra, sexual piquancy.

Two played it now. There was the will of the rider, that spoke down the length of the rein, from the gloved hand to the warm and tender tongue under the bit [...] And there was the will of the animal to shrink and start, to toss aside the restraint of bridle and saddle and the firm legs across her, to shake the confident equipoise,[4] awake him to the intense life and the will to combat under him. (*Helena* 22–3)

Constantius, lolling on the couches opposite her, is also daydreaming, riding victorious at the head of his troops. 'At the entry into possession' their eyes meet.

They gazed at one another, unknowing, separate, then running together like drops of condensed steam on the ewer, pausing, *bulging* against one another, until, suddenly, they were one and ran down in a single minute cascade. (*Helena* 25, my italics)

Waugh wrote to John Betjeman, seeking his wife's advice: 'I am

writing [Penelope's] life under the disguise of St Helena's [...]
She is 16, sexy, full of horse fantasies. I want to get this right
[...] I have no experience of such things, nor has Laura. I make
her always the horse & the consummation when the rider
subdues her. Is this correct? Please make her explain. And is
riding enough or must she be driven? Are spurs important or
only leather work' (L 207). Betjeman never passed on the
queries. Later, Waugh wrote directly to Penelope for corrections
of the published 'hipporastic passages [...] the fruit of my
unaided invention'. She had none.

Like Waugh, Helena wants to get her fantasies right. The next
morning she encounters Constantius in the stables just as she's
trying out the feel of a bit in her own mouth. Her undeniable
sexuality is strikingly modern. Helena associates herself with
white-armed Helen, fair among women of Homeric legend, but
Waugh has plucked her straight out of Betjeman's contemporary pantheon – 'the golden hiking girl / With wind about her
hair, / The tennis-playing, biking girl, / The wholly-to-my-liking
girl' with a hearty appetite and a mind of her own, expressed in
resonantly contemporary schoolgirl slang.[5]

'IT'S ALL BOSH, ISN'T IT?'

Waugh sets Helena up as the voice of scepticism and the
reader's unambiguous touchstone. We first hear her arguing
with Marcias, her tutor-slave, about Homer's Troy. Why does
nothing survive of it now, except poetry? There is a tourist town,
Marcias concedes, where guides can show you anything you
want – Achilles' tomb, Paris' bed, one leg of the great wooden
horse...But why didn't people dig, Helena demands. Some of
Troy's bound to be down there still. 'When I am educated, I shall
go and find the real Troy.' A pointedly prophetic exchange.[6] But
first she must complete her education.

Helena's disappointing marriage to chilly, ambitious Constantius carries her across the Channel to the over-extended
Roman Empire and an education in false religions. At home she
had been brought up in undiscriminating devotion to Druid
fertility rites and Roman deities. In Ratisbon she's left as an
army wife and hears gossip of all-male initiation rituals, secret

meetings, Asiatic trances, lustrations in warm bull's blood, the cult of Mithras. 'It's all bosh, isn't it?' she asks of the Governor's wife. 'It's disgusting.' 'Yes, but it's bosh, too, isn't it?' Later, Constantius becomes Governor of Dalmatia, returns to these rituals, and initiates their son Constantine. Women are debarred. When Helena is told the myth of Mithras, her questions are inconveniently basic:

> 'Where?'
> 'Where?'
> 'Yes, *where* did it happen? You say the bull hid in a cave and then the world was created out of his blood. Well, where was the cave when there was no earth?'
> 'That's a very childish question.'
> 'Is it? And *when* did this happen? How do you know, if no-one was there?' (*Helena* 97)

It's the same when she encounters Gnosticism in the highbrow circles of Trèves. Here Helena's tutor-slave Marcias resurfaces as a bearded mystagogue, whose impenetrable discourse of Aeons, Demiurges, and the mensual thirty-nine gives Helena the giggles. At question-time, in her 'clear, schoolroom tone', she demands again, 'When and where did all this happen? And how do you know?' Nor is she browbeaten by his lofty, tautologous snub: 'These things are beyond time and space. Their truth is integral to their proposition and by nature transcends material proof.' Later she turns to the Christian Lactantius:

> 'I couldn't understand a word he said. It's all bosh, isn't it?'
> 'All complete bosh, your Majesty.'
> 'So I supposed. Just wanted to make sure. Tell me, Lactantius, this god of yours. If I asked you when and where he could be seen, what would you say?'
> 'I should say that as a man he died two hundred and seventy-eight years ago in the town now called Aelia Capitolina in Palestine.'
> 'Well, that's a straight answer anyway. How do you know?'
> 'We have the accounts written by witnesses.' (*Helena* 130–1)

Satisfied at last, at some unknown date Helena is baptized. But her awkward questions persist. When she finally reaches Rome, her son Constantine proudly shows her the standard under which he fought the Battle of the Milvian Bridge.

143

Tradition has it that the cross appeared to him as a celestial sign on the eve of battle. Constantine had his soldiers change the markings on their shields, and under an improvised standard in the shape of a cross he conquered his co-Emperor Maxentius and won the Empire to Christianity. Constantine's historic Labarum is described in dispassionate detail. It is an elaborate gold-plated cross surmounted by a jewelled wreath enclosing the holy monogram XP. Medallion portraits are embroidered on its satin banner. Helena observes it with growing bewilderment, and objects: how could it have been knocked up overnight by the camp carpenters? It must have taken months.

> 'Two or three hours, I assure you. The jewellers were inspired. Everything was miraculous that day.'
> 'And whose are the portraits?'
> 'My own and my children's.'
> 'But my dear boy, they weren't all born then.'
> 'I tell you it was a miracle,' said Constantine huffily. (*Helena* 202–3)

Slowly, it becomes apparent that Helena's questions, and her commonsensical responses, are Waugh's as he picks his way through suspect myth and miracle to create a credible legend. He's still at it as Helena makes her way to Jerusalem in search of the Cross on which Christ died. What wood would it have been made of? A Coptic elder proposes a universal composite allowing the entire vegetable world to participate in the Redemption. *'Oh, nonsense,' said Helena*. A young clergyman objects that the vegetable world was neither redeemed nor capable of redemption. The Copt offers an alternative theory of four timbers indigenous to Palestine, each symbolizing... *'Rot,' said Helena*. Another launches into a long narrative involving three seeds planted in dying Adam's mouth, Moses, and the Archangel Gabriel. *'Bosh,' said Helena [...] 'It's just this kind of story that I've come to disprove.'*

As Waugh explained, in a talk preceding the BBC's dramatization of *Helena*, 'Everything about the new religion was capable of interpretation, could be refined and diminished; everything except the unreasonable assertion that God became man and died on the Cross [...] at a particular moment in time, at a particular geographical place, as a matter of plain historical fact.' Helena's timely discovery of the True Cross confronted the supersubtle speculations dividing the early church, and turned believers 'back to the planks of wood on which their salvation hung'.[7] This fundamental fact was her unique gift to Christianity.

POWER WITHOUT GRACE

Helena's life was bare of event until her discovery of the Cross in old age. She tagged about Europe with her husband Constantius, who, for all his aspirations, remained on the threshold of power. On Waugh's broad historical canvas the interminable sequence of Caesars jockeying for supremacy is seen through the unimpressed eyes of a contemporary – a note Waugh establishes with Divine Valerian, the first Emperor to be mentioned. 'A great joke' in Old King Coel's court, Immortal Valerian's historic fate is a 'shocking business' to the Romans: 'First a mounting-block, then a footstool, now a dummy, skinned, tanned, stuffed full of straw, swinging from the rafters for the Persians to poke fun at.' Divine Valerian, immortally stuffed; then barely Divine Claudius, less rackety Divine Quintilius – neither of Constantius' boasted ancestors impress bluff King Coel. He's just another 'relation of the Divine What-d'you-call-him – awful fellow who was Emperor not long ago' (*Helena* 30–2). In due course the latest Immortal, divine Aurelian, is murdered, and succeeded by a faster flow of Caesars – nonentity Probus, with Carus, Diocletian, Maximian, and Galerius jostling him 'in the inmost cell of the foetid termitary of power', the heart of a dying Empire.

> The oblivious Caesars fought on. They marched across frontiers, made treaties and broke them, decreed marriages and divorces and legitimizations, murdered their prisoners, betrayed their allies, deserted their dead and dying armies [...] All the tiny mechanism of Power regularly revolved, like a watch still ticking on the wrist of a dead man. (*Helena* 139)

And Waugh's focus tightens on Constantine, his court, and his wife Fausta.

Waugh's blurb drew attention to his art of compression and selection. Fausta is its best example. In Fausta Helena recognizes not the woman of dubious morality she certainly was, but 'something even more unlovely: an epitome of the high politics of the age'. Fausta is an avid follower of fashion; her silliness is the pretentious opposite of Helena's bluntness. The Christian Church, Fausta says, must keep up with sophisticated times: 'It's no use trying to puncture the horologium.'[8] The martyrs' simple faith is *passé*. 'Of course everyone admires them tremendously. It's wonderful what they went through. But, I mean, just having one eye out and a foot off doesn't qualify one in theology.' Her fatuous babble parodies the inspissated controversy over the nature of Christ preoccupying the first Council of Nicaea in 325 AD.

> 'I mean, we must have Progress. Homoiousion is definitely dated. *Everyone* who really counts is for Homoousion – or is it the other way round? If Eusebius were here he'd tell us. He always makes everything so clear. Theology's terribly exciting but a little muddling. Sometimes I almost feel nostalgic for the old taurobolium, don't you?' (*Helena* 152)

Fausta has indeed got it all the wrong way round. In the Nicaean debate Homoiousion was the latest thing, and the side that lost; Homoousion was definitely dated, and won.[9] Waugh deliberately makes neither side clear, because this was a dispute over the unknowable, *things beyond time and space, whose truth is integral to their proposition and by nature transcends material proof* – like the Gnostics' guff. Fausta would have done better to stick with the *démodé* brutalities of Mithraic initiation rites and the taurobolium.[10]

Yet vicious Fausta's ruthless ambition is absolutely of her time. Waugh creates a chilling image of Constantine's inbred court, loveless and faithless through multiple marriages, and divorces, of convenience; riddled with spying; rotten with denunciations, liquidations, and endemic dread. At its heart is Fausta, sexy, sleek, pouting and lethal. 'Like a great goldfish', Helena thinks, but when Constantia, Constantine's half-sister, visits with her son Licinianus, heir of the conquered and killed co-Emperor Licinius, the child's fear of Aunt Fausta loosens his bowels and makes him wet the floor. In due time he too is eliminated, like so many others, a terrified twelve-year-old sent into exile for treachery along with Constantine's favourite son Crispus, his obvious heir and most brilliant general. Before Constantine can recall them, both are murdered on the evidence of a witch's ambiguous denunciation, opportunely glossed by Fausta.

In the grim *tour de force* ending this chapter, Constantine takes his revenge. The historical sources only say Fausta was stifled in her bath. Waugh brings that flat fact to life with characteristic precision. He is adept at imagining luxury, and hated central heating. In the hot dry room of Fausta's suite of baths – tepidarium, sudatorium, laconicum – there's only a cloudless mirror, and a couch with cushions of silky goatskin, impermeably perfumed with sandalwood oil. Even the door is just a polished cedar slab. (The original ivory and tortoiseshell inlay fell to pieces; bronze grew too hot.) Here Fausta lies back, sweat moist between her breasts, meditating on her singular blessedness. 'Why was she, alone among women, so uniquely privileged? [...] Unworthily, perhaps, but most conveniently, she was the elect of God; His own especial favourite and consort.'[11] Her enemies are scattered. 'Heaven had spoken to her as it spoke to Constantine at the Milvian Bridge.' The room grows hotter; no servant answers her bell. The floor blisters her feet; on stepping-stones of cushions she struggles to the door – and finds it locked.

> No use now to push or ring or knock. The good hour was over. She slid and floundered and presently lay still, like a fish on a slab. (*Helena* 193)

The end of a very low form of life indeed.

Fausta's hubris and infernally overheated death prefigure her damnation. Yet Constantine is little better. After the publication of *Helena*, Waugh turned down a commission to write a life of Constantine, saying he didn't like him much. In his introductory talk for *Helena*'s radio dramatization, he is frankly critical of the first Roman Emperor to become a Christian:

> Power was shifting. In the academies of the Eastern and South-Eastern Mediterranean sharp, sly minds were everywhere looking for phrases and analogies to reconcile the new, blunt creed [...] with the ancient speculations that had beguiled their minds, and with the occult rites which had for generations spiced their logic. [...] Constantine was no match for them. Schooled on battlefields and in diplomatic conferences where truth was a compromise; [...] busy with the affairs of state; unused to the technical terms of philosophy; Constantine, not yet baptised, [...] not quite sure that he was not himself divine, not himself the incarnation of the Supreme Being, [...] was quite out of his depth. (*Holy Places* 11–12)

In *Helena*, Fausta's catty gossip encapsulates Waugh's criticism and establishes Constantine's position in the verdict of history. He just wasn't up to it. 'He can get on all right giving orders and all that [...] – garrison Greek they call it – but when the professional rhetoricians get going, the poor boy is quite lost. He hadn't the least idea what was going on at Nicaea. All he wanted was a unanimous vote...' Moreover, Waugh's Constantine is just as vicious and hubristic as Fausta. He is complicit in her murders and on his orders Fausta fries. Stung by popular rhymes calling him a second Nero, he complains, naively: 'Nero thought he was a God. A most blasphemous and improper idea. I know I am human. In fact I often feel I am the only real human being in the whole of creation.' 'When I die... if I do die,' he suspects God will have an ascension like Elijah's in store for him. When Helena warns him that he's suffering from 'Power without Grace', he assumes she only means he should get baptized at once. He has a better idea – to postpone baptism till the last moment, and make sure of Heaven. 'That's strategy, you see [...] That's tactics.' His Christianity is solely pragmatic.

Furthermore, he embodies both Power without Grace, and Power without Taste. In the novel's funniest scene Constantine, in a green wig, grotesquely overdressed, grumpily reviews the drawings for his Triumphal Arch. All Waugh's venom against fashionable modern art fuels the architects' lofty defence of their 'broad mass broken by apertures' with 'certain decorative applications' – viz, a rudimentary frieze of identical dwarves in which diminutive Constantine is unrecognizable. 'I was not aiming at direct portraiture, sir' – 'And why not, pray?' – 'It was not the function of the feature.' If the best sculptor in Rome can do no better than that, Constantine retorts, let them pull off the bas-reliefs from Trajan's arch, a far finer monument from two centuries back, and stick them on *his* Arch.

Today's reader may well assume that this is a flight of Waugh's fancy. It is not.

THE INVENTION OF THE TRUE CROSS

Waugh's style changes when Helena reaches Jerusalem in search of the Cross. It is perceptibly quieter, more prosaically factual. His dramatized summary of the conflicting opinions of Christian, Roman and Hebrew historians, Talmudic scholars and archaeologists has the suspense and satisfaction of a very rational detective story (a genre Waugh always enjoyed). Helena's questions tease out the probabilities of what the Cross might have been made of, how constructed, how and why disposed of, by whom and where... till she can go no further. There is no indication where, in the vast building site that once was Golgotha, she should look. An abandoned cistern, a well, the cellar of a house ruined three hundred years ago? Only prayer remains. Here, as once before in this novel, Waugh steps off the time-line.

Earlier, Waugh used that image when Fausta's witch, a seasoned young charlatan, falls into a genuine trance. 'She had stepped off the causeway of time and place into a trackless swamp.' She is possessed by music that compresses past and present, 'drumming from beyond the pyramids, wailing from the *bistro* where the jazz disk spun'. Her prophetic chant unites despots from Tito, Mussolini, the Mexican General Cárdenas and Hitler, to Constantine and Napoleon:[12]

> Zivio! Viva! Arriba! Heil!
> Plenty big chief from the Rhine to the Nile.
> He got two gods and he got two wives [...]
> The world was his baby but baby got sore.
> So he lost the world and plenty lives more [...]
> Lost to the world on Helena's isle [...]
> Nothing but ocean for mile upon mile.
> Played for a sucker by British guile,
> Tied up tight in durance vile
> And left there to rot on Helena's isle.
> Ave atque vale! Heil!

> (*Helena* 187–8)

Helena's moment out of time is the opposite of this seedy warning. In a dream that she knows is of God, she finds herself alone on a 'timeless morning [...] empty and silent and brilliant as a mountain peak'. She meets a 'businessman', an ageless travelling salesman in incense, who remembers the day Christ was crucified, his own indifference as Christ stumbled under the cross he bore, and Christ's rebuke: 'Tarry till I come.'[13] He shows Helena where the Cross was hidden – for free. The next

149

morning she finds the spot, marked by what looks like a (cloven) hoof print. She replaces it with a cross of pebbles. And commands the workmen to dig there. The Invention of the True Cross is a mixed blessing. She foresees the tide of tat relics it will bring to the world.

Helena's discovery of three crosses follows tradition, but is delivered as something entirely downbeat and ordinary. 'Now that her quest was at last accomplished [...] she was as practical about arrangements as though some new furniture had been delivered at her house.' The miraculous becomes prosaic. The novel's closing image returns to Helena, the keen young horsewoman of Coel's court, in a last, typically oblique metaphor once again asserting that her discovery called believers away from controversy, back to the blunt facts of Christ's life:

> Hounds are checked, hunting wild. A horn calls clear through the covert. Helena casts them back on the scent. (*Helena* 265)

The Catholic festival, The Invention of the True Cross[14] derives its name precisely and correctly from the Latin *invenire*, meaning to find. It is a small instance of the virtue Lactantius admired, using a word in its first and purest sense. With equal precision, however, Waugh calls on the later, semantically degraded connotations of *invention* with *lies* and *fiction*. This pun marks the paradox at the heart of his enterprise. 'Ellen's Invention', the ironic title of his final chapter, celebrates a chronicled event that was a miracle, uniting what he called 'the opposed faces of history and myth'. With classic, etymological precision the modest final sentence of his Preface had already warned the reader of the paradoxes to come.

> The story is just something to be read; in *fact* a *legend*. (*Helena* xiii, my italics)[15]

*

Conventional historical novels tend to concretize fiction with well-researched period detail. They risk being waxworks in fancy dress, a cliché in a toga, like Fausta's leaking *horologium*. Waugh chooses not to clutter the past with the past, but make it present. *He* didn't specify the tepidarium, sudatorium, and laconicum in Fausta's Roman baths. He simply described her 'hot, dry room', and we recognize a sauna. Bored in

Constantine's provincial home town, Helena borrows 'the few rolls of poetry in the bank-manager's library'. Exiled in Dalmatia, she visits the building site of Diocletian's latest palace on the Adriatic shoreline. 'They were shown the cranes, the concrete mixers, the system of central heating, all of the latest pattern.' Waugh introduced his wilful, obvious anachronisms not as a mere decorative rhetorical device. Reality is itself anachronistic. Human nature doesn't change much and neither do building sites or the Dalmatian coast where Helena was exiled and Waugh served in 1944–5.[16] The Romans had (wooden) cranes and under-floor heating and wigs and libraries too. In 1945, with Mussolini – self-styled Duce of a new Imperium – obscenely hung by the heels beside his murdered mistress, the shadow of decadent Rome fell sharply across conquered Italy. Auden's poem, 'The Fall of Rome', is contemporary with Waugh's *Helena*, and also exploits the double exposure of past on present:

> Fantastic grow the evening gowns;
> Agents of the Fisc pursue
> Absconding tax-defaulters through
> The sewers of provincial towns.
> [...]
> Caesar's double-bed is warm
> As an unimportant clerk
> Writes I DO NOT LIKE MY WORK
> On a pink official form.

Helena, however, is laced with not one but two unexpected kinds of reversal. Certainly Waugh's anachronistic realism transcends time. He is also surreptitiously accurate when he seems most fantastic. His past is present and his fictions are true. The stuffing of Divine Valerian is documented fact. The description of Constantine's improbably ornate Labarum, with its portraits of children as yet unborn, comes directly from Constantine's contemporary court historian, Eusebius of Caesarea, a hypocritical Arian toady whom Fausta dotes on and Helena dismisses as 'creepy-crawly'. As he really was.[17] Helena prefers Sylvester, the quiet Pope of the time, who marvels, 'People believe [nonsense] here and now while the Emperor and I are alive and going about in front of their faces. What will they believe in a thousand years time?' Waugh surprises our latter-day credulity by palpable fictions that turn out to be true. Constantine's triumphal arch celebrating the victory of the Milvian Bridge is still standing. It really is a fatuous hotchpotch with friezes of primitive miniature manikins like a playschool paper chain, disproportionately flanked by beautiful big bas reliefs snitched from Trajan's nobler arch. Constantine really did postpone baptism till the last moment, in the hope of slipping into heaven on the sly. He did have one of the nails from the True Cross turned into a snaffle for his horse. On one of his massive statues another of the nails was indeed 'set as a ray shining from the imperial cranium'.

Waugh was clear about the difficulties of his 'unhistorical life of St Helena'. 'It will be interesting only to the very few people who know exactly as much history as I do. The millions who know more will be disgusted; the few who know less, puzzled' (*L* 206, 310). He knew perfectly well that the *millions* and the *few* should be interchanged. Now, however, he is trapped in his own irony. Millions really can find all they want on the internet. Check out the photos of Constantine's arch, and laugh. Wikipedia's reader-friendly scholarship reconciles Waugh's knowledge to our ignorance, illuminates his ironies, and can explain at least some of the many 'hints and allusions and little jokes tucked away' in his mischievous hybrid[18] – if we realize that they are waiting to be found. Waugh's daughter Harriet said it was the only book of his own that her father read to his children. 'Nobody appreciated it so he decided that [we] should read it at the highest possible level [...] He read it to us and explained all the different layers as he went along.' Lucky things.

Helena was badly reviewed. It was too unlike everything Waugh's readers had come to expect of him. They had just rediscovered the familiar, wickedly satirical Waugh in *The Loved One*. With some irony, Waugh wrote to Nancy Mitford, '*Loved One* is being well-received in intellectual circles. They think my heart is in the right place after all. I'll show them' (*L* 273). *Helena*, for all its boasted tricksiness, does have its heart in what most people could comfortably call the right place. Initially at least, it can and should be read quite simply and directly, without false expectations.

11

Men at Arms
1952

In 1946, at the advanced age of forty-three, Waugh pessimistically reckoned: 'I have two shots in my locker left. My war novel and my autobiography. I suppose they will see me out.' (*L* 238) Then *Helena* intervened, and unexpectedly took four more years to complete.

At long last, in June 1951, Waugh wrote to Laura, 'Yesterday I spent reading all my war diaries & recapturing the atmosphere of those days. Today I began writing & it came easy.' (*L* 351) Not so easy, though. Within days he discovered that his new method of uninterrupted composition didn't suit him – 'I hate leaving a trail of unfinished shabby work behind me' – and reverted to his old practice, perfecting each page before moving on. Even then, his letters show growing discontent. The novel in progress is 'unreadable & endless. Nothing but tippling in officers' messes and drilling on barrack squares. No demon sex. No blood or thunder.' 'A great bore.' 'A book in poor taste, mostly about wcs and very very dull.' It is 'slogging, inelegant, the first volume of four or five, which won't show any shape until the end.' When the proofs finally arrived in May 1952 he dismissed it simply as 'my fiasco'.[1]

There were obvious difficulties. In *Put Out More Flags* Waugh had already given a brilliant, panoptic image of England during the Phoney War. The fact that many of its highly individualized characters were drawn from his earlier novels innocently appeared to confirm their reality. They had pasts of their own. The novel further benefited from Waugh's military training – both as a soldier who lived at close quarters with men of all ranks, and as an Intelligence Officer who, like Guy in *Men at*

Arms, 'read his map easily and had a good eye for country'. *POMF*'s social range was thus unusually wide for Waugh, while the rural terrains surveyed by the marauding Basil were evoked with a military tactician's precision. Moreover, for its immediate contemporaries the novel recognizably recreated familiar recent realities – the social upheavals just brought by slum evacuees like the Connolly children and wartime profiteers like Basil; the fatuities of the Ministry of Information; the spy-panic that drove Ambrose to Ireland. At the same time Waugh's humdrum experiences in early training were accurately transferred to Alastair Digby-Vane-Trumpington, and the dispiriting shambles of one particular embarkation attributed to Cedric Lyne. However, past successes like these now created problems, as the new novel was forced to retrace old ground.

POMF had reverted to the succinct, impersonal style of Waugh's early work. The authorial voice was satirically detached. Only rare moments of interiority were allowed to his three *alter egos*, Alastair, Cedric, and Ambrose. In *Men at Arms* he returned to the neo-Victorian mode he had begun to explore in *Work Suspended,* and over-indulged in *Brideshead Revisited.* Guy Crouchback's story is given a meditative, third-person interiority closer to John Plant's candid first-person narrative in *Suspenders* than Ryder's self-deceiving account in *Brideshead.* This ruminative interiority establishes a significant difference from *POMF.*

However, there is little impetus to the external facts of Guy's early training. Consequently he is deliberately subordinated to Apthorpe, proud possessor of the porpoise boots and brass-bound field latrine. As in Shakespeare's second Henriad, Guy's moral development, like Hal's, is subordinated to the Falstaffian Apthorpe who provides the novel's ostensible main narrative. Guy's persistent disappointments and dim achievements are intermittently reflected in reverse in the novel's single, structurally dominant arc of Apthorpe's rise and fall. Thus Waugh effectively decoys the reader's attention away from the experiences already captured in *POMF,* towards Apthorpe's broad comedy.

Waugh also distances *Men at Arms* from *POMF* by enlarging its scope a few months beyond the period of the Phoney War, to climax in his first offensive action, the planned atttack on Dakar in September 1940. This aborted exercise is conflated with

Waugh's second offensive action, the commando raid on Bardia (which actually took place in April 1941, beyond the novel's ostensible time-frame). Waugh also appears to draw on later commando training (not his own) in Scotland for the period spent under canvas at Penkirk in *Men at Arms*.[2] Both transpositions provide refreshing new material for the author.

So Waugh remedied his perceived omissions. In Dakar Brigadier Ritchie-Hook's booty of a decapitated Negro's head provides comic-grotesque blood and thunder. Demon sex sidles in with Guy's attempted seduction of his ex-wife Virginia. Virginia is joined by other, ostensibly insignificant characters who will emerge as dominant figures in the trilogy's subsequent volumes, finally gathering this comic fiasco into a shape Waugh completed – with difficulty.

APTHORPE GLORIOSUS, FURIBUNDUS, IMMOLATUS

The Latinate titles of the novel's three books simultaneously suggest Apthorpe's status as the novel's hero, and undercut it by signalling his mock-heroic literary forbears. He is first introduced as a *Miles Gloriosus*, the boastful buffoon of Plautus' comedy.[3] In the Campaign of Connelly's Chemical Closet he is elevated into an epic hero like Ariosto's Orlando Furioso, fiercely engaged in fantastical warfare – defending his field latrine.[4] Detonated by Brigadier Ritchie-Hook while seated on his loo, he is finally carried off by Guy's inadvertent *coup de grâce* – a whisky bottle smuggled into his hospital bed. Thus the little sweep of his story passes from modest comedy to high farce to tragic bathos. It is plaited with two other strands: Guy's parallel course as a trainee officer with the invented Halberdiers (the largely accurate equivalent of Waugh's training as a Marine), and the domineering role played by their Brigadier, the one-eyed Ritchie-Hook. All fade out together as the novel ends, though Guy and the Brigadier, the two men who immolated Apthorpe, will live to fight again.

In the novel's first book Apthorpe's comedy is muted. He is showily fluent in technical acronyms, an ostentatious know-all of army training manuals; he's given an obsession about boots; he gets drunk often and absurdly. At the Halberdier Barracks, the equivalent of Waugh's first three months training at

Chatham, Apthorpe and Guy, both 'Uncles' as the oldest of the new recruits, benefit from the respect due to age, which is the only distinction of rank in this happy, old-fashioned company. But when they move into Kut-al-Imara House, a requisitioned minor public school, in the new year of 1940, both return from leave crippled by coincidental knee injuries and the pair become a laughing stock. A contrapuntal pattern is set up between them, where one rises as the other falls. Guy fails dismally at shooting practice while Apthorpe sails through. Earlier, conversely, in a typical episode of mistaken identity, Ritchie-Hook confuses Guy with Apthorpe, approving of him as the tough chap with African experience (a boast of Apthorpe's), while Guy's history as a softie who spent years in Italy is transferred to Apthorpe. Then Ritchie-Hook discovers Apthorpe's chemical closet and starts his campaign of harassment.

When Waugh arrived at Kingsdown, the original of Kut-al-Imara, in January 1940, his letters and diary dispiritedly described their barren new quarters as 'a hideous, derelict Victorian villa without carpets, curtains, or furniture, one bath, one wc without a seat and another without a plug'. Or, more hyperbolically: 'one bath for sixty men, one washbasin, the WCs all frozen up and those inside the house without seats' (L 134, D 461). Lavatories mattered to Waugh. The one he installed at Piers Court was a magnificent Victorian throne with upholstered leopard-skin armrests.[5] No wonder he made Apthorpe lug his brass-bound mahogany portaloo about Kut-al-Imara's grounds from shrubbery to potting shed to find private easement, with the one-eyed Brigadier in hot pursuit.

Guy, like Waugh, is enchanted by this fantastical campaign. He speaks for them both when interrogating Apthorpe, who has just escaped injury from a falling flowerpot by wearing his helmet while at stool. 'Apthorpe, do you always wear your tinhat on the thunder-box?' he demands. 'You don't start out wearing it? [...] And when do you put it on, before or after lowering the costume? I must know.' Why is Waugh a consummate artist? Because, like Guy, he *must know*. And good taste be damned.

When Waugh first encountered his own brigadier, Ritchie-Hook's original, he told Laura that 'Our brigadier St Clair Morford looks like something escaped from Sing-Sing & talks

like a schoolboy in the lower-fourth' – repeating himself in the
Diaries with the happy addition – 'teeth like a stoat, ears like a
faun, eyes alight like a child playing pirates. "We then have to
biff them, gentlemen."' (*L* 134, *D* 461).[6] The motif of schoolboy
war games instead of real warfare, already set up in *POMF*, is
central to *Men at Arms*, and parallels between the two are
constantly foregrounded. Training takes place in a requisitioned
school; the trainees are 'day-boys' or 'boarders', depending on
whether they stay in camp or abscond to married quarters in
lodgings. Ritchie-Hook's campaign against Apthorpe is an
exercise in biffing founded on the practical jokes common in
St Clair-Morford's married life.[7] 'For this remarkable warrior the
image of war was not hunting or shooting; it was the wet sponge
on the door, the hedgehog in the bed; or rather, he saw war
itself as a prodigious booby-trap.'

So Waugh diversifies the dead period from January 1940 to
the fall of Finland at the end of March, by focusing instead on
the tiny personal combat which 'was being played against the
background of the Brigadier's training methods [...] and itself
formed their culminating illustration'. In Ritchie-Hook's lec-
tures, Waugh drily observes, 'it appeared' that booby-traps were
vital to the defence of the Western Front. As Ritchie-Hook
expounds trip-wires, detonators, anti-personnel mines – and an
explosive goat he himself loosed behind enemy lines – his
campaign against the unfortunate Apthorpe follows the same
tactics of homicidal surprise, culminating finally in Apthorpe's
near escape, blown up as he sits down on his aptly-named
thunder-box.

This homely campaign is the novel's funniest sequence.
When the brigade forms at Penkirk, in Scotland, for final
training under canvas, Waugh fills dead time by inventing less
funny twists to Guy and Apthorpe's contrapuntal relationship.
Apthorpe's boots fetish is taken for another tired turn about the
block. Ditto his Boot-like weakness for heavy baggage. In the
ascendant in their shared tent, Apthorpe lies at his ease on a
high collapsible bed, surrounded by portable camp furniture,
while Guy freezes on the ground with a rolled up blanket for a
pillow. Shamelessly finessing chronology, Waugh links April
Fool's Day with the elevation of both Apthorpe to Headquarter
Company Commander *and* Churchill to the Premiership.[8] While

Guy lags behind, an insignificant platoon commander, Apthorpe becomes insufferable, ostentatiously celebrating his promotion before it is official, lording it over Guy, evicting him from their shared quarters. Impervious to absurdity, he demands smart salutation from all supposed inferiors, and is ragged by the men's refusal, or – in Guy's case – blatantly mocking compliance in 'one of those pathetic spasms of fourth-form fun that came easily in military life'.

Apthorpe's fictional value wanes as France falls. He's left inland and off-stage when Guy's men go to coastal defence. He plays no visible part in the expedition against Dakar. When Guy is left to dispose of the Brigadier's gruesome trophy, a Negro head, in another spasm of fourth-form fun he thinks – 'Apthorpe's cabin? No' – and deposits it in Ritchie-Hook's in-tray instead. The rejection is symptomatic of Apthorpe's dwindling role. He belongs to the world of theoretic training manuals and unportable kit, not real action. After Dakar the brigade encamps in Freetown, but Apthorpe disappears on leave up-country. Rumours of his sickness precede his re-appearance, borne on a sling between native bearers as in 'a Victorian woodcut from a book of exploration'. Dying in hospital, 'doing nothing, staring at the sunblind with his hands empty on the counterpane', he is reminiscent of Falstaff in his last moments. His death is full of comic pathos. The impeccable regimental pomp of his funeral is an absurd, elegiac farewell to the out-dated world of military valour where he would have liked to belong.[9]

TRUSLOVE, DAKAR, AND THE RAID ON BARDIA

Waugh's schoolboy theme comes to a climax with the Dakar expedition. When Brigadier Ritchie-Hook welcomed his newly-formed company at Penkirk with the thrilling words, 'Gentlemen, tomorrow you meet the men you will lead in battle', Guy recognized 'the old, potent spell, big magic' that 'set swinging all the chimes of his boyhood's reading':

'...I've chosen your squadron for the task, Truslove.' 'Thank you, sir. What are our chances of getting through?' 'It can be done, Truslove, or I shouldn't be sending you. If anyone can do it, you can. And I can tell you

this, my boy, I'd give all my seniority and all these bits of ribbon on my chest to be with you [. . .]'
The words came back to him from a summer Sunday evening at his preparatory school. (MA 208)

In *Men at Arms* Waugh gives Dakar the Truslove treatment. But let's begin with the facts.

At the end of August 1940, after the fall of France and the English flight from Dunkirk, Waugh's brigade finally went into action, sailing in a large Anglo/Free French convoy from the Orkneys to Freetown on the west coast of Africa. Their mission was to install De Gaulle and his forces in Dakar, which was in the hands of the Vichy government. However, the town was antagonistic, and better defended than they expected. Faulty intelligence, poor communications and persistent mist held them at bay for two days. On 25 September they withdrew. In Waugh's *Diaries* this episode is first ironically termed 'the battle of Dakar' and ends as 'the Dakar fiasco' (*D* 481–2). It marked a decisive point in his disillusion with the Marines.

'Bloodshed,' he wrote to Laura, 'has been avoided at the cost of honour.' And, with considerable honesty, he confessed that 'during the time when we expected to be sent into an operation which could only be disastrous, I realised how much you have changed me because I could no longer look at death with indifference. I wanted to live and was pleased when we ran away.' In retrospect, it is clear that in the letter preceding this one he was tactfully giving her instructions to cover his potential death, or capture. Disappointed of honourable action, he set the tone for the rest of his war: 'I know that one goes into war for reasons of honour & soon finds oneself called on to do very dishonourable things. I do not like the R[oyal] M[arine] Brigade's part in this war and I do not like the war, but I want to be back in Europe fighting Germans' (*L* 141). He had already begun negotiations to transfer to the Commandos, and successfully renewed them on his return. Meanwhile, on the slow troopship home, he added:

> I do wish sometimes I could meet an adult. They are all little boys. Some of them naughty little boys like the Brigadier, most of them delicious & just what I want Bron [his son] to be at the age of ten, but not one of them a mature man. (*L* 142)

159

A decade later, recognizing the need for blood and thunder to bring his novel to a close, Waugh extended the Dakar non-event by a simplified reminiscence of his next offensive action, in April 1941. The Commando raid on Bardia, a small town on the Libyan coast, is dryly summarized in one paragraph of Waugh's unofficial *Memorandum on LAYFORCE: July 1940–July 1941*.[10] Allied intelligence said that 2,000 enemy troops held the town with large concentrations of transport and some coastal defence guns. The raid was to invade on four separate beaches. However, where Dakar had turned out to be unexpectedly resistant, Bardia was deserted; its only vehicles were abandoned trucks. In three hours' occupation the only visible enemy was a single motorcycle patrol which two parties of Commandos failed to stop. All the raid's other incidents were, Waugh observed, 'caused by our own incapacity'. The parent-ship refused to approach closer than four miles from the coast, causing the loss of 60 men. The first boat couldn't get in the water and the next 'preferred to go to Beach A' instead of B, which got no landing party. On Beach A Waugh's party encountered an unexpected ditch and a rough, steep wadi (a dry watercourse leading inland). The men supposedly covering their retreat panicked, 'fired a few shots at their officer, killed him, and disconcerted the parties climbing the wadi'. Of the other raiding parties one found the coastal defence guns already disabled. Another was 'content to burn some motor tyres' in an abandoned Italian camp. Another destroyed a small footbridge. No detachments reached the town. Returning from the mission, one party missed its rendezvous; another went down the wrong wadi and was left behind. A grounded boat had to be destroyed by a grenade in its petrol tank. The flames lit up Waugh's boat, its ramp jammed, drifting round the bay, a sitting target full of seasick men.

After his return, Waugh wrote an officially sanctioned propaganda account of the raid to publicize the newly-created Commandos.[11] It makes very funny reading by the side of the flat, disgruntled *Memorandum*. The mission's unexpected difficulties are exaggerated to heroic odds, its failures minimized or spun as successes. It is, in fact, a blueprint for the hyped fiasco of Trimmer's Operation Popgun in *Officers and Gentlemen*, and an echo in miniature of Britain's upbeat presentation of the retreat from Dunkirk.[12] The impassable ditch, precipitous wadi, and (a

160

new detail) deafening din of falling stones all testify to the climbing Commandos' toughness. The covering party's disastrous burst of fire is attributed to the enemy and nobody is killed. The escape of the motor-cycle patrol is 'really very lucky' because 'it was through them that the enemy learned, as we particularly wanted them to learn, that a landing was taking place'. The bonfire of abandoned tyres turns into *new* tyres, 'a precious thing in the desert', which 'blazed gloriously' for the same specious purpose of alerting the gullible enemy. Hoodwinked into believing the town was in enemy hands, they 'did exactly what the British higher command wanted' and sent reinforcements to repel the phantom invasion.

In *Men at Arms* the Dakar expedition follows its real original until it is aborted and the ships withdraw to general relief. Waugh's inventions begin when Ritchie-Hook, fretting for action, is miffed by his Halberdiers' ignominious stand-by role, supporting the supporting brigade of despised Royal Marines 'and a unit of unknown character called a "commando"'. Guy is summoned by the Brigadier, the ship's Captain, and Colonel Tickeridge, all looking 'gleeful and curiously naughty', to discuss a 'little bit of very unofficial fun'.

'Can you find a dozen good men for a reconnaissance patrol?'
'Yes, sir.'
'And a suitable officer to lead them?'
'Can I go myself, sir?' he said to Colonel Tickeridge.
This was true Truslove-style. (*MA* 282)

In Ritchie-Hook's unauthorized landing party the Bardia raid of several hundred men is diminished to one small boat-load, whose only task is to prove that Dakar's beach isn't wired as Intelligence maintains. (It is.) This pure schoolboy prank replays Waugh's own landing on Bardia's Beach A, adding all the vital, inessential particularities missing from Waugh's military records – from the steamy breath of the sea when the sally-port is opened, to Guy's sense of intense exhilaration as he stumbles ashore ahead of his men, waist deep through tepid water, to his first foothold on enemy soil. The Truslove thrills of Ritchie-Hook's incognito participation in the landing, his butchering the poor Negro sentry with hand-grenade and machete, are ballasted by the realism of Waugh's own experiences. Particularly when, as in Bardia, Guy's covering party panics, fires three rounds from its Bren gun alarmingly close, and Guy finds himself repeating the act of contrition but also thinking, 'what a preposterous way in which to get oneself killed.' But the whole operation is preposterous, and in the last of four references, Guy ruefully dismisses it as 'Operation Truslove'.[13]

At Truslove's first mention, we were told that 'Pathans were Captain Truslove's business'. Those fierce Afghan warriors came from the same stable as the Zulus of Waugh's first fiction, written and illustrated by him when he was eleven and the First World War was just beginning. For 12-year-old Guy, as for the young Waugh, 'Troy, Agincourt and Zululand were more real than the world of mud and gas'. Childhood memories of 'Truslove' epitomize the schoolboy fantasies impelling Waugh and many other young Peter Pans when they first enlisted for the Second World War.[14]

In *POMF* Basil Seal also half-expected a tougher version of Truslove's appointment. He'd be summoned to an obscure address in Maida Vale, where a lean, scarred man with hard grey eyes would say: 'We've followed your movements with interest ever since that affair in La Paz in '32. You're a rascal, but I'm inclined to think you're the kind of rascal the country needs at this moment. I take it you're game for anything?' 'I'm game.' In *POMF*, as in *Men at Arms*, both dreams come partially true, and Colonel Plum recognizes Basil in just the right style ('Jibouti 1936, St Jean de Luz 1937, Prague 1938. You won't remember me...').

Alas, at this point Ritchie-Hook seems to be on his way out. Even before Dakar, when he talked to Guy at dusk, he was 'barely visible in the failing light' and was immediately juxtaposed to Leonard, a good soldier who had been looking 'like a ghost for some time'. Soon after Leonard is wiped out in the Blitz. Dakar looks like the Brigadier's last escapade. Colonel Tickeridge says he's too old to be an *enfant terrible* any more, and he's not a national hero either: 'It's the end for him.'

The real Brigadier St Clair-Morford's short military record refers to his conspicuous gallantry in hazardous operations in the First World War and, repeatedly, to his recklessness. After his retirement, in 1944 he was put in command of R. M. Military School, Thurleston, where 'he unfortunately looked out of a tank hatch on the live firing range and was hit in the head by a bullet'.[15] That sounds familiar. Early in Guy's training, Waugh describes Ritchie-Hook, bored by the live firing range safety routines, running up and down the trench, raising and lowering his hat on a stick for the men to shoot at.

> All missed. Enraged he popped his head over the parapet shouting: 'Come on you young blighters, shoot me.' He did this for some time, running, laughing, ducking, jumping, until he was exhausted though unwounded. (*MA* 173–4)

It's nice to think of Waugh's real Brigadier, dead at 51, immortalized and laughing, a schoolboy to the last.

GUY'S STORY

Originally Waugh was uncertain how long his war trilogy would be. He threatened Nancy Mitford with 'four or five volumes', and promised Cyril Connolly that 'all the subsidiary characters' would have a book each. The imprecision of his intentions is compounded by his terminology. A 'book' may mean an entire novel, or subsections of it, as *Brideshead* is divided into two or three books, and *Men at Arms* into three. 'Anyway', he added, 'the theme will see me out – that is the humanising of Guy' (*L* 383).

For Waugh had the *broad* outline planned from the start. The Prologue, like the final trilogy, is titled 'Sword of Honour', and prepares for the completed arc of Guy's story. Its tender opening – three pages of Waugh's finest writing – delicately introduces the theme of delayed sexual fulfilment that will find completion only in the trilogy's last volume. The 'sad gap' between Gervase and Hermione, Guy's Victorian grandparents, on their honeymoon, was healed as they sailed up the coast of Italy, 'and there, one night in their state room, all came right between them'. Fulfilment delayed in love is set against fulfilment disappointed in war, as Guy leaves Castello Crouchback to enlist in England, praying first at the mediaeval tomb of Roger of Waybrooke, 'il santo Inglese' who died in Italy, never reaching the Crusade he left England to join.

The Prologue, then, deliberately prefigures the two arenas of Guy's future failure and fulfilment, in love and war. It also quickly establishes Guy's spiritual sterility eight years after his wife's desertion, replicating Waugh's suffering between his first wife's betrayal in 1929, and his marriage to Laura in 1937. Waugh's account is resolutely unemotional. Guy is simply 'handicapped'. 'It was as though eight years back he had suffered a tiny stroke of paralysis; all his spiritual capacities were just perceptibly impaired,' and 'lately he had fallen into a habit of dry and negative chastity which even his priests felt to be unedifying'. From this wasteland Guy sets out on his crusade.

*

Waugh endows Guy with a bent for self-critical introspection which lets us follow his development with sympathetic ease. Initially his growth seems merely social. Unlike Apthorpe, and in spite of embarrassment, he quickly adopts the Halberdier toast – 'Here's how' instead of 'cheers'. Dutifully socializing after his first Ensa show,[16] he unintentionally snubs an aging tenor and goes to bed asking himself 'Was that the real Halberdier welcome expected of him? *There was much to repent and repair.*'[17] Lamed and alone in Kut-al-Imara's dispiriting quarters, he finds a single room he longs for – but, remembering Leonard's comradely help with his kit, welcoming him into a room for four, he contritely rejects it. (Apthorpe snaps it up.) After a day of humiliating incompetence at the firing range, he buys himself a drink before cleaning his gun; is bawled out by an officer and then mocked by Trimmer, a tick. Waugh – no stranger to sudden rages – memorably conveys Guy's helpless fury, carrying him into 'a red incandescent stratum where he was a stranger', but ends with him standing '*in shame and sorrow*', last in the queue for hot water, 'leaning on his *fouled* weapon' – a technical term whose larger moral connotations are obvious. Near the novel's end, Guy regrets his inability to commiserate with a white-whiskered Goanese steward wearing a Catholic medallion like himself, and recognizes his paralysis is more than merely social. His heart 'opened towards him'; 'he yearned to show his own medal' as other men would have done, '*better men than he.*'

At its best, military training is itself moral, as the image of the fouled weapon suggests. When Guy joins the Halberdiers' barracks, the first thing he warms to, and learns from, is their tradition of democratic courtesy. In sharp contrast, Kut-al-Imara is lowering primarily because it lacks that *esprit de corps*. Under its corrosive indiscipline and indifferent rote-learning even the men lose individuality and become bad soldiers. Whereas at Penkirk, when the latest Army Training Memorandum is distributed to the trainee officers, their responses to its hundred and forty-three questions are at first like a game of 'Happy Families' ('How many men in your platoon have *you* earmarked for signallers?') Moreover, for Guy the questionnaire becomes a lay catechism, an opportunity for critical self-scrutiny: '*How many of your men do you know by name and what do you know of their characters?*' He has already registered his dislike of scroungers like Sarum-Smith, ticks like Trimmer, the debilitating effect of a selfish wife on a good colleague like Leonard. As he acquires authority he has to apply these discriminations.

There is a telling difference between Guy and Waugh here. France has fallen, England expects invasion hourly; for days the company has been confined to shipboard under two hours' notice to sail, when Guy – and Waugh – receive an urgent request for shore leave on compassionate grounds. Halberdier Shanks, a first-class soldier, *must* go to Blackpool to compete in the slow valse competition. He's been practicing with his girl for three years; they won at Salford last year. As Company Commander, Guy regretfully refuses, wondering 'Was this the already advertised spirit of Dunkirk? He rather thought it was.'

And Waugh? 'In defiance of the Colonel's orders I relented. Yesterday he came back with a silver cup as big as himself.'[18] Guy shares his creator's sympathies, but lacks Waugh's defiant independence.

Waugh knew well enough how unjust military systems of preferment and promotion could be. In *Commando Raid on Bardia* he commented: 'There is a universal danger in all armies that, when volunteers are called to leave their regiments for special service, the worst get sent. No company commander wants to lose good men; they all have some troublesome fellow they are glad to pass on' (*EAR* 263–4). In *Men at Arms* Guy and Major Erskine confide to each other that both have put up their immediate subordinates – two bad lots – for promotion for precisely these reasons. 'Jolly sort of army we're going to have in two years time when all the shits have got to the top.' (This duly comes about in *Officers and Gentlemen*.) Erskine also explains that Apthorpe's promotion as HQ Commander will lead nowhere but 'GSO2(Q) or something wet like that' while Guy is earmarked to command a fighting company but first needs experience leading a platoon. His apparent rejection is, in fact, a delayed promotion. At about this time in Waugh's own military career, his commanding officer reported on him in comparable terms: 'A natural commander and experienced man. He works hard and gets good work out of his subordinates [...] Possesses any amount of moral courage [...] with more military experience [...] he will make a first class Company Commander.'[19] Both Guy and Waugh did subsequently get their captaincies, but in odd circumstances, and neither kept them for long. As Erskine predicts to Guy, 'You will [get a rifle company] before we go into action, unless you blot your copy book in a pretty sensational way.' Guy's subsequent leadership of Ritchie-Hook's unauthorized raid on Dakar earns a black mark against him, and Colonel Tickeridge warns him that in spite of his bravery, dragging the wounded Brigadier to safety under enemy fire, he's marked for life: 'when your name comes up, someone is bound to say: "Isn't he the chap who blotted his copy-book at Dakar in 40?"' He loses his captaincy before he even knew he had it. Something similar happened to Waugh.[20]

*

Guy's vicissitudes in his military career are paralleled by just two episodes in his love-life: his two meetings with his ex-wife Virginia, who left him eight years earlier, and has been through a couple of marriages and many liaisons since then. Both these plot-strands are deep-buried conduits for Waugh's prime concern: the workings of providence, which will become manifest only as the trilogy ends. His long-term plan echoes that of *Brideshead*, runs the same risks of readers' incomprehension and, additionally, is vulnerable to his own changes of mind.

The question of divine providence is lightly raised, and challenged by Guy, when Mr Goodall, an *aficionado* of Catholic heraldry, tells him about one of Guy's distant relatives of ancient Catholic stock, whose wife left him for another man, but then had a brief fling with her first husband, and bore his son to her unsuspecting second husband. For Goodall, that son is, 'in the eyes of God, the rightful heir to all his [true] father's quarterings'. Guy can't resist asking, 'Do you seriously believe that God's Providence concerns itself with the perpetuation of the English Catholic aristocracy?' but Goodall is unperturbed. 'But of course. And with sparrows too, we are taught.'[21]

This episode is immediately followed by Guy's second meeting with Virginia. In their chance first encounter, Guy happily found that they could see each other without rancour – she had all the spontaneity he lacked, and the affection he dared not express ('Guy, pet ... '). In their second meeting, Guy is fired by Goodall's contention that his relative's one-night-stand with his ex-wife was not adulterous because the Church recognized neither the couple's divorce nor the wife's subsequent marriage. Assuming this theological indulgence, Guy intends to take Virginia's affectionate reconciliation as far as he can. But his intentions are thwarted by a series of drunken phone calls from Apthorpe. The contemporary reviewer who criticized the couple's encounter for being 'like a scene from some shabby and tasteless bedroom farce' was, however inadvertently, quite right: that is the desired effect.[22] There is something undeniably shoddy in Guy's intentions, which offend Virginia. When they quarrel, his insult about her loose life is as unforgivable as hers about his inadequate performance on their wedding night. The formal hotel bedroom plus drawing-room set, where Guy's seduction fails to take place, has been provided by Tommy Blackhouse, his successor and Virginia's second of many more ex-husbands, who has just spent the night with her and is now, in effect, pimping her to Guy.

All these moral shadows darken the undeniable, but painful comedy of this scene. They create real unease, which promotes the gravitas of Waugh's unspoken subtext, that Man proposes, but God disposes. Yet Virginia, like Waugh in his happy-go-lucky pre-Catholic youth, can see nothing but inconsequent chance at work. 'How things just do happen to one!' she exclaims, sitting on the floor, her eyes wide and amorous, as Guy slides down beside her:

> It was all going as Guy had planned, and, as though hearing his unspoken boast, she added: 'It's no good planning anything,' and she said again: 'Things just happen to one.' (MA 159)

Then Apthorpe rings once more, Guy and Virginia quarrel, and as Apthorpe interrupts for the third time, she leaves. It is not here, now, or thus, that they are meant to come together, nor for this purpose alone. Not long after this débâcle, Guy goes down to Matchet to visit his father for Holy Week. There is a lovely image of Mr Crouchback in vigil on Good Friday morning, staring straight into the candlelight, just turning to smile as Guy joins him. Then the curtains are drawn from the eastern windows and 'brilliant sunlight blinded their eyes'. There are many kinds of blindness. This devout scene is immediately juxtaposed with a most secret nocturnal meeting where two officials in counter-intelligence are hard at work. A spy's garbled report of Guy's conversation with Apthorpe about the thunder-box has been transmogrified into a suspect politician called Box and identified as Guy's brother-in-law, Box-Bender. 'Thus two new names were added to the Most Secret index' and later 'dispersed into a dozen indexes in all the Counter Espionage Headquarters of the Free World [...] Then they, too, took down the black-out screens and admitted the dawn.' So Waugh starts yet another thread in his plot. Grace-Groundling-Marchpole, the assiduous assistant in this scene and the personification of purblind authority, will re-appear in later volumes, quickly acquiring the status of an agent of disorder, the antitype of providence or its human parody. And Guy will be trapped in his ever-expanding web.

12

Officers and Gentlemen
1955

'Lent [1953] began well. I wrote first pages of novel, very good too. White's [his London club] in an air raid. Then the fog closed in' – not just literally either. On Ash Wednesday, Waugh 'resolved to give up opiates for Lent'; less than a month later his diary confessed: 'Have abandoned resolution to give up narcotics and am giving up wine instead.' Always mercilessly self-aware, he had recently noted his increasing dependence on drugs and drink to alleviate chronic insomnia, his deteriorating work routines, and uneasily observed 'A flaw somewhere' (*D* 716, 714). Slimming in August can't have helped ('I am light as a feather and feeble as tissue paper', *L* 408). A fog descended. Over the summer and autumn his letters and diary entries reveal regretted quarrels with old friends, twinges of paranoia, and disconcerting lapses of memory whose details were precise, sharp – and wrong. In December he admitted to Nancy Mitford, 'I am stuck in my book from sheer boredom. I know what to write but just cant make the effort to write it'. After New Year he pathetically told his daughter Margaret, 'Oh I have been ill since you left. First a cold & then agonising rheumatism. So I am jumping into the first available ship. She goes to Ceylon. I shant come back till I have finished my book.' (*L* 415, 417) On board he suffered the acute attack of insanity later described in *The Ordeal of Gilbert Pinfold*. Yet by Lent 1954 he was back on form, and in November shared his elation with Nancy Mitford: 'This book is done at last [...] It is short and funny & completes the story I began in *Men at Arms* which threatened to drag out to the grave' (*L* 433). However, he had radically curtailed his original, ambitious plans for a *magnum opus* in 'four or five volumes which won't show any shape until the end.'

Officers and Gentlemen is divided into two parts. Book I, *Happy Warriors*,[1] is primarily concerned with Guy's training as a Commando in Scotland and covers the equivalent period in Waugh's life from November 1940 to January 1941. *Interlude*, and Book II, *In the Picture*, draw on Waugh's experiences in Cape Town, Egypt, and during the fall of Crete from February to June 1941.

It is not certain when the novel was interrupted by Waugh's Pinfold episode. It is worth comparing it to *Vile Bodies*, which he felt to be broken-backed by his first wife's defection, also in mid-composition. The literary impact of both disturbances must have been blurred both by the cumulative nature of experience, and by rewriting after the event. Yet Waugh attempted to unify *Vile Bodies* by a sense of 'cumulative futility'. The Bright Young Things' irresponsible world finds its logical conclusion in the novel's bleak prophetic panorama of the Second World War. By contrast, the two halves of *Officers and Gentlemen* differ markedly on stylistic grounds and make a less convincing whole. It seems likely that Waugh's period of insanity fell between Books I and II.[2] By the end of Book II, fearing the possibility of another mental breakdown, he published it with a blurb claiming '*Officers and Gentlemen* completes *Men at Arms*. I thought at first that the story would run to three volumes. I find that two will do the trick.' But he left the possibility of a continuation open, 'If I keep my faculties'.

The opening is, as Waugh says, very good indeed, succinctly shrinking the Blitz to inappropriate analogues which would have outraged the Londoners of 1940.

> The sky over London was glorious, ochre and madder, as though a dozen tropic suns were simultaneously setting round the horizon [...]; now and then a huge flash momentarily froze the serene fireside glow. Everywhere the shells sparkled like Christmas baubles.
>
> 'Pure Turner,' said Guy Crouchback, enthusiastically [...]
>
> On the pavement opposite Turtle's a group of progressive novelists in firemen's uniforms were squirting a little jet of water into the morning-room.[3] (*OG* 1)

In this exhilaratingly topsy-turvy world, the air-raid is 'best left to the civilians'; Air Marshal Beech cravenly hides under the club billiard table, and happy under-officers drink and joke above his head.

After this crisp opening, Book I sinks into a heavy sequence of disjunctive episodes, the laborious invention Waugh noted in his letter to Nancy Mitford. In a careless review Cyril Connolly had criticized *Men at Arms*, drawing on the formal guest night at the Halberdier Barracks to conclude: 'One raises the silver loving cup expecting champagne and receives a wallop of ale.' Waugh humbly acquiesced: 'You have clearly defined all that I dislike in the book. "Beery" is exactly right.'[4] Now he writes to Connolly, in the surviving fragment of a letter, 'I work away at my brewery. Another cask of...' Beer, presumably.

Book II is strikingly different. Two strong narratives – Trimmer's sham heroism and the Allies' shameful withdrawal – are tightly interwoven. The touch is light, the action nimbly shifting. The welcome reappearance of Mrs Stitch sharpens Waugh's satirical edge. The fall of Crete is as harrowing, flat and true as John Andrew's deliberately prosaic death in *A Handful of Dust*. Waugh seems at the height of his powers again.

BOOK I: *HAPPY WARRIORS*

Waugh described *Men at Arms* as 'the first comic turn of a long music-hall show, put on to keep the audience quiet as they are taking their seats' (*L* 379). To Connolly he added, unapologetically, 'nor will the pace quicken much' in following volumes, where 'all [!] the subsidiary characters, like "Trimmer" & "Chatty Corner" & "de Souza" will each have a book to himself' (*L* 383). Waugh follows his dangerous plan in *Officers and Gentlemen*'s Book I, whose first seven sections are recast as a single chapter, helpfully re-titled *Apthorpe Placatus*, in the final trilogy.

Guy returns to England to fulfil Apthorpe's deathbed bequest to Chatty Corner, his taciturn, ape-like guest at the Halberdier Guest Night. He amasses Apthorpe's unwieldy legacy of tropical kit, and with the help of Jumbo Trotter, a Halberdier officer-and-gentleman of the old school, they requisition a staff car, chauffeur, and lorry – and fail to find the legatee. Meanwhile Jumbo, a fine new comic character, seems all set to usurp the distinctly unfunny Chatty Corner and take over his book. It's only after Jumbo and Guy have reached Guy's new posting with the Commandos on the Isle of Mugg that Guy chances on Chatty Corner, and in their very brief, only encounter, persuades him to sign a receipt for his *un*delivered bequest, sight unseen. Guy feels his duty is discharged, but its hasty incompletion leaves the reader unsatisfied. Has Waugh simply lost interest?

Such uncertainties are a recurrent problem in Book I. The gravity of Guy's task was magnified at the beginning of the novel: it was 'the second stage of his pilgrimage, which had begun at the tomb of Sir Roger [. . .] An act of *pietas* was required of him; a spirit was to be placated.'[5] There is a perceptible disparity between comic Apthorpe and Sir Roger Weybrooke, the failed crusader. The reference to two unquiet spirits of classic epic[6] also seems rather overblown, as does Guy's sense of failure, when he can't find Chatty to fulfil his duty: 'Ever prone to elaborate his predicament rather fancifully,' he imagines himself standing on guard over Apthorpe's kit year after year, like the Imperial Russian sentry keeping perpetual watch over the spot where Catherine the Great had once admired a wild flower. It is not quite clear whether Waugh is being deliberately mock-heroic.

Guy's tendency to fanciful over-elaboration is partly an implicit confession of authorial weakness. In *Men at Arms* 'the spell of Apthorpe' was said to 'bind [Guy] and gently bear him away to the far gardens of fantasy' (*MA* 166). In *Officers and Gentlemen* Waugh frequently alleviates his monotonously military material by flights of fancy, never more so than in *Happy Warriors*. When Guy finally locates Chatty Corner – locally known as King Kong – on his first evening in Mugg, he is 'so confounded between truth and fantasy' that he expects to find 'a *tableau* from some ethnographic museum, some shaggy, prognathous hypothetical ancestor, sharpening a flint spear-head among a heap of gnawed bones between walls scrawled with imitation Picassos'. Instead he meets an ordinary, if hirsute man, with no interest in Apthorpe's hoard of tropical gear. And Apthorpe, according to Chatty Corner, turns out to have been no expert in jungle warfare, just a city worker in a tobacco company, and a poor shot. A fair parallel, in fact, to Sir Roger of Waybrooke, the failed crusader.

These shifts between fantastical hyperbole and bathetic reality have always been an element of Waugh's style, and their tone clarifies as Book I progresses. The funniest episode in *Happy Warriors* is Guy and Tommy Blackhouse's dinner with the gunpowder-hungry Laird of Mugg and his mad Nazi daughter (indubitably, and tactlessly, deriving from Unity Mitford),[7] in a castle with a skirling Highland piper, baying dogs, and 'objects of furniture constructed of antlers'. Here, too, Waugh tethers ballooning fantasy to precise, prosaic realism. The 'baronial severity of the furniture was mitigated by a group of chairs clothed in stained and faded chintz'; the dogs range from deerhounds to 'an almost hairless pomeranian'; a crazy dinner-table conversation of cross purposes and mistaken identities distracts Guy from his struggle with a 'totally unassimilable' hunk of gristly venison.

However, Waugh does not seem fully in control, especially in the handling of his plot. R. M. Davis's detailed study of the authorial manuscript supports this impression.[8] Plot lines are laid, and abruptly snapped. Guy can't find Chatty Corner; when he does, Corner is indifferent to his bequest. Apthorpe is a popped bubble. Ivor Claire and Guy are delighted to see Mrs Stitch's yacht approaching Mugg – but she isn't on it. The Laird of Mugg spends his time plotting to steal explosives from the Commandos, in order to blow up the rocky coastline he blew down from the crags in the first place, and turn his inhospitable island into a well-beached holiday resort. The detonation of this extended narrative fuse is delayed till it fizzles out, a negligible damp squib, in the second half of the novel, where we hear enigmatic rumblings from the higher authorities: 'That explosion at Mugg...' 'The security precautions at the embarkation...' That plot rustle you can just make out at the limits of hearing is the sound of loose ends being tied up. Nothing more is said. In the trilogy's final version, *Sword of Honour*, Waugh kills off the story in a single decisive sentence closing *OG*'s Book I: 'The great explosion which killed Mugg and his niece was attributed to enemy action' (*SH* 380). All these dangling plot lines support the impression that the novel was interrupted by Waugh's Pinfold experience at about this point.

Yet unfulfilment is also the leitmotif of the trilogy. The reader's narrative expectations are as implacably thwarted as the novel's characters, in their respective hopes of high comedy, heroic promotion, and honourable death.

Human aspirations are subject to providence. Waugh's characters are subject to the *fiat* of their author. When Virginia, abandoned by her latest lover, embarks on a brief fling in a fog-bound, seedy Glaswegian grand hotel, she believes that Trimmer, formerly 'Gustave', her sympathetic masseur-cum-hairdresser on many Atlantic crossings, is 'the guide providentially sent on a gloomy evening to lead her back to the days of sun and sea-spray and wallowing dolphins'. In this delusion, her casual 'providentially' is authorially loaded. For her it means no more than 'conveniently'. In fact the liaison, destined to become a penitential bore for her, is part of the author's divine plan. On the same page, Virginia's tawdry brief encounter is pointedly capped by the re-appearance of Grace-Groundling-Marchpole, now head of the most secret department in counter-intelligence, filing the Nazi propaganda hidden in Guy's car by the Laird of Mugg's mad daughter, and triumphantly adding another black mark to Guy's name. Everything, he believes, is falling into place. He only needs proof of the connections between Guy and Box-Bender, Salzburg and Mugg, Cardiff and Santa Dulcina, and his 'private, undefined Plan' will be vindicated. 'Somewhere in the ultimate curlicues of his mind, there was a Plan. Given time, given enough confidential material, he would succeed in knitting the entire quarrelsome world into a single net of conspiracy [...] and there would be no more war.'

The Vanity of Human Wishes! Marchpole's hubris was earlier lightly prefigured by Mr Goodall, the expert on Catholic aristocracy, in church on All Souls' Day, 'popping in and down and up and out and in again assiduously releasing *toties quoties* soul after soul from purgatory. "Twenty-eight, so far," he said. "I always try and do fifty."' The delusion of mortal aspirations, something more than mere unfulfilment, is the ultimate theme of the trilogy.

MR CROUCHBACK'S ROLE

Guy's ever-accumulating, unmerited black marks echo the fate of his recusant ancestor. In the novel's first pages, old Mr

Crouchback, now doing war work as a Latin master (like Waugh's father), is decoyed from a tricky translation by questions about the Blessed Gervase Crouchback, martyred in the time of Tudor persecution. Was he betrayed by the steward in his house of hiding? Certainly not, says Crouchback; a historian misread the Jesuit records 'and the mistake has been copied from book to book...'. Perpetuated errors like this are endemic in army records, and recurrent in hagiographic bibliography. More broadly, in the twentieth century, the religious persecutions of the Renaissance were replicated in the racial and ideological persecutions of Communist Russia and Nazi Germany. Priest holes, fugitive hideaways, the betrayal of innocents, mass murder, unjust trials and executions without trial, span the centuries. F. J. Stopp, Waugh's first biographer-critic, quotes Waugh verbatim, when Waugh explained to him that old Mr Crouchback's function was

> to keep audible a steady undertone of the decencies and true purpose of life behind the chaos of events and fantastic characters. Also to show him as a typical victim (parallel to the trainloads going to the concentration camps) in the war against the Modern Age. (Stopp 168)

In *Men at Arms*, Waugh repeated the motif of the doomed trainloads travelling east and west three times, carefully locating the terms and chronological placing of his references in order to encompass, simultaneously, the imminent Soviet massacres of Poles, and the later Nazi holocaust of the Jews, without specifying either.[9] Beyond these loaded references, throughout the trilogy, Waugh deliberately and scrupulously avoids focusing on any aspects of the war outside his own range of experience. And at each point he plays off these references to distant and as-yet-unknown horrors against the ignorant security of Guy, his fellow trainee-officers, and the public at large. Instead, he conveys the trainee-officers' initial oblivious-ness about contemporary events, which was common among Waugh's fellow men-at-arms.[10] Only twice in *Men at Arms* does he identify episodes as 'a microcosm' of larger trends. In *Officers and Gentlemen* Mr Crouchback serves this microcosmic purpose when Miss Vavasour, a fellow-guest at the seaside lodging-house in Matchet, warns him that the proprietors are planning

175

to evict him, making him *a typical victim, parallel to the trainloads going to the concentration camps*. He is sublimely unaware of his danger, even when the sterling Jumbo has dealt with the billeting officer threatening the seizure of his living-space. This episode is a fine example of Waugh's capacity *not* to swell the ordinary to fantastical proportions, as he does in the comic scenes on Mugg. On the contrary, and very simply, here he shows us the world in a grain of sand at Matchet.

THE COMMANDOS

When Waugh returned from Dakar in the winter of 1940, he was seconded from the Royal Marines to the Commandos, joining them for training first in Largs, near Glasgow, and then on the Isle of Arran, the Mugg of *Officers and Gentlemen*. In February 1941 they sailed for Egypt via Cape Town and the Suez Canal. In 'Commando Raid on Bardia', Waugh explained that their original function was to fulfil the current need for small groups of elite fighting troops capable of independent action in 'sharp little counter-attacks on their own'. There was, he added modestly, 'nothing peculiar about our men. They were simply the best types of the regiments from which they came', and included several sons of the First World War's foremost leaders – 'Jellicoe, Keyes, Beatty, and Churchill' (*EAR* 263–4). The Commandos' buccaneering appeal was well conveyed in *POMF*'s last pages, where Waugh's leading men are enticed by the schoolboy attractions of toggle-ropes, tommy guns, rope-soled shoes and blacked-up faces.

'The officers are divided more or less equally into dandies and highly efficient professional soldiers,' Waugh told Laura. 'All the officers have very long hair and lapdogs & cigars & they wear whatever uniform they like [...] As a result of [their] being so very rich I have been able to set myself up as a poor man.' (*L* 145–6) His friend and fellow-commando, Randolph Churchill (son of Sir Winston Churchill), had a Pekinese, lost over £400 in a single night's gambling,[11] and, like other toughs at Largs, frequented expensive Glasgow hotels at weekends (as in Trimmer's idyll with Virginia). When they reached Egypt, Waugh told Laura that 'all' his rich friends 'have bought racehorses' (L 151). Waugh, like Guy, was more circumspect, gambling for low stakes, and his diary is critical: 'The standard of efficiency and devotion to duty, particularly among the officers, is very much lower than in the Marines. There is no administration or discipline [...] Officers have no scruples about seeing to their own comfort or getting all the leave they can' (D 488). His informal *Memorandum on Layforce* concludes: 'After RM Brigade the indolence and ignorance of the officers seemed remarkable [...] no-one even pretended to work outside working hours [...] Two night operations in which I acted as umpire showed great incapacity in the simplest technical ideas.' Nevertheless he was, at this stage, torn between affection and disapproval: 'On the whole, however, I saw few symptoms of their later decay. They had a gaiety and independence which I thought would prove valuable in action' (D 490). Many aspects of this mixed picture are seen in Waugh's *Happy Warriors*. They are epitomized in Ivor Claire.

'I remember well my impression on first joining,' Waugh wrote in 'Commando Raid on Bardia'. 'The commando was at that time living in Scotland and the officers' mess was at a seaside hotel. I had come from the austerity and formality of the Royal Marines [... where] it is thought disgraceful to sit down before six in the evening [...] I found a young troop leader wearing a military tunic and corduroy trousers. He was reclining in a comfortable chair, a large cigar in his mouth. Then I noticed above the pocket of his coat the ribbon of the Military Cross' (EAR 264). *Happy Warriors* replays this scene, elaborately fantasticated. At his arrival in the Mugg officers' mess, Guy finds Ivor Claire reclining on a sofa, his head turbaned in bandages, his feet in embroidered velvet slippers, nursing a white Pekinese and a glass of white liquor: 'The pictorial effect was of a young prince of the near East in his grand divan in the early years of the century.' (Many of Waugh's deliberately fanciful elaborations in this particular novel rely on arty analogues.)[12] Later, Trimmer asks Guy, 'Did you spot his M.C.? Do you know how he got it?' A significant question, whose answer the reader, hurried on by the narrative, is likely to miss.

But even at this early stage the Commandos clearly lacked the *esprit de corps* Guy loved and respected in the Halberdier

Barracks (and Waugh at RM barracks at Chatham). Claire encourages Guy to snap up the hotel room just about to be vacated by an injured Commando, so forestalling several other officers who hurry back from the afternoon's climbing for the same purpose. Seeing to their own comfort, in fact, in a way Guy felt ashamed of in *Men at Arms*, when he moved into Kut-al-Imara House and was briefly tempted to seize the only single room for himself. Later, Tommy Blackhouse, Guy's commanding officer, deliberately organizes a night exercise designed to 'make Ivor do some work for a change', allotting his troop a taxing cross-country route to rendezvous on the remotest northern corner of the island. In less than an hour Ivor's troop truthfully signal their arrival – by hired bus via the unauthorized coastal road. This, too, is Waugh's fantasticated version of the actual night exercises he umpired and judged technically deficient. In the novel, however, Ivor argues that he wasn't cheating but following the Commando code of independent initiative by exploiting local resources. In real operations 'there would probably be a bus lying about somewhere'. This was not a convenience they were to find in Crete.

Guy is as charmed by Ivor Claire as he was fascinated by Apthorpe. When he first meets him in elegant repose, he recognizes 'a young show-jumper of repute' whom he once saw completing a faultless round in the Concorso Hippico in Rome, 'leaning slightly forward in the saddle with the intent face of a pianist'. This entrancing memory recurs three times (57, 146–7, 295), Ivor always intent, 'concentrated as a man in prayer', an ideal of manhood. 'Ivor Claire, Guy thought, was the fine flower of them all. He was quintessential England, the man Hitler had not taken into account, Guy thought.' These are the last two sentences of the novel's *Interlude*, before the Commandos finally find themselves *In the Picture* at the fall of Crete. The repetition suggests that *Guy thought* wrong.

Earlier, neglected hints support this suspicion. As early as *Men at Arms*, the story of Truslove, the hero of Guy's childhood reading, included another fine rider, 'a showy polo-player named Congreve' who withdrew from the regiment to avoid foreign service. His fellow-soldiers felt 'tainted' by his coward-ice; his name was banned, and their subsequent acts of heroism were motivated by the impulse to redeem the regiment's honour. Ivor's behaviour, for all its charm, is already evidently tainted by self-interest like Congreve's. As for his Military Cross, as Trimmer admiringly tells Guy, it was won 'At Dunkirk, for shooting three territorials who were trying to swamp his boat. Great chap old Ivor.' Trimmer – coward, liar and poseur – is not a good judge of truthfulness or bravery. It is difficult to detect any conceivable heroism in Ivor's murder of three fellow soldiers trying to join his boat in the flight from Dunkirk.[13] This, too, is ominous.

BOOK II: *IN THE PICTURE*

This book is the finest of the trilogy, displaying in tandem two opposed pictures: the comic false image of Trimmer as a people's war hero, and the dismally true likeness of the fall of Crete. The contentious influence of biographical material on literary analysis can also be seen at its best and worst in these two narratives. The identification of Trimmer's living original enriches our enjoyment of this episode, while the precise details of Layforce's withdrawal from Crete have been the source of significant historical error and interpretative confusion. Donat Gallagher's research is based on original sources. It significantly enhanced our understanding of both episodes.[14]

Gallagher's identification of Trimmer with Lord Lovat is summarized in the following section of this chapter. His essay on the evacuation of Crete corrects Antony Beevor's erroneous accounts, which have been followed, and even magnified, by Waugh's biographers and critics in order to accuse Waugh and his commanding officer, Bob Laycock, of malpractice. Gallagher's exhaustive research into the military records covering the embarkation from Sphakia definitively demonstrates that, contrary to Beevor's allegations, Laycock and Waugh's withdrawal, with their men, followed specific orders. They did not force their way ahead of other, higher-priority troops. Waugh did not falsify the war dairy in order to cover up Laycock's alleged disobedience of orders.[15] Gallagher's research is rich in documented detail, giving a strong sense of the shame shared by many soldiers at the Allied débâcle; the confused orders and counter-orders governing their flight; the pickets and cordons attempting to control the huge surge of regular soldiers, legitimate base-camp personnel and the lawless miscellany of defectors and free-booters pressing into Sphakia's bottleneck on the last night of evacuation. By the time the last ship sailed, over 4,000 men had been lifted off the island. Another 6,000 were left behind, to surrender at dawn on 1 June and be bombed by the enemy, as in both the novel and *Diaries* (*OG* 302, *D* 510).

GUSTAVE-TRIMMER-SCOTTIE-MCTAVISH

In his distant past Trimmer was 'Gustave', a phoney French hairdresser on the trans-Atlantic liner, *Aquitania*, where Virginia was one of his customers. He first appears in *Men at Arms* as Trimmer, a lazy tick who aroused Guy's incandescent fury and failed to complete the Halberdier officers' training. In *Officers and Gentlemen* he resurfaces masquerading as a Highlander of indeterminate officer status, and enjoys a brief liaison with Virginia. Waugh's contemporaries identified him with Simon Fraser, 15th Lord Lovat, who was to have a strong negative impact on Waugh's military career in 1943.

Gallagher confirms the rumoured identification, particularly after Trimmer's appearance on Mugg as the hyper-Scottish 'McTavish'. In his surprising new guise, 'in the kilt and uniform of a highland regiment, [carrying] a tall shepherd's staff', Trimmer recalls the well-known public image of the kilted Lovat with 'the shepherd's crook he always carried and looking like Britannia'.[16] Gallagher's initial parallels between the undistinguished early careers of Lovat and Trimmer are cogent and straightforward. Notably, both were sacked from their regiments, in Lovat's case, his own familial regiment of the Lovat Scouts. Crucially and conclusively, Gallagher then relates Trimmer's 'Operation Popgun' to Lovat's 'Operation Abercrombie', an early failed Commando raid he led against the occupied French seaside town of Hardelot in April 1942. Both tally closely in detail. 'Both turn out fiascos but are nevertheless lauded in the press, both leaders receive the Military Cross, both are employed in wartime propaganda.' The main differences between fact and fiction are that Trimmer's bungled exploit makes farcical comedy while Lovat's was a popular success; and that Trimmer – 'Fine and free, nosy and knowing,' in Waugh's words – is irredeemably vulgar, while Lovat, as Gallagher points out, was a member of the Scottish Catholic aristocracy who despised Waugh as a parvenu. Waugh's caricature of Lovat under the guise of a 'horrible hairdresser' (Lovat's own admission) adroitly attacks Lovat's snobbery. Moreover, from our present historic perspective, Lovat appears a self-promoting exhibitionist with a shocking disregard for the safety of his men and the lives of his prisoners, whom Waugh came to dislike with good reason.[17] I would add that Trimmer, by contrast, is a pathetic, lovelorn coward who becomes almost likeable by the end of *Officers and Gentlemen*.

Gallagher's argument is definitive. Yet the appeal of Trimmer's story chiefly lies in Waugh's inventive camouflage of his association with Lovat. In later years Waugh enjoyed scanning the press for potentially libellous references to himself. He was canny in hiding his own tracks. Dispersing traits of his original among different characters is natural to the writer of fiction and can hardly be thought of as a ploy. For instance, I suspect that Lovat's dubious MC is initially paralleled by Ivor Claire, rather than by Trimmer. Lovat's incredulous acknowledgement, 'for I am Trimmer, you know' stresses what was, for Lovat, the patent improbability of a Scottish aristocrat's kinship to a horrible hairdresser.[18] Trimmer's first appearance in *Men at Arms*, as an insignificant skiver whose probationary commission is speedily terminated, is unremarkable. In *Happy Warriors* his seedy idyll with Virginia in the Glasgow hotel is better realized than his unexpected appearance on Mugg, where his caricature Scottish persona simply seems unlikely to readers unaware of his original. However in Book II, his story is consolidated and completed with astonishing speed, economy, and persuasive local detail. Trimmer the People's hero is convincing as a genuine propaganda sham, and Trimmer the womanizer is true to life.

The structure of Book II is simple. In the first half Trimmer predominates; the second half concentrates on Crete. Trimmer's story is both military, and personal. The department of Hazardous Offensive Operations (HOO) is threatened by a sceptically hostile higher authority. General Whale and his press liaison officer, Ian Kilbannock, enlist Trimmer for Operation Popgun in a last-ditch attempt to secure the survival of HOO. This military context is matched by a better realized feminine counterpart – a domestic group of four women. They are Ian's wife Kerstie (dependable, faithful and economical), her lodger-friends Zita, Brenda – and Guy's ex-wife Virginia (undependable, loose-living, and improvident). Virginia lives on Kerstie's hospitality. Trimmer, known to them as 'Scottie', is a *habitué* of the canteen where they work. He flourishes in Kerstie, Brenda and Zita's indulgently unimpressed company. When Virginia meets him in the canteen, this unwelcome ghost from her past accentuates poor Trimmer's unacceptable commonness, and her own failing fortunes.

An interesting change in narrative tone occurs. In Glasgow, Waugh was straightforwardly disparaging. Trimmer on the prowl had 'all the panache of a mongrel among the dustbins'. In London, when Scottie's true past as the *Aquitania's* hairdresser, is revealed, Kerstie is kinder: 'I mean there's nothing very funny about his being what he is when one knows what he is – is there? – if you see what I mean.' Trimmer acquires something of the dignity discovered by Parolles in *All's Well That Ends Well*, when he too dropped his bravado, accepting what he was. 'Simply the thing I am / Shall make me live.' Enlisted for Operation Popgun to save HOO's future by a Commando success, Trimmer is glumly acquiescent, not even pretending to be brave.

Consequently the comedy of Operation Popgun seems amiably broad rather than satiric. Like a tamer version of the Dakar landing closing *Men at Arms*, the aptly-named Popgun is radically shrunk to something easily imaginable. A mini-raid of eight sappers led by Trimmer, supervized by Ian, must land on a tiny island off occupied Jersey to disable a suspected radar post. Lost in the mist, the submarine accidentally lands them on French soil where Ian and Trimmer disturb a farmhouse and run away. The sappers blow up a local railway track while waiting for their officers. In Ian's report citing Trimmer for a decoration, each detail of the shambles is translated into heroic officialese. 'On landing [Captain McTavish] showed a complete disregard of personal safety which communicated itself to his men.' (That is, he allowed them to smoke and did so himself.) 'While carrying out his personal reconnaissance he came under small arms fire. Fire was returned and the enemy post silenced.' (The reverse: startled by a dog barking, Trimmer accidentally let off his gun and both bolted. Shouting 'Sales Boches!' the farmer's wife fired once, and went back indoors.) They 'identified the line of the railway' (Trimmer fell over it). 'Heavy traffic in strategic materials was noted' (they hid from a passing goods train). 'A section of the permanent way was successfully demolished, thereby gravely impeding the enemy's war effort' (the sappers blew up the line on their own initiative). Trimmer throughout 'showed remarkable coolness' (his teeth were chattering). For Ian, an experienced journalist, writing this 'was jam'. Waugh, also a dab hand in the art of spin, wrote his upbeat version of the Commandos' Bardia Raid soon after his return from Crete. By then he was bitterly aware of the gulf between real warfare in defeat, and the specious triumphs of a propaganda exercise.

In the subsequent round-up of responses to Trimmer's triumph, old Mr Crouchback's is a telling variant on this Book's title and leitmotif, *In the Picture*. In his innocence he believes the press splash, and when Miss Vavasour cuts out Trimmer's photo to keep on her dressing table, Mr Crouchback approves. 'He deserves a frame.' Poor Trimmer has indeed been framed to appear the hero he is not, and he hates it.

In Section 6 Waugh cuts away from the desolate Cretan scenes of flight to their ironic opposite, Trimmer the hero being paraded to three drunken American journalists. The story is dead; Ian has difficulty maintaining the American journalists' interest, when they hit on a new line. On the *Aquitania* Gustave the hairdresser worked for American womanhood. 'It's the casual personal contacts that make international alliances. The beauty parlour as the school of democracy.' But Trimmer, obsessed by Virginia, refuses to cooperate. What American women did he meet on board? Not Virginia, Ian prompts, more typical ones: the journos aren't interested in Virginia.

> 'Old trouts mostly,' said Trimmer. 'Mrs Stuyvesant Oglander. There were smart ones too, of course – Astors, Vanderbilts [. . .]'
> 'What I had in mind for my readers, Colonel, was something a little more homey.'
> Trimmer had his pride. He awoke now from his reverie, sharply piqued.
> 'I never touched the homey ones,' he said. (*OG* 291)

Trimmer's refusal to say what the papers want is later paralleled by Guy, resisting Mrs Stitch's cajolery, 'the hypodermic needle of her charm', to lie about Ivor Claire's desertion. In their very different ways, both have their pride, each a commitment to his own truth. This tiny moment of comic rebellion is one of several small touches that mitigate Waugh's portrait of Trimmer.

CRETE

When Waugh began work on *Officers and Gentlemen* he advertised for 'detailed information POW routine from then junior officer taken prisoner unwounded France 1940'.[19] The specifications are very precise. Waugh must have been planning to fictionalize the experiences of Guy's nephew Tony, after he was taken prisoner at the novel's beginning, possibly to match Guy's impending surrender at the novel's end – but gave it up. 'I should have realised that one cannot live other people's experience.' Conversely, the intricate jigsaw of fact and fiction in his version of the fall of Crete is neatly constructed from his own experiences, as recorded in his diary for the last days of May 1941.

In *POMF* Waugh transferred the Cretan landscape to a barren northern terrain with just two brushstrokes ('Deep snow in the hills, thin ice in the valleys'). His diary vividly logs distracted orders and the slow tide of flight, but it also allows fleeting glimpses of Crete as it really was in late spring ('In an arbour of sweet jasmine I found Bob and Freddy...'). In *Officers and Gentlemen* Waugh dwells on this poignant incongruity. Under aerial bombardment exhausted men lie 'deep in the scrub, feeling the sun, breathing the spicy air'. Guy beds down 'behind a boulder among thorny sweet shrubs'. Cistus and jasmine flower among the farm buildings of a ruined village, sour with the smell of dirty men. 'On a fragrant hillside', dizzy with hunger, Guy's commanding officer, poor Fido Hound, loses his dignity for a lump of flaky, fat bully beef he carries off, doglike, to swallow alone.

While Waugh was working on the novel, he advised a correspondent against seeking publication for a family memoir: 'The visual scene is not always precise,' he writes; 'I was unable to *see* the Yorkshire house as I wished' (*L* 401). Conrad comparably said his task was, 'by the power of the written word, to make you hear, to make you feel, [...] above all, to make you *see*. That – and no more, and it is everything.'[20] The novel's additions to the material from Waugh's diary make us *see* the umbrella pines, abandoned courtyards, and the slit trenches cut between the irregular trunks of a wide vineyard, 'full of tiny green fruit just formed'. We *hear* the 'low monotone' of demoralized troops, and 'the flat undertone' of the retreating soldiers, a weird thing. The 'faint crescent hum' of approaching aircraft brings with it 'a nearer, louder, more doleful, scarcely more human sound, echoed from man to man along the dusty road: "Aircraft. Take cover. Take cover..."'. Waugh's narrative equably accommodates the mix of this desolate sound, the plane's burst of fire, and its disappearance into an incongruously 'silent, quattrocento heaven'.

Waugh's fictional reworking of his raw diary is best seen in its most memorable episode. He has gone off by himself.[21] Independent, exhilarated and alone, he comes to a village:

a pretty, simple place with a well in the square. I wanted to fill my bottle but the rope had been cut and the bucket stolen. I asked a peasant, in gesture, for water; he went away grumbling a refusal but I followed him into his cottage and after a bit he gave me a cupful from a stone jar.

In the square a peasant girl came and pulled at my sleeve; she was in tears. I followed her to the church, where in the yard was a British soldier on a stretcher. Flies were all over his mouth and he was dead. There was another girl by him also in tears. I think they had been looking after him. There was also a bearded peasant who shrugged and made signs that might have been meant to describe the ascent of a balloon, but which told me what I could already see. Again with signs I told them to bury him.

Then I went on. (*D* 503-4)

In the fictional version, Waugh cuts both peasants and sets the scene in sharper detail. The well is 'built about with marble steps and a rutted plinth'. In a nearby house (not 'cottage') he finds 'an earthenware jar of classic shape', and removes the straw stopper. 'He heard *and felt* a hum and, tilting it to the light, found it full of bees and a residue of honey' (my italics). In the gloom an old lady gazes at him, ignoring his requests for water, 'quite blind [...] quite deaf, quite alone'. Imperceptibly, Waugh is drawing us backwards to a timeless, classic place. Guy goes back into the sunshine, and a girl – 'ruddy, bare-footed', and in tears – takes him 'frankly' by the arm and leads him to a yard once used for livestock, where another girl is also in tears by a young English soldier on a stretcher.

The novel's pace slows. The diary's two short paragraphs are over. The soldier lies at rest, his limbs disposed like those of Sir Roger at Santa Dulcina, not awkwardly sprawled like other dead Guy has seen. He looks unhurt. 'Only the bluebottles that clustered round his lips and eyes proclaimed that he was flesh.' (Not 'dead'. Nor living 'flesh and blood'. *Flesh*, that is as grass, covered by flies.) 'Why was he lying here? Who were these girls? [...] Guy would never know.' The three stand silent beside his body, 'stiff and mute as figures in a sculptured Deposition'.

To make us feel ... Guy thinks of the boy's parents waiting, year after year, to hear of him. He kneels by the body, takes the red identity disk from his breast and leaves the green one behind, remembering the precept from his army training: 'If in doubt, gentlemen, remember that green is the colour of putrefaction.' He reads the young soldier's number, name and Catholic designation; commits his soul to God's mercy, salutes, and passes on.

*

We know from Waugh's correspondence with his researcher, how important chronology was for him.[22] Throughout the trilogy the passage of time is delicately marked by the Christian calendar, particularly Lent and Holy Week. In *Men at Arms* the limbo of Phoney War was also calibrated alongside distant major events – the invasion of Finland; the fall of Norway; the fall of France; Dunkirk. Geographical accuracy, and status were less important. Waugh's complicated progress between ranks and postings is cut and simplified in Guy's career. However, the fall of Crete was an important historical event. For Waugh there were just five days to cover, from the early hours of 28 May to the morning of 1 June, and one forty-mile retreat, from Canea on Crete's north-western coast, over the mountains and down a gorge to Sphakia on the south. For those that were there, defeat and disorder, bombardment by day, flight by night, exhaustion, hunger and fear reduced those five days over difficult terrain into an overwhelming image of timeless confusion. Waugh's task was to combine factual precision with that subjective perception.[23]

It is very hard to follow the movements of Guy, Hound, and their men, as they set out against the tide of fugitives from Canea and then with it – forwards, and then backwards – with stragglers, Guy observes, in advance of the retreating front lines in this battle.[24] The chronology, on the other hand, is there, but occluded. It is hard for the reader to keep count. In fact it is possible to chart the novel's five days against the undated diary, and to log the diary's details against those that Waugh invents.[25] This exercise reveals a paradox: Waugh follows actual chronology exactly, while recreating in the reader's mind, with equal accuracy, the fleeing army's exhausted sense of interminable, undifferentiated time. How does he do it?

The two terminal points are clearly marked. Guy and his men land on the night of 27 May. In the morning he notes on his pad: *28/6/41. Adv. Bde HQ established on track west of road* [. . .] Four days later, on the eve of surrender, Waugh writes, 'On 31 May, Guy sat in a cave overhanging the beach of Sphakia [. . .] By his watch it was not yet ten o'clock but it seemed the dead of night.' Even this apparent clarity contains confusion: Guy's note misnumbered the month. The slip is trivial, symptomatic of his tiredness, but also of Waugh's agenda. The night of that first day is marked by Guy watching the moon rise, 'a fine, opaque, white brush-stroke on the rim of her disc of shadow'. (The new moon was three days old on 28/5/41.) The second night is identified by a variation on that delicate image ('It was the moment of evening when the milky wisp of moon became sharp and luminous.') The next morning Guy leaves Hound to deliver orders on his own. That day and the next the narrative follows Hound: a jerky sequence with a whole day dropping out of the picture as he sleeps ignominiously curled up in a drain. In the next chapter the narrative returns to Guy, and the same days are re-traversed through his eyes. For the reader the long, bewildering sequence of night and day is doubled. Even though periods of daylight and darkness are distinguishable, they are no longer numbered, and the reversal of men sleeping by day and moving painfully forward at night intensifies the confusion.

It is finally worse confounded by a distracting singsong linking Guy marching (who knows when, now?) to Trimmer on his way to the American journalists, crooning Cole Porter's popular lyric.

> Night fell. [...] Guy found the remnants of his headquarters [...] They fell in and set out into the darkness. They marched all night, one silent component of the procession of lagging, staggering men. Another day; another night.
> 'Night and day,' crooned Trimmer, 'you are the one. Only you beneath the moon and under the sun.' (OG 283)

'Another day, another night' is deceptive. It does not refer to the succession of nights and days Guy has just traversed. It signals an entire further day and night that Waugh does not describe at all. By the time we leave Trimmer, Guy is at Sphakia, and it is the night of 31 May.

*

Waugh's argument moves slowly below his sparkling surface. His underlying concern is to convey the breakup of Allied discipline and morale. Gallagher quotes many participants' sense that they 'had taken part in a disgrace and were tainted by it'.[26] A brigadier condemned the Allied commanders for being 'utterly without offensive spirit'. A private spoke bitterly of the 'strange lethargy [...] cravenness of spirit and blind incompetence' preventing his unit from attacking vulnerable enemy positions. Guy, like Waugh, observes a steady sequence of enemy bombers following 'some insect-plan' of their own, and suggests they could be picked off by a single Bren gun, but nothing is done.[27]

For peacetime readers Waugh clarifies the extent of the Allied breakdown by inventing counter-examples of men who do not behave badly. There is Colonel Tickeridge, 'in high good humour', with his Halberdiers in perfect military order, carrying out a textbook 'battalion in defence'. 'They say it's *sauve qui peut* now,' says Fido Hound. 'Don't know the expression,' says Tickeridge. At a field conference he asks, 'cheerfully', 'Is this a last man, last-round defence?' No, it's a planned withdrawal. Later Guy comes across Tickeridge again, unloading injured men from a lorry, Halberdier Shanks, star of the slow valse, among the wounded, equally unperturbed.[28]

Guy passes two men by the roadside, one very old, one young, working with spades. It is the Greek General Miltiades with his interpreter. The general's driver was wounded, the young man explains. The general would not leave him. Two hours ago the driver died, and they have just buried him. Then there is the striking appearance of a dusty Cretan sports car, an exhausted New Zealand brigadier and his driver in front, a wounded brigade major sprawled in the back, 'upheld by a kneeling orderly, as though in gruesome parody of a death scene from grand opera'.

All these exemplary soldiers show care for their fellow-men and a hospitable *esprit de corps*. They drink together and share their food. They care for their dying and dead. They obey the humanizing rules of war that protect the wounded, and see to the burial of the dead – the burial parties whose instructions Guy only recently recalled. 'If in doubt, *gentlemen*, remember that green is the colour of putrefaction.' These gentlemen, not all of them officers, contrast with the rabble of an army in flight.

Fido Hound, alas, is no gentleman. Claiming urgent, non-existent reports to deliver, he ousts the New Zealanders' young driver and is reluctantly ferried by the brigadier over the mountains toward Sphakia and the sea. Hound is Waugh's painful anatomization of military discipline in breakdown, of the Allies' demoralized disorder. He is everything Waugh's paradigms of courtesy are not: frightened, greedy, driven by instinct, helplessly self-serving; a filcher of food, the deserter of his men. Hiding in his culvert under the road, he feels two deep needs, 'food and orders. He must have both or perish'. Unhappy, untrustworthy Fido is the antithesis of Felix, old Crouchback's golden retriever. He is a bad dog who's been 'off on his own, rolling in something nasty'. There is an ingratiating, craven pathos to Hound: 'He wanted to fawn and lick the correcting hand.' Yet Waugh's portrait also has compassion. The exhaustion and hunger Hound suffers and Waugh describes so well, were his own. Waugh, like Hound, knew a mind 'that curled up and slept [as] the swing of his body carried him forward from one numb foot to the other', 'eyes dazzled and befogged, a continuous faint shrilling in his ears as though from distant grasshoppers'. On the last lap of exodus, in the spectacular Imbros gorge leading to Sphakia, Waugh, like

Hound, was drawn by 'the thunderous organ tones of Kitchen' till he found the cave of fugitive Spaniards and their bubbling cauldron of 'chickens and hares and kids, pigs and peppers and cucumbers and garlic and rice and crusts of bread...' and was made welcome.[29]

However, Waugh also knew the dangers of behaviour like Hound's. Lieutenant-Colonel Colvin, Hound's original, is first mentioned in Waugh's *Diaries* after the failed raid on Bardia. Waugh did not pass on complaints that Colvin had 'behaved badly' to his commander, Bob Laycock, because 'I thought no one had behaved well enough for them to be able to afford a post mortem [...] Perhaps if I had we might have been spared some shame in Crete' (*D* 496). Not only shame. Dereliction of duty in an officer endangers his men. Communication and mutual support between troops are jeopardized by unscheduled, unreported movements. In the initial stages of breakdown Hound issues orders with no hope of having them obeyed, nor does he check their fulfilment. His reports degenerate into meaningless formulae. (Guy, conversely, is frank about having nothing to report.) Colvin and Hound both panic and lead Waugh and Guy, and their men, on a forced night march far beyond their scheduled point of retreat. In both the novel (darkly) and the *Diaries* (more clearly), there is a moment of confusion just before, implying that Hound tried to steal a motorcycle and was shot at by his men, stopping him fleeing on his own.[30]

At the evacuation from Sphakia, in the novel as in reality, specified fighting troops in good order, under their commanding officers, had priority over stragglers. The navy was capable of carrying off less than half of the 11,000 men funnelled into that tiny fishing village. An absconding officer, therefore, robbed his men of the right to escape. When Hound ousts the young New Zealand driver of the Cretan sports car, the driver is left by the roadside 'looking desperate', not merely because he'll have to make the long journey to Sphakia on foot.

Ludovic, a sinister corporal major first introduced in Book II, is pleased to find Hound, his commanding officer, unmanned and at his lowest ebb, because they need each other to get off the island. 'We both made a miscalculation,' Ludovic tells Hound. Both are deserters – but armed pickets guard the beach. There was a shambles in the night, 'Men looking for officers, officers looking for men [...] With your help we shall get off very nicely, I believe. I've got the men all lined up for parade tonight – rather a motley crowd, I fear, sir.' They are the rabble of hospitable Spaniards. We hear no more. The narrative jumps to Guy. He finds his headquarters in good order; they fall in and march for two days and nights to the sea. 'He did not enquire for Major Hound.' Six years later, Waugh provided a retrospective *Synopsis of Preceding Volumes* to introduce his final volume, *Unconditional Surrender*. It summarized Hound and Ludovic's meeting, the 'irregular body of Spanish refugees', and concluded: 'Nothing more is ever heard of Hound. It is to be supposed that Ludovic perpetrated or connived at his murder.'

It is to be supposed recurs twice in the *Synopsis*. Hound's opaque end is just one among an exceptional number of ambiguities, innuendoes, lacunae and loose ends closing this novel. There is a simple biographical reason for this. Waugh gave up his plans for a trilogy and on the dust-jacket for *Officers and Gentlemen* said that it completed Guy's story, which began in illusion and ended in disillusion. However, after he had written *Pinfold*, he returned to the trilogy with renewed confidence. On the dust-jacket of *Unconditional Surrender* he confessed that he had not been 'quite candid. I knew that a third volume was needed. I did not then feel confident that I was able to provide it.' Six years had passed. Waugh's provision of a *Synopsis* for the readers of his final volume was a practical necessity.

Moreover, there were historical reasons for the ambiguities closing *Officers and Gentlemen*. Before both Waugh and Guy's troops had even landed on Crete, their ship was boarded by a 'haggard, unshaven, shuddering Lieutenant-Commander' incoherent with panic and exhaustion. Wounded and dying pressed aboard before the fresh troops could disembark. In both fact and fiction, fighting spirit was undermined from the outset. Signallers ditched their equipment before even going ashore. The men arrived on an island where the Allies had already suffered defeat and were in retreat. On their first day both Waugh and Guy's commanders learned that their task was merely to cover the retreat, and leave last of the fighting troops. In this demoralizing situation discipline was lost, and, unsurprisingly, in the disorder of flight many crimes were committed or suspected. Many more were unguessed and unknown. Waugh's narrative gestures towards such incidents.

Several times in the *Diaries*, he mentions a martinet officer named Pedder, who appears in the novel as Prentice, 'a glaring, fleshless figure' – 'awfully mad' in Ivor Claire's words. By the time they're encamped in Egypt (from where they sailed to Crete), Prentice's men are 'on the verge of mutiny'. In both the novel and the *Diaries* Pedder/Prentice is reported to have died in a fierce engagement, probably shot from behind by his own men,[31] just as Hound thinks he is shot at as he makes his solitary escape down the mountainside to Sphakia, and probably earlier too. Waugh specifically names one deserter in his *Diaries*.[32] In the novel, among many nameless, Roots and Slimbridge from Guy's own troop abscond when volunteering to forage for food. In both *Diaries* and novel Waugh and Guy give a lift to an officer with a 'preposterous haw-haw voice' later suspected by both of being a private soldier in stolen uniform. All these specified figures are cut or unnamed in the final *Sword of Honour*. Too many men behaved badly for individual censure. Against a dark background of dubious practice *Officers and Gentlemen* focuses on the fully realised figures of Hound, Ludovic, Ivor Claire, Mrs Stitch and Guy. Deliberate ambiguities concerning them add to the confusing Cretan ambience, where all 'is smothered in surmise, / And nothing is but what is not'.[33]

HOUND AND LUDOVIC

In *Officers and Gentlemen* Waugh floats a number of unresolved possibilities about Hound's death. We last see him replete with the Spaniards' food, in their cave, being watched over by Ludovic, who makes clear their need of each other to escape from Crete, Hound acting as commanding officer, with Ludovic and his rabble of fugitives as Hound's legitimate fighting force. Hound could have been killed by the Spaniards, whose lawlessness was suggested when the company was encamped in Egypt pending their departure to Crete, and the lightly buried body of a taxi driver with his throat cut was found near their lines. *Or* Hound could have been shot by one of the checkpoints guarding access to the beach, because either his or

Ludovic's rabble didn't pass muster. Before Hound and his company had even got ashore on Crete, the haggard lieutenant-commander boarding their ship turned to Hound and 'with an awful personal solicitude' warned him, 'You've got to know the password, you know [...] They'll shoot you as soon as look at you, those sentries'. Historically, at Sphakia there were cordons keeping the rabble back at bayonet point. *Or* Hound could have been killed by Ludovic when Ludovic's ruse failed, *or* if Hound refused to acquiesce. Among many possibilities and no certainties, Hound simply drops out of the picture. Ludovic's murder of Hound is made clear in the later *Synopsis* preceding *Unconditional Surrender* ('It is to be supposed that Ludovic perpetrated or connived at his murder'), but the facts still remain murky. Later, planning *his* novel, one of Ludovic's guilty nightmares is his heroine's possible fate 'immured in a cave or left to drift in an open boat'.

More ambiguities surround Ludovic. A menacing figure of obscure origins, he first appears as a hanger-on from Ivor Claire's barracks who volunteered as a reservist claiming the rank of corporal of horse. Clear implications that his claim was false are capped by as yet indecipherable innuendos suggesting an unwelcome connection, possibly homosexual, possibly black-mail, between Ludovic and Claire, which Claire breaks by the usual ploy of unmerited promotion.[34] Ludovic has a strong gift for self-preservation; he is adept at threatening insinuation. Guy says he 'looks like a dishonest valet'; Waugh duly gives him a plummy Jeevesian servility with disconcerting lapses into harsh vernacular. He takes control of poor Hound, vulnerable in his extremity, capturing and feeding him in order to exploit his officer status, threatening him with disclosure if he refuses. Ludovic also tries to manipulate Guy, when Guy finds him on the beach at Sphakia in the last hours before surrender. Ludovic uses the same euphemism he employed with Hound ('we both made a miscalculation'), in a failed attempt to insinuate his and Guy's shared guilt as deserters:

> 'I thought you'd deserted us?'
> 'Did you, sir? Perhaps we both made a miscalculation.'
> 'Have you seen Major Hound?'
> *'Oh yes, sir. I was with him until – as long as he needed me, sir.'*
> *'Where is he now? Why have you left him?'*

'Need we go into that, sir? Wouldn't you say it was rather too early or rather too late for enquiries of that sort?' (*OG* 299, my italics)

The italicized lines were cut in the *Sword of Honour* text, as was the give-away *Synopsis*, so sustaining the mystery of what had happened to Hound well beyond the confines of *Officers and Gentlemen*, and deep into the last book of the trilogy.

In the last hour before surrender Ludovic joins Guy and several others in the small fishing smack a sapper sets afloat to try and sail from Crete to Egypt (as some, not all, did successfully, according to the *Diaries*).[35] Waugh does not explain how the sapper dies. Maddened by extreme exposure, fearing Ludovic is planning to kill him, he begs Guy for his gun. Guy drops the gun overboard. The next morning the sapper is gone. The *Synopsis* elucidates. '*It is to be supposed* that Ludovic precipitated him.' That elucidation is also eliminated from *Sword of Honour*'s final version, leaving us smothered in surmise. May we conclude that the delirious sapper had indeed over-heard Ludovic plotting to kill him? The neutral narrative does not preclude it.

IVOR CLAIRE

Claire, like Hound, vanishes from sight in Crete. Where did he go? From his first appearance on Mugg, bandaged and at his ease on a divan, he was always adept at seeing to his own comfort. Breaking camp in Egypt, he spent two weeks in a private nursing home with a twisted knee, supposedly incurred leading a party 'armed with tent-mallets' against Arab marauders (an easy innuendo to unpick: he was playing polo). In Crete he only reappears on the last night, driven into Sphakia's stranglehold with all the remaining troops, waiting to surrender as ordered at dawn. Claire tries to persuade Guy that the orders are confused: 'I was at Dunkirk you know. Not much fuss about priorities there. No inquiries afterwards.' His plea confirms suspicions of Claire's guilt at Dunkirk. Guy is inflexible: he has the orders in writing. Claire switches tack, arguing that honour is a temporal, not absolute, virtue. At one time it would have been dishonourable to dodge the challenge to a duel. Now Guy would laugh at it. Isn't the same true of desertion?

'And in the next war [...] I expect it will be quite honourable for officers to leave their men behind. It'll be laid down [...] as their duty – to keep a *cadre* going to train new men to take the place of prisoners.'
'Perhaps men wouldn't take kindly to being trained by deserters.'
'Don't you think in a really modern army they'd respect them the more for being fly?' (*OG* 295)

Guy and Waugh's revulsion is left unspoken, and once again Waugh leaves the episode in the air. 'Ivor stood up saying, "Well, the path of honour lies up the hill" and strolled away.' Up, or down? Down to the harbour to surrender? Or up into the hills, like the single sturdy soldier the next morning who shouldered his pack and went back up the mountain alone to join the Cretan guerillas?

Neither. Once again the later *Synopsis* clarifies: 'That night Clare [sic] deserts his troop and insinuates himself into the embarkation.' Downhill to disgrace. Even Trimmer, running away from Operation Popgun, wasn't allowed to leave without his resourceful men. He had to wait for their return to the rendezvous, and they boarded their craft together.

In *Men at Arms* Waugh set up both 'Truslove', the aspirational hero of the children's war books admired by Guy as a schoolboy, and Truslove's fictional antithesis, the 'showy polo-player named Congreve', who funked foreign service and resigned from the cadre. His name was banned; his fiancée broke off their engagement; his entire company felt 'tainted' by his defection (*MA* 275). Congreve's real function was to introduce a predictive fictional parallel to polo-playing Ivor Claire, so associating Guy's distress at Claire's desertion with the schoolboy idealism that motivated Guy and many of his fellow soldiers at the beginning of the war.

Early in his writing career Waugh realized that his personal morality was out of kilter with his times. On his first visit to Addis Ababa, he was startled by the egotistical vanity of a fellow visitor, remarking in his diary, 'I think I must be a prig, people do shock me so' (*D* 334). He went on worrying at this problem in *Remote People*, the travel book covering the Abyssinian trip: 'It seems to me that a prig is someone who judges people by his own, rather than by their, standards' (*RP* 51). This was certainly a problem for Waugh. In 'Fan-Fare' it lies behind his denial of being a satirist, because satire depends on a stable society with 'homogenous moral standards', while the society for which he writes no longer shares an (actually, *his*) established moral system (*EAR* 104). After *Officers and Gentlemen* was published, Waugh echoed this preoccupation when he wrote to Anthony Powell conceding that 'Crouchback junior (not so his admirable father) is a prig. But he is a virtuous, brave prig. If he had funked, the defection of "Ivor Claire" could not have had the necessary impact on him' (*L* 443). Guy's revulsion at Claire's defection is personal, instinctive and absolute, an instinct deriving from Waugh's own priggishness. In the eyes of Tommy Blackhouse and Mrs Stitch, Guy's disapprobation is irrelevant and unsustainable.

MRS STITCH

Mrs Stitch is a profoundly ambivalent figure. Her attractions are obvious, 'a beauty' leaning against Guy, 'light and balmy', bubbling with cultured chatter, a dazzling hostess, an impenitent eccentric. She is also deeply flawed. Even in *Scoop* she had feet of clay.[36] Her first meeting with Guy twice sounds an ominous bossy note ('Take it, fool'; 'Other side, fool'). Waugh's uneasy relationship with her acknowledged original, Diana Cooper, is very evident in their lifelong correspondence. When they first met, she later told Waugh, she determined to bind him to her 'with hoops of steel'. Thereafter Waugh teasingly signed a letter to her with 'Hoops of Steel, Bo' (his nickname). She *was* steely – irresistibly demanding, outspokenly judgemental, while playing a Baby's frail feminine role (her pet name for herself). Waugh had a difficult relationship with her husband, the prominent politician Duff Cooper; in the Pinfold period interrupting this novel, he was suspicious of her manipulation and reluctantly acquiescent to her cajolery. In *Officers and Gentlemen*, in order to protect Ivor Claire from the disgrace of his desertion, Mrs Stitch lies on Claire's behalf, and ships him out of trouble to India. She tries and fails to persuade Guy to confirm the story she concocted for Claire. Through her unofficial power in high places, she secretly organizes Guy's unwilling departure by slow ship to England, instead of joining his beloved Brigadier Ritchie-Hook and the promise of real offensive action at last.

This episode, the novel's dénouement, differs from those discussed above because what is hidden from Guy is clear to the reader. His vulnerable naïveté arouses our anxiety; his slow resistance to Mrs Stitch's cajolery relieves us. His integrity appears secure – until her last, devastating deceit. We know that she knows that Guy has documents disproving Claire's story. We fear she will steal them. We are anxious and then relieved when she takes Guy to her own house to recuperate after his escape from Crete. This moment is full of conflicting signs. Her hospitality is marred by his lodgings – an unfurnished basement room, only the bare feet of Berber servants visible in the kitchen courtyard outside, and Mrs Stitch, her arms full of fragrant tuberoses 'dancing lightly from cockroach to cockroach across the concrete floor', to make it perfectly habitable.

In the Prologue to *Men at Arms* (*MA* 8) Waugh had described 'an almost etiolated cow in an underground stable from which sometimes she escaped' at Castello Crouchback. The cow is a perfect example of Waugh's bizarre leitmotifs spanning this trilogy – an even wider range of texts than in *Brideshead* – to suggest lightly what is never directly stated. Early in *Officers and Gentlemen* Waugh describes the cow's escape during Mrs Stitch's single, chance visit to Castello Crouchback many years before the war. Mrs Stitch was the only guest in the party visiting the Castello to join in the chase, 'grasp the halter and lead [the cow] back with soothing words to her subterranean stall' (*OG* 124–5). When Mrs Stitch meets Guy in Alexandria, she reminds him of that distant episode – her first words, in idiomatic Italian and a rich Genoese accent, are 'The cow has escaped' '*C'è scappata la mucca*' (*OG* 166). After Guy's escape from Crete, she visits Guy in hospital in Alexandria, recovering from exposure, and changes the refrain to idiomatic Italian for 'The Captain has escaped' '*C'è scappato il Capitano*' (*OG* 310). Guy has escaped from Crete, but not in the same way as Claire. She then helps Claire escape further, and takes the etiolated Guy, still recovering from extended exposure, prisoner in her subterranean stall.

But she does *not* search his room and filch his papers, as we fear. Instead, she sends Guy home before he can report Ivor's defection to Ritchie-Hook, who is notoriously implacable in his pursuit of deserters. And then comes the reversal. At his departure, Guy asks Mrs Stitch to post an envelope addressed to

Central Headquarters, not thinking to explain that it contains the dead young soldier's identity disk. She takes it benignly, waves Guy off, turns back into the house and drops it into the waste-paper basket, her famously huge blue eyes 'one immense sea, full of flying galleys'.

Waugh had to explain the implications of this to Nancy Mitford: 'Mrs Stitch threw away Guy's letter because she thought it contained the incriminating war diary of Hookforce in Crete. War Diaries had to be sent to CHQ Records by Intelligence Officers' (L 446). For the bemused, unhappy reader, the main point is nevertheless painfully clear. The compassion in those lovely eyes is ruthless, and is lavished on a coward who fled. Guy will never know that his trust was betrayed and his duty thwarted to protect Ivor Claire, a friend whom he no longer honours. The young soldier's family will never be told of his certain death. A second restless spirit entrusted to Guy's care, a far cry from Apthorpe's – another unburied Palinurus or Elpenor – has joined the millions of nameless, unacknowledged dead.

GUY AND WAUGH

A cluster of modern commentators has settled on Ivor Claire's defection. It has been fly-blown into a covert confession that Waugh funked, illicitly insinuating himself into the embarkation like Claire, together with his commanding officer, Bob Laycock. Hence the shame, otherwise inexplicable to these critics, which Waugh embodies in Guy.

Waugh did not need to commit a crime to be ashamed of Crete. Even the tiny failure of Dakar had left him feeling dishonoured, 'with head unbloody but bowed' (L 145). From the beginning of the war he, like Guy, had been driven by the yearning to serve a just cause. 'Why was the young soldier lying still unburied in the deserted village of Crete, if it was not for Justice?'

Encamped in Egypt before Crete, Waugh had gone into Alexandria for his Easter confession, '& had to have the priest arrested for asking questions of military significance' (L 151). In the novel Guy reports this experience to Hound, who does nothing about it. When his omission is discovered Hound writes a report in glib officalese insinuating the opposite of the truth, that Guy has been investigated *for* a breach of security, not that he had reported a threat *to* security. In due course Grace-Groundling-Marchpole adds the report to his growing file that will incriminate Guy. Ironically enough, this epitomizes the intrepid scepticism of Waugh's Grace-Groundling-Marchpole-like detractors: they will not be taken in by his high ideals and unaccountable shame, convinced that a mendacious, bullying hypocrite lurks below.

Waugh was a clear-sighted, fallible romantic idealist who found the timeless security he needed in his faith. In his early middle age he sought and sporadically found a lesser, human haven in military *esprit de corps*. He loved some of his fellow soldiers and commanders 'deeply and tenderly'. Disappointments in his own career came often. Some are passed on to Guy and described without rancour. Like Waugh, 'he had twice put up captain's stars and twice removed them; their scars were plainly visible on his shoulder straps' (*US* 5). Yet there is no hype over Waugh's sense of personal disappointment, neither when he fails himself, nor in his larger, shared shame when participating in the collapse of an entire army. When Guy recognizes that his ideals are a hallucination, he takes his war diary to the incinerator in Mrs Stitch's kitchen courtyard, and burns it. It is 'a symbolic act'. He will not pursue Claire for the sake of Justice. He is likened to the man stripping his gun at Sphakia harbour, and dropping it, piece by piece, 'splash, splash, splash, into the scum'. Burning the true record of his diary is Guy's symbolic surrender to the fly world of Claire, Trimmer, Kilbannock and Mrs Stitch, which Waugh associates with cockroaches, dustbins, garbage, and scum.

13

The Ordeal of Gilbert Pinfold 1957

Officers and Gentlemen was sent off to the publishers in November 1954. In January 1955, fleeing the English winter again, Waugh took another sea journey to Jamaica, where he began the first chapter of *Pinfold*. Many distractions, including two libel suits which Waugh won, interrupted its progress. It was finally written and completed between September 1956 and January 1957.

The events leading up to Waugh's brief bout of madness are well documented, and accurately recounted in what he pointedly called a 'novel' only in inverted commas.[1] It was not a novel because it was not fiction. As Waugh assured both correspondents and later interviewers, its material was all true, but selectively summarized. Hence the work's subtitle, 'A Conversation Piece'. It is a conversation piece because it is all about Pinfold's Voices. After the event, Waugh's aural hallucinations also provided a rich topic for his own conversation. Consequently, it is very difficult not to read Pinfold as Waugh, particularly when he privately noted that 'The book is too personal for me to be able to judge it' (*D* 769).[2]

Waugh suffered from insomnia all his life. By 1953 he was using a soporific concoction of bromide and choral, roughly mixed and as strong as the whim took him. To mask its unpleasant flavour he began lacing it with *crème de menthe*, adding repeated doses as required during the night. By day, it proved effective against new, unexplained pains in his legs.

His friendships began to suffer. On a visit to Diana Cooper in Paris, he quarrelled sharply with her husband, also an irascible man. Lady Diana mended the breach. In July the rift deepened in a serious, barely healed quarrel with Lady Diana. Randolph Churchill, Waugh's old companion-in-arms, rashly involved himself as an ineffectual peacemaker. Christopher Sykes, another old friend, found Waugh inexplicably distant. On New Year's Eve Duff Cooper died as revellers on shipboard to America caroused outside his cabin. Lady Diana was deeply offended by Waugh's brief letter of commiseration. *Officers and Gentlemen* had been going badly for months. Waugh was worried about money. His futuristic dystopic novella, *Love Among the Ruins* (a slight work lovingly and indeed finely illustrated by Waugh himself), had been published to what Waugh identified as 'curious claims to intimacy', particularly in the noticeably unanimous, hostile Beaverbrook press. He responded by a general essay on deteriorating standards in literary reviews, specifically detailing and ironically parrying the Beaverbrook journalists' insults.[3] Not to be browbeaten, he then agreed to an interview for *Personal Call*, a radio programme, which was conducted in Waugh's library at Piers Court. Stephen Black, the interviewer, seemed supercilious; his questions were personal and slightingly unliterary. Waugh's son Auberon, who listened to the recording in the radio van outside, shrewdly noted that the interviewer 'did not seem to like my Father much'.[4] Waugh forbade the programme's transmission in the UK and USA. Yet in September he agreed to another interview, once again with Black, now reinforced by two others, for a different series called *Frankly Speaking*. In a mutually cordial, concessive exchange the BBC guaranteed no 'pseudo-intimacy,' while Waugh promised to answer 'any' questions on 'general subjects'. The resulting interview also displeased him. He requested, and got, a rerun. With his permission the BBC spliced the two texts. Even now, in toneless transcript, Waugh's interrogation sounds shocking. His indistinguishably hostile interviewers take advantage of the agreed conditions to ask general, non-literary questions designed to prove him the cartoon monster of his popular reputation. Waugh achieved a difficult balance – refusing to duck out of rebarbative opinions attributed to him, while remaining ruthlessly rational in his dry replies. Raising Waugh's reputed approval of capital punishment, for instance, one questioner asks blandly:

And you yourself would be prepared to carry it out?
Do you mean actually do the hanging as such?
Yes.
Very odd of them to choose a novelist for such a task.

Later:

Do you find it easy to get on with the man in the street?
I've never met such a person.
[...] *How do you find people of various countries* [...] *are they all much the same as you were now saying?*
I clearly cannot make myself understood [...] There is no such thing as a man in the street, there is no ordinary run of mankind, there are only individuals who are totally different.[5]

Finally, in December, came Betjeman's Great Benefaction. Knowing Waugh's love of ornate Victoriana, Betjeman offered him the magnificent gift of an elaborately decorated washstand by William Burges.[6] Waugh inspected it minutely at the home of a mutual friend, accepted with delight – and on its arrival found it lacked one vividly recollected detail, a serpentine ornamental pipe which he draws for Betjeman, pathetically asking 'Did I dream this or did it exist' (*L* 417). Although comparable lapses of memory were also worrying him, he maintained his intellectual robustness, dismissing the Box, a contemporary fad favoured by a neighbouring friend, which was reputed to effect long-distance cures via the patient's tissue samples, radar, and transmission of 'Life Waves'.

All this back-history fed into the Pinfold experience. In late January 1954, face empurpled, hands blotchy, leaning heavily on two sticks, Waugh stumbled aboard the *Staffordshire*, bound for Ceylon. As he finished off the last of his soporifics, the voices began. His first letter to Laura mentions the noises in his cabin which 'my p.m. [Waugh's familiar spirit, persecution mania] took for other passengers whispering about me'. Yet he tries to appear optimistic. 'It was at 50 that Rosetti's chloral taking involved him in attempted suicide, part blindness & part paralysis. We will avoid all that' (*L* 418). He did not know that withdrawal triggered aural hallucinations, which had also afflicted Rossetti.

*

Waugh wrote his first book, a biography of Rossetti, when he was twenty-five. In hindsight it offers a disconcertingly close analogue to Waugh's current sufferings.[7] In 1869 Rossetti, like Waugh, *appeared to those outside his own circle as a very prosperous and self-satisfied man, so accustomed to praise as to invite criticism.* Yet, like Waugh, he was *tortured with insomnia,* melancholic and unstable. When he was forty (not fifty, as the fifty-year-old Waugh remembered), his doctor introduced him to chloral, then a novelty narcotic reputedly free of negative side-effects. Like Waugh, Rossetti was an insouciant self-medicator. *He took it in fabulous quantities.* The more his friends diluted it, the more he drank. Like Waugh, *to make matters worse, since he found the taste of the drug disagreeable, he acquired the habit of gulping large glassfuls of neat whisky after each dose.* Both Rossetti and Waugh found reliable sleep essential for their creative work. As Rossetti wrote to Ford Madox Brown: *'The fact is that any man in my case must either do as I do or cease from necessary occupation, which cannot be pursued in the day when the night is stripped of rest.'*

In both Rossetti and Waugh, mild paranoia was aggravated by hostile professional criticism. After the dissemination of Buchanan's notorious attack on 'The Fleshly School of Poetry', Rossetti *was devoured by the distressing and not uncommon delusion that the whole world was banded together against him in a conspiracy of infinite ramifications.* He ended his long friendship with Browning through misreading the last lines of 'Fifine at the Fair' as a personal insult. In Lewis Carroll's harmless 'Hunting of the Snark' *he discovered an elaborate satire on himself.* As other reviews echoed Buchanan, *malevolence stared at him in the eyes of strangers in the street; every tiny mishap in his every day life [...] had become in his mind the work of his enemies.* His friends took him into their care, and watched over him. One night, *on retiring to bed he heard himself addressed by a voice in his room in terms of 'gross and unbearable obloquy'. Despairing of ever freeing himself from his ubiquitous and insuperable enemies, he* [took] *poison and rolled over to sleep.*

Rossetti's friends resuscitated him. He survived, initially severely crippled. Waugh, limping heavily aboard the *Staffordshire,* was made of stronger stuff.

AT SEA

There is only one published letter, partially quoted above, from Waugh to Laura on shipboard, when he had already given up his medication and, in spite of the incipient voices, was feeling better. His tone is lucid and painfully tender: 'When I wake up which I do 20 or 30 times a night I always turn to the other bed and am wretched you aren't there & puzzled you are not...'. As his aural hallucinations grew louder, he fell silent.

We can turn instead to the little-known recollections of a sympathetic fellow-passenger, known only as Gwen.[8] On the bitterly cold day when everyone boarded, Waugh came into the lounge, looking so 'oh – awful' that another passenger said, 'It's a bit much coming on drunk at this time of day'. Gwen simply thought he was ill. Nor, later, did she think he drank much ('Everyone drinks on ships'). His behaviour certainly was eccentric. At breakfast 'people were saying there's something odd about that man, he's talking to the toast-rack. There were little lamps on the tables with pink shades and he'd have a long conversation with those.' At other times he appeared to be perfectly normal. 'We weren't against him. We really did try...'. One afternoon, he was sitting looking rather lost in the small bar lounge while Gwen was doing a crossword, 'so I looked across to him and said, Mr Waugh, you ought to know this. How do you spell Naiad? Is it N I A I D or N A I A D and he looked up and smiled and he said, "That's always a word that puzzles me. What are you doing?" so [...] I went over to him and he was perfectly all right. He was absolutely lucid then. And we discussed children's books, *The Wind in the Willows*, and *Alice...*'. That choice of books is indisputably true to Waugh.

Waugh's cabin looked onto the promenade deck; Gwen's was on the deck below. Throughout the ten days and nights from Liverpool to Port Said, their first port of call, she was disturbed by his knocking at her door asking for a Miss Margaret Black.[9] A nurse on her way to Colombo managed to quiet him one difficult morning, but 'he seemed to go off in the evenings'. Once Gwen passed Waugh on her way to the dancing, and asked whether he would join them. 'He put his hands over his ears and said, No. I, it's the noise. All this noise, music in my ears, I think I'm going mad...'. Another frightening night, he hurled a stool down at her as she made her way up to the promenade deck. She told the captain, whom Waugh was pestering about untransmitted wireless messages and an unknown Commander Campbell.[10] A tough Lancashire businessman, Gwen's helpful neighbour on the lower deck, was disembarking at Port Said, and Waugh was put ashore under his care. He drove Waugh to Cairo, and after two days managed to get him on a flight to Colombo. Gwen's last glimpse of Waugh was on the high verandah of Colombo's main hotel, looking down at his fellow-passengers in the dining room below. 'Oh Lord,' she says she thought, 'I hope he doesn't throw a chair onto one of the tables...'.

From the novel it appears that Waugh did not realize his own potential for violence. Pinfold is portrayed as leaving the ship of his own accord, with dignity. Gwen's other details tally with the novel. Pinfold uses the little pink-shaded lamp on his dining table as an intercom to his persecutors. He searches for the bluff old soldiers conjured from his voices. He makes enquiries about missing telegrams home. He accepts the apparently casual friendliness of Mr Murdoch, the fellow-passenger whom he suspects to be a secret agent. This is Gwen's tough Lancashire man ('His manner was genial and his voice richly redolent of the industrial North'), who offers to take him in his company car from Port Said to Cairo. It is clear, if we read the details carefully, that many people were anxious about Pinfold/Waugh, and were taking care of him.[11]

In the novel, Pinfold is surprised to hear that he has been at sea only for four days, and has sent his wife one telegram rather than a dozen. Time is as fluidly undistinguishable as it once was in Crete. Waugh appears to have written only one letter to Laura from the *Staffordshire*. The next is from Cairo, the last three from Ceylon. In these three weeks Waugh struggles to find rational explanations for his paranoia. Like Pinfold, he is determined to reduce the irrational to explicable order, preferring to accept the malice of others because he thinks it is a factual reality, rather than believe in his own madness. From Cairo he writes:

> I must have been more poisoned than I knew. Then when I was beginning to rally I found myself the victim of an experiment in telepathy which made me think I really was going crazy [...] I don't know what I wrote to you on the ship or even if I wrote to you at all.

I was semi-delirious all the time so disregard whatever I wrote
except my deep love [...] Hand is steady today and the malevolent
telepathy broken for the first time [...] Please don't be alarmed by
the references to telepathy. I know it sounds like acute p.m. but it is
real & true. A trick the existentialists invented – half mesmerism –
which is most alarming when applied without warning or explanation to a sick man. (L 418–9)

From Colombo:

> My Darling,
> It is rather difficult to write to you because everything I say or
> think or read is read aloud by the group of psychologists whom I
> met in the ship. I hoped that they would lose this art after I went
> ashore but the artful creatures can communicate from many
> hundreds of miles away. Please don't think this is balmy [sic]. I
> should certainly have thought so three weeks ago but it is a fact &
> therefore doesn't worry me particularly. [...] It is a huge relief to
> realise that I am merely the victim of the malice of others, not mad
> myself as I really feared for a few days. (L 419–20)

His next letter ends 'As I write this I hear the odious voices of
the psychologists repeating every word in my ear. As they are in
Aden & I am here it is a more remarkable feat than Tanker's Box
[...] You must realise that this is the reason for the rather cold
tone of this letter.' In the last, equally constrained letter, 'I am
still grossly afflicted by the psychologists'.

RETURN

Laura, understandably anxious, confided in their friends,
Frances and Jack Donaldson. Jack agreed to fly to Colombo
and bring Waugh home, but Waugh arrived in London while
Jack was still waiting for the required inoculations. Laura went
alone to meet Waugh at the Hyde Park Hotel, and quickly
convinced him that 'Margaret' had no relationship to Stephen
Black. On Waugh's instructions she rang the BBC, who told her
that Black was in hospital, not on a cruise to Colombo. The
Waughs then invited their friend, Father Caraman,[12] to join
them for dinner, without explaining why. For him, the dinner-
table conversation was enough: Waugh 'was as mad as a coot'.
Caraman rang his friend, Dr Eric Strauss, head of psychiatry at

St Bartholomew's and a Roman Catholic, who joined them to make his diagnosis. After a polite exchange, Strauss asked about Waugh's drugs and alcohol intake, and quickly concluded that Waugh's aural hallucinations were caused by excess of phenobarbitone and alcohol. They would have faded faster had he been able to eat and sleep properly. Laura was sent to fetch a prescription for paraldehyde, a safe soporific, from the night chemist, and as Strauss and Caraman saw the Waughs into the lift up to their room, Strauss said to Caraman, 'Wouldn't it be wonderful if the voices stopped tonight!' As they did, more or less.

All subsequent accounts of this evening derive from three primary sources.[13] Father Caraman was the sole witness at the Hyde Park Hotel (Strauss died soon after). His written account is quoted in Sykes's biography of Waugh, and its gist is repeated, in less detail, in Caraman's later interview with Nicholas Shakespeare. Immediately on their return from London, the Waughs invited the Donaldsons to dinner at Piers Court, and told them what had happened. Frances Donaldson vividly describes this occasion in her clear-sighted *Portrait of a Country Neighbour*. Sykes quotes both first-hand sources at length, and adds peripheral details from his own later conversations with Waugh. All three interconnecting accounts tally, barring one noticeable anomaly unique to Caraman, and not repeated in his Nicholas Shakespeare interview:

> Almost immediately after sitting down [to dinner] Evelyn [...] leaned across and asked me abruptly to exorcise him: this (he explained) was the reason why I had been invited to dinner. He said he was being tormented by devils; then he repeated aloud to me what the voices had just told him about myself: nothing insulting but (as far as I recollect) simply that I was a priest who had the power to put his tormenters to flight. My first reaction was to suppose that Evelyn was acting the madman. Only when he persisted and became pressing in his demand for an exorcism did I begin to fear he might be in earnest. (Sykes 364)

When Waugh left the dinner table to go to the lavatory, Caraman asked Laura if he was serious. She told him about Waugh's letters from Ceylon. On Waugh's return, Caraman made it clear that there could be no exorcism until he had seen a doctor.

Judging by Frances Donaldson's account, the Waughs said nothing of this to them. Yet Waugh certainly feared he might be possessed. His only other published personal letter from Ceylon was to Diana Cooper, repeating the substance of his letters to Laura but ending, 'Oh dear, you will think me insane or possessed by devils. Perhaps you have something there' (*Wu/ Stitch* 188). After *Pinfold's* publication, other sufferers from aural hallucinations wrote to Waugh. His sympathetic reply to Robert Henriques[14] can hardly have been reassuring: 'My voices ceased as soon as I was intellectually convinced that they were imaginary. I do not absolutely exclude the possibility of daemonic possession as the source of them' (*L* 494).

Frances Donaldson's account of Waugh's manner immediately on his return to Piers Court is insightful. He was thin, which suited him, and 'extremely pleased with himself. He had the air of someone who had brought off an unexpected coup, or discovered in himself some unexpected gift' (Donaldson 61). That coup was his victory over the voices; the gift – a hamper full of fresh literary material. Both Sykes and Donaldson were surprised by his uninhibited public boasts that 'I have been suffering from a sharp but brief attack of insanity'; 'I've been off my head'; 'Yes, I've been quite mad'.[15] But, as Donaldson observes, Waugh was 'immensely attracted to madness'. She compares him to Dennis Barlow in *The Loved One*, catching his breath when he first sees Aimée, 'her eyes greenish and remote, with *a rich glint of lunacy*' (*LO* 46, my italics). While writing *Pinfold*, Waugh told his friend, Daphne Fielding, that he'd met and failed to recognize her son at a party. But 'then I saw his mothers lovely mad eyes and [...] goodness I fell in love [...] I say, talking of mad, I am full in the middle of writing an account of my going off my rocker. It seems funny to me. Would you think it awful cheek if I dedicated it to you?' (*L* 476) She didn't. It is duly dedicated TO DAPHNE IN THE CONFIDENCE THAT HER ABOUND-ING SYMPATHY WILL EXTEND EVEN TO POOR PINFOLD.[16]

Yet there is little self-indulgence in Waugh's portrayal of poor Pinfold. Frances Donaldson says that on that first evening,

> he told [his] story with a detachment and a mockery that if he had been speaking of some other person would have seemed, as he often did seem, inhumanly cruel and insensitive. It was not merely that the element of self-pity was entirely missing; although he had

recovered his senses only two or three days before, he quite clearly regarded his misadventures as outrageously funny. In him the sense of the ridiculous was much stronger than the kinder emotions. (Donaldson 62)

Waugh's vision, particularly when directed on himself, is unsparing. Pinfold is a comic grotesque, just as Waugh often saw himself in his diaries. Like Waugh, he drinks to get through the tedium of family Christmas, and once, 'catching sight of himself in the looking-glass, thus empurpled and wearing a paper crown, he took fright at what he saw'. Hence Waugh's uncharacteristic wish to reproduce an ultra-modern Francis Bacon painting for the book's dust jacket. Something specially commissioned would be prohibitively expensive, he says, but 'an existing horror' would do nicely.[17]

THE 'NOVEL'

The Ordeal of Gilbert Pinfold occupies an anomalous position in Waugh's *oeuvre*. A rough division can be made between his earlier, predominantly satiric works, and the later, overtly Catholic novels, even though in chronological terms the two overlap. On the one hand we have *Decline and Fall, Vile Bodies, Black Mischief, A Handful of Dust, Scoop, Put Out More Flags*, and *The Loved One*. On the other, *Work Suspended, Brideshead Revisited, Helena*, and the *Sword of Honour* trilogy. The satiric works tend towards the surreal and absurd; the Catholic novels are predominantly rational and realistic. In *Pinfold* the two extremes become one, because Pinfold's phantasmagoric experiences are a subjective reality and Waugh's illusions were a biographical fact. Furthermore, all the satiric novels present a disordered world whose apparent chaos is artistically controlled. Scrutinize the kaleidoscope, and a perfect pattern is revealed. In *Pinfold*, on the contrary, no coherence underpins the chaos. Waugh's original blurb was explicit. In Pinfold's world 'on the borderline of sanity, the reason remains strenuously active but the information on which it acts is delusory'. In interview he repeated: 'It was not in the least like losing one's reason, it was simply one's reason working hard but on the wrong premises.'[18] Thus in this novel alone, apparent formlessness is its appropriate form, and irrationality its *raison d'être*.

This paradox is sharpened by the supremely rational self-portrait opening the novel. Chapter One, 'Portrait of the Artist in Middle Age', is Waugh's direct riposte to the spurious intimacy claimed by the Beaverbrook press and Stephen Black's BBC interviews. The impertinent camaraderie promised by catchy titles like *Personal Call, Frankly Speaking,* and even the later *Face to Face,* is repudiated by Waugh's uniquely authoritative portrait of himself as Gilbert Pinfold. Instead of the cartoon grotesque of the radio interviews, Waugh offers an objective analysis of a complex, often absurd figure solidly based on his own reality. There is no navel-gazing, no subjective self-indulgence, and no false modesty either. Pinfold stands 'quite high' among the novelists of his own generation; like them, he is notable for 'elegance and variety of contrivance'. Assiduous students seek in vain for contemporary fads and cosmic significance in his work, because 'Mr Pinfold gave nothing away. Not that he was secretive or grudging by nature; he had nothing to give.' His aesthetic is modest and impersonal: 'He regarded his books as objects which he had made, things quite external to himself to be used and judged by others.' Thus his friends, family, and the reader are beckoned in, and held at arm's length: 'He offered the world a front of *pomposity mitigated by indiscretion* that was as hard, bright and antiquated as a cuirass' (my italics). The terms of this lapidary self-assessment are characteristically disenchanted. In relation to *Pinfold* they require a positive inflexion. Waugh's impenitent indiscretion has the penitential honesty of the confessional. Linguistically, the articulate 'pomposity' of the (self-)portrait's controlled and savoured style has the serene precision of a Holbein.

It is significant that the title of the first chapter – 'Portrait of the Artist in Middle Age' – gestures towards James Joyce's *Portrait of the Artist as a Young Man.* In his youth Waugh flirted with Modernism. Like Joyce, he was fascinated by the early cinema. His first, highly experimental short story, *The Balance* (1925), displaced traditional narrative by recasting it as the action of a silent film (in roman type), punctuated by the film's explanatory captions (in capitals), intercut by comments from the cinema audience (in italics), spliced with traditional third-person narrative and internal monologue.[19] Waugh matured into an inveterate *enfant terrible,* with a healthy scorn for his literary forbears. Two years before his death, in a rare, happy interview, he teasingly ridiculed Joyce as a 'poor dotty Irishman', once a good writer, latterly hired by the American avant-garde to write 'gibberish'. ('If you read *Ulysses*, it's perfectly sane for a little bit, and then it gets madder and madder.') In his youth, he explained, many talented authors were deflected into stream of consciousness, that 'tremendous blind alley in which they gave what everyone was thinking and feeling apart from what they were saying or doing'. This is precisely what Waugh avoided from his earliest novels to his last. His aesthetic is classically objective and simple, following the precept of showing, not telling:

> The novelist deals with speech and action, and time sequence. It isn't the novelist's business to feed readers with emotions. If your novel's any good the reader should get emotions from it, perhaps not the ones you intend, but they should be there.[20]

Pinfold achieves its paradoxical combination of detached intimacy by precisely these conventional means. This is true not only of the first chapter's portrait of the artist, but also of the selective transcription of Pinfold's deranged experiences aboard the *Caliban*. The traditional, realist narrative recounts recognizable speech and action in a fuddled time-sequence. And yet, the ironic detachment of the first chapter echoes Joyce's self-*Portrait of the Artist as a Young Man*, and a distant kinship links the nightmare film-script of the 'Circe' episode in *Ulysses* to the hallucinatory scenarios and illusory voices resounding through the pipe-work of the *Caliban*.

In 'Circe' Joyce lowered his bucket deep into the human mind, to dredge up the taboos, lusts and secret fears of his drunken protagonists. In his carnival of the subconscious Stephen finally faces his mother's reproachful ghost, and the cuckolded Bloom is goaded into enacting his masochistic transsexual fantasies in a circus ring. Joyce's narrative imitates the subconscious as it fantasticates, extrapolates and exaggerates. In direct contrast, Waugh's forensic documentation of his aural hallucinations is lucid and unadorned. His literary mode is laconic, his sexuality reticent, his obedience to social norms less flagrantly transgressed than in Joyce's practice. A restraining intelligence is shared by author and victim, curbing Pinfold's liveliest delusions. Thus, for instance, in 'Circe', Blazes Boylan, Bloom's cuckolder, tosses his hat onto Bloom's antlers, inviting him to watch through the keyhole and play with himself while Blazes 'goes through' his wife a couple of times. The servile Bloom eagerly acquiesces. Pinfold, on the contrary, is appalled by involuntarily overhearing a scene of religious bullying:

> 'Billy, you know what we talked about last time. Have you done it again? Have you been impure, Billy?'
> 'Yes, sir. I can't help it, sir.'
> 'God never tempts us beyond our strength, Billy. I've told you that, haven't I? Do you suppose I do not feel these temptations, too, Billy? Very strongly, at times. But I resist, don't I, Billy?'
> Mr Pinfold was horror-struck. He was being drawn into participation in a scene of gruesome indecency. His sticks lay by the bunk. He took the blackthorn and beat strongly on the floor. (*Pinfold* 38)

Throughout his ordeal, Pinfold struggles *strongly* to resist the voices that assail him. Yet his 'soul's well, sexual department', like Joyce's, is no less murky than any other man's.[21] His enflamed imagination creates the orgiastic scene in which a hapless lascar sailor is tried for rape, tortured 'slowly and deliberately [...] with undisguised erotic enjoyment', and accidentally killed by Captain Steerforth and his lover, the harsh-voiced 'Goneril' of Pinfold's fantasy. Many of Pinfold's nightmare scenarios are semi-literary in origin. His imagination instinctively reaches for his reading. Goneril cries, 'Tie him to the chair', and Pinfold promptly identifies *King Lear*'s 'Bind fast his corky arms' though he cannot remember who says it. More tellingly, he recognizes that the scene derives from 'the kind of pseudo-American thriller he most abhorred'. It certainly recalls the sado-erotic torture scene in *Casino Royale*, Ian Fleming's first Bond novel, published just before Waugh's Pinfold experience.[22]

More shamingly, Pinfold is titillated by the prospect of an assignment with the besotted 'Margaret', supposed sister of his prime tormenter, and daughter of one of the retired military men Pinfold has already identified among his voices. In a scene which Frances Donaldson found frankly embarrassing, the general encourages his daughter to lose her virginity to the aging Pinfold.

'Go in and get him lass. How do you think your mother got me? Not by waiting to be asked, I can tell you. She was a soldier's daughter. She always rode straight at her fences. She rode straight at me, I can tell you.' (*Pinfold* 132)

Some years later, reading a report of the *Chatterley* trial, Waugh came across the 'ludicrous' scene between Mellors and Lady Chatterley's father, and recognized 'the germ of the hallucination I suffered and described in *Mr Pinfold*. This father of Lawrence's was the father I had heard urging his daughter to my cabin' (*D* 781). The resemblance is obvious, but Waugh's general is more convincing than Lawrence's toe-curling Sir Malcolm, with his 'little squirting laugh' –

'How was the going, eh? Good, my boy, what? [...] I'll bet it was! Ha-ha! My daughter, chip of the old block, what! I never went back on a good bit of fucking, myself. Though her mother, oh, holy saints![...] But you warmed her up, oh, you warmed her up, I can see that. Ha-ha! My blood in her! You set fire to her haystack all right!'[23]

Waugh was well aware of the disturbing strength of his own affection for his favourite daughter Margaret. Post-Pinfold, he was relieved by his psychiatrist's reassurance that it was now likely to wane. Yet he transfers something like it to both the general, and to Pinfold himself, with the unabashed frankness and robust self-mockery that so struck Frances Donaldson. The general, his voice thick with Celtic sentiment, encourages his diffident daughter to Pinfold's cabin because 'An old man can show you better than a young one. He'll be gentler and kinder *and cleaner*' (!) and 'I'd like dearly to be the one myself to teach you'. Perhaps this is why Frances Donaldson found the episode so embarrassing, but Waugh is impervious to embarrassment. On the contrary, this extended scene is the funniest in the novel.

In the first chapter, Waugh had described the insomniac Pinfold padding down to the library to make a minute correction to his manuscript, returning to his bed to 'lie in the dark dazzled by the pattern of vocables'. When people praise Waugh's vaguely designated 'style' they usually mean identifiably fine writing like this, or like the 'pungent judgments' quoted by his friends as 'typical Pinfolds' – for instance Pinfold's self-defensive social carapace as the antiquated cuirass of

213

'pomposity mitigated by indiscretion' quoted earlier. Yet even this memorable phrase epitomizes a prime feature of Waugh's style, which dances perpetually from high to low, tripping the slow-witted reader in its fancy footwork between the two. This is well illustrated as Pinfold waits for Margaret's visit. Some anticlimaxes are broad, like the general's final irritable advice that his daughter should get going, if she really wants Pinfold, 'but for God's sake come on parade looking like a soldier. Get yourself cleaned up. Wash your face, brush your hair, *take your clothes off*' (my italics). Other slithers of tone are more finely controlled. Erotically stirred, a little apprehensive, Pinfold contemplates Margaret's impending visit. Inadvertently, irreversibly, his language transforms her welcome from steamy high romance to the installation of an unwieldy piece of furniture, neatly summarized in a classic *tricolon diminuens*.[24]

> She must not find him reclining like a pasha. He must be on his feet. There was one chair only. Should he offer it to her? Somehow he must dispose her, supine, on the bunk. But how to get her there, silently and gracefully? *How to shift her? Was she portable? He wished that he knew her dimensions.* (*Pinfold* 133, my italics)

In fact, the novel's structure, if any, rests on a comparable commerce between the high melodramas of Pinfold's delirium, and the comforting reality of prosaic days at sea, regularly marked by the steward's gong and brisk walks about the decks.

THE HALLUCINATORY NARRATIVE

Pinfold's delusions multiply in a world of timeless flux. His watch runs down, unwound, on his first night aboard. Dozing and waking, he finds it difficult to count the days. He is haunted by a dizzying sequence of increasingly lurid scenarios. The pseudo-priest and Billy, the unchaste sailor. A deckhand entangled in heavy machinery, indifferently injured as he's cut free. The coloured steward tortured and accidentally murdered by the captain and Goneril. Two drunks besieging Pinfold's cabin all night, threatening assault. An international incident between Spain and Gibraltar. Pinfold's planned fate as the unwitting substitute for a secret agent sought by the Spaniards. The ship is also – aptly, it seems – called the *Caliban*.

Like Prospero's island, it is full of noises. Not, however, Caliban's 'sounds and sweet airs, that give delight and hurt not' but noise, Waugh's anathema. The maddening three-eight jazz rhythm of the Pocoputa Indians and a snuffling crypto-dog in the neighbouring cabin. The 'ghastly sounds' of drunken vomiting; 'the whimpering sob of the injured seaman and the murdered steward'; the weeping Margaret; a babel of vicious voices. All re-echo through the ironically misnamed *Caliban*.[25]

In this fluid world characters proliferate, coalesce and reform in brief relationships prompted by Pinfold's strenuously rational lunacy, and his professional instinct for tidy plotting. A kindly nurse comforts the wounded deckhand. She reappears as 'a kind of Cordelia' grieving over the murdered steward. She stabilizes as 'Margaret', tenderly pursuing Pinfold. She acquires the general for a father, and a plaintive mother, modelled on Pinfold's Anglican maiden aunts. One drunk turns out to be Margaret's brother, and Goneril is her sister-in-law. Identities are unstable; old scenarios dissolve as new relationships are surmised. Initially Pinfold thinks of the captain as an ally: he is duty-bound to him by a vestigial instinct of solidarity from his military days. Unmasked as a sadistic murderer, the captain turns into a lecherous, treacherous, smiling villain, like *Hamlet*'s Claudius. Threatened by the Spanish designs on Gibraltar, the captain becomes heroic again; to Pinfold he now seems 'a simple sailor obliged to make a momentous decision [...] for the peace of the world'. Then it transpires that he plans to substitute Pinfold for the secret agent sought by the Spaniards. Pinfold is to be 'written off' without consultation.

The boundaries between factual narrative and hallucinatory delusion are equally fluid. Brooding on the unwelcome prospect of Spanish captivity, Pinfold's first, rational thought leaps across the narrative divide straight into his hallucinations. 'It was the General who voiced the thought uppermost in Mr Pinfold's mind. "Why Pinfold?" he asked.' His tireless imagination immediately provides plausible answers. Pinfold's a sick man, the captain says, and therefore expendable. He's a Catholic, therefore less likely to be harmed by Spain. Above all, he looks exactly like a secret agent...

Absurdities like this last justification comically betray Pinfold's loose grip on reality. As he struggles to rationalize his increasingly complex nocturnal melodramas, the novelist in him is dimly aware that his voices embody familiar fictional types, but not that he is their creator. Waugh states disingenuously: '*From the voices*, clear, precise, conventional,' of the general and his military friends, Pinfold 'had formed a clear idea of their appearance' – and, in quick succession, their complete back-histories. They are retired major-generals, gallant officers in the First World War '– line-cavalry probably –', too old for active command in 1939... They are drawn, in short, from Waugh's senior officers when he joined the Marines, models for old stagers like Jumbo Trotter in Waugh's own fiction. 'He did not find them on deck or in any of the public rooms,' because they are merely the detritus of Pinfold's novelistic imagination, still unstoppably at work.

There is an identifiable line of descent from the precise, morally loaded allusions (for instance, to Victorian melodrama) in *Brideshead*, to the fantastical literary pastiche just for entertainment's sake (particularly in the laboured Scottish half of *Officers and Gentlemen*), to the sub-literary caricatures erratically peopling Pinfold's nightmares. Listening, puzzled, to the two louts outside his cabin, Pinfold concludes again that '*By their voices* they seemed to be gentlemen of a sort'. He's 'pretty sure' Fosker was in the jazz band. Surely he glimpsed him flirting in the saloon-bar? A superfluity of supplementary details crowd in. Fosker is tall, shabby, shady, vivacious – *bohemian*. He has long hair, a moustache – and *side-whiskers*, like 'the dissolute law students and government clerks of mid-Victorian fiction'. The rapidly self-generating details leave him slightly bewildered: 'When Mr Pinfold came to consider the matter at leisure he could not explain to himself how he had formed so full an impression during a brief, incurious glance [...] The image, however, remained sharp cut as a cameo.' Figures like Fosker, the general, Goneril, the villainously smiling captain, derive from familiar classics and second-rate fiction: had the drunkards' scene appeared on stage, 'Pinfold would have thought it grossly overplayed'. Here, their very spuriousness is evidence of Waugh's psychological insight. And, indeed, the accuracy of his dispassionate recall.

However, as Pinfold's mind grows stronger, the quality of his hallucinations changes. The melodramatic playlets he unwillingly witnesses, but never participates in, give way to the voices' concerted character assassination of Pinfold alone. It begins with Fosker and his drunken friend's reckless slanders, backed by the general's maturer censure, quickly spreading to the gossip Pinfold hears from the dozing, knitting figures everywhere about the ship. He is a butch homosexual, a bogus aristocrat, the derisory 'Lord of the Manor of Lychpole'. He's impotent, suicidal, a coward, an immigrant Jew called Peinfeld with a dozen pairs of shoes. He only pretends to be religious because he thinks it's aristocratic. He's a typical alcoholic; there's a petition to get him off the captain's table. He says he was at Eton and Oxford, but really he's one of 'a lot of nasty people who crept into prominence during the war', when he was a fascist, a quisling, a blackshirt. His mother got him out of his debts but he gave her a pauper's funeral. 'That cowardly, common little communist pansy' is extremely rich. 'The long-nosed, curly-headed gentlemen don't pay taxes like us poor Christians, you know...'

Only two accusations seem valid. Pinfold 'is written out.' 'He's tried every literary trick. He's finished now and he knows it' is a coarser restatement of Pinfold's opinion, stated at the beginning of the novel, that even the best writers had only a couple of books in them, and 'all else is professional trickery' – a truth painfully close to Waugh's flagging practice at this very time. Fosker also says Pinfold will enjoy them ragging outside his cabin because Pinfold himself did so. He was sent down from Oxford for making a row outside the Dean's room, accusing him of 'the most disgusting practices' (as Waugh actually did, though he wasn't sent down).[26] Many of the slanders are self-cancelling. Some are wisps of half-remembered literature; some are rationalized and expanded by Pinfold himself. He not only typifies the decline of rural England but is a reincarnation of the new men of Henry VIII's reign, who despoiled the Church and peasantry. ('Mr Pinfold, not [the hooligans], drew the analogy.') In the last days of Pinfold's sea journey, absurd 'operations' are designed to distress him. Operation Storm and Operation Stock Exchange are singularly ill-suited to frighten Pinfold, an excellent sailor with zero business acumen. In these last days Pinfold is subjected to intensive interrogation by an inquisition furnished with 'a huge but incomplete and wildly inaccurate dossier' covering the whole of his private life. Pinfold knows he could make a better case against himself, than his detractors. 'It was very odd [...] that these people could go to so much trouble to investigate his affairs, and know so little about them.' Exactly the same can be said of Waugh's BBC interviewers in 1953, and the journalists of the Beaverbrook press whose animus he had aroused, identified and attempted to counter in the same year. Their slurs re-emerged in force after Waugh's death, and have been repeated and exaggerated ever since. It is highly ironic that *Pinfold* is itself a prophetically accurate nightmare. Perhaps the last word on that should go to Philip Toynbee, *Pinfold's* most insightful contemporary reviewer:[27]

> The ultimate horror in the recesses of Mr Waugh's mind is the same horror which has obsessed many of us who have experienced the normal torments of public school life. For the bully, of course, is an enemy not only of weakness, [...] sensitivity, [and ...] loving kindness, but also of intelligence. It is the appalling, nagging, shrewd *stupidity* of the imaginary persecutors which is best brought out and will haunt my own imagination for many days.

REALITY, THE COUNTER-NARRATIVE

Pinfold, and the reader with him, turn with relief to the orderly, commonplace world on the decks of the *Caliban*. 'Here was light and liveliness, a glitter of cool sunshine and a brisk breeze.' Pinfold's mood regularly improves on his walks around the decks, finding 'a kind of paschal novelty' in the scene and rejoicing in it. He 'benevolently' watches the young playing deck-quoits, Mrs Benson and Mrs Cockson in their usual deckchairs – 'They liked their glass, that pair, thought Mr Pinfold with approval; good sorts. He greeted them. He greeted anyone who met his eye. He was feeling very much better.'

Not many fellow-passengers wanted to meet poor Pinfold's dotty eye. Yet he is very appealing. On his first evening he 'submissively' follows the steward down to dinner. He gazes 'sadly' at his curry, 'wishing to be pleasant'. Attempting to entertain the company, he talks familiarly about acquaintances on the Government front bench, realizes he appears to be showing off, and stops in mid-sentence, 'silent with shame'.

Pinfold is appealing because his real nature is very different from the public persona he – or rather, Waugh – adopted in middle-age, which made him, more than Pinfold, so remarkably unpopular. Rather surprisingly, Waugh writes of Pinfold, 'It was his modesty which needed protection and for this purpose, but without design, he gradually assumed this character of burlesque'. Other men have to defend themselves against adversity, but Pinfold had been 'over-rewarded' in his early years of literary success, when 'diffidence had lent him charm'. Now, to avoid conceit, his beleaguered modesty takes refuge behind a caricature persona that keeps critical and adulatory strangers at bay.

Waugh's detractors might be surprised by the idea of his modesty and diffidence, or that he could be silent with shame. Yet his letters, particularly in the aftermath of the Pinfold experience, show him anxiously attempting to make amends to various friends. The 'novel' itself, like the *Diaries*, does not present the image of a modest man (who understates his own good qualities), so much as of one used to ruthlessly dispassionate self-assessment. Now he makes it in public for the first time. Listening to two old gossips early in the narrative, Pinfold lies back smoking 'without resentment. It was the sort of thing one expected to have said behind one's back – the sort of thing one said about other people.' That note of unrepentant, accurate self-knowledge recurs in a later character-analysis, when we are told Pinfold 'was not what is generally meant by [...] a "philanthropic man"; he totally lacked what was now called "a social conscience". But apart from his love of family and friends he had a certain basic kindliness [...] He rather liked Mrs Scarfield, Mrs Cockson, Mrs Benson [...] and all those simple, chatting, knitting, dozing passengers.' 'In an old fashioned way he was also patriotic', and these sentiments sufficed for 'what are generally regarded as the higher loyalties.' Pinfold/Waugh is no self-deceiving sentimentalist. Thinking of Margaret with 'tender curiosity' introduces a frank summary of Pinfold's sexual mores. 'He had never, even in his bachelor days, been a strenuous philanderer...' – which is a fairer version of the impotence attributed by his voices. As a young man Pinfold patronized brothels abroad with a traveller's curiosity for tasting the exotic (as Waugh had an affectionate relationship with the Berber prostitute in Fez). In England (evidently a different

219

matter), he was 'rather constant and rather romantic in his affections. Since marriage he had been faithful to his wife.' After conversion, he 'developed what approximated to a virtuous disposition', but his reluctance to commit 'grave sins' came not from a fear of Hell but because 'he had assumed a personality to which such specifically forbidden actions were inappropriate'. This commendably lukewarm personal assessment is a powerful answer to the spite of Waugh's detractors.

Pinfold's courage combating his delusions is also (in its mad way) impressive. He beats strongly on the floor to silence the bogus chaplain's prurient bullying. He unlocks his cabin door and waits, all night, cudgel in hand, for the hooligans to beat him up. Alone in his haunted cabin again, expecting imminent abduction by the Spaniards, he assesses the situation with military detachment, coolly changes into tweeds, and pockets his passport and travellers cheques for every eventuality. If he must be sacrificed to the enemy, he will go of his own volition. He rather resents the intrusion of Margaret's family, pimping her to him, and roundly tells her mother to 'shut up, you old bitch', much to the general's delight ('Good for Pinfold'!). He has only one moment of atavistic panic, when he goes on deck to forestall the Spaniards' approach, and finds deserted decks and a dark world at peace. Fearing insanity for the first time, he cries, like Lear, 'O let me not be mad, not mad, sweet heaven.' Goneril's malign laughter comes as a relief, signifying to him that 'It was all a hoax [. . .] He might be unpopular; he might be ridiculous, but he was not mad.' His reason is of supreme importance to him, more than his dignity or conventional morality.

In the ship's daylight world of banal routines, Pinfold repeatedly attempts to re-assert his grip on reality. As dawn breaks after the hooligans' siege, he calmly lies on his bunk, 'his rage quite abated,' his 'orderly, questing mind' logically dismantling the many accusations made against him. Pondering paranoid suspicions of the captain, he begins to shave – a 'prosaic operation' recalling him to 'strict reason'. Shifting to another enigma, 'Mr Pinfold gazed at his puzzled, soapy face' – and finds a rational excuse for that puzzle as well. His gift for virtuoso ingenuity replaces one inadequate explanation for his experiences by another. And as his search for a conclusive explanation usurps the false suspense of each successive hallucinatory scenario, Waugh tempts his readers with the resolution promised by this rational counter-narrative. So the form of *Pinfold* is the form of the detective novel – with its calculated provisionality, its fecund revisions, its relentless readjustments, the narrative satnav perpetually recalculating. When Pinfold finally fingers the ringleader, Margaret's brother, as Angel, the interviewer from the BBC, he feels 'as though he had come to the end of an ingenious, old-fashioned detective story he had read rather inattentively'. Backtracking over the past in this new light, 'he carefully assembled the intricate pieces of a plot more modern and horrific than anything in the classic fictions of murder. He heard so much, directly and indirectly; he reasoned so closely; he followed so many clues and reached so many absurd conclusions; but at length he knew the truth.'

Pinfold's letter explaining this 'truth' to his wife is a marginally more coherent replay of Waugh's letters to Laura from Colombo, with their bewildered farrago of scantily understood, contemporary voodoo from the Box to psycho-analysis, psychologists and Parisian existentialists. It is yet another irony of the novel's reception that many critics were nonetheless tempted to analyse it in psychoanalytic terms.[28]

Of course that isn't the truth either. The promised detective story turns into a shaggy dog story whose prosaic anticlimax is the doctor's diagnosis of 'a perfectly simple case of poisoning'.

The novel also ends with an unresolved, supernatural subtext. We know that Waugh continued to suspect he might have been possessed even after the novel was finished. That fear is mooted in the text: Pinfold writes to his wife that he wants to consult Father Westmacott on his return because '*he knows all about existentialism and psychology and ghosts and diabolic possession. Sometimes I wonder whether it is not literally the Devil who is molesting me.*' A number of divine allusions are touched in, early on: the kindly nurse lulls the injured deckhand, and Pinfold, to sleep with the words of the 'Angelic Salutation' (the words of the Angel Gabriel in the Annunciation). Pinfold's lameness vanishes simultaneously with the death of the tortured native steward, and he is uncertain 'whether he had not been healed by the steward's agony' (an oblique echo of Christ's agony on the cross). Conversely, the approaching end of the novel is spotted with infernality. Pinfold's omissions of Mass and prayerless nights are inconspicuously noted throughout, till we are finally told that 'he had given up any attempt at saying his prayers; the familiar, hallowed words provoked a storm of blasphemous parody from Goneril'. Pinfold writes to his wife that the treatment he suffered, of vilification followed by psychoanalytic interrogation, is *a hellish invention in the wrong hands*. Twice he says to Angel 'Who the devil said you might use my Christian name?' 'Who the devil said I needed help?' (The obvious answer is, 'The Devil said...'). And when Pinfold says, '*I* am leaving *you*, my good Angel,' Goneril interrupts with 'We'll give you hell for this, Gilbert...'

It is a Renaissance theological commonplace that the devil can assume the shape of an angel.[29] Is Angel the devil, or does Pinfold's phrase, 'my good Angel' express an inadvertent truth, acknowledging him as Pinfold's guardian angel? Angel compares himself and his accomplices to the Guardians in T. S. Eliot's *Cocktail Party*[30] – 'a little band doing good' in secret, not driving Pinfold mad but curing him: 'We're driving you sane'.

The voices are too malignant, flawed and unreliable for that to be credible. Yet the novel does suggest that Pinfold's ordeal was spiritually regenerative. The final chapter is titled 'Pinfold Regained', an analogy with Milton's *Paradise Regained*, which recounts Christ's victory over the devil's temptations in the wilderness. Pinfold himself believes that 'he had endured a great ordeal and, unaided, had emerged the victor'. His victory – which is the true climax of the story – comes when Angel offers to switch off what Pinfold calls 'that infernal Box' and never trouble him again, if Pinfold will lie to his wife and keep Angel's activities secret. But the lie Angel offers Pinfold is the truth Pinfold had never even contemplated: 'Tell your wife you had noises in the head through taking those grey pills...' Here, at last, is real suspense as Pinfold considers Angel's temptation on his long flight home. 'There were strong attractions in the bargain. Could Angel be trusted?' Surely not! Only en route to London, in the unromantic borough of Acton, does Pinfold reject Angel's bad bargain, so saving himself from a lifetime's uncertainty by refusing the voice of temptation.

Waugh wrote his novels in longhand, on foolscap, and had

them beautifully bound. There is one oddity about the manuscript of *The Ordeal of Gilbert Pinfold*. It contains a single leaf from St John Chrysostom's Fifth Homily on Matthew I.22–3 in the original Greek with two Latin translations, inserted loose between chapters 4 and 5. Since it has been trimmed to fit the bound pages of the manuscript, its insertion must be deliberate.[31] The one striking moment in this extract is its opening, an exhortation to study the scriptures daily, in a discipline of sustained interpretation. In order to understand what is being said, the reader must 'know accurately *the connexion of the thoughts*, which we are busy in *weaving together* for you [. . . and] *by continued remembrance make the things laid before you* [. . .] *into a kind of chain'*. It is comparable to the precise hermeneutic demands Waugh set his readers in *Brideshead*, and which took mad control in *Pinfold*.

More broadly, the homily is a commentary on Matthew's account of the Angel's Annunciation, one of the texts of the Divine Salutation that lulled the wounded lascar and Pinfold to sleep. It suggests a mystery reaching beyond the confines of the novel. Waugh's experiences seem to have initiated a perceptible moral change, which later allowed him to refer, however facetiously, to his 'great new goodness' after the survival of his ordeal.

THE COMFORTERS

Two-thirds of *Pinfold* were completed and in the hands of his literary agent, when Waugh was sent a young author's first novel for comment. By an extraordinary coincidence the heroine of Muriel Spark's *The Comforters* also suffers from aural hallucinations. Waugh's response was frank, succinct and generous. The book is 'remarkable'; the 'mechanics' of the hallucinations 'well managed'. They are of particular interest to him 'since I am myself engaged on a similar subject'. Unasked, he adds: 'She can report me as saying: 'brilliantly original and fascinating' (L 477). The latest edition still carries Waugh's well-deserved praise.

Spark had suffered from a period of visual hallucinations from which the aural hallucinations of her heroine distantly derive.[32] Her 'machinery' differs from Waugh's because the novel is meta-fictional, post-modern, and ultimately unrealistic. The voices heard by the heroine are prompting, or repeating, the narrative of a novel, this novel, inadvertently being written by the heroine, to the voices' dictation. Once this has been clearly suggested early on, the voices cease to be heard, giving way to a lively, complicated plot circling round an eccentric group of diamond-smugglers. Waugh's wholly realistic narrative is entirely devoted to his actual experience; the aural hallucinations are sustained to the end with what Philip Toynbee called 'a dreadful vividness which wholly persuades us that [the voices] are no less real than the events of the voyage' – as, of course, they are, being real hallucinations.

Both authors are aware of the absurdity of their protagonists' delusions. Waugh habitually marks this by slipping in and out of literary pastiche. Spark, on the other hand, offers a variety of interpretations of her hyper-fictional core narrative through a range of commentator-participants. At the end three opposed alternative readings are offered: one comically commonplace; another psychoanalytic; a third supernatural. Spark, like Waugh, is a Roman Catholic. Both authors' fictional *alter egos* fear possession. In Spark, this is darkly confirmed in a stormy climax where the novel's antagonist, a robustly repellent religious hypocrite, fails to drown the heroine, and is herself drowned. Waugh's markedly understated ending is the antithesis of Spark's melodramatic dénouement. But in their different ways both authors conclude with the victory of an innocent protagonist over a diabolical adversary. In both, the adversary is euphemized by name. Angel and the Comforters are as implacable as the Eumenides, the Kindly Ones. It is another, unanswered question, whether or not the unkindly ones are divinely controlled, and the delusions a purgative call to order.

14

Towards
Unconditional Surrender
A Recapitulation, 1941–61

Unconditional Surrender was finally written, and published in 1961. Twenty years, six novels, two travel books, and a biography separate this novel from the raw experiences it was based on. The impacted biographical substrata of a third of Waugh's life and more than a third of his total literary output provide the foundations for his last novel. Let us take the layers chronologically, one by one.

1941–43

After the fall of Crete, Waugh, like Guy, returned on a troopship looping its way around half the world from Egypt to England via Cape Town and Iceland. Always a happy sailor, he was cheered to find a complete set of his novels in the ship's library, most of which he re-read with unmixed pleasure. Meeting those forgotten, familiar faces fuelled *Put Out More Flags*, which Waugh began and finished by the time he docked in Liverpool, 20,000 miles and seven weeks later. In September 1941 he returned to barracks for routine training, and continued to write up his military experiences – publicly and patriotically, in the up-beat 'Commando Raid on Bardia', and a belligerent polemic in *Horizon* arguing against Cyril Connolly's proposal for special, soft conditions for writers.[1] Waugh's anonymous riposte was ostentatiously signed 'Combatant'. Privately, in his personal *Diaries* and against military regulations, he copied his detailed notes on training for the Commandos, the failed Dakar and Bardia raids, and the flight from Crete. His *Memorandum on LAYFORCE: July 1940–July 1941* later became a first-hand resource for *Men at Arms* and *Officers and Gentlemen*. In the retrospect which opens *Unconditional Surrender* Waugh dismissed the period after his and Guy's return (1941–3) as 'two dead years'. He cut the phrase from *Sword of Honour*, but it accurately conveys a long period of pointless re-training, frustrated attempts to get back into active service, cheerful drunkenness, and desolation. 'I wish I could recapture some of that adventurous spirit with which I joined at Chatham,' he had written to Laura, soon after his return to England, plaintively adding: 'There is no one here with any sense of humour but they never stop laughing' (*L* 157). Colonel Cutler, Waugh's superior officer and 'a pompous booby [...] with no interest in the war or warfare', who consistently blocked his attempts at promotion, was later turned into the pettifogging, nameless commanding officer in the Prologue to *Brideshead Revisited*. The *Diaries'* mixed bag equably accommodates Waugh's enviable capacity for impenitent enjoyment with moments of appalled self-knowledge. 'A beautiful day of overeating and overdrinking' *follows* a drunken evening when 'I saw myself in a mirror afterwards, like a red lacquer Chinese dragon, and saw how I shall look when I die' – later recycled in *Pinfold*.[2] In the same entry, in October 1942, he admires his commander, Bob Laycock, for tearing a strip off his troop leaders without incurring resentment, whereas 'If I did it I should be sarcastic and so [...] do no good at all but only harm' (*D* 529). On the same page, 'Sharp and triumphant row with Shimi on a matter of maps' is followed by '[I] meditate starting a novel'.

Shimi is Lord Lovat, Trimmer's original; the novel is probably *Brideshead*. The two are significantly linked in the second of Waugh's two dead years, culminating in his enforced resignation from the Special Service Brigade in July 1943. Many commentators believe this affected him as profoundly as his first wife's desertion. Here, as in his departure from Crete, Waugh has come in for much negative commentary. The documented facts of his resignation have only recently been established by Donat Gallagher. I am indebted to him in the following brief summary.[3]

TRIMMER'S TRIUMPH

By April 1943 Waugh's prospects had improved. Bob Laycock, Waugh's commanding officer, was to lead 'Operation Husky' in North Africa, preparing for the Allied invasion of Italy, and Waugh was to join him as intelligence officer. Meanwhile he was serving as temporary liaison officer at Combined Operations Headquarters (COHQ) in London, representing Laycock's scant enthusiasm for a proposed merger of the Marine, and Army, Special Service Brigades. In *Officers and Gentlemen* Waugh transferred Laycock's embattled position to General Whale. Just as Whale reluctantly acceded to the publicity stunt of Trimmer's 'Operation Popgun', in order to preserve the independent status of his Hazardous Offensive Operations, so Waugh was responsible for managing 'Operation Coughdrop', an ill-conceived bombing raid on a submarine depot on the French coast whose cover, according to intelligence reports, had already been blown. (In *Unconditional Surrender* Operation Coughdrop resurfaces again, much more recognizably and fleetingly, as Operation 'Hoopla', aimed at 'some prodigious bomb-proof submarine pens in Brittany'.) In both contexts Waugh, as liaison officer, had to represent views unacceptable to General Haydon, the officer in charge of Combined Operations. Waugh was well aware that relations with him were strained ('General Haydon shows himself ill-intentioned', D 536).

Meanwhile Laycock's relationship with his deputy, Lord Lovat, was equally fraught. Lovat was even more headstrong than Waugh is currently reputed to be, treating his subordinates with arrogance and his superiors with insubordination. Lovat resented Laycock's attempts to control him, while one of Laycock's fellow-officers twice wrote to Laycock in exasperation at 'your prima donna', Lovat.

Finally, relations between Waugh and Lovat were, by now, also antagonistic. Lovat was Waugh's junior by eight years. A year previously, Waugh had recorded his admiration for Lovat's conduct in the Commando raid on Dieppe; ('Shimi Lovat did brilliantly, the only wholly successful part of the raid' (D 525)). Since then matters between them had deteriorated. In that diary entry Waugh had dismissed a story that Lovat had claimed to have led the raid himself, and boasted of executing all but four of his prisoners. In 1976 this passage was cut from the *Diaries* by their editor, prior to publication, under threat of legal action from Lord Lovat.[4]

On 8 May 1943 Laycock informed Lovat of a replacement for Waugh at COHQ, who was to take his place as soon as Waugh's embarkation orders for Operation Husky arrived. At a subsequent meeting Lovat requested a different replacement for Waugh, and Laycock agreed. In the memorandum of this meeting Laycock confirmed the change, but reiterated his order to Lovat that Waugh should join him (Laycock) on Operation Husky, as soon as the new substitute could take Waugh's place. A third communication from Laycock to Lovat, on the day he left for North Africa (24 June), ordered Waugh's batman to accompany Waugh 'in the first reinforcements to Husky'. And then, on 26 June, most unexpectedly, Waugh's father died.

Waugh was given a fortnight's compassionate leave to put his father's affairs in order. Two days before leave ended, Lovat ordered him – via a subordinate, in itself an insult – to report to the Commando depot at Achnacarry for training as soon as his replacement arrived. Waugh wrote back to Lovat repeating Laycock's explicit, thrice-repeated orders that he should remain as liaison officer at COHQ till his embarkation orders arrived and then be sent to join Husky. Lovat replied that the order of 8 May was 'automatically cancelled' by the change of Waugh's replacement (a lie), and that General Haydon had approved Waugh's demotion to more training. Lovat's bluntly tabulated letter left Waugh no room for negotiation, grimly ending: 'You will not proceed overseas unless passed physically fit by Achnacarry.' In his memoirs, Lovat himself terms the depot 'a trial by ordeal centre for sorting out new recruits'. Other Commandos confirm that the posting was unprecedented for an experienced officer of Waugh's age and length of service. Waugh made the same point more forcefully in a letter to Laycock.[5] Not surprisingly, then, Waugh immediately appealed to General Haydon: 'If doubt exists about the fitness of an officer for foreign service, it is usual to refer him to the Medical Authorities. I do not understand why an exception is being made in my case. May I please come and see you about this?' The interview was not a success. According to Waugh, General Haydon 'was already in a highly excited condition' when he arrived; he said Laycock had 'made a great mistake' in asking for Waugh at all; that Waugh should train at the depot until fit, and then go on to a further course in intelligence. This would have delayed Waugh's departure by three months, too late to be of use to Laycock. As Waugh wrote to Laycock, General Haydon 'ended by saying I had done nothing but discredit to the Brigade since I had joined it and for the Brigade's good he advised me to leave as soon as possible. I have therefore tendered my resignation to the Deputy Commander' (*D* 544). Which he did, in a letter of acid servility addressed to Lt.-Col. The Lord Lovat, DSO, MC.

17 July 1943

My Lord,
   I have the honour to inform you that I have this morning had an interview with the GOCO in which he advised me to leave the Special Services Brigade for the Brigade's good.
   I therefore have the honour to request that I may be posted to the Royal Horse Guards.
   I am
      My Lord,
         Your Lordship's obedient servant.

Small honour, heavy irony. As in the trilogy's bitter title – *Sword of Honour*.
   Waugh inserted all the letters leading to his resignation into his *Diary* (*D* 539–545), concluding: 'A fine pompous letter to Lord Louis Mountbatten should follow here but Diana Cooper lost it. E. W.' Many years later, when planning the second volume of his autobiography, Waugh asked Laycock for a copy of the lost letter, which Laycock evidently provided. In it Waugh had clearly summarized the facts culminating in his enforced resignation, described General Haydon's 'severe but vague strictures' and answered the few specific accusations made against him. Lovat's name was not mentioned. Waugh's letter ended, poignantly, with what mattered most to him: 'I therefore respectfully request that an investigation may be made into how, why, and by whom these allegations were made which so gravely affect *my honour as an officer* and have produced so unwelcome a change in my military career.'[6]
   In the diary of the time, nothing more was said of the lost letter to Mountbatten. Yet Waugh's apparently insignificant, but

pointedly initialled note is startling. It suggests comparison with another lost letter, the one that Mrs Stitch – Diana Cooper's fictional incarnation – destroys at the end of *Officers and Gentlemen*. Bruised by his own recent experiences with Lovat, Waugh might well have suspected Diana Cooper of malicious interference in his military career. As the wife of Duff Cooper,[7] she was as well-placed as Mrs Stitch to meddle for motives of her own. Waugh did finally manage to obtain an interview with Mountbatten, which was amiable but ineffective, being too long delayed after Waugh's forced resignation, and falling just prior to Mountbatten's own departure from England. Shortly after, Waugh spent a weekend with Diana Cooper, they quarrelled, and he left 'sad and cross with no inclination to be reconciled'. All these events were recorded in the next two pages of the *Diary* (*D* 545–6). It seems likely that, over a decade later, immediately post-Pinfold, and still prone to paranoia from his past, Waugh recast them at the end of *Officers and Gentlemen*. There Mrs Stitch destroys Guy's letter to GCHQ, on the mistaken assumption that it contained Guy's incriminating war diary, and adroitly decoys Guy into his lengthy voyage home, so pre-empting his meeting Ritchie-Hook, who would have brought justice on Claire.

Nor was that the end of it. Poor Waugh's p.m. – his admitted persecution mania – was justifiably triggered by Lovat's open hostility. Long after the event, and indeed after Waugh's death, Lovat maintained that Laycock had never wanted Waugh to join him in Operation Husky. This was not true.[8] But Waugh might well have feared it at the time. The letters he inserted into his diary include two of the formal instructions Laycock sent Lovat, quoted above. But Waugh was also well aware that he was becoming a difficult colleague. Back in August 1942 he had confessed 'I began to trace a decline in my position in Bob [Laycock]'s esteem'. In March 1943 two fellow officers were promoted above him, and Laycock had to take him aside to explain that 'I am so unpopular as to be unemployable' (*D* 525, 532). Waugh was clearly upset when the brigade left without him: 'I was angry with Bob for leaving me behind so easily' (*D* 539). His suppressed suspicions of Laycock, like his distrust of Diana Cooper, cast a personal shadow over the end of *Officers and Gentlemen*.[9]

Lovat's triumph had extended consequences. Haydon and Lovat's animosity was undisguised and Waugh's initial response was uncomplicated: he dismissed Haydon as 'the poor mad General' and spoke openly of Lovat's 'personal malice'.[10] His lasting revenge came only with Lovat's demeaning caricature as Trimmer. Laycock and Diana Cooper, on the other hand, were his friends, but also his social and military superiors. Uncertain about their attitudes towards him and out-manoeuvred by Lovat's strategies, Waugh was understandably jumpy. A decade later, his paranoid delusions in the Pinfold period interrupted the composition of *Officers and Gentlemen*, and obscured the Cretan climax. Waugh's schoolboy sense of military honour was profoundly shaken by the surrender of Crete. There is no doubt that Laycock and his senior officers were evacuated from the beach at Sphakia legitimately. Yet in the novel, Guy's last discussion with Claire voices Waugh's revulsion from the contemporary trend sanctioning officers to abandon their men. It is very likely Waugh felt the same thing personally, when Laycock appeared to have given up on him for Operation Husky. 'I was angry with Bob for leaving me behind so easily.'

Waugh did not allow himself to smart for long. In mid-August, his first diary entry after his resignation maintains that 'The indignation I felt a month ago has subsided and I have got bored with the whole thing' (D 545). Yet he still fretted for a satisfactory outcome, hoping that 'justice may be done', that Laycock would command a Mediterranean Commando Force 'while Shimi will be packed off to the Far East [...] Nothing could be funnier than that' (D 547). 'That' seems to have been the standard disposal route for problematic officers. Brigadier St Clair-Morford, Ritchie-Hook's original, left the brigade in disgrace a year earlier, to Waugh's regret, and was packed off to assist the Indian Government,[11] just as Mrs Stitch arranges Ivor Claire's discreet posting to India to cover up his desertion. Waugh, meanwhile, was pursuing Bill Stirling for a commission in the SAS, naively believing that 'after my treatment by Haydon I must "make good" as a soldier. Nothing can upset him more than to find me promoted as a result of his intemperance' (D 551).

Forlorn hope! Nothing upset Haydon. Waugh was not promoted. Lovat 'won every point & escaped going to Far East

& is just where he wants to be as Palais de Danse Hero' (*L* 172). And Laycock was made Chief of Combined Operations. Waugh's congratulatory letter compared him, 'not quite sincerely, to the righteous flourishing like a green bay tree. There is no shade for me under those wide branches. We lunched together [...] but there was a curtain of reproach between us' (*D* 553–4).

1944–5

BRIDESHEAD REVISITED

In the remaining months of 1943, Waugh continued to seek active service with diminishing hope. He found Bill Stirling the diametric opposite to Laycock – 'vague, mystical, imaginative, unsmart, aristocratic,' he tells Laura, but his similar diary entry also adds '*more moral*' (my italics, *L* 172, *D* 550). At the same time he was impatient to write. Vague intimations of a new novel – a kind of Arcadia – culminate in the August diary entry beginning with his hope for justice to be done, and ending with irritable clarity:

> I dislike the Army. I want to get to work again. I do not want any more experiences in life [...] I am not impatient of [the world's] manifest follies and don't want to influence opinions or events, or expose humbug [...] I don't want to be of service to anyone or anything. I simply want to do my work as an artist. (*D* 548)

At the same time a number of disparate events impacted on Waugh's spiritual life. His father's death was followed, unexpectedly quickly, by the death of his friend and contemporary, Hubert Duggan. In November he attended a parachuting course on his own volition, in preparation for his unfulfilled hopes of joining the SAS. Although he missed the first two days' simulated training through illness, he rashly joined in two real jumps on the fourth day, the first arousing 'the keenest pleasure I remember'. On the second he landed badly, and was hospitalized with a cracked fibula. Sick of 'a more and more limited life in the vicious spiral of boredom and lassitude', he finally put in a successful appeal for three months' unpaid leave to write, and began *Brideshead* on 1 February 1944.

Back in April 1943 Hubert Duggan was casually mentioned as due to die in two years but still vigorously talkative. On 25 September he suddenly resurfaces, 'frightfully ill'. On successive visits Waugh finds him 'in despair', 'pathetically ill'. The diary entry for 13 October is the source for Lord Marchmain's deathbed scenes: the family divisions – 'big Catholic trouble' as Julia Flyte calls it; the debated hiding of a holy medal in the sickroom; and, at the end of the day,

> Father Devas very quiet and simple and humble, trying to make sense of all the confusion, knowing just what he wanted [...] and patiently explaining, 'Look all I shall do is just to put oil on his forehead and say a prayer. Look at the oil in this little box. It is nothing to be frightened of.' And so by knowing what he wanted and sticking to that, when I was all for arguing it out from first principles, he got what he wanted and Hubert crossed himself [...] So we spent the day watching for a spark of gratitude for the love of God and saw the spark. (*D* 553)

Hubert Duggan died twelve days later. Waugh was out of London that day; his diary records only Laycock's promotion and their uneasy lunch together.

It is hard to avoid impertinence in speaking of Waugh's spiritual life. What can or should we guess? He avoids overt introspection. Even in the semi-private diaries, the tone is detached and factual. He is ostentatiously hard-boiled about Lovat's victory ('I have got bored with the whole thing'). Two days after the memorable scene at Duggan's bedside, he flatly notes: 'No news of Hubert. I have done all in my power in that matter.' He says virtually nothing of his father's death in his published letters and barely mentions it in his diary. The successful parachute jump is merely recorded as keenly pleasurable. Yet his father's life and death will lie behind the moving portrayal of Guy Crouchback's father and his exemplary death. The parachute jump reappears with increasingly transcendental connotations in *Pinfold* and *Unconditional Surrender*. Hubert Duggan's death provides the narrative climax of *Brideshead* and the novel's telos, its desired end. In each case what was drily recorded in the diaries is invested with powerful emotional and spiritual colouring in its fictional form. Lovat's victory, on the other hand, is an absent presence haunting the war trilogy. Waugh's intentions in relation to it seem to have swollen and subsided in the long course of composition.

Critics and biographers wishing to equate the impact of Lovat's (and possibly Laycock's) presumed betrayal with the breakdown of Waugh's first marriage, can point to a potential parallel in the Prologue opening *Brideshead Revisited*. The first shockwaves of Waugh's cumulative sense of disillusion in 1943, his fourth year of army life, are memorably registered in Ryder's extended metaphor of marital breakdown:

> Here my last love died [...] and [I] felt as a husband might feel, who, in the fourth year of his marriage, suddenly knew that he had no longer any desire, or tenderness, or esteem, for a once-beloved wife; no pleasure in her company, no wish to please, no curiosity in anything she might ever do or say or think; no hope of setting things right; no self-reproach for the disaster [...] We had been through it together, the Army and I. (*BR* 12)

In *Work Suspended* Waugh had written powerfully of emotional reticence: 'first a numbness, then a long festering, then a scar ever ready to open' (*WS* 41). It took Waugh five years to recast Evelyn Gardner's infidelity in *A Handful of Dust*. In *Brideshead*, apart from the marital metaphor, there is no hint of the Lovat débâcle. Instead, the Prologue establishes Waugh's broader perception of a worthless civilization in its final throes, by deploying a futuristic perspective on the present. Ryder's military camp, clearly based on Waugh's at Pollock in May 1942 (*D* 522), is a planless maze of barrack-huts and wavering short cuts superimposed on an unfinished housing scheme neatly quartered by roads and drainage ditches. In Ryder's jaundiced, Wellsian fantasy, the 'Pollock diggings' will provide future archaeologists with '*a valuable link between the citizen-slave communities of the twentieth century and the tribal anarchy which succeeded them. Here you see a people of advanced culture, capable of an elaborate drainage system and the construction of permanent highways, over-run by a race of the lowest type*' (*BR* 15). The highest achievements of contemporary culture are nothing more than tarmac roads and municipal drains. The military are subnormal. That is why Ryder's laid-back fellow-soldiers are on such friendly terms with the inmates of the neighbouring lunatic asylum: 'Cheerioh chum, we'll be seeing you'; 'We won't be long now'. Nothing has a rational purpose in this army of lunatics, led by pompous boobies like Colonel Cutler (and, in reality, Haydon, the poor mad general). Having established as much in *Brideshead*'s Prologue, Waugh turns his back on the present to trace the purposeful workings of divine providence in the pre-war past. He does not return to Ryder's present until his brief Epilogue, when Brideshead Castle is about to be despoiled by military anarchy, now seen with resignation *sub specie aeternitatis*. The light burning in the chapel's modest tabernacle, Ryder muses, is 'the flame which the old knights saw from their tombs, which they saw put out' in the fall of Jerusalem, and yet 'there I found it this morning, burning anew among the old stones' (*BR* 381).

That final, strongly positive image is another example of a motif reappearing with increasingly spiritual significance in Waugh's last works. In an interview of 1949, he first mentioned his intentions for 'a far-off novel whose theme will be chivalry during World War II'.[12] In 'Sword of Honour', the Prologue to *Men at Arms*, Ryder's old knights in their tombs are particularized in the effigy of Sir Roger of Waybrooke, failed crusader, whose prayers Guy Crouchback invokes before setting out on his personal crusade against Germany and Russia, the enemies of Christendom. The theme of chivalry will be especially important in *Unconditional Surrender*.

YUGOSLAVIA, 'COMPASSION'

Waugh finished *Brideshead* in June 1944. His attempts to find active posting were resolved by Randolph Churchill's opportune choice of him as fellow-officer in the allied military mission to Yugoslavia. At the beginning of July they set out on what was to be Waugh's last military assignment, and the raw material for the final part of *Unconditional Surrender*. En route, they stayed with Duff and Diana Cooper at the British Embassy in Algiers, a 'charming Arabesque villa' with peacocks and palms and 'tiled courtyards not unlike Mexico,' Waugh told Laura. 'D & D very popular and happy, good food, one lavatory, one bath, everyone in pyjamas all the morning' (*D* 570; *L* 185). But Waugh was still smarting. Later he transformed this short idyll into Guy's convalescence in the Stitches' official residence in Egypt, at the bitter end of *Officers and Gentlemen*. On the next stage of their journey Waugh and Randolph's plane crashed while landing in Croatia. Several passengers died. Waugh was burned on his hands, legs and head but anaesthetized by shock. In *Unconditional Surrender* this experience is expanded into a toneless, semicomic episode and transferred to the morally null Ian Kilbannock (*L* 186, *D* 573–4, *US* 274–9). Randolph and Waugh were sent back to Italy to recuperate, but in Rome Waugh was hospitalized again for 'a far worse trouble' – a carbuncle on the back of his neck, which reduced him to 'an extremity of pain & depression'. It was only in September, after two months' delay, that they finally reached their destination.

Topusko housed the Partisan headquarters of the largely Catholic region of Croatia. Hence, partly, Randolph Churchill's invitation for Waugh to accompany him there. The allied military mission's main function was to send observing officers and wireless operators to Tito's communist partisans as the Germans withdrew, to organize flights of personnel in and out of the local airfield, and to pick up drops of supplies. Waugh describes the situation succinctly at the beginning of his short story, 'Compassion' (1949), which is later woven into the last book of *Unconditional Surrender*. In Yugoslavia the first stirrings of a spiritual change (later re-apparent after the Pinfold experience) began to make themselves felt. Initially Waugh appears barely to have been aware of them. Retrospectively, five years later, he traced their growth in his fine, critically neglected short story, 'Compassion'.

Major Gordon finds himself responsible for the welfare of one hundred and eight Jews who are introduced on the short story's first page, and appear – casually – in Waugh's first published letter to Laura from Topusko. 'We also arrange for the evacuation of distressed jews' (*L* 187). Their miserable history encapsulates a miniature summary of wartime Yugoslavia. These Jews are the survivors of anti-semitic massacres by the Ustaše (members of the Croatian Revolutionary Movement, a fascist terrorist organization). They were rounded up by the invading Italians and held in a concentration camp until the Italians in their turn surrendered to the Croatian communist partisans, who conscripted the Jews still capable of work, and then fled from the German invaders with their remaining prisoners. 'And here they were, a hundred and eight of them, half-starving in Begoy.' In the course of the story the communist partisans intern this miserable remnant once again, in the camp where the Germans and Ustaše had previously held Jews, gypsies, communists and royalists for slave labour, killing the few still alive when they also fled. At the end of 'Compassion', Madame Kanyi and her husband, the two most worthwhile members of the hundred and eight Jews are unjustly executed by the partisans.

The story's central theme is the growth of Major Gordon's compassion, the partisans' indifference to compassion, and the curious byways compassion takes to reach the human heart.

Major Gordon, Waugh's *alter ego*, is a Scottish rationalist. He has little sympathy for the Jews seeking his help. Unlike Waugh, 'Major Gordon was not an imaginative man,' but – rather more like Waugh –

> [...] He saw the complex historical situation in which he participated, quite simply in terms of friends and enemies and the paramount importance of the war-effort. He had nothing against Jews and nothing against communists. He wanted to defeat the Germans and go home. Here it seemed were a lot of tiresome civilians getting in the way of this object. ('Compassion', *The Month*, August 1949, 82)

Major Gordon is also sceptical of his official predecessor's warning that the interpreter serving the military mission is a spy for the Serbo-Croat Secret Police, because 'such things were beyond his experience'. In the course of 'Compassion' experience opens his eyes to communist secret surveillance, and modifies his attitude to the Jews. When UNRRA, the United Nations Relief and Rehabilitation Administration, requests the Jews' details prior to arranging their evacuation, he visits their cramped quarters, 'little nests of straw and rags' in a derelict schoolhouse, and leaves, half-stifled and shaken, because

> Another part of his mind was [...] slowly being set in motion. He had seen something entirely new, which needed new eyes to see it clearly: humanity in the depths, misery of quite another order from anything he had guessed before. He was as yet not conscious of terror or pity. His steady Scottish mind would take some time to assimilate the experience. ('Compassion' 86)

Aristotle defined tragedy as inspiring pity and terror. Waugh introduces the concept of tragedy obliquely, avoiding a term impoverished by overuse and employing his logical narrative structure to compensate for the understatement. In the next scene Major Gordon suspects the Jews' spokeswoman, Madame Kanyi, of protecting her own interests at her fellow Jews' expense, and is ashamed when she catches him out. She tells him gravely, 'It is not always true that suffering makes people unselfish. But sometimes it is,' and the major returns to his quarters 'in a reflective mood that was unusual to him'.

The truth of Madame Kanyi's rebuke is quickly borne out when he is publicly reprimanded by the Yugoslavian commissar for visiting the Jews in accordance with UNRRA's instructions. Smarting with resentment, his concern sharpens as approaching winter and the partisans' impassive stonewalling thwart his attempts to liberate them.

> Major Gordon did not forget the Jews. Their plight oppressed him [...] The Jews were numbered, very specially, among his allies and the partisans lapsed from his friendship. He saw them now as a part of the thing he had set out hopefully to fight in the days when there had been a plain, unequivocal issue between right and wrong. Uppermost in his mind was resentment against the General and the Commissar for their reprimand. By such strange entrances does compassion sometimes slip, disguised, into the human heart. ('Compassion' 89)

All the passages quoted above are cut from the story's final reappearance, broken up and redistributed but otherwise barely changed, in the last part of *Unconditional Surrender*.

'Compassion' is an objective portrayal of Waugh's own change of heart. Its spurs – resentment at a slight, obstinate resilience against discomfiture, the pain of failure – are all familiar from Waugh's recent military history. Turning back to his diaries and letters from Yugoslavia, alerted by 'Compassion', we can see Waugh's dispassionate detachment gradually being worn away. He does not trace his Jews' story, but they resurface with quickening concern: 'Our poor jews stay in increasing distress. The more airmen arrive the smaller their chance of getting out.' 'Every evening last week Major Clissold has hoped for an aeroplane and has been disappointed [...] On Friday we took fifty-six Jews out in intense cold and sent them back to their straw after two hours wait' (*L* 192, *D* 584). When Waugh is transferred from Topusko to Dubrovnik in late December, nothing more is heard that might relate to his poor Jews, beyond two references to 'Partisan refusal to accept Unrra or AML [Allied Military Liaison] help, if distributed by our observers' and 'Saw the unrra representatives, no good' (*D* 596, 616). But he is much occupied with a variety of other humanitarian, charitable undertakings, writing to Laura, 'My work consists solely in doing good. I distribute food to the needy and get a sense of vicarious generosity in the process. A great number of prayers are being put up on my behalf [...] I do not think there is any military appointment so congenial – good architecture, good food, wine, blameless life, and for once in my life a sense of being very popular'.[13]

The *Diaries* (595–618) give a daily picture of Waugh's benefactions to an extraordinary miscellany of suppliants – a communist French widow of forbidding appearance, a priory of hungry Dominicans, a Berlin stockbroker, a Norwegian widow, a distracted Chilean engineer with a stowaway daughter. He employs and feeds an unneeded Jewish interpreter, on three successive days referred to as 'my poor Mr Sen', who knows no English and is 'literally an agoraphobe, he led me to the hills by back alleys, from the habit of fear'. 'I also adopted a Maltese widow, castigated a Canadian for concealing his marriage [...] A Partisan came to say he had a pain, could I give him jam to cure it. The nuns got a fine load of mixed foodstuff and twittered like sparrows.' 'Looking back on the last two days I find that everything I have done, which is not much, has been benevolent...' Finally, in summary, there is his letter to Laura, 'my sweet whiskers', in February 1945:

> My life has been clouded. I boasted too soon of my happy situation. The partisans are now seeking to expel me and I think they will succeed [...] the bloodiness of the partisans and my uncertain position depress me continually; more than that there are so many unhappy people who look to me for help which I can ill supply. It seems to comfort them to come & tell me how miserable they are; it saddens me. But is it not odd? Would you have thought of me as having a kind nature? I am renowned for my great kindness here. At our headquarters in Bari however I am looked on as very troublesome and offensive. (*L* 200–1)

Waugh returned to England shortly after: the happy resolution of his prayers to be 'in my own home, at my own work, and at peace' before another year was out. He had alienated the partisans by his officially sanctioned (and later, officially ignored) investigations into religious persecution in Croatia. His paper on 'Church and State in Liberated Croatia' was tactically inopportune for the Foreign Office and his military superiors, who maintained a friendly policy towards Tito and the partisans well beyond the end of the war.

1945–65

So why did it take Waugh twenty years to begin and complete the final book of his war trilogy?

As soon as he was demobbed and *Brideshead* published, he began *Helena*. It was, partly, a Roman reflection of the modern world at war, with Brigadier Fitzroy Maclean, Waugh's military commander in Yugoslavia, providing the model for Helena's husband Constantius.[14] *Helena* was interrupted by Waugh and Laura's trip to Hollywood to discuss the projected film of *Brideshead* with MGM. Fascination with Forest Lawn took over as the negotiations failed, leading directly to the swift composition and publication of *The Loved One* in 1947–8. In 1949 he returned to his most recent war experiences in 'Compassion', and began thinking about a war novel on the theme of chivalry. *Helena* was finally finished and published in 1950. *Men at Arms* was written in 1951, published in 1952, and *Officers and Gentlemen* begun in 1953. It ran into the sand, probably about halfway through, as Waugh's health declined and he suffered his Pinfold experience in the winter of 1953–4. On his return from Ceylon, the demons routed, he completed *Officers and Gentlemen*, which was published in 1955. *Pinfold* was begun in the winter of 1955–6, and finished in 1957, when Waugh began planning *Unconditional Surrender*. That gave way first to the authorized *Life* of his recently deceased friend, the Right Reverend Ronald Knox, which was researched and written in 1958 and published in 1959; then to the last of his travel books, *A Tourist in Africa*; then to the Revised Edition of *Brideshead* (both published in 1960). *Unconditional Surrender* came out at last in 1961, followed in 1965 by the war trilogy's final recension as the one-volume *Sword of*

Honour. An impressive tally for two decades, which also included another travel book and the first volume of his autobiography. He was working on the second when he died in 1966.

This steady output is partly explicable on pragmatic financial grounds. Waugh took care not to earn too much in any particular year by timing his publications to avoid punitive post-war income tax, while continuing to earn enough to maintain his large family. However, a closer view reveals a more complicated picture.

There are relatively simple biographical factors governing the delay between 1957 and 1960. Waugh had admired Ronald Knox from his days at Oxford. When it became clear that he was dying, Waugh took on himself the difficult task of acting as Knox's companion during several dismal periods of convalescence in out-of-season seaside hotels. Even more generously, he agreed to act as Knox's literary executor, which also committed him to the significant chore of writing Knox's biography. The compassion Waugh learned in Yugoslavia is evident here. Indeed, there is a strong impression that Waugh took on these tasks as a conscious moral and even penitential duty, rather as he took on his life of Campion while hoping and waiting for the Vatican annulment of his first marriage. They required a selfless patience that did not come naturally to him. Researching Knox's biography took Waugh to Rhodesia, a journey that was funded by *A Tourist in South Africa*, which he disliked as a potboiler. Finally, he repudiated what he had once seen as his *magnum opus*, in his cut and modified version of *Brideshead Revisited*. This was, then, a period of pause and critical reassessment.

At the same time the multiple strands of Waugh's literary undertakings also began to get increasingly tangled as novels leapfrogged each other, one interrupted by the next. This study has perforce omitted the travel writings, journalism, and most of the short stories, but even within an exclusive focus on the novels and personal writings, finer criss-crossing strands proliferate, as Waugh reads and rereads his diaries and his wartime letters to Laura (which he told her to keep), raiding his full larder at will. The pillaging can be unrelated to the chronology linking Waugh's life to individual works. For instance, a fellow officer in Yugoslavia, variously appearing as

Brigadier O'Brien Twoigg, Taowig ('pronounced Twigg'), Brig. O. Twig, with 'the eyes and forehead of an orang-utang', a moustache like Osbert Lancaster's and gleaming 'little ape eyes' (*D* 600–11), is snapped up very early on, to figure as Chatty Corner in *Men at Arms*. Similarly, ideas are tried out in one novel, jettisoned, and reappear in entirely different contexts. Another example: in the manuscript of *The Loved One*, Mr Joyboy is given a back-history as an ex-hairdresser on a trans-Atlantic liner. Ultimately that becomes instead a richly suggestive part of Trimmer's past in *Officers and Gentlemen*.

Writing a trilogy presented further problems. From his earliest work, Waugh routinely set up thematic motifs that were first introduced inconspicuously in a novel's earliest pages, reappearing in many ingenious variations, until they emerged from the wings to appear with full force, centre stage. The cannibal motif in *Black Mischief*, first obliquely suggested when the barefoot Azanian soldiers eat their unwelcome consignment of army boots, is Waugh's first acknowledged example of this rapidly refined technique. In the trilogy, Waugh's intentions changed from novel to novel and promised plot strands lost interest or even significance. Chatty Corner makes the transition from *Men at Arms* to *Officers and Gentlemen*, as originally intended, but his comedy has worn thin and he is summarily hustled off-stage. The very structure of the trilogy changed as Waugh's spirits rose and fell. Having promised a trilogy at the end of *Men at Arms*, he published *Officers and Gentlemen* as the last of only two volumes, leaving the carefully composed prologue to *Men at Arms* bereft of its expected resolution. This could not do, and after marked delays Waugh completed his original design in *Unconditional Surrender*.

There are two major moments when Waugh's steady output falters – in the period on either side of the Pinfold experience, which broke the composition of *Officers and Gentlemen* in two, and in the logical next step of *Unconditional Surrender*, which was postponed until not one, but three other literary assignments had jumped the queue. This is unlike Waugh. In 1943, his letter requesting leave to write *Brideshead* stated: 'It is a peculiarity of the literary profession that, once an idea becomes fully formed in the author's mind, it cannot be left unexploited without deterioration. In fact, if the book is not written now it will never be written' (*D* 557, n.1). The warning of *Work Suspended* must have been fresh in his mind. In 1939 he had willingly abandoned it to join the Marines, but on returning to it when circumstances allowed, he found that its time had passed. In its 1942 introductory epistle, Waugh says regretfully that in spite of it being 'my best writing, [...] the world in which and for which it was designed, has ceased to exist'. The last sentence of its 1949 Postscript consigns it to even deeper oblivion, 'a heap of neglected foolscap at the back of a drawer'. No wonder that when Waugh discovered Forest Lawn's mine of literary gold, he put aside *Helena*'s patient excavations, preferring to set to work at once on Dennis Barlow's shapeless chunk of experience while it was still fresh.

Curiously, Waugh fictionalized the same response at the end of *Pinfold*; Gilbert takes out the neat manuscript of his unfinished novel from its drawer, glances through it, and puts it aside. 'He knew what had to be done. But there was more urgent business first, a hamper to be unpacked of fresh, rich experience – perishable goods.' Yet when Waugh returned from Ceylon, he did not set straight to work on *Pinfold*; he finished *Officers and Gentlemen* first. The delays came between *Pinfold* and *Unconditional Surrender*. The point is, not that Waugh always wanted to gobble up the experience closest to hand, but that '*once an idea becomes fully formed* [...] it cannot be left unexploited without deterioration'.

I would like to suggest that Waugh's ideas for the trilogy were discomposed by two traumatic experiences. First, in the military context, were the two blows inflicted on his moral core – something more than his *amour propre* – by the flight from Crete, and then by his enforced resignation. These prompted the delay in writing the Cretan episode, and the even greater delay in coming to terms with the tussle with Lovat, which he ultimately chose to omit altogether, except that he satirizes Lovat's earlier career, prior to his harassment of Waugh, in Trimmer's 'Operation Popgun' in *Officers and Gentlemen*. Secondly, in the personal sphere, were the unwelcome revelations of Pinfold's hallucinatory voices. Waugh's period of insanity and enforced self-scrutiny seem to have prompted an unexpected change of plan in the ending of *Officers and Gentlemen* – not to harry Ivor Claire over his desertion. Then he withdrew, giving time for his steady mind to reassess his last years as a soldier, and his work as an artist, before setting out, at last, on *Unconditional Surrender*.

JUSTICE, COMPASSION, AND THE BENEFIT OF THE DOUBT

Guy's decision *not* to pursue Ivor Claire by reporting his desertion is surprising because everything earlier in *Officers and Gentlemen* promoted Guy's admiration of Ivor, and consequently deepened his final revulsion from Ivor's self-serving cowardice. Guy's decision to ignore Claire's conduct – which precedes Mrs Stitch's unnecessary interference on Claire's behalf – comes as a shock to the reader, who is left in some uncertainty about the moral rightness of Guy's decision to avoid responsibility. 'For Julia Stitch there was no problem,' Guy thinks. 'An old friend was in trouble. Rally round.' As for the cheerfully pragmatic Blackhouse, 'Tommy had his constant guide in the precept: never cause trouble except for positive preponderant advantage'. In the field Tommy would have shot any man endangering a position without compunction, but 'This was another matter. Nothing was in danger save one man's reputation. Ivor had behaved abominably but he had hurt no one but himself.' Guy, on the other hand, 'lacked these simple rules of conduct. He had no old love for Ivor, no liking at all, for the man [...] had proved to be an illusion. He had a sense, too, that all war consisted in causing trouble without much hope of advantage.' And yet why were his fellow-Halberdiers prisoners of war, and why did the unknown soldier lie dead, 'if it was not for Justice?' Guy does nothing.

When Germany turns on its ally and invades Russia in late June 1941, all Guy's illusions dissolve together. There is no longer a single, recognizably evil common enemy. Guy is back in 'the old ambiguous world', where not only priests are spies and gallant friends prove traitors, but one enemy has itself turned into an unwelcome friend. The incineration of Guy's war diary is his abdication from the battle for Justice, though he will continue to serve as a soldier. It is not an act of compassion for Claire.

Yet Waugh suggested an alternative morality in a curious little scene that is planted earlier in the second half of *Officers and Gentlemen* (200–02). Guy's father is umpiring a home cricket match. He is increasingly elderly, feeling the chill, inattentive. The fast bowler of his school's team traps the last batsman LBW, but Crouchback calls 'Not out', inadequately apologizing, 'I'm sorry, I just wasn't looking, I'm afraid. Have to give the other fellows the benefit of the doubt, you know.' The cross little bowler takes a fast run up to his next ball, Crouchback sees his foot well over the line, hesitates to give a 'no ball', the wicket goes down and the match is won by the home team of Our Lady of Victories – significant name. Old Croucher was wrong first time, as the schoolboys recognize, but 'Anyway, what's the odds?' His two faulty verdicts and the errors of both teams cancel each other out. He returns to the guest house at Matchet, to celebrate the exemplary bravery of Trimmer – who may look like what he is, a hairdresser, but who carries out what Guy's father expansively misdesignates 'one of the most daring exploits in military history'.

Old Crouchback's many misjudgements are governed by generosity of spirit, courtesy, charity, giving the other fellow the benefit of the doubt. Something Guy still has to learn – and does so, in *Unconditional Surrender*.

15

Unconditional Surrender 1961 *Sword of Honour* 1965

PROLOGUE

Lovat's trivial triumph over Waugh is quickly dispatched in the Prologue to *Unconditional Surrender*, where Waugh contrives a nod to his own degrading rejection in Guy's comparable discomfiture. In 1941 'A draft of reinforcements was sent out' to Ritchie-Hook's battalion, biffing its way across North Africa, but 'Guy was not posted with them'. His omission is implicitly explained in the novel's first, retrospective paragraph, which raises the familiar 'rumours that [Guy] had "blotted his copybook" in West Africa'. In *Sword of Honour*, the novel conflating all three novels of the trilogy into a single volume, that opening retrospect and a reference to Guy's following 'two blank years' are cut and briskly replaced. Instead, we are told that by 1943 the forty-year-old Guy 'grew scant of breath so that on field exercises he was prematurely exhausted and impatient' (*SH* 542). Consequently, in August 1943 Guy's nameless brigadier legitimately refuses to take him overseas, because he is now too old to go into action. Thus Waugh camouflages his personal history by two explanations for Guy's declining military career – on the one hand his accumulation of unmerited black marks collected by Grace-Grounding-Marchpole, which was set up and sustained from *Men at Arms* onwards. And, on the other hand, the humdrum reality of his increasing age and physical limitations, which are no different from Waugh's.

At the end of *Men at Arms*, when Apthorpe died from Guy's smuggled bottle of whisky, it was the nameless brigadier who warned Guy that he never wanted to see him again. Guy's present rejection thus acquires an absurd significance: he feels that Apthorpe's ghost was *not* laid by the merely notional delivery of his bequest to Chatty Corner. 'That ghost [...] walked still in his porpoise boots to haunt him; the defeated lord of the thunder-box still worked his jungle magic.' The dropped stitch of *Officers and Gentlemen* has been neatly picked up, initiating a curious voodoo motif that becomes important in this novel.

Guy's pagan superstition is promptly countered by his father's rational, humane values. In Gervase Crouchback's conversation with his son, Waugh raises the moral issues that will dominate and finally resolve *Unconditional Surrender*. Italy has just surrendered. Guy is dismissive of the Church's role in Italy's recent confused past, and is rebuked by his father: 'you're really talking the most terrible nonsense, you know. That isn't at all what the Church is like. It isn't what she's *for*.' And when Guy says he's not interested in victory because it no longer seems important who wins, his father repeats his rebuke in a military context: 'That sort of question isn't for soldiers.' Later the same question recurs, when Virginia views the London crowds: 'What good do they think they're doing?' she asks herself, as she surveys the passing uniforms and gasmasks. 'What's it all *for*?' And again, when Guy attends his father's funeral, remorse for his own failings towards his father are 'not what he was here for. There would be ample time in years to come for these selfish considerations.' Waugh's own italics ensure that the question's force spans all these repetitions in their various contexts.

After their meeting, Guy's father provides several answers to the vast question – 'What's it all *for*?' – in a letter warning his son that he has not long left to live. His words therefore carry special authority. He begins with the Romans' resentment at their Piedmontese invaders in the nineteenth century, 'And of course, most of the Romans we know kept it up, sulking'. That word is loaded; later in the same letter Guy's father repeats it in relation to Guy's resentment at being abandoned by his nameless brigadier: 'I know you are cut up at being left behind in England. But you mustn't sulk.' For old Mr Crouchback, 'that isn't the Church. The Mystical Body doesn't strike attitudes or stand on its dignity. It accepts suffering and injustice. It is ready to forgive at the first hint of compunction.' *That* is what the Church is for. And that is what its believers are also for, whereas sulking is a demeaning human impulse to strike attitudes and vainly insist on one's dignity.

It is difficult for non-Catholics to follow Guy's argument with his father because it draws familiarly on Italian history, seen in precisely such humdrum human terms. For Guy, the Lateran Treaty,[1] by which the Catholic Church made terms with the Italian State, was an ignoble compromise. His father sees it within an entirely different scale of values, asking his son, 'When you spoke of the Lateran Treaty did you consider how many souls may have been reconciled and have died in peace as the result of it? How many children may have been brought up in the faith who might have lived in ignorance? Quantitative judgements don't apply. If only one soul was saved that is full compensation for any amount of loss of face.' Parts of this key passage are repeated at several important moments in the narrative to come.

A false sense of dignity, striking attitudes, smarting at loss of face – all these are painfully familiar elements in the slow failure of Waugh's military aspirations. Gervase Crouchback's letter to his son closes with the quaint valediction, 'Ever your affec. father, G. Crouchback' – precisely the way in which Waugh himself ended letters of paternal advice to his adolescent children. Between 1955 and 1959, the period running up to this novel's composition, first his eldest son, Auberon, and then his favourite daughter Meg went through difficult periods. Auberon was fretting to change schools, leave Downside, go into the restaurant trade, anything. Then Meg in her turn was also unhappy, frightening the nuns of Ascot by accidentally imbibing a pipette of mercury in a science lesson. Waugh's letters to both share the tone and values of Crouchback's advice to his son. To Bron: 'I should hate you to be low-spirited and submissive, but don't become an anarchist. Don't above all things put on side [...] Enough of this, but pay attention to it

[...] Your affec. papa E. Waugh.' And again, 'My Dear Bron Don't write in that silly tone. No one has any motive with regard to you except your own welfare [...] If you go [to Stonyhurst] determined to sulk, it would be hopeless.' Meg was more affectionately teased for similarly absurd self-regard. Waugh wishes her a happy birthday despite the savage persecution of the headmistress – 'You have certainly made a resourceful & implacable enemy in that holy lady [...] Sweet Meg, don't be a donkey. Everyone loves you – particularly I – me? Which I wonder is grammatical.' He, meanwhile, has prepared her room (they had just moved to Combe Florey): 'I am having a bottle of quicksilver put on your wash hand stand. The stomach pump will be kept in the cellar.' But for all his affection Waugh was unyielding. 'I don't like it at all when you say the nuns "hate" you. That is rubbish. And when you run down girls who behave better than you. That is mean. Chuck it, Meg [...] Don't whine.' And again, 'You wrote a very ignoble letter to your brother Auberon but since it was not addressed to me I will not tell you how much I despise you for your discontent self-pity detraction of others etc etc [...] All love Papa' (*L* 437, 441, 490–1, 483, 527). Gervase and Guy Crouchback are Waugh at sixty and forty, the father of the present chiding his younger self, just as his own children are chidden.

Gervase Crouchback espouses the nursery morality Waugh cherished from his youth. In *Unconditional Surrender* Guy's father encourages him to disregard his loss of face and accept the diminished prospect of settling in the family's 'Little Hall', or 'Lesser House' at Broome after demobilization. In the Prologue's second section, Jumbo Trotter is an exemplar of such virtues. In *Officers and Gentlemen*, when Ritchie-Hook left Jumbo behind on the isle of Mugg, he too suffered the blow that now falls on Guy, but 'he no longer bore resentment'. Jumbo accepts that he is on the shelf, while 'the threat of just such a surrender' overcasts Guy. Jumbo Trotter didn't sulk, and when he offers Guy temporary lodgings – 'come and stay at my little place' – Guy makes the link with Broome's 'Little Hall? Lesser House?' No – its equivalent, Number 6 Transit Camp, the unemployed officers' pool, and the dregs of the military backwater. Guy too must accept surrender to the inevitable.

But what does this surrender mean?

LOCUST YEARS

Unconditional Surrender is dedicated to Waugh's daughter Margaret, 'Child of the Locust Years', and – lest that be missed – the Prologue is also subtitled *Locust Years*. The striking Old Testament image[2] alludes to Churchill's celebrated speech to the House of Commons in November 1936, castigating the squandered opportunities of 1932–6, when Germany first started building up its military power and Britain did nothing. Now, Churchill says in his rhetorical climax, the First Lord of the Admiralty reassures them that 'We are always reviewing the position, [...] everything is entirely fluid'. So the Cabinet persists 'in a strange paradox, decided only to be undecided, resolved to be irresolute, adamant for drift, solid for fluidity [...] So we go on preparing more months and years – precious, perhaps vital to the greatness of Britain – for the locusts to eat.' Meg, born in 1942, is a child of the locusts' second swarm. In Waugh's dedication to *Unconditional Surrender*, Churchill's derision is turned against him, because Churchill, no less than Chamberlain, squandered *his* locust years of 1941–5 by temporizing with Stalin, rather than Hitler. *Unconditional Surrender* reverses expectation by not focusing on the unconditional Axis surrenders ending the war. Instead, it is concerned with, and by, the Allies' unconsidered surrender to communism. Churchill made his belated stand against the Soviet Union only when he was out of power, in the Iron Curtain speech of March 1946.

The unopposed advance of atheist communism is introduced inconspicuously in the novel's opening pages. In a reprise of the American cult of the sham in *The Loved One*, devout crowds are shown shuffling into Westminster Abbey to pay homage to the ceremonial sword of Stalingrad. George VI's gift to the Soviet defenders of the Siege of Stalingrad really did evoke a semi-religious popular response, as in the prize-winning poem Waugh partially quotes ('I saw the Sword of Stalingrad, / Then bow'd down my head from the Light of it, / Spirit to my spirit, the Might of it / Silently whispered – O Mortal, Behold ...').[3] The sword's spurious sanctification is lightly pressed home in Waugh's prose: at its *apotheosis* in the Abbey it is displayed *for adoration* by its *devotees*, mounted between candles on *a table counterfeiting an altar*. As in Renaissance iconography, the idolatry of its perverse worship is signalled by inversion – several of the novel's clever-clever characters point out that the escutcheon would be upside down if the sword were to be worn, as it should be, on a baldric. As was indeed the case.

Seemingly just as harmless as the sword of dishonour is the figure of Sir Ralph Brompton, civilian dandy and retired ambassador, nonchalantly twirling a single eyeglass on its black cord. We first meet him, ubiquitous and inexplicably influential, on his daily tour of Hazardous Offensive Operations HQ in the Royal Victorian Institute, where Guy shares his office with a gigantic plaster megalosaurus. In his own underemployed days as liaison officer at General Combined Operations HQ, Waugh was reduced to forwarding letters to himself and tracking their return to his desk (*D* 527). Both HOO and GCO are dinosaurs that have outgrown their usefulness. Meanwhile Brompton, the diplomatic adviser to HOO HQ, is occupied in 'the self-imposed task of "political indoctrination"'. With post-war hindsight, Waugh's original readers would have quickly recognized that Brompton's partisan views predict imminent communist take-overs worldwide. As Brompton blandly states, 'Tito's the friend, not Mihailovich. We're backing the wrong horse in Malaya. And in China [...] Chiang is the collaborationist', while real resistance is Mao's in the northern provinces, 'Russian trained and Russian armed, of course'. Brompton may seem 'a figure of obsolescent light comedy rather than of total war', yet as he speaks of political prejudice, 'not in the highest quarters, or among the People, but *half-way down*,' he gazes at Guy through his single eye-glass, 'without animosity seeing him with his back to the wall, facing a firing squad [Waugh's italics]'. In Yugoslavia Guy will come to learn that such outcomes are no metaphor but a routine reality.

In *Officers and Gentlemen* Waugh prepared for the cult of 'the People' in a brief night scene on Mugg when Ian Kilbannock, very drunk, harangues Guy about the war's current needs for propaganda purposes. Guy and his lot are no good: they're irredeemably out-dated, 'last-war stuff [...], the "Fine Flower of the Nation" [...] and *it won't do*'. 'Prophetically drunk', he noisily starts declaiming, 'This is a People's War [...] The upper classes are on the secret list. We want heroes of the people, to or for the people, by, with and from the people.' From shipboard

Ritchie-Hook hears the row, shouts for silence, and Ian hides 'cowering among the quayside litter' as Guy returns to his quarters.

Ian's prophesy is fictionally fulfilled in his creation of Trimmer as the archetypal 'People's hero'. Historically it was fulfilled in May 1942 – the year preceding the opening of *Unconditional Surrender* – by US Vice-President Wallace's speech hailing the new era to come with the end of the war, as 'the Century of the Common Man'. It became a popular term Waugh abhorred, because it reduced the individual to the mass (see *D* 531, 537). Readers have often misunderstood Waugh's derision. His scorn is not motivated by snobbery but by his commitment to the individual – the principle prompting him to prefer the anarchist to the socialist because 'a writer's material must be the individual soul (which is the preconception of Christendom)'.[4] For Waugh, 'the Marxist can only think in classes and categories, and even in classes abhors variety. The disillusioned Marxist becomes a Fascist; the disillusioned anarchist, a Christian'.[5] On the same principle he wearily parried the BBC interviewer's innuendo that he despised the man in the street (another variant on the Common Man), saying: 'There is no such thing as a man in the street, there is no ordinary run of mankind, there are only individuals who are totally different.'

The first two books of *Unconditional Surrender* give a broad image of unopposed British capitulation to institutionalized communism. In the last, Yugoslavian section communism is seen in grim close-up. Throughout, Waugh works via individuals rather than generalizations.

On Guy's parachute training course a fellow Halberdier, the appositely named Frank (de Souza) reappears, a debonairly indiscreet socialist under the covert surveillance of his political warder and social inferior, the apparatchik Gilpin. Socialist infiltration of the army at all levels, evident in the incongruous coupling of Gilpin and de Souza, is later paralleled by Sir Ralph Brompton, finely suited, languidly long-legged, confabulating with his shoddy antithesis, a caricature officer in a canvas-belted, crumpled off-the-peg uniform, no ribbons on his plump breast, a pipe insecurely clasped between false teeth – a 'rather suddenly gazetted brigadier', clearly promoted on ideological rather than military grounds. For all their differences, 'their political sympathies were identical'. Now Brompton's activities are more acidly identified: 'Liberation was Sir Ralph's special care. Wherever those lower than the Cabinet [...] adumbrated the dismemberment of Christendom, there Sir Ralph might be found.' Liberation, Waugh says, had not yet become a dirty word. Brompton and his shoddy anti-type comfortably agree that Frank de Souza (party member, politically sound) and Guy (traditionalist, an unwitting smoke-screen) are both suitable as liaison officers for the British mission to the Anti-Fascist Forces of National Liberation in the Balkans – that is, Tito's partisans.

When Guy arrives in the mission's headquarters in Bari, a telling scene interrupts his induction by the idealistically pro-partisan Major Joe Cattermole, and Brigadier Cape's bluff (and later historically corroborated) alternative view, that 'the Jugs' are 'a suspicious lot of bastards', their supposed partisan victories to be taken sceptically, their prime motive being the introduction of a communist state rather than the defeat of the retreating Germans. In the intervening scene, the baffled reader hears a confusing exchange between Cattermole and Cape about a presentation watch inscribed to the Royalist leader Mihailovich (at that time being discreetly sidelined by the British in favour of the apparently more proactive Tito and his partisans). The watch is ostensibly a gift from the émigré Yugoslav government in London; it was being transported by a Serb but fell into the hands of an American. Who informed Cattermole. Who informed the partisans. Who arrested the Serb. Who 'was dealt with'. That is, shot.

'This isn't soldiering as I was taught it,' says Cape. The sub-text of this tale is probably a partisan piece of anti-Mihailovich discreditation; the reader, as yet unversed in the unsavoury politics of the region, can only be sure that some innocuous Serb has been killed on incomprehensible grounds. Cape, like the British higher command and indeed Churchill himself, prefers to turn a blind eye on the dishonourable political practices of their temporary allies:

> Now remember, we are soldiers not politicians. Our job is simply to do all we can to hurt the enemy. Neither you nor I are going to make his home in Jugoslavia after the war. How they choose to govern themselves is entirely their business. Keep clear of politics. That's the first rule of this mission. (US 215)[6]

At the very end of the novel and the war, as Guy is about to return to England, Waugh mentions a British officer 'busy dispatching royalist officers – though he did not know it – to certain execution'. The pragmatic British cultivation of ignorance is one of its most shameful wartime derelictions of responsibility. In 1945 the Allies' forcible repatriation of prisoners of war to the USSR and Yugoslavia delivered them up to mass executions, death through forced marches, starvation and death in labour camps.[7] In *Unconditional Surrender* Britain is thus 'led blundering into dishonour', and liberation is merely a euphemism for the dismemberment of Christendom and its Christian values.

After the alliance with Russia, to Guy as to Waugh, personal honour alone remained. But before we come to this – the novel's main narrative – we must deal with its main source of comedy.

LUDOVIC THE CLOWN

Waugh's blurb for *Sword of Honour* explained that the trilogy was always intended to be read as 'a single story' describing the Second World War as experienced by 'a single, uncharacteristic Englishman'. 'For this purpose,' he adds, 'I invented three clowns who have prominent parts in the structure of the story, but not its theme.' Waugh's theme was the chivalry of a modern religious crusade. Apthorpe is the dominant clown of *Men at Arms*; Trimmer of *Officers and Gentlemen*; and Ludovic of *Unconditional Surrender*. Each fulfils a prominent structural purpose as Guy's antithesis. Their histories contrast with his, providing comedy and narrative drive. Unlike him, none of them are remotely chivalric.

Ludovic's enigmatic back-history, hinted at in *Officers and Gentlemen*, is confirmed in a leisurely account coupling him with Waugh's latest creation. He was once Sir Ralph Brompton's valet, secretary, sexual protégé, and – unmistakeably, his blackmailer.[8] It was for this reason, we may assume, that Brompton wished Ludovic onto Ivor Claire, who was probably another of Brompton's many young acolytes. Now less sinister and apparently less potent than he was in Crete, Ludovic allows Waugh to balance the novel's account of Britain's political infiltration with its cultural decline. Initially Ludovic is a vehicle for Waugh's mockery of Cyril Connolly, the editor of *Horizon*. Subsequently he turns into a parody of Waugh himself, while his novel, *The Death Wish*, is a travesty of *Brideshead*. During Waugh's period in Yugoslavia, he was baffled by references to 'Grave' in Nancy Mitford's bright, chatty letters. So she sent him a copy. Waugh read Connolly's *The Unquiet Grave* with ferocious attention, copiously annotated his copy and had it bound. In his diary it is summarized as 'half commonplace book of French maxims, half a lament for his life [...] badly written in places, with painful psychological jargon' (*D* 608). His final verdict on its flyleaf is more self-revealing: 'Cyril is the most typical man of my generation. There but for the Grace of God, literally... He has the authentic lack of scholarship of my generation [...] the authentic love of leisure and liberty and good living, the authentic romantic snobbery, the authentic waste-land despair, the authentic high gift of expression.'[9] Waugh's aposiopesis omits the phrase's standard completion, 'There but for the Grace of God go I'. Here this empty formula is genuinely significant. Connolly did not share Waugh's faith; nor does Ludovic share Guy's.

In *Officers and Gentlemen* Ludovic kept a journal where he recorded his aphoristic, coldly derisive observations. In *Unconditional Surrender* Everard Spruce publishes Ludovic's *pensées* in *Survival*, under the fashionably contemporary title, *Notes in Transit*. At this point Waugh makes Spruce begin to usurp Ludovic's role as a caricature of Connolly. Spruce and his four secretaries – who wear their hair long and enveloping, King's Road style, particularly one who 'went bare-footed as though to emphasise her servile condition' – are immediately recognizable from the Mitford/Waugh correspondence. In it, both often refer to Smarty-Boots Connolly and his female acolytes, particularly one whom Waugh nicknamed 'Bluefeet'.[10] *Survival* has the same seedy offices as *Horizon*, the same noxious drinks parties, the same brown-nosing of influential literati and the cultural elite, the same editorial commitment to the left. Spruce, like Connolly, is pro-Marxist, and follows the Ministry of Information's guidelines by promoting abstract modern art, because it is supposedly anti-fascist (the British equivalent of the CIA's promotion of Abstract Expressionism because it was the opposite of Soviet

Realism). 'Ah, *modern*', remarks Guy's Uncle Peregrine without hostility, glancing at ten shiny pages of squiggles in the latest *Survival*, and passing on.

Ludovic's *Notes in Transit* is manifestly a version of *The Unquiet Grave*, particularly in Spruce's summary – no apparent plan, a mixture of 'more or less generalised aphorisms' and 'particular observations'. In *Grave* Connolly's authorial persona was Palinurus, the drowned Virgilian sailor, whose unquiet grave provided his title, and whom Waugh burlesques in Apthorpe's restless spirit. When Ludovic first visits the *Survival* office, he is still haunted by his murders of Hound and the sapper (in whose boat he and Guy escaped from Crete). Waugh mocks Connolly's pretensions via Spruce's literary allusions, which mean nothing to Ludovic:

> 'there seemed to me two poetic themes which occur again an again. There is the Drowned Sailor *motif* – an echo of the *Waste Land* perhaps? Had you Eliot consciously in mind?'
> 'Not Eliot,' said Ludovic. 'I don't think he was called Eliot.' (*US* 57–8)

And the Freudian psychology of the Cave image? Another blank. For Ludovic, guiltily flinching away from memories of Hound's death, 'there was nothing psychological about the cave.'

With continued irony, Waugh makes Spruce praise Ludovic's 'extremely acute and funny' personal observations, adding cautiously; 'are they in any cases libellous?' Waugh was, by this time, well practised in litigating against others' libels of himself, while protecting his own satirical vivacities. It would be difficult for Connolly to protest at an old friend's teasing in his portrait as Spruce, when Waugh was about to be so much more critical of himself by turning Ludovic into a denigratory version of himself.

Ludovic works obsessively over his *pensées*, 'curtailing, expanding, polishing; often consulting Fowler, not disdaining Roget' (Waugh used both). His manuscripts are an accurate replica of Waugh's, written and re-written 'in his small clerkly hand on the lined sheets of paper which the army supplied'. Both share an ignorance of fashionable contemporary icons comparable to the authentic lack of scholarship Waugh identified in his and Connolly's generation. So, for instance, Ludovic is flattered by Spruce's back-handed compliment that *Notes in Transit* reads 'as though Logan Pearsall Smith had written Kafka', not realizing that Pearsall Smith was a dated littérateur,[11] and Kafka an exemplar of contemporary Angst (partnered with Kierkegaard among Waugh's pet hates). Some years earlier, Waugh was comparably discomfited by Diana Cooper's allusive and inaudible dinner conversation about O'Neill's *Mourning Becomes Electra*. Waugh, just settling in to Piers Court and preoccupied by its faulty wiring, misheard it as 'a morning with the electric'. 'She said it was a play everybody was excited about and she made me feel a bumpkin and wanted to' (*D* 429).

Ludovic's feverish composition of his novel, *The Death Wish*, is nearly identical to Waugh's when writing *Brideshead*. Like Waugh but a little earlier, 'Since the middle of December [1943] he had without remission written 3,000 words a day' (also Waugh's output when in his stride). For safety he posts the manuscript in batches to a distant, Scottish typist, suffering 'deep qualms of anxiety' till the separate, duplicate typescripts are safely returned. 'Now at the beginning of June [1944] he had it all complete, two piles of laced and paper-bound sections.'

All this is like Waugh.

But Ludovic abandons the care originally taken over his *pensées*. 'He felt no need now to find the right word. All words were right. They poured from his pen in disordered confusion [...] He barely applied his mind to his task.' Ludovic settles down to read the last chapter, 'not to polish or revise, for the work seemed to him perfect (as in a sense it was)'. Like *Brideshead*, it is 'a very gorgeous, almost gaudy, tale of romance and high drama' set in the high society glimpsed in his younger days as Sir Ralph Brompton's companion, valet and secretary. The costly *merchandise* of Brideshead Castle reappears in what Waugh terms the *equipment* of Ludovic's characters, and his *splendidly caparisoned* heroine. It is 'pure novelette', 'egregiously bad'. Waugh's frank repudiation of *Brideshead*'s weaknesses in the Preface to the novel's 1960 Revised Edition informs this parody. But the failures of *The Death Wish* also throw into relief the main difference between Ludovic's work, and Waugh's.

Ludovic has no idea where his novel is going. 'He was

possessed, the mere amanuensis of some power making for – what? He did not question.' He doesn't know what the novel's title will be, till he finishes it. He doesn't know what his heroine, the improbably named Lady Marmaduke Transept, will die of, though he knows she must die. Her lingering decline has no moral function, whereas Lord Marchmain's death is *Brideshead's* spiritual climax and its *raison d'être*. It is tonic; *The Death Wish* is merely morbid. In the language of a publisher's puff, Waugh proclaims: 'Nor was it, for all its glitter, a cheerful book. Melancholy suffused its pages and deepened towards the close.' *Brideshead*, on the other hand, ends distinctly cheerfully – in its very last words Ryder's second in command tells him 'You're looking unusually cheerful today'. *Unconditional Surrender*, and the entire trilogy compacted in *Sword of Honour*, end positively, like *Brideshead* – in spiritual rather than worldly terms. All three works encompass material disappointment and personal dis-illusion, and yet are sanguine at the close, because they are an expression of Waugh's faith.

CHIVALRY AND VIRGINIA

In the very first pages of the Prologue to *Men at Arms*, prophetically titled 'Sword of Honour', Waugh established the two themes that were to find resolution in the long delayed completion of his trilogy. As befits an epic, they are chivalry in love and war.

The Prologue opens with the honeymoon of Guy's Victorian grandparents, Gervase and Hermione, in Italy. Waugh suggests their unfulfilled union with great delicacy. Everywhere the couple are praised and petted, but 'all was not entirely well with them [... When] they mounted to their final privacy, there was a sad gap between them, made by modesty and tenderness and innocence, which neither spoke of except in prayer.' As their yacht slowly travels up the coast of Italy, 'one night in their state room, all at last came right between them and their love was joyfully completed.' At dawn, standing together at the moist taffrail, the exultant lovers take in the thronged harbour of Santa Dulcina delle Rocce, and claim it as their future home. Castello Crouchback is based on the Herberts' Villa Altachiara in

Portofino, where Waugh first met a 'white mouse called Laura' in 1933, and where they began their own honeymoon four years later. ('Lovely day, lovely house, lovely wife, great happiness.' *L* 80, *D* 422). Delayed consummation in love is swiftly paralleled by the armed effigy of Sir Roger of Waybrooke, the English knight who set out from Genoa on the Second Crusade, was shipwrecked at Santa Dulcina delle Rocce, and, his 'great vow unfulfilled', became its uncanonized *Santo Inglese*. Unfulfilled, unconsummated, unsanctified – all prefigure Guy Crouchback, by spiritual disposition an idealist, by name a cripple, crippled indeed by his failed marriage and family tendency to suicidally introspective melancholy. In *Unconditional Surrender*, disappointed by his frustrating war, Guy seeks personal honour in two private crusades: in the field of love by knowingly re-marrying the pregnant Virginia and taking on paternity for Trimmer's child; in war by his Mosaic attempt to lead the Jews out of captivity in Yugoslavia. Both are undertaken in the light of his father's advice that *Quantitative judgements don't apply.* If even one soul is saved, that is enough.

Virginia's story is the best narrative strand in this novel. She is vital, sharp, ramshackle and intensely likeable. She is unafraid of unpalatable truth. Waugh twice commends her 'fine, high candour'– or, earlier, her 'high incorrigible candour', for instance when she speaks to the witch-doctor, Dr Akonanga, of 'Women like myself [...] who want to get rid of babies'. 'Guy, *pet*' she says to her estranged husband with abundant, throw-away affection in *Men at Arms*, and again, to Guy of his pedantic uncle Peregrine in *Unconditional Surrender*, 'What an old pet. Why did you never let me meet him before?' During Guy's failed overtures on Valentine's Day in *Men at Arms*, her eyes change without warning from 'wide and amorous' to 'sharp and humorous' (*MA* 159–60). She is at her most attractive in the equally volatile scene – the best in *Unconditional Surrender* and thematically the least necessary – when staid Peregrine unexpectedly invites her out to dinner. To his bemused surprise she teases him into the 'cavalier grace' of confessing that he had thought of bedding her, and – in her case – was sure he wouldn't need the aphrodisiacs used by his friends. Alongside Waugh's more obviously creditable heroines (Roman Helena,

Brideshead's Cordelia, *Work Suspended's* innocently infatuated Julia), and closely relating to his many bright, dynamic women friends (Diana Cooper, Nancy Mitford, Ann Fleming, Penelope Betjeman, Frances Donaldson), Virginia's easy morals and chequered sexual career offer Waugh's most interesting answer to critics complaining of his male chauvinism.

Waugh is careful to sustain thematic continuity prepared for in Guy's failed rapprochement with Virginia in *Men at Arms*, and completed in Virginia's overtures to Guy in *Unconditional Surrender*. On both occasions Virginia remarks, 'How things just do happen to one!' and again, 'It's no good planning anything. Things just happen to one' (*MA* 159) and finally, shuddering over her unwilling relationship with Trimmer, 'The things that happen to one!' (*US* 165). Her acquiescent fatalism is a strong element in her make-up and part of Waugh's theme. Initially it is presented as a voodoo variant of Guy's fear of Apthorpe's unplacated ghost. 'The defeated lord of the thunder-box still worked his jungle magic,' Waugh reminds us, at the beginning of this novel, when Guy was refused service abroad. Similarly, now, Virginia is haunted by Trimmer's favourite song, Cole Porter's 'Night and Day',[12] interminably crooned by him in *Officers and Gentlemen*, and now echoed in the 'jungle rhythm' of Dr Akonanga's tom-tom as she climbs the stairs to his office, hoping to find a doctor willing to rid her of Trimmer's child. In a nightmare after his refusal, Virginia dreams she is headless, covered with bloody feathers, splayed like the sacrificial chicken used in Akonanga's incantations, a voice from her womb repeating 'you, you, you'. She gives up looking for an abortionist; to Kerstie Kilbannock she talks about Fate. But when she hears that Guy, currently bedridden by his parachuting accident, has inherited unexpected wealth from his father, she woos him – and, when that fails, frankly confesses her pregnancy and wins his charity. She is fatalistic but not passive. In Waugh's divine plan, she fulfils her destiny.

Kerstie Kilbannock is furious when she hears that Guy intends to marry Virginia, assuming she hasn't confessed her pregnancy. London life with Ian 'had not entirely atrophied her susceptibility to moral outrage'. But when Guy reassures her that he knows what he's doing, she is still shocked: 'You poor bloody fool [...] you're being *chivalrous* – about *Virginia*. Can't you understand men aren't chivalrous any more?' Thus Waugh underlines the chivalric theme of his war trilogy, and introduces a late denial of *A Handful of Dust*'s disillusion. Guy's quixotic idealism, unlike Tony Last's, is authorially sanctioned, even though Virginia is no mediaeval damsel in distress. Guy tries in vain to persuade Kerstie of his motivation. This, his first 'single, positively unselfish action', is not sought out by him but 'something most unwelcome, put into my hands,' something beyond the call of duty, 'not the normal behaviour of an officer *and a gentleman*' (my italics). Something, indeed, that will make him a laughing-stock at Bellamy's. But – Guy hesitates, and rephrases his prime concern, the soul of the unborn child, to fit Kerstie's secular scale of values – 'there's another life to consider'. Kerstie is unmoved; her 'granite propriety' only goes so far. 'My dear Guy, the world is full of unwanted children. Half the population of Europe are homeless [...] What is one child more or less in all that misery?' When she leaves, unpersuaded, Guy turns back to his father's letter: *Quantitative judgements don't apply. If only one soul was saved, that is full compensation for any amount of 'loss of face'* (*US* 194).

Guy's deliberate legitimization of Trimmer's child convincingly fulfils one half of Waugh's chivalric theme, chiefly because this romantic plot is vividly unromantic at every stage. Guy and Virginia both frankly confess the limitations of their interest in each other, and understand each other well. It is an adult relationship, whose precise parameters agitate the curiosity of their friends, but the truth is 'simple enough', and simply told. Liberated by the *Chatterley* trial's lifting of sexual censorship, Waugh is able, for the first time, to describe lovemaking with the precision denied him in *Brideshead*. Even there he managed to differentiate clearly between Ryder's sex with Celia, and with Julia. Here, he delicately balances the trilogy's tender opening description of Gervase and Hermione's shy delay and exultant consummation, with Guy and Virginia's prosaic reunion at the trilogy's close. On their return from the registry office, Guy hobbles back to bed, Virginia joins him there, 'and with gentle, almost tender, agility adapted her endearments to his crippled condition'. Who but Waugh would have made that fine distinction between *gentle*, and not quite *tender*? 'She was, as always, lavish with what lay in her gift.

Without passion or sentiment but in a friendly, cosy way they had resumed the pleasures of marriage.' In their few weeks together Guy's knee mended and 'the deep old wound in Guy's heart and pride healed also'.

THE LOST BATTLE

Guy's other chivalric crusade is less successful, both for him, and for Waugh. In 'Compassion', the story of Major Gordon's attempted rescue of the Jews at Begoy is compact and entire. Almost all of it reappears in the last, Yugoslavian book of *Unconditional Surrender*, but it is broken up to make way for inferior material. Many of the interruptions are ostensibly comic. Tension is dissipated and the cumulative impact of the short story lost. Waugh was aware of this.[13]

Unconditional Surrender's final book accommodates the composition of Ludovic's novel and its instantaneous popular success. It is titled *The Death Wish*, apparently referring to Ludovic's novel by the same name. However, this is deceptive. *The Death Wish* identifies a larger and graver phenomenon. As Guy awaits orders to leave the British Mission's Headquarters in Bari for Yugoslavia, he recalls his high hopes as he prayed at the tomb of Sir Roger, and their unfulfillment. 'Half an hour's scramble on the beach near Dakar; an ignominious rout in Crete. That had been his war.' Depression descends. A slight acquaintance unexpectedly identifies his problem: 'Crouchback has the death wish.' In confession before his departure for Yugoslavia Guy admits he wants to die, and is indifferently told by the priest that it is 'a mere scruple [...] To wish to die is quite usual today'. Other, minor characters sustain this despondent leitmotif as the trilogy draws to its end.

In *Sword of Honour* the title of this final book was changed to *The Last Battle*. Each novel of the trilogy ends with the pairing of a historic military fiasco with its fictional *reductio ad absurdum*, shrunk to absurdity. *Men at Arms* established the pattern with the real, failed raid on Dakar, and Brigadier Ritchie-Hook's diversionary escapade with his gruesome trophy of a decapitated negro's head. In *Officers and Gentlemen* the fall of Crete was counterpointed by Trimmer's Operation Popgun. At the end of

Unconditional Surrender, Waugh reintroduces an unexpected ghost – the sadly depleted figure of Ritchie-Hook, military *persona non grata* after a bust-up with Monty, dreading retirement, still straining to snap at the enemy. The novel's fictional engagement derives from a 'battle' actually laid on for the officers of the mission soon after Waugh's arrival in Yugoslavia.

Waugh, unimpressed, mentions it briefly in his diary and a letter to Laura. On a fine autumn day they were driven through beautiful countryside 'to see a battle', 'picnicked on the side of a hill with a desultory, inconclusive little battle going on a mile below us & drove home by dusk and moonlight' (*L* 188, *D* 581–2). It was clearly a meaningless publicity exercise. *Unconditional Surrender*'s battle is also staged to impress allied observers, including an American general and Brigadier Ritchie-Hook, and win American support. The object of the engagement is a solid little fort manned by Domobrans, the local Croatian nationalist home-guard, tendentiously glossed as 'fascist collaborators' for the observers' benefit.

As at the end of *Men at Arms*, Ritchie-Hook is impatient to fight and secretly arranges a diversionary attack of his own, with a Montenegrin fellow officer and a small band of his men. The battle is brief and bathetic. Two allied jets laid on for show overshoot their target. One group of partisans fall victim to friendly fire. The main partisan force run away at the first, false rumour of an advancing German division. Ritchie-Hook's little company of partisans slink away behind him as he leads their surprise attack. Oblivious and alone, he continues at a steady trot, never looking behind him, falls at the Domobrans' first burst of fire, rises and limps on. 'He was touching the walls, feeling for a handhold, when a volley from above caught him and flung him down dead.'

Two German staff cars roll up to find four dead partisans in charred woodland, a slightly dented fort, and what looks like 'the single-handed attack on a fortified position by a British major-general'. There is more to this than anyone might realize. The fortified position was once 'part of the defensive line of Christendom against the Turk' (*US* 284). Ritchie-Hook's futile death in an unworthy cause is another link uniting the beginning of the trilogy to its end. Sir Roger of Waybrooke enlisted under an Italian Count 'who promised to take him to the Holy Land but led him first against a neighbour, on the walls of whose castle he fell at the moment of victory' (*MA* 6).

Ritchie-Hook's last stand is the bathetic parallel to the novel's last real battle – Guy's Mosaic struggle to liberate his little band of Jewish survivors, stranded in hostile Yugoslavia. Characteristically, Waugh pulls the focus of his understated narrative from the ragged crowd of one hundred and eight 'displaced persons' in Guy's yard, to their three representatives – a grocer, a schoolmaster, and Mme Kanyi. She is the only one Guy can communicate with directly, in Italian (French in 'Compassion'), so avoiding the spy-interpreter Bakic's surveillance. She is articulate and intelligent; her husband, an engineer, is employed by the partisans to maintain their derelict electricity generator. For this the couple have a hut of their own and marginally better conditions than the other semi-starved Jews. Mme Kanyi is a moral touchstone like Guy's father. When warning Guy to deal with the Yugoslavs, not her, in his negotiations with UNRRA, she is disconcertingly direct:

'[. . .] It is better that you do nothing except through the Commissar. I know these people. My husband works with them.'

'You have rather a privileged position with them.'

'Do you believe that for that reason I do not want to help my people?'

Some such thought had passed through Guy's mind. Now he paused, looked at Mme Kanyi and was ashamed. 'No,' he said. (*US* 234–5)

Towards the end of Guy's service in Begoy, the grocer and schoolmaster are sent as representatives to UNRRA in Italy. The Kanyis are refused permission; the partisans need them for their electricity. Adverse weather aborts three separate attempts to have the remaining a hundred and six air-lifted out. Fearing for their survival as winter approaches, Guy makes a last, successful appeal for an air-drop of earmarked relief supplies. The partisans object. Guy's message countermanding the drop is ignored. The supplies are impounded. The Jews finally get their charitable aid. They alienate the locals by trailing around in their cast-off greatcoats and using their supplies to barter for food. In their turn they are herded into the camp once imprisoning the Četniks' victims. The tabulation of this dispiriting sequence has the dead accuracy of the fatal meet in *A Handful of Dust*. Finally, shortly before his departure from Begoy back to Mission Headquarters in Bari, Guy meets Mme Kanyi by chance and helps her carry home a load of firewood from the forest, trailed by Bakic. As he leaves, in a last act of kindness, Guy asks a subordinate to pass on a bundle of American illustrated magazines to the Kanyis, thinking they may provide welcome reading in the winter months. The next spring, he finally traces his Jews, now transported to yet another displaced persons' camp in Italy. The Kanyis are not with them.

At Mission HQ Gilpin, the communist apparatchik, informs Guy that the Kanyis were not sent to Italy with the rest of their people. He has the last word on their story. 'The woman was the mistress of a British Liaison Officer [...] The husband was guilty of sabotaging the electric light plant. A whole heap of American counter-revolutionary propaganda was found in their room.' And when Guy presses him further, 'What happened to the Kanyis?' Gilpin is sourly triumphant: 'What do you suppose? They were tried by a People's Court. You may be sure justice was done.'

That is, they were shot.

In *Put Out More Flags*, Sonia attempted to explain why her husband Alastair joined up, and died. 'He thought that perhaps if we hadn't had so much fun perhaps there wouldn't have been any war [...] He went into the ranks as a kind of penance or whatever it's called religious people are always supposed to do.' (*POMF* 124) In *Unconditional Surrender* Sonia's tentative inarticulacy is rephrased by Mme Kanyi, in her last meeting with Guy:

> 'Is there any place that is free from evil? [...] It seems to me there was a will to war, a death wish, everywhere. Even good men thought their private honour would be satisfied by war [...] They could assert their manhood by killing and being killed. They would accept hardships in recompense for having been selfish and lazy. Danger justified privilege [...] Were there none in England?'
> 'God forgive me,' said Guy. 'I was one of them.' (*US* 300)

Waugh was one with Alastair and Guy, and with the death of justice their last battle is lost.

Let us turn away from the failure of human institutions to Waugh's abiding theme.

ESCHATOLOGY

On *Brideshead Revisited*'s first dust-jacket, Waugh boldly identified his general theme as 'at once romantic and eschatological', an 'ambitious, perhaps intolerably presumptuous [...] attempt to trace the workings of the divine purpose in a pagan world'. His ultimate intention was to bring comfort to his hero and any sympathetic readers – 'a hope, not, indeed, that anything but disaster lies ahead, but that the human spirit, redeemed, can survive all disasters'. Both aims continue to sustain Waugh's final trilogy.

Eschatology is the part of theology concerned with death, judgement, and the destiny of the human soul. It's not surprising that many 'pagan' readers resisted *Brideshead*'s theme. We hate literature that has a palpable design on us.[14] In the last volume of his trilogy Waugh concerns himself with divine purpose, but effectively disperses its discussion throughout a range of human responses to what is variously seen as fortune, fate, doom, natural law and, finally, as providence.

For the sake of analytical clarity, let us take the hierarchies of belief in their natural succession, and in the rough sequence Waugh deploys, from primal superstition to faith, moving towards an approximation of the Four Last Things (traditionally Death, Judgement, Heaven and Hell).

JUNGLE MAGIC

As has already been noted, in the earlier part of *Unconditional Surrender* there is a subdued motif of primitive voodoo. The jungle magic of Apthorpe the avenger, in his porpoise boots pursuing Guy; the throb of Dr Akonanga's tom-tom echoing in Virginia's ripening womb. At the parachute training-camp, where Ludovic has reached his final ranking as camp commander, De Souza glimpses Ludovic's pallid face in hiding at an upper window, nicknames him Colonel Dracula, and launches a casual fantasy that Ludovic is a zombie, one of those men 'who are dug up and put to work and then buried again. I thought perhaps he had been killed in Crete or wherever it was.'

For Ludovic, however, it is *Guy* who is the un-dead, another restless spirit come from the underworld to haunt him. *Guy* was the sole witness of his murder of the sapper in the boat drifting from Crete; Ludovic carried him ashore in Egypt apparently dying of exposure. When the all too living Guy hails him at a *Survival* party, amicably inviting him to dinner, Ludovic is horrified: 'It was as though Banquo had turned host.' When Guy reappears at the parachuting school Ludovic commands, Ludovic's first instinct is to go into hiding, as he does for the duration of Guy's course. His second is to kill him.

In his early years as Brompton's catamite, Ludovic was fed books on Marxist economics (which he found tedious), and books on psychology, the latest voodoo. Ludovic is a pagan, a man without faith; he has no Grace to give at dinner, and goes to bed unshriven. His responses when Guy unexpectedly reappears at the parachute training camp draw indiscriminately on old and new superstitions. He 'had read enough of psychology to be familiar with the word "trauma"'. Guy's reappearance is 'an evil omen'. 'Things had been done by [Ludovic], which the ancients believed, provoked a doom.' His sense of impending doom reaches from classical antiquity to embrace all humanity. Ancient and modern, all proclaim 'this grim alliance between the powers of darkness and justice. Who was Ludovic [...] to set his narrow, modern scepticism against the accumulated experience of the species?'

DOOM

At this point Waugh gives himself time to dwell on his burgeoning theme. Ludovic consults his 'sacred scriptures', his dictionary and his Thesaurus. They are comfortless. His dictionary defines *Doom* as 'irrevocable destiny (usually of adverse fate) [...], destruction, ruin, death'. Roget's indiscriminate *Thesaurus* offers a variety of disheartening analogues – '*Nemesis*: Eumenides [...]; *lex talionis*; ruthless; unforgiving, inexorable; implacable, remorseless.' Moreover, Ludovic's moral world does not even unite the powers of darkness with the ancient laws of retributive justice (*lex talionis*). When Guy is invalided out of his parachute course, Ludovic's instinct, as in Crete, is to kill – without justification. And 'with deliberation'. In his role as camp commandant he rephrases the instructor's succinct report ('*NBG – Too old. Spirit willing – flesh weak*') into a certain death sentence, praising Guy's 'outstanding aptitude', and recommending him 'for immediate employment in action *without further training*' (my italics). Ludovic thinks he can impose his own irrevocable doom on *his* unwitting nemesis.

The wartime world of anonymous officialdom is, of course, thronged with individuals exerting what they believe to be their Doom on others. Not all, by any means, were as pettish in their malevolence as Lovat was to Waugh. Ludovic's intentions are thwarted by Grace-Grounding-Marchpole, who rejects Ludovic's recommendation for Guy's immediate, untrained employment in action, on the evidence of the secret files he has already collected against Guy. (Waugh reminds the reader of this in his Synopsis preceding *Unconditional Surrender*.) Marchpole's rejection is rejected, in its turn, by Sir Ralph Brompton and his seedy military counterpart, deliberately thwarting 'the fatuity of the security forces'. To his pleased surprise, Guy finds himself sent to Yugoslavia after all. Grace-Grounding-Marchpole's elaborate suspicions of Guy, which swelled to hubris in *Officers and Gentlemen*, dwindle to nothing towards the end of *Unconditional Surrender*.

Unlike other plot strands set up earlier in the trilogy and later abandoned, this happens for good reason. Guy's military carer was legitimately blocked by a nameless brigadier ever since Guy's gift of whisky triggered Apthorpe's death in *Men at Arms*. Now the nameless brigadier crops up in Yugoslavia, more cordial than usual. As always, Guy can't read his signature, and when he signs Guy in for drinks at the military club, Guy finds even his own name illegible. He shares 'a vicarious anonymity' with his host. Ian Kilbannock, a bolder man than Guy, simply asks the anonymous brigadier his name. It is 'Marchpole. Grace-Grounding-Marchpole, to be precise. I dare say you know my brother in London [...] He's a secret big bug. I'm just a cog in the machine.' But the big bug, the cog, and Guy – the nonentity ground between them – are all equally powerless, and nameless, in the big wheels of war.

Yet this is also the world of *Brideshead Revisited*. The heavy wheels stir and the little ones spin – not in vain, but in obedience to God's unknown, greater design.

PROVIDENCE

Waugh's variants on primitive superstition, doom and chance are strung on a network of parallels and contrasts. 'At the same time as Ludovic was contemplating the arcane operation of Nemesis in the lowlands of Essex,' Waugh writes, 'Kerstie was causing dismay' in her household by revealing 'the effects of causality in the natural order' – that is, Virginia's pregnancy. Natural law is the rationalist's equivalent of fate. Virginia fails to find an abortionist and after three attempts succumbs to her fate as a mother. But she also accepts the Catholicism required by her remarriage to Guy with a surprised ease that is the antithesis of Rex Mottram's willing suspension of disbelief. 'The whole thing is as clear as daylight to me,' she says, and after her first confession, repeats, 'Why do people make such a *fuss*? It's all so easy'. It takes her fifteen frank minutes to confess 'half a lifetime's mischief'. Afterwards, she tells Peregrine that 'it is rather satisfactory' to feel she will 'never again have anything serious to confess as long as I live'. Sceptical Uncle Peregrine holds his peace. 'He preferred to leave such problems in higher hands.' He had already abdicated responsibility in deciding ticklish questions of doctrine, when Virginia asked him what difference it might have made, had she become a Catholic on her first marriage to Guy. He 'hesitated between his acceptance in theory of the operation of divine grace and his distant but quite detailed observation of the men and women he had known'. Similarly, Waugh's own faith allows him to create credibly wayward characters encompassed in the wide embrace of providential care.

Virginia's first confession is juxtaposed with Guy's in Bari before flying to Yugoslavia. He confesses his death wish, and the sin of presumption. 'I am not fit to die.' Virginia, conversely, is fit to die, even if her newly shriven innocence seems too frail to last. 'The same words were said to her as were said to Guy. The same grace was offered.' Lying in London at night, she listens to the doodlebugs overhead with curious fatalism: 'Is that the one that's coming here?' Later one does, and she is killed.

Waugh was in London in June 1944 when the first V1 flying bombs were launched, and, hearing one fly near and low one night, confessed in his diary to being afraid for the first, and he hoped the last, time in his life (*D* 568). They must have been a test of faith for many contemporaries. The godless Everard Spruce, and his acolytes, Frankie and Coney, simply fall silent and draw back from the window. Later, Virginia's Catholic friend, Eloise Plessington, and her sister-in-law Angela (Guy's sister), discuss their instinctive prayers as this, the most random of fates, passes overhead. Eloise confesses that she can't consider Virginia's death 'as purely tragic' because, 'God forgive me for thinking so,' she died at the one time in her life when she could be sure of heaven – eventually. 'There's a special Providence in the fall of a bomb,' she says.

Her misquotation is a grim reapplication of Hamlet's stoic consolation: 'We defy augury: there is a special providence in the fall of a sparrow.' And Hamlet's aphorism refers us back to *Men at Arms* and Mr Goodall, the aficionado of ancient Catholic aristocracy.[15]

Mr Goodall inadvertently prompted Guy's first, attempted rapprochement with Virginia by his story of a distant relative of Guy's, whose Catholic marriage failed. In the course of her second marriage this woman had a brief fling with her first husband and conceived a child. The second husband assumed the baby was his own. For Goodall the child was, 'in the eyes of God, the true heir' to his natural father's heraldic title. Guy voices the reader's incredulity: 'Do you seriously believe that God's Providence concerns itself with the perpetuation of the English Catholic aristocracy?' Goodall is unperturbed. 'But of course. And with sparrows too, we are taught.'

Now, in Waugh's final volume, this resolution is set the right way up. Guy knowingly fathers Trimmer's bastard son, and takes him into the household of the faith, a family of inestimably greater value than the aristocracy. Moral order is established, and conventional validations of legitimacy and inherited class rejected.[16] This is, incidentally, another answer to those who accuse Waugh of snobbery.[17]

Hamlet expanded on the special providence in the fall of a sparrow, when he added that 'there's a divinity that shapes our ends, / *Rough-hew them how we will.*' Unlike Milton's fallen angels, debating 'Fix'd Fate, Free Will, Foreknowledge Absolute [...] in wand'ring mazes lost', Shakespeare twice embraces the combined concept of divine providence working with human agency. 'The fated sky / Gives us free scope.'[18] Virginia's death is an illustration of this; she sent her baby, in whom she had absolutely no interest, into the country to be cared for by Angela's nanny. An act of pure egotism on her part providentially saves the baby for further purposes, while Virginia, Peregrine, and the housekeeper all die. Waugh holds his peace about their fates, turning to Guy and his father as spokesmen in the delicate exploration of human attentiveness to the promptings of providence.

It takes time for Guy to recognize how the general statements of his father's letter can guide his own conduct. At Gervase's funeral, Guy's first intimations come to him, as he thinks of his prayers as reporting for duty, saying to God 'I don't ask anything from you. I am here if you want me'. That, he recognizes now, is his deadly core of apathy, which his father had noted with concern. Meditating quietly as the Requiem proceeds, Guy comes to the realization Waugh had already expressed in *Helena* and *Brideshead*: 'that somewhere, somehow, something would be required of him; that he must be attentive to the summons when it came. [...] One day he would get the chance to do some small service which only he could perform, for which he had been created. Even he must have his function in the divine plan.' And Guy prays: 'Show me what to do and help me to do it.'

Word for word, Guy's all-encompassing prayer was Waugh's in the diseased apathy of his pre-Pinfold limbo (*D* 722, 3 January 1954). For Guy, clarification comes slowly, and it is only when Virginia fails to seduce him and comes clean about her pregnancy that his way is clear.

The deployment of this theme is Waugh's final fictional testament of faith. Yet its resolutions are not easy ones. The ways of providence are hard to accept. Divine Justice is unfathomable in the unjust tragedies epitomized by Guy's dead, unknown soldier lost in Crete, in the deaths of the Kanyis specifically and all the world's innocent victims of war and persecution, in the deaths of Virginia, Peregrine, and his housekeeper as the V1s fell. And Waugh's judgements can be surprising. When Guy hears of Virginia's death, he writes: 'The news did not affect Guy greatly; [...] *far less than the departure of his two Jewish protégées*' (the Kanyis, whom he erroneously supposes to be

271

saved). Yet four pages earlier, Waugh says Guy 'felt compassion [for his band of Jews]; *something less than he had felt for Virginia and her child* but a similar sense that here again, in a world of hate and waste, he was being offered the chance of doing a single small act to redeem the times' (my italics in both quotations). The contradictory vacillation between more and less echoes Peregrine's prosaically hedged responses to Guy's grilling about his *tête-à-tête* dinner with Virginia. Did Peregrine enjoy himself? 'Yes and no. More no than yes perhaps.' Virginia was in cracking form? 'Yes and no. More yes than no. She laughed a lot.' But, Peregrine warns, she has *designs* on Guy. Should Peregrine have repeated that to Guy? 'In the circumstances, yes.' Not yes and no? 'Just yes.' Judgement is a tricky thing.

JUDGEMENT

At his father's funeral, Guy meditates on the Requiem Mass's praise of the dead: *In memoria aeterna erit justus.* He thinks the phrase is apt: 'His father had been a "just man"; not particularly judicious, not at all judicial, but just in the full sense of the psalmist.' What that implies is well illustrated by his father's umpiring of the cricket match at Our Lady of the Victories, which was initially injudicious (rash and mistaken), but completely unjudicial (not judgemental, giving the other chap the benefit of the doubt), and ultimately just (the home team had already won before he gave them the victory). Waugh's linguistic sensitivity, like an artist's heightened sense of colour, exploits differentiations that are perceptible to the observer, but hard to articulate without clumsiness.

At his father's funeral, Guy also watches Box-Bender's well-meaning eagerness to do all that must be done, to sit, stand, kneel, and pray when others do, and reflects, 'Well, "the Grace of God is in courtesy"'.[19] Waugh's moral judgements in his last piece of fiction are also softened and humanized by courtesy. In the round-up of the novel's epilogue, Ivor Claire is forgiven, having collected a DSO and 'an honourably incapacitating wound' after six months' gruelling service in Burma. He is welcome at Bellamy's, with 'his brief period of disgrace set aside and almost forgotten'. Tommy Blackhouse, too, has prospered, advancing into posts of ever greater eminence, 'never seeming to seek advancement, never leaving rancour behind him'. Yet this conclusion is not like the vinous optimism descending on the end of *Scoop*. There are minor ironies, veiled reservations. Tommy Blackhouse retires with a worldly bonanza – many decorations, 'a new, pretty wife', the rank of major-general. (Unlike Waugh, he can do nothing wrong.) Trimmer is nowhere to be found. He 'flopped everywhere' on his American tour and is said to have jumped ship in South Africa. Gilpin has gone into politics (like Lord Lovat) and is an unpopular under-secretary. Ludovic inhabits Guy's Castello Crouchback, bought with the American sales from *The Death Wish*.

Above all, between *Unconditional Surrender* and *Sword of Honour*, Waugh makes two significant alterations, both concerning Guy. Both complicate a previously simplistic presentation of providential judgement.

In *Unconditional Surrender* a brief recapitulatory paragraph recorded the failure of Guy's military ambitions as he waited in the limbo of Bari. 'He had left Italy four and a half years ago. He had taken his leave of the crusader, [...laying] his hand on the sword that had never struck the infidel. He wore the medal which had hung round the neck of his brother, Gervase, when the sniper had picked him off on his way up to the line in Flanders.' In *Sword of Honour* this passage is cut. Instead, the medal is lost. When Guy is recovering from near-death by exposure in hospital in Egypt, and Blackhouse tells him he should be recommended for 'an MC or something', Waugh inserts the following reply from Guy:

> 'I had a medal once. It belonged to my brother. My father gave it to me.' He put his hand into his pyjama coat and felt the place on his breast where it should have hung. 'It seems to have gone.' (*SH* 526, cf. *US* 217)

In the trilogy's final form, at the very end of his life, Waugh doggedly returns to, *and reaffirms* Guy's sense of moral failure. A medal – metaphoric memento of bravery and sacrifice, a spiritual heirloom – was unequivocally lost by Guy in Crete.

Unconditional Surrender, on the other hand, is generously benign. In particular, Guy is given a happy ending. Virginia sent her baby out of London to be looked after by Guy's sister,

273

but it was Virginia's new Catholic friend, Eloisa Plessington, and Eloisa's unmarried daughter Domenica, who grew fond of the child. On the last page we learn that Guy married Domenica on his return from Yugoslavia; they have two more sons of their own. They are happily settled in the Lesser House at Broome; Domenica manages the home farm; Peregrine's bequest to Virginia's boy has left them moderately well off.

In the only modification of *Sword of Honour*'s ending, Waugh robs the couple of their sons by one cut and an outsider's inserted remark: 'Pity they haven't any children of their own.' Waugh, polyphiloprogenitive paterfamilias *par excellence* and firm believer in primogeniture, would not have thought this was an entirely happy ending.

The novel's last sentence, delivered by Guy's brother-in-law, is unchanged from *Unconditional Surrender*, but acquires new irony:

> 'Yes,' said Box-Bender, not without a small, clear note of resentment, 'things have turned out very conveniently for Guy.'
> (*US* 240, *SH* 796)

In Guy's childless days Box-Bender had hoped that the estate at Broome would eventually pass to his and Angela's children. In *Unconditional Surrender*, his resentment is well-founded if unsympathetic. Things have indeed turned out well for Guy. In *Sword of Honour*'s version, Waugh avoids the pat distribution of punishment and reward tempting every author-creator. Guy and Domenica have no children of their own. Box-Bender does not know that he has been cheated of Angela's potential patrimony by a child who is not a Crouchback. His resentment is ill-founded and appears doubly mean. Peregrine knew, and nonetheless made the boy his heir.

Guy, too, is content; if he were to be asked whether he was satisfied with the dispensation of providence, he might say 'more yes than no'; more probably it would be 'yes'.

HEAVEN

Waugh's blurb for the dust-jacket of *Sword of Honour* ends sadly.

On reading the book I realized that I had done something quite outside my original intention. I had written an obituary of the Roman Catholic Church in England as it had existed for many centuries. [...] It never occurred to me, writing SWORD OF HONOUR, that the Church was susceptible to change. I was wrong.

Even in *Unconditional Surrender* in its original form, there is a strong elegiac note that is at its most poignant in the Requiem Mass for Guy's father. This sustained *tour de force* is full of affectionate humour and nostalgic tenderness. The convent school's funeral tea where 'what was lacking in nourishment was compensated for by ingenuity of arrangement [...] slices of spam were cut into trefoils'. The solitary drifting leaves in Broome's tree-lined avenue, bringing memories of Guy's boisterous November days leaf-catching with his mother in his 'wholly happy childhood' (a personal memory deriving from the earliest days of Waugh's courtship of Laura).[20] It is warm with love – 'To Guy his father was the best man, the only entirely good man, he had ever known'. It is rich in Guy's devout attention to the words of the Mass, half in Latin, half translated and embellished in Guy's ruminations.

A valedictory melancholy colours this section, titled *Fin de Ligne*. Guy, as Miss Vavasour sadly notes, is the last of his line. Broome Hall itself lies at the end of a road, its drive a continuation of the village street, narrowing to a little frequented track overgrown by hedges. Lesser House, where his father suggested Guy should end his days, is at the end of another cul-de-sac, although at the back it is open to the park. There is an open vista to this retreat, like the sunlit solitary peace revealed from Guy's drifting parachute, before gravity and his accident claimed him.

It is noticeable that in *Unconditional Surrender* Waugh twice deliberately applies the orthodox perception of paradise to Virginia and Guy's mundane experiences. Humanity can have no other sense of the divine. At Gervase's funeral Guy meditates on several passages from the traditional Latin requiem, but Waugh withholds its description of paradise. Shortly after, he applies it, translated into English, to Virginia's capacity in a diverse world to find her own place 'of coolness, light and peace'. Much later Guy makes his parachute jump, momentarily loses consciousness, and comes to himself enveloped in hazy November sunlight and absolute solitude:

He experienced rapture, something as near as his earthbound soul could reach to a foretaste of paradise, *locum refrigerii, lucis et pacis.* The aeroplane seemed as far distant as will, at the moment of death, the spinning earth. As though he had cast the constraining bonds of flesh and muscle and nerve, he found himself floating free; the harness that had so irked him [...] now almost imperceptibly supported him. He was a free spirit in an element as fresh as on the day of its creation.

All too soon the moment of ecstasy ceased. He was not suspended motionless; he was falling fast [...] At one moment he had the whole wide sky as his province; at the next the ground sprang to meet him. (*US* 128–9)

This is more than an accurate description of Waugh's own parachute accident. It is a compelling image of Guy's frustrated longing for death, which he shared with Waugh. A foretaste of liberation from Broome's Lesser House, from Jumbo Trotter's little place, from Piers Court and Combe Florey.

*

The changes brought about by the Second Vatican Council were debated and ratified between 1962–5. Their intention was to make the Church more popularly accessible. Latin gave way to the vernacular; the priest celebrating mass was to face the congregation instead of the altar; the congregation were to participate audibly in their prayers – what Waugh, a lover of silent, private prayer, called 'making a row'. Waugh objected to these and other changes on strong rational, emotional, aesthetic and democratic grounds. He bitterly regretted the loss of Tenebrae, which is so important to the structure of *Brideshead Revisited*; he also mourned the loss of Easter as a feast of dawn, and Christmas as the Holy Night. Far from enjoying the publicly shared celebration of Mass, Waugh more than once asserted that in his youth he had been drawn to Catholicism not by its splendid rituals, but by the 'spectacle of the priest and his server at low Mass, stumping up to the altar without a glance to discover how many or how few he had in his congregation; a craftsman and his apprentice; a man with a job which he alone was qualified to do'.[21] It is precisely the description Guy had applied to the providential summons he hoped, some day, to hear.

As for the 'active participation' called for by the Second Vatican Council, Waugh's personal protest was characteristically blunt, according to his daughter Hatty. 'He couldn't bear the changes in the Mass; he used to go out during Mass and sit in the car. Every time he thought the priest was about to say "Lord be with you" and the congregation responded "And you too", he used to beat the horn for the "you too"...'[22]

From 1964–6 Waugh's correspondence with Cardinal Heenan, friends, family, and his dwindling diary entries all chart his growing desolation. 'Every attendance at Mass leaves me without comfort or edification.'[23] 'I find the new liturgy a temptation against Faith, Hope, and Charity' (*L* 631). 'I shall not live to see things righted' (*D* 793). Finally, in late March 1966, 'The Vatican Council has knocked the guts out of me [...] Easter used to mean so much to me [...] they destroyed the beauty of the liturgy. I have not yet soaked myself in petrol and gone up in flames...' (*L* 638–9).

Ten days later, on Easter Day like Rossetti, Waugh died. In the morning he had attended Latin Mass, in the manner of the Old Faith. His daughter Margaret wrote to Diana Cooper:

> Don't be too upset about Papa. I think it was a kind of wonderful miracle. You know how he longed to die and dying as he did on Easter Sunday, when all the liturgy is about death and resurrection, after a Latin Mass and holy communion would be exactly as he wanted. I am sure he had prayed for death at Mass. I am very happy for him.

Her sister, Hatty, had prayed that they would not be able to resuscitate him.

Appendix A

Appendix B

LAYCOCK AND IVOR CLAIRE

The potential association of Bob Laycock with the fictional Ivor Claire is complicated. It illustrates the dangers inherent in all simplistic one-to-one identifications, even in cases as luminous as Lovat's links with Trimmer/McTavish. It is further complicated by Waugh's understandable changes of mind in the twenty years embracing his wartime experiences, and their gradual recreation in the *Sword of Honour* trilogy. Waugh's feelings about Laycock seem to have changed more than once; his presentation of Claire also undergoes readjustments in the course of the three novels and their final single-volume recension.

In *Men at Arms* Waugh clearly sets up a long plot-trail by establishing Guy's schoolboy sense of honour through his memories of the Truslove story, and its antithesis in Truslove's fellow-soldier, Congreve, whose shameful cowardice casts a permanent shadow over his company. In *Men at Arms* the obvious parallel to Congreve appears to be Leonard, the trainee Halberdier whose wife persuades him to avoid combat abroad and take a cushy home posting in canteen work. Retribution follows swiftly via an authorial thunderbolt killing him in the London Blitz.

However, in *Officers and Gentlemen*, the showy polo-playing Congreve's true function emerges as the predictive parallel to Ivor Claire, hero of the Corso Hippico in Rome. Claire's desertion from Crete, the night before the Allied surrender, casts its shadow of proxy shame over Guy, just as Congreve's fellow-soldiers felt tainted. To the non-specialist reader it

279

appears to have nothing to do with Bob Laycock, who is amply and clearly fictionalized in Guy's commanding officer, Tommy Blackhouse. And Blackhouse – to his irritation – is kept out of the entire Cretan débâcle by falling on the eve of their disembarkation and being shipped back to Egypt with a broken leg.

Consequently, to most readers it must come as a complete surprise to hear that, shortly after the publication of *Officers and Gentlemen* in July 1955, Ann Fleming sent a telegram to Waugh ending 'Presume Ivor Claire based Laycock dedication ironical Ann'. In his diary for 6 July Waugh records 'horror' at her message, quoted verbatim. He concludes, 'I replied to say that if she breathes a suspicion of this cruel fact it will be the end of our friendship'. His letter to her corroborates the diary entry, omitting the crucial phrase, 'this cruel fact': 'Your telegram horrifies me. Of course there is no possible connexion between Bob and Claire. If you suggest such a thing anywhere it will be the end of our beautiful friendship [...] For Christ's sake lay off the idea of Bob = Claire [...] Just shut up about Laycock, Fuck You, E. Waugh.' Ann Fleming's prompt reply is cheerfully impenitent: 'Dearest Evelyn Panic is foreign to your nature and you rarely use rough words. Why do you become hysterical if one attempts to identify your Officers and Gentlemen? [...] May I have permission when rereading the book to imagine that Trimmer McTavish is Lord Lovat? – I won't tell anyone else [...] Love and thankyou and Fuck you.' The friendship was not broken off.[1]

The diary's reference to 'this cruel fact' apparently contradicts Waugh's contention that 'there is no possible connexion between Bob and Claire'. Gallagher draws on the *OED*'s recorded usage of 'fact' to mean 'alleged fact', and tentatively suggests that 'Waugh already knew the gossip about Laycock's "take-off" from Crete, and that it was baseless. He also knew that Fleming (a mischief-maker as he was) would enjoy spreading the rumour that *Officers and Gentlemen* endorsed the gossip, which could destroy his friendship with Laycock and his wife. He therefore boiled over.'[2]

However, the association between Laycock and Claire also seems to be inadvertently reaffirmed by a verbal echo uniting the real, and the fictional figures, in similar contexts. On the eve of surrender, Claire argued that in later, wholly democratic times, it might be perfectly honourable for officers to leave their men – it might indeed be laid down in the King's Regulations as their duty, to train up reinforcements. Guy's objection, that men might not take kindly to being trained by deserters, was smoothly parried by Claire: 'Don't you think that in a really modern army they might respect them the more for being fly?' In Waugh's diary covering the period after his return from Crete, he noted that Laycock was reported missing while cutting communications behind Rommel's line. 'It looks unlikely that he has survived, but in White's everyone says he is too "fly" to be caught' (D 517). I have only found this word used once elsewhere by Waugh.[3]

At this point in the diaries there is no sign that Waugh disapproved of the attitude generally held in White's. Moreover, Waugh had expressed no compunctions about his and Laycock's flight from Crete in his letter to Laura, written from Egypt, the day after they were lifted off from Sphakia: 'I shall have a great deal to tell you when we meet which I cannot write now. Meanwhile be profoundly grateful to God & his saints for my preservation during the days May 28 – June 1st (operating largely through the forceful personality of Bob Laycock)' (L 153, 2 June 1941).

It is apparent from Gallagher's account that there *was* negative gossip about Laycock's departure from Crete, although Gallagher's evidence, drawn from contemporary military documents, shows this gossip to be baseless.[4] For a suspicious reader it would be possible to read Ann Fleming's suggested irony into Waugh's Dedication of *Officers and Gentlemen*, which begins auspiciously, 'To Major General Sir Robert Laycock, K.C.M.G., C.B., D.S.O. That every man in arms should wish to be' – but continues with an unusually comprehensive disclaimer: "*He* [i.e. Laycock] *will recognize this story as pure fiction: that is to say of experience totally transformed. No real character is portrayed [. . .] No unit, formation, command, organization, ship or club, no incident, civil or military*' – nothing, in fact – '*is identifiable with the realities of those exhilarating days* **when he led and I lamely followed**' (Waugh's italics, my bold).

However, I believe Gallagher is right to maintain that it needed no illicit flight for Waugh to feel shamed by the Cretan defeat, and also that he did not want to spoil his friendship with Laycock and his wife Angie. Consequently he refrained from any overt criticism of Laycock, just as Guy refrains from pursuing Ivor Claire. But it is also probable that Waugh's later feelings, and writing, were affected by his subsequently wounded *amour propre* in 1943, when Laycock failed to take him on Operation Husky and Lovat engineered his forced resignation. It was *this* that fed Waugh's suspicious resentment, and seeped into his long-meditated and planned retribution: the creation of Trimmer, of Ivor Claire, and the introduction of Mrs Stitch's unsavoury role at the end of *Officers and Gentlemen*.

The prospective difficulty of dealing with this intractable chunk of experience may well have added to the other factors triggering Waugh's Pinfold breakdown at the crucial point in mid-composition of *Officers and Gentlemen*. There is a comparable, and opposite diminution of tension when Waugh resumed his story six years later, in *Unconditional Surrender*. Here 'the full culpability of Claire's desertion' is covered in the Synopsis, but Claire then vanishes from view, only to be heard of at the end of the novel, his reputation ostensibly restored by six months' guerilla service with the Burmese Chindits, a DSO, and 'an honourably incapacitating wound'. Ironies are still audible, however: 'He was often in Bellamy's now. His brief period of disgrace was set aside and almost forgotten.' Blackhouse's retirement from service in the Epilogue closing *Unconditional Surrender* is also ambivalent: his many decorations, pretty new wife, and increasing eminence seem the fruit of a happy disposition, rather than particular courage – 'never seeming to seek promotion, never leaving rancour behind'. Blackhouse seems altogether much more like 'Lucky' Laycock (as Wikipedia records him) than the somewhat seedy Ivor Claire.

There are even more clearly identifiable changes of attitude when Waugh finally cut and adjusted the three novels to create his coherent, single-volume trilogy, *Sword of Honour*. Here all references to Truslove and Congreve are cut from the *Men at Arms* chapters. There are also several significant cuts in Guy and Tommy Blackhouse's discussion of Claire's desertion, when both meet in hospital in Egypt after the fall of Crete. These cuts diminish Claire's culpability and moderate Guy's excessive high-mindedness. *Sword of Honour*'s Blackhouse no longer tells

Guy, 'Ivor's put up a pretty poor show. *We* know that – you won't find me applying for him a second time' (missing from *SH* 527). And when Guy muses on Blackhouse's laid-back response to Claire's desertion, so different from his own sense of abhorrence, the following parenthesized and italicized lines are cut from *Sword of Honour*'s version:

> Tommy had his constant guide in the precept: never cause trouble except for positive preponderant advantage [...] This was another matter. Nothing was in danger save another man's reputation. Ivor had *[behaved abominably but he had]* hurt no one but himself. He was now out of the way. *[Tommy would see to it that he was never again in a position to behave as he had done in Crete.]* His troop was out of the way too, until the end of the war. It did not much matter, as far as winning the war went, what they said in their prison camp. *[Perhaps in later years when Tommy met Ivor in Bellamy's he might be a shade less cordial than of old. But to instigate a court martial on a capital charge was inconceivable; in the narrow view it would cause endless professional annoyance and delay; in the widest it would lend comfort to the enemy.]* (*SH* 529–30, cf. *OG* 319–20)

Most significant is Waugh's addition to *Sword of Honour*'s text of this conversation. Tommy is delighted by Guy's escape, congratulating him with 'They ought to give you an MC or something', except that such honours are handed out after victories, not defeats. Guy responds,

> 'I had a medal once. It belonged to my brother. My father gave it to me.' He put his hand into his pyjama coat and felt the place on his chest where it had hung. 'It seems to have gone.'
> Tommy said, 'The R.A.M.C. no doubt' and turned to more practical matters. (*SH* 526, not in *US*)

For Blackhouse the loss of Guy's medal is a matter of indifference; the Royal Army Medical Corps probably stole it. For Waugh, it is symbolic.

When Cyril Connolly reviewed *Men at Arms*, he predicted the medal would play an important part in the promised trilogy: 'I should guess one of its themes to be the particularly Catholic way in which a holy medal preserves the hero from sin' (*CH* 337). Connolly is, in fact, merely appropriating Gervase Crouchback's comment when he gave Guy the medal; such medals had helped soldiers avoid the temptation of prostitutes.

Waugh quickly quashed Connolly's suggestion: 'The medal is not, as far as I know, going to play much part in the novel' (*L* 383). It reappears late in *Unconditional Surrender*, in a brief recapitulatory paragraph introducing Guy's visit to the confessional in Bari, prior to his transfer to Yugoslavia.

> He had left Italy four and a half years ago. He had then taken leave of the crusader whom the people called 'il santo inglese'. He had laid his hand on the sword that had never struck the infidel. He wore the medal which had hung round the neck of his brother, Gervase, when the sniper had picked him off on his way up the line in Flanders [...] (*US* 217)

All this, and a little more, Waugh cut from *Sword of Honour*, introducing instead Guy's loss of the medal during the Battle of Crete. At the end of his life, Waugh deliberately suggests the loss of honour that Crete symbolized. It was a disgrace far larger than the misbehaviour of any single individual. Where was the bravery of their brothers, fallen in the First World War?

Notes

CHAPTER 1. *DECLINE AND FALL*

1. Opening quotations from *ALL* 171, followed by 'Our Children's Corner', *The Isis* (2 May 1923), 7; 'Children's Corner, *The Isis* (20 June 1923), 16 (both unsigned); and 'The Union', *The Isis* (3 March 1924), 9. See also p. 287, n.5.
2. I will follow Waugh's practice in using this generally accepted title uniting Carroll's two volumes, *Alice's Adventures in Wonderland* (1865), and *Through the Looking Glass* (1872).
3. According to legend, after a series of defeats during his campaigns fighting for Scottish independence, Robert the Bruce hid in a cave, where he watched a spider repeatedly re-climbing its thread to make its web. The lesson learned, he defeated the English at Bannockburn, and won the Scottish crown.
4. 'Grimes sought to enliven me with stories of his ups and downs [...] Every disgrace had fallen on this irrepressible man [...] Grimes always emerged serenely triumphant' (*ALL* 229).
5. Waugh published his analysis of Firbank's technique *after* the publication of *Decline and Fall*, in March 1929 ('Ronald Firbank', *EAR* 56–8).
6. i.e. a beanfeast. In Wales, Waugh had noted 'a pleasing Curzonism' – Lord Curzon's pretentious mispronunciation of 'beano' as though it were some grand Latin term, 'bayāno' (*D* 213).
7. W. Pater: essay on Leonardo da Vinci in *Studies in the History of the Renaissance* (1873). Pater's meditation on the Mona Lisa begins: 'She is older than the rocks among which she sits; like the Vampire, she has been dead many times, and learned the secrets of the grave ... '. She is, then, another death-defying rider on the Great Wheel, an older, more attractive sister to the indestructible Grimes. Grimes's pederasty is frankly unveiled in *ALL* 277–8.
8. Another of Waugh's childhood favourites. 'The Happier Hunting Ground', the name of the pets' cemetery in *The Loved One*, may have

come from *The Wind in the Willows,* ch.9 ('Sicily is one of my happy hunting-grounds,' says the Sea Rat). But it is also an American Indian name for the afterlife.

CHAPTER 2. *VILE BODIES*

1. I am indebted to Nicholas Shakespeare for the full, unpublished pre-production transcript of 21 interviews for his 3-part biography, *The Waugh Trilogy,* Arena, BBC 2 (1988), hereafter *NS Interviews.* Since the pagination in this composite text runs in several separate batches, each reference is also identified by the name of the interviewee; here *Lady Pansy Lamb,* 68–9.
2. *NS Interviews, Harold Acton,* 47; H. Acton: *Memoirs of an Aesthete* (London: Methuen, 1948), 204.
3. In his film, *The Scarlet Woman,* Waugh played the Dean of Scone College in a silly wig, and Lord Borrowington, a penniless peer and pimp with burnt-cork moustache, shadowed cheeks and low eyebrows. See photo 5, *ALL* 214. In *DF* Grimes and Prendergast's wigs suggested transformative resilience (but Prendy was also hampered by a wooden leg). In *VB* they acquire a negative moral resonance.
4. Waugh refers to Brian Howard as 'Poor old Hat' (*D* 315). In *VB* he is mocked as Johnny Hoop, a very minor character whose party invitations are adapted from *Blast* and Marinetti's *Futurist Manifesto,* with 'two columns of close print; in one was a list of all the things Johnnie hated, and in the other all the things *he thought he liked*' (*VB* 51. My italics). This is an accurate description of Brian Howard's 16 inch high invitation to his party, 'The Great Urban Dionysia' on 4 April 1929. See *Brian Howard, Portrait of a Failure,* ed. Marie-Jacqueline Lancaster (London: Anthony Blond, 1968): Hat hoax, 272–5; parties, 267–8; Brian's Hat-art and party invitation reproduced between 300 and 301. Brian Howard later reappears as Ambrose Silk in *POMF*; see p. 294 n.8.
5. See Waugh's review of a biography of Northcliffe, August 1930, *EAR* 98.
6. Both epigraphs come from Lewis Carroll's *Alice's Adventures in Wonderland* (1865), II: *Through the Looking Glass,* chs. 2 and 4 respectively.
7. My italics. 'Do you, or do you? [...] Are we, or are we?' (53); 'Do you, or do you' (82); Haven't you, or haven't you?' (86); 'Don't you think so, or don't you?' (49); 'Don't you think?' (84: after Adam and Nina sleep together for the first time); 'Don't you think, or don't you? (58, 59, 188).

8. According to Harold Acton (*NS Interviews*, Acton, 44).
9. The body of the deceased is committed to the grave, 'earth to earth, ashes to ashes, dust to dust, in sure and certain hope of the Resurrection to eternal life, through our Lord Jesus Christ; who shall change our vile body, that it may be like to his glorious body'.
10. 'Tess as a Modern Sees It', *Evening Standard*, 17 January 1930, 7.
11. Waugh is uncannily prescient in Father Rothschild's prophecy: 'Wars don't start nowadays because people want them. We long for peace, and fill our newspapers with conferences about disarmament and arbitration, but there is a radical instability in our whole world order, and soon we shall all be walking into the jaws of destruction again, protesting our pacific intentions' (*VB* 144).

CHAPTER 3. *BLACK MISCHIEF*

1. *RP* 14.
2. First published under the title *The Autobiography of Emperor Haile Selassie I* (1976). Quotations from the introduction, xiii, and chapter 12, pp. 65, 66.
3. *WA* 134.
4. Riszard Kapuściński: *The Emperor* (London: Picador 1983), 143–4.
5. 'Father Knox showed how from the anthropological considerations of our present ideas about food and drink, the apportionment of work between men and women, burial customs and drama, we were rapidly approaching the civilisation of the savage', 'The Union', *The Isis* (5 March 1924), 9. Waugh also said this speech showed 'the same training' as the one picked out for special praise, quoted on p. 5 above. Waugh later became a friend of Ronald Knox, whose authorized biography he wrote in 1959.
6. Joab was David's commander, a serviceable, sometimes self-serving subordinate who silently engineered the expeditious execution of two rivals, Abner and Amasa, and the deaths of Uriah (whose wife David desired) and Absalom (David's treacherous son). Major Joab is closely modelled on him, see 2 Samuel, chs ii, iii, xi, xviii and xx. In the *Book of Ruth*, Boaz is a benevolent patriarchal figure offering kinship and concubinage to Ruth. This pastoral idyll finds its degenerate equivalent in *Black Mischief*'s corpulent Boaz and his coarser courtesan, Madame 'Fifi' Fatim Bey.
7. Jack Driberg: *The Savage as He Really Is* (London: Routledge 1929), 1. The arresting opening to an eloquent, first-hand plea for cultural understanding of 'savages'. The King of Rabbah's 'naïve remark suggests a profound truth [. . .] For it cuts both ways. It applies to the civilised man as well as to the savage.' (Both suspect each other

of barbarism.) Before leaving for Abyssinia, Waugh contacted his Lancing friend Tom Driberg for an introduction to his older brother in Addis Ababa (*L* 50).

8. 'An Open Letter to his Eminence The Cardinal Archbishop of Westminster', May 1933. Although 'allegedly withdrawn before publication' Waugh had at least 5 copies bound and distributed. See R. M. Davis et al: *A Bibliography of Evelyn Waugh* (New York: Whitston, 1986), 7. Hereafter *Bibliography*.

9. See p. 16.

CHAPTER 4. *A HANDFUL OF DUST*

1. It is now owned by a family Trust controlled by the children of the last Countess of Beauchamp, and lived in by the daughter of the penultimate Lord Beauchamp's youngest son.

2. Paula Byrne points out that the dining room, with its hammer beam roof and minstrels' gallery, where the local choir sang at Christmas, is described 'exactly' in *HD*. See her *Mad World: Evelyn Waugh and the Secrets of Brideshead* (London: HarperPress, 2009), 160.

3. 'Angels in printed cotton smocks, rambler-roses, flower-spangled meadows, frisking lambs, texts in Celtic script, saints in armour, covered the walls in an intricate pattern of clear, bright colours [. . .] the altar steps had a carpet of grass-green, strewn with white and gold daisies' (*BR* 47–8). See also p. 48.

4. 'Fan Fare', April 1946, *EAR* 303. 'Other sorts of savage at home' continues the theme of *BM*.

5. Mr Christie predicted the nature of his rare visitors by his premonitory visions: 'Sometimes I see a pig or a jackal; often a *ravaging tiger*', *Ninety-Two Days* (1934, repr. Penguin 1987) 63, my italics. Hereafter *92 Days*.

6. All italics mine, apart from '*everything*'.

7. M. Bradbury: *Evelyn Waugh* (London: Oliver and Boyd 1964), 62, 55, 67.

8. Divorce on hotel evidence was achieved by Wallis Simpson in order to marry the abdicated King Edward VIII, and by Waugh's friend, Diana Guinness, to live with and later marry Oswald Mosley. In both cases the acquiescent husband played out the seaside charade to exonerate his adulterous wife.

9. See Donat Gallagher: '*Holy Deadlock* and *A Handful of Dust*: A. P. Herbert, Evelyn Waugh, and Divorce Law Reform in the 1930s' in *The Happy Couple: Law and Literature*, ed. Neville Turner and Pamela Williams (Sydney: Federation Press, 1994). Waugh believed that the Christian religions, all of which were opposed to divorce, should

teach the sanctity of the marriage bond (which Waugh upheld) to their own members, but that the law should cater for the secular majority, which wanted the right to divorce.

10. Artemis Cooper (ed.), *Mr Wu and Mrs Stitch: The Letters of Evelyn Waugh and Diana Cooper* (London: Hodder & Stoughton, 1991), 43–4. Hereafter *Wu/Stitch*.

11. The allusion to Proust's *À la recherche du temps perdu* in two chapter headings, i. *Du Côté de Chez Beaver*, and vi. *Du Côté de Chez Todd*, seems highly ironic. Neither Todd nor Beaver inhabit *le temps perdu*, the lost chivalric time nostalgically sought by Tony. Waugh did not rate Proust. Later he confessed, 'I remember how small I used to feel when people talked about him & didn't dare admit I couldn't get through him' (*L* 270), while his first wife was gushing 'I do adore Prousty-Woosty' (*NS Interviews; Pansy Lamb,* 81). Waugh tried Proust again in 1948, and dismissed him as 'a mental defective' with 'absolutely no sense of time […] And as for the jokes!' (*L* 273–4).

12. (*L* 88). Henry Green was the *nom de plume* of Henry Yorke. He is indexed under Yorke in Waugh's *Letters*, and most critical texts on Waugh.

13. The chapters' numbered titles are: i. *Du Côté de Chez Beaver*; ii. *English Gothic*; iii. *Hard Cheese on Tony*; iv. *English Gothic – II*; v. *In Search of a City*; vi. *Du Côté de Chez Todd*; vii. *English Gothic – III*. Waugh's early taste for the bizarre and surprising, expressed in his Union review while an Oxford undergraduate (see p. 5 above), is also 'Gothic'.

14. Two days before 'Fan-Fare' was published, Waugh reviewed George Orwell's *Critical Essays* under the title 'A New Humanism' (6 April 1946, *EAR* 304–7). It casts light on Waugh's conception of humanism. Orwell's essays are of 'absorbing interest' because 'they represent at its best the new humanism of the common man', evident in Orwell's democratic catholicity of subject matter. Their 'one serious weakness' is that Orwell 'seems never to have been touched at any point by a conception of religious thought and life'.

15. *92 Days* 116. Waugh enjoyed reading 'most of Dickens' aloud to his two daughters, Margaret and Harriet, every evening for two years when they attended a local day-school (*NS Interviews, Harriet Waugh,* 57).

16. Tony's inserted speech begins 'You would hear better and it would be more polite if you stood still when I addressed you', and ends with the lines quoted here (*HD* 206–7). His confusion of Brenda with Rosa earlier in this speech is a significant implicit recognition of his own fault as a husband. See my essay on 'Waugh's *A Handful of Dust*: Right Things in Wrong Places', *Essays in Criticism* (January 1982), 65–6.

17. Hebrews 13. xiv, predicting the Fall of Jerusalem. In *BR* Waugh returns to the Fall of Jerusalem when Cordelia quotes the Lamentations of Jeremiah I.i: *'Quomodo sedet sola civitas'* ('How doth the city sit solitary...'). See pp. 108–9.
18. In 1925 Colonel Percival Fawcett disappeared with his son while searching for a lost city in Brazil. His nameplate and compass were later found with two different Indian tribes. In 1932 a Swiss trapper in the Brazilian jungle discovered 'a captive, and very disconsolate', tall, blue-eyed, white-bearded white man in an Indian village, who managed to talk to the Swiss while the Indians were preoccupied by a drinking bout. His signet ring, and the name he gave of his backer in São Paolo, were later corroborated. This prompted Peter Fleming, the brother of Ian Fleming, to undertake an unsuccessful search for Fawcett in 1932, published as *Brazilian Adventure* (1933, repr. Northwestern University Press: The Marlboro Press, 1999). Waugh consulted Fleming before setting out on his own Brazilian journey in December 1932, and reviewed his book after his return (August 1933, *EAR* 136–8). See *Brazilian Adventure* 29–30 for the Swiss trapper's account of Fawcett's discovery, and 157–8 for Fleming's final conclusion: that Fawcett would either have tried to escape, and died in the attempt; or, after eight years in captivity, he had lost his mind or his memory. Fleming's balanced account extends little hope for Tony Last.
19. Waugh 'goes out of his way to establish grounds for Brenda's dissatisfaction. Tony is a prig and a bore, an amiable half-baked schoolboy living in a world of arrested development. The focus of the tragedy has moved beyond questions of personal responsibility [...] Waugh uses Tony as a foil to the barbarities of modern civilization while refusing his ideology heroic status. He is lamentably weak, suffers from misplaced tolerance, and is a feeble shadow of the gentlemanliness he supposes himself to represent', Martin Stannard: *Evelyn Waugh: The Early Years 1903–1939* (London: Dent, 1989), 361, 381.
20. Bradbury, op. cit. 62.
21. See *Bibliography*, 67. The still active copyright for *The Man Who Liked Dickens* was a practical reason for its alternative ending.

CHAPTER 5. *SCOOP*

1. *'Suppose that this particular district is crossed, on an average, by two strangers a year; one in every two hundred Indians knows some English; one in every fifty Indian houses possesses surplus food; most Indians go to Bon Success once in every five years; there is one Indian house every fifteen miles;*

on February 21st, 1933, a stranger's horse gave out within a quarter of a mile of an Indian house, whose owner spoke English, had food, and was that day setting out for Bon Success. When is this likely to recur?' (*92 Days* 111)

2. 'Message to call on Diana; found her with face expressionless in mud mask'; 'On Thursday 15th [October 1936] made a very good start with the first page of a novel describing Diana's early morning' (*D* 391, 409).

3. Christopher Sykes: *Evelyn Waugh; A Biography* (London: Collins, 1975), 163. Hereafter Sykes. See 123–4, 132–3, 152, 160–3 for his account of Waugh's divorce proceedings and the reasons for their delay. Waugh's pilgrimage to the Sanctuary of St Patrick, Lough Derg, Co Donegal, is not mentioned by his biographers, but is included in his own unpublished list of major events in his life from 1927–39. The list, in reverse chronological order, is highly selective; the inclusion of the pilgrimage suggests its importance to him. The document can be found in the Evelyn Waugh Collection in the Harry Ransom Humanities Research Center at the University of Texas (*Diaries* 1940–42, Box 12, Folder 13).

4. *L* 96–7, *Scoop* 73.

5. *Wu/Stitch* 58 and Sykes 157. Waugh's misremembered acquaintance was married to the British Legation's Counsellor in Tehran.

6. In *Scoop's* opening, John Boot visits Mrs Stitch still in bed and in a mud mask. She turns towards him 'her face of clay' – Waugh's covert reversal, in this novel's mode, of the usual 'feet of clay'. The novel's opening was then published as a short story, titled 'Mrs Stitch Fails for the First Time'. Her machinations to get John Boot sent to Ishmaelia fail at the beginning of the novel; at its end she accepts responsibility she doesn't have for getting John Boot onto the honours list, in itself an error for William Boot, Lord Copper's intended honorand. Waugh's wary scepticism about Diana Cooper's influence in high places recurs more gravely on pp. 196–8 and 229–30.

7. See Waugh's 'Memorandum on *Scoop*', cited in full in 'Notes on the Film Adaptations of *Brideshead Revisited* and *Scoop*', ed. Donat Gallagher, *Areté* 14 (Summer 2004), 19–29. Hereafter *Memoranda*.

8. The pioneering black journalist, J. A. Rogers (1890–c.1980) was in Addis Ababa in 1930 for Selassie's coronation and in 1935 for the Italian-Ethiopian War. Waugh would certainly have encountered him. Rogers' main interest was the history of racial mixing, in all nations and periods, from mulattos and negritos to whites of black origin, like Pushkin and Beethoven (supposedly). See Darryll Pinkney: *Out There: Mavericks of Black Literature* (NY: BasicCivitas Books, 2002), 1–53.

9. Lord Rothermere supported Hitler's annexation of the Sudetenland in 1938.

CHAPTER 6. *WORK SUSPENDED*

1. See also pp. 88 and 293 n.4.
2. See pp. 28–9 above for *Alice* and Abyssinia. The mad inconsequentiality and injustice of the Knave of Hearts' trial (*Alice's Adventures in Wonderland* ch. 10), lies directly behind Tony's hallucinations in the jungle, just prior to meeting Mr Todd (*HD* 201–3).
3. Stannard I.490, repeated by Artemis Cooper in *Wu/Stitch* 69.
4. *L* 158; dedicatory letter to the first edition of *WS* (1942). Quotations come from this, rather than the final, abbreviated and reconfigured text of 1948, unless specified otherwise.
5. *WS* 5 and 45; second time cut from *WS* (1948).
6. Letter to Waugh, cited in Martin Stannard: *Evelyn Waugh* (vol II): *No Abiding City 1939–1966* (Dent, 1992, repr. Glasgow: HarperCollins, 1993) 74–5. My italics.
7. Waugh spent his solitary evenings in Fez visiting a brothel where, he tells Mary Lygon: 'I have formed an attachment to a young lady called Fatima [. . .] she is brown in colour and her face is tattoed all over with blue patterns v pretty [. . .] I gave Fatima that milk ring you gave me . . . ' (*L* 84). Compare *WS* 28–30, where Plant keeps his friendly, but not v pretty Berber at a distance.
8. John Plant is 33 (34 in the second version); Waugh and Laura first met when he was 30.
9. 'Knowing my tastes, you can imagine the abject state I was reduced to by Julia' (letter to Waugh, cited in Stannard II.74).
10. See p. 73.
11. The work of Plant's father identifiably mimics the *oeuvre* of Charles Spencelayh, who first began exhibiting at the Royal Academy in 1892, and continued to do so till his death at 93 in 1958. Waugh and Diana Cooper eagerly followed Spencelayh's work in the salerooms (*Wu/Stitch* 66, 89, 237), while Mrs Stitch buys Plant Senior's picture of the year for 500 guineas (*WS* 21). When Waugh cut and rewrote *WS* in 1948, he changed Plant's unfinished last work, to *Again?* – 'a one-armed veteran of the First World War meditating over a German helmet' (*WS* 1948, 119). It is the close equivalent of Spencelayh's *Why War?* – showing an old man contemplating a newspaper headlining the Munich crisis, his WWI gas-mask on the breakfast table beside him. Both pictures, Plant's and Spencelayh's, are dated 1939. For a reproduction of *Why War?* see Aubrey Noakes: *Charles Spencelayh* (London: Chaucer Press 2006), 75.

12. *WS* (1942) 2; cut from *WS* (1948) 139.
13. *NS Interviews; Harriet Waugh*, 91–3.
14. F. J. Stopp: *Evelyn Waugh: Portrait of an Artist* (Chapman & Hall, 1958), 106. Hereafter Stopp. Waugh was a lifelong reader of detective stories, including those by Agatha Christie, whose husband had been at Lancing with him. Christie's *The Murder of Roger Ackroyd* (1926), probably Christie's best novel, is still a textbook example of unreliable narrative, since the murder is committed by the narrator, who successfully obscures his role from the reader throughout, without lying. It might well have had some seminal influence on Waugh's plans for *WS*.

CHAPTER 7. *PUT OUT MORE FLAGS*

1. 'Each time [Laura] gave birth he ensured his absence' (Stannard II.23), repeated with slight modification by Selina Hastings: *Evelyn Waugh: A Biography* (London: Sinclair-Stevenson, 1994), 366. Not so. He was there for Teresa (1938), and Auberon (1939), and arrived within 24 hours, from military training in Scotland, just too late for the premature birth and death of Mary (1940). Margaret was born when he was on service in Scotland (1942), but he returned home as soon as permitted. He was in retreat writing *Brideshead* at the birth of Harriet (1944), in Madrid at the birth of James (1946), and in London for Septimus (1950).
2. 'Thank you for a lovely leave, I think the happiest two days of my life,' (*L* 134), 'the happiest forty-eight hours of my life...Another soft night' (*D* 461).
3. 'I had little dreamt that English children could be so completely ignorant of the simplest rules of hygiene, and that they would regard the floors and carpets as suitable places upon which to relieve themselves' (Oliver Lyttelton, programme note to Dennis Potter's *Blue Remembered Hills*, National Theatre, May 1996).
4. The Harknesses are closely related to the Pennyman couple in 'William and the Tablet', *William – The Detective* (1935), 81ff. The Pennymans have 'a mission in life [...] to get away from the ugliness of modern civilisation and back to the morning of the world' by 'the wearing of handwoven garments of curious design, the eating of strange food out of crockery that had been baked in a kiln by Mrs Pennyman [...] and the use of furniture made by Mr Pennyman.'
5. *New Statesman*, October 1939; my italics. In a review of *Enemies of Promise* in 1938 Waugh praised Connolly's classification of esoteric modern literature as 'the Mandarin School' (*EAR* 238).

6. The Penguin edition mistakenly read 'conventional' for many years.
7. Chamberlain: 'You can imagine what a bitter blow it is *to me* that all *my* long struggle to win peace has failed' (my italics).
8. Brian Howard of the Bruno Hat hoax and Johnny Hoop's giant party invitations in *Vile Bodies* (see p. 286, n. 4) lies behind Ambrose Silk. Both Brian and Ambrose had, and lost, a German Hitler-Jugend boyfriend (Toni, and Hans, respectively). Ambrose's *Monument to a Spartan* gestures kindly towards Brian Howard's *Notes on Civilians at Bay*, a vivid, long account of his flight from Marseille as the Germans marched into France, which was spread over three issues of *Horizon*, September to December 1940.
9. Reused in *OG* 273; see p. 185–6. The *Diaries'* misreading of 'dependent' as 'despondent' has been emended.
10. Waugh is deliberately ambiguous: 'Early in his military career, [Basil] lamed himself, shooting away the toes of one foot' while demonstrating a device for demolishing railway bridges, and was discharged from the army. *Basil Seal Rides Again* (1963), 6.

CHAPTER 8. *BRIDESHEAD REVISITED*

1. All references are to Waugh's final Revised Edition of 1960 unless specified otherwise.
2. Waugh reverts to the 'Author's Note' prefacing *Decline and Fall* at his publishers' request, which said the novelette 'was meant to be funny'. *Brideshead Revisited*, he now says, 'is *not* meant to be funny. There are passages of buffoonery, but the general theme is at once romantic and eschatological. // It is ambitious, perhaps intolerably presumptuous; nothing less than an attempt to trace the workings of the divine purpose in a pagan world, in the lives of an English Catholic family, half-paganized themselves, in the world of 1923–39 [. . .]'
3. In his *Memorandum on Brideshead* for MGM, Waugh described Ryder's relationship with Sebastian as 'romantic affection'. See *Memoranda* for the full text. Waugh singles out Richard Pares and 'Hamish Lennox' (actually Alastair Graham) as 'the friend of my heart' during his Oxford days. Waugh's hard-drinking friendship with Hamish and his relationship with Hamish's mother resemble Ryder's with Sebastian and Lady Marchmain; see *ALL* 191–2. Male love is common in classical pastoral, e.g. Virgil's *Eclogue II*.
4. Originally titled *A Child's World* (1886), by Sir John Everett Millais, *Bubbles* depicted a boy blowing bubbles with a clay pipe. Acquired as an advertisement for Pears Soap, it later became ridiculous.
5. D. L. Patey: *The Life of Evelyn Waugh: A Critical Biography* (Oxford:

Blackwell, 1998), 234. Hereafter Patey.

6. This was the predicament of Lady Mary Lygon (Maimie or Blondie to Waugh), fifth child of Lord Beauchamp, the original of Lord Marchmain. In 1928 she seemed likely to marry the bisexual Prince George, fifth child of King George V (see Byrne: *Mad World*, 137–9). Later she married Vsevolode Joannovitch, an émigré Russian prince turned wine merchant.

7. Simeon's prophecy to Mary at the Presentation in the Temple, '(Yea, a sword shall pierce through thy own soul also)', Luke 2.35, is related to seven events in Mary's life as *Mater Dolorosa* (grieving mother), traditionally depicted as seven swords piercing her.

8. *Schatten – Eine nächtliche Halluzination* (1923), an early German expressionist psychodrama, with Fritz Rasp as footman. In 1924 Waugh thought it 'quite superb' (*D* 189).

9. Quotation from *BR* (1945), 191; mistakenly altered to 'I'm not sure' in the Revised Edition (1960), 241, and subsequent reprints.

10. Matthew 5.2–11.

11. '[...] when people wanted to hate God, they hated mummy [...] she was saintly but she wasn't a saint' (*BR* 245–6).

12. *Quomodo sedet sola civitas / plena populo / facta est quasi vidua / domina gentium ... How doth the city sit solitary that was so full of people; how is she become a widow that was great among nations*: the opening verse of the Vulgate Lamentations of Jeremiah, Book 1, and Waugh's translation from his *Life of Rossetti*, 1928. Waugh was describing Rossetti's *Beata Beatrix*, the portrait of his dead wife: 'On the frame, designed by Rossetti himself, are inscribed the first words of the quotation which Dante uttered when Beatrice's death "despoiled the city of all dignity". *Quomodo sedet sola civitas!*' (*Rossetti* 130–1). By *Brideshead* Book Three Ryder has heard the lament sung by a half-caste choir in Guatemala, and echoes it in worldly terms on his return to London from the South America jungle: 'Here I am [...] where wealth is no longer gorgeous and power has no dignity. "*Quomodo sedet sola civitas.*"'

13. From mediaeval times, the choir stalls around the altar had tip-up seats with a small ledge on the underside, often projecting over decorative carvings invisible when the seat was lowered, which provided a small shelf (or 'mercy seat') to rest against during long services supposed to be served standing. The *strepitus* was created by a variety of means from stamping to clapping prayerbooks shut; the Downside tradition created a resounding, awe-inspiring crash.

14. Quotation from the end of G. K. Chesterton's 'The Queer Feet' in *The Innocence of Father Brown* (1911).

15. Open presentation of sex in literature was first legalized in November 1960, when Penguin Books published D. H. Lawrence's

unexpurgated *Lady Chatterley's Lover* and were acquitted from contravention of the 1959 Obscene Publications Act. Too late for Waugh, whose Revised Edition of *Brideshead* was completed in 1959 and published in 1960.

16. This is introduced in the Revised Edition, replacing the anodyne First Edition, p. 202, in which there is no suggestion of sex between them; Celia merely boasts of her 'self-restraint': 'I may say I've been tormented with visions of voluptuous half-castes [...] But I determined not to ask and I haven't.' 'That suits me,' Ryder replies.

17. 1945 version, pp.228–9: 'Now on the rough water, *as I was made free of her narrow loins and, it seemed now, in assuaging that fierce appetite, cast a burden which I had borne all my life, toiled under, not knowing its nature – now, while the waves still broke and thundered on the prow, the act of possession was a symbol, a rite of ancient origin and solemn meaning'* (my italics).

18. The First Edition begins 'So, at sunset I took formal *possession* of her as her lover' (cut in 1960; my italics).

19. Roger 'did not, as some husbands do, resent his wife's pregnancy. It was as though he had bought a hunter at the end of the season and turned him out [...] He had summer business to do; the horse must wait till autumn.' Moreover, Roger is himself incommoded 'by the habit, long settled, of regarding sex relationships in terms of ownership and use. Confronted with the new fact of pregnancy, of joint ownership, his terms failed him' *(WS* 117).

20. See his Introduction to *Brideshead Revisited* (Everyman's Library 1993), xiv.

21. Sykes, 250. *Orphans of the Storm* (1921), dir. D. W. Griffith, starring Lillian and Dorothy Gish, was a silent film, with early experimental colour techniques.

22. *Memoranda* 14, 24.

23. Waugh's trans-atlantic liner derives from the *Queen Mary*, which brought the newly-wed Waugh and Laura back from Mexico, a stormy passage from New York on 4 October 1938. Its first class lounge had bronze doors embossed with classical images of bulls and dolphins, and corridors walled in simulated wood. See David Cliffe: 'A Companion to Evelyn Waugh's *Brideshead Revisited*', www.abbotshill.freeserve.co.uk/ (accessed 2013), notes to Book 3, ch.1, 223, 235.

24. Romans 6.23 continues, 'but the gift of God is eternal life.' There is strong irony in Ryder's mistaken response, misreading a heavenly gift as an earthly due to be *demanded*.

25. The *Titanic* collided with an iceberg and sank with a loss of 1,500 lives on her maiden voyage in April 1912.

26. Waugh used Hunt's title for what is now known as *The Awakening*

Conscience (1853). For Hunt's account, and Ruskin's commentary – an early *tour de force* of iconographic criticism – see William Holman Hunt: *Pre-Raphaelitism and the Pre-Raphaelite Brotherhood* (2nd ed., London: Chapman & Hall, 1913) I. 255 and 302–3.

27. Waugh's postscript to the reconfigured *Work Suspended* was written well after he had finished *Brideshead*, in September/October 1947. See R. M. Davis: *A Catalogue of the Evelyn Waugh Collection* (New York: Whitstone, 1981), 160, E560. Hereafter *Catalogue*.

28. A once popular party game combining musical chairs with blind man's buff. Players representing different towns are seated around the room; the Postmaster General decrees an exchange of letters between two locations, whose representatives try to swap seats without being caught by the blindfolded Blindman. Postcards hop, letters run; lots of running around, chasing and changing places.

29. Saul, a Roman, persecuted the Jews till he was struck down by a blinding light on the road to Damascus. 'And when we were all fallen to the earth, I heard a voice speaking unto me, and saying in the Hebrew tongue, Saul, Saul, why persecutest thou me? It is hard for thee to kick against the pricks' (Acts 26.14). Waugh, an experienced rider, clarifies the image for the modern reader.

30. Latin for 'Who?' In Waugh's youth, it was a public-schoolboy's way of offering something unwanted, answered by the other kids jumping up and down shouting, 'Ego!' Me, me!

31. 'Then the devil taketh him up into the holy city, and setteth him on a pinnacle of the temple. And saith unto him, If thou be the Son of God, cast thyself down: for it is written: He shall give his angels charge concerning thee: and in their hands they shall bear thee up […] Jesus said unto him, It is written again, Thou shalt not tempt the Lord thy God' (Matthew 4.5–7; also Luke 4.9–12).

32. *D* 553, and see further pp. 232–3.

33. See 'How I Lived in a Very Big House and Found God', *Times Literary Supplement* (20 November 1981), 1352 (a review of the television version of the novel), and Amis at 24, to Philip Larkin in 1946: 'Over the Knobworthy mantelpiece was a superb Schleimikunt of the Klapstruck period, flanked by Pederasti engravings. I […] went across the rich Pewbicke hair carpet,' etc. See *The Letters of Kingsley Amis*, ed. Zachary Leader (London: HarperCollins, 2000), 97.

34. See M. Stannard (ed.), *Evelyn Waugh: The Critical Heritage* (London: Routledge & Kegan Paul 1984), 233–70, particularly E. Wilson ('his cult of the high nobility is […] so rapturous and solemn that it finally gives the impression of being the only real religion in the book,' 246), D. O'Donnell ('In Mr Waugh's theology, the love of money is not only not the root of all evil, it is a preliminary form of the love of God,' 260), and D. Pryce-Jones on the 1960 Revised

Edition for wide-spectrum impercipience (272–6).
35. See Stannard II.144, n. 146; extract from unpublished letter by Green to Waugh, 25 December 1944 (my italics).
36. Letter to the Editor of *The Bell*, reprinted in *L* 255, *Critical Heritage* 105-6.
37. Waugh's fears and their relief are both confirmed in M. Waterson (ed.), *The English Country House Remembered: Recollections of Life Between the Wars* (London: Routledge & Kegan Paul 1985), particularly ch. 1, 14–28, concluding that 'Although the catalogue of destruction during the last fifty years [1935–85] is a depressing one, there has not been the wholesale dissolution, comparable to that of the abbeys in the sixteenth centuries, which might have been expected.' Ryder appears to have become a society artist in the mould of Rex Whistler: see the photograph of Whistler painting a mural in the Marchioness of Anglesey's dining room (24). Waugh knew and met Whistler, for instance on a house visit to the Marchioness of Bath in 1942 (*L* 165).
38. See *D* 558–9, 560–1, 564, 566–7. 3,000 words a day was his top speed.
39. See p. 6, and compare Acton on *The Temple at Thatch* as 'too English for my [. . .] taste; too much nid-nodding over the port' (*ALL* 228) to Blanche on Ryder's jungle art as 'creamy English charm, playing tigers'.

CHAPTER 9. *THE LOVED ONE*

1. For full details of the negotiations, see J. Heath: '*Brideshead*: The Critics and the Memorandum', *English Studies* 56 (June 1975), 222–30; R. M. Davis: 'Anglo-American Impasse: Catholic Novel and Catholic Censor', *Dalhousie Review*, 72 (Winter 1992–3), 467–81; and D. Gallagher: 'What Was Biting Mr Breen?', lecture delivered to Union Club, Sidney, 23 June 2009.
2. Adipocere: 'a greyish waxy substance formed by the decomposition of soft tissue in dead bodies subjected to moisture'.
3. After W. B. Yeats's poem, 'The Lake Isle of Innisfree': 'I will arise and go now, and go to Innisfree, / And a small cabin build there, of clay and wattles made; / Nine bean rows will I have there, a hive for the honeybee, / And live alone in the bee-loud glade.' The next, biblical quotation comes from 1 Corinthians 15.55.
4. The term was coined by the biologist-philosopher Ernst Haeckel (*Haeckel's Riddle Universe*, tr.1902), and had a brief vogue. See *OED*'s citations under 'thanatism'.
5. *Othello* II.iii.256. A year earlier, Waugh told Nancy Mitford saints were 'simply men & women who have fulfilled their natural

obligation which is to approach God. It is in this that all mankind has a different nature from the rest of creation' (*L* 233).

CHAPTER 10. *HELENA*

1. *The Loved One* and *Pinfold* are both shorter, but Waugh avoided calling either a novel. *LO* is subtitled *An Anglo-American Tragedy; Pinfold* is '*A Conversation Piece*'.
2. Waugh's prefatory note to the first three chapters, published as a short story: *St Helena Meets Constantius: a Legend Retold* (*Tablet*, 22 November 1945), 299. Waugh acknowledged that Constantius was based on Fitzroy Maclean, with whom Waugh clashed over the British position in Yugoslavia. See *Wu/Stitch* 83, and pp. 240, 311 n. 14.
3. MS *Helena*, final page, later replaced by Gibbon's 'history'. See Patey 297, and for the Gibbon quoted by Constantine, Patey 294.
4. Another pun.
5. In a postcard of 4 November 1950, Waugh wrote to Eddie Sackville-West: 'Modern slang. If one is writing of, say, Pepys's England one knows pretty much how they spoke, but surely in a remoter age & a foreign tongue one can only make the characters speak as the sort of people one sees them as, speak now. As Shakespeare made his Romans do. The crowds in Julius Caesar speak contemporary Elizabethan English do they not? Or am I wrong? Is it stylized?' (PC in the collection of Georgetown University Library. I am indebted to Alexander Waugh for bringing this to my attention.) Earlier quotation from John Betjeman's poem, 'Senex'.
6. It points forward to both her discovery of the True Cross, and Schliemann's 1871 excavation of the historic city of Troy. Till then, like Marcias, scholars had assumed Troy was wholly legendary.
7. *Holy Places* 12. Radio 3 dramatization by Christopher Sykes, performed on 15 December 1951.
8. i.e. turn the clock back. If the bottom of an inflow clepsydra (water clock) sprang a leak, it would show time running backwards.
9. In the Nicaean debate, the traditionalists, who won, held that Jesus was consubstantial (homoousios) with God. The progressive Arians held that Christ, being God's Son, was merely of similar substance (homoiousios) to God.
10. Rites involving bull-sacrifices. The last recorded taurobolium preceded Fausta's speech by some thirty years, so it too was *passé*.
11. Patey points out that Fausta blasphemously echoes the Annunciation: 'Hail, thou that art highly favoured, the Lord is with thee, blessed art thou among women' (Luke 1.28). Earlier, she tried to

insinuate that Helena was responsible for the deaths of Crispus and Licinianus, and inappropriately compared herself to Christ's parable of the Sower when Constantine refused to take the hint (Mark 4.3–20, and *Helena* 185). Her insinuations, like the Sower's seeds, fell on stony ground and Constantine's stony silence preceded her assassination.

12. *Zivio* and *Heil* are all-hails for Tito and Hitler. *Viva* and *Arriba* are Italian and Spanish equivalents. Constantine was married to Minervina, divorced her to marry Fausta and make alliance with her father the Emperor Maximian, who was then conveniently assassinated. His two gods were Roman, and then Christian. Napoleon was tricked by the British and imprisoned on the island of St Helena till he died. *Ave atque vale* says hail and farewell to them all, in Latin.

13. The unnamed Wandering Jew of legend, condemned to wander the earth till the Second Coming, is based on Waugh's old Oxford acquaintance, Brian Howard, also the original for Ambrose Silk in *POMF*.

14. In Waugh's saddened lifetime Pope John XXIII removed this festival on 3 May from the Roman Calendar to avoid duplication with Holy Cross Day on 14 September.

15. Another etymologically precise usage, legend deriving from the Latin *legendum*, meaning something *to be read*.

16. He tried to visit the palace when he was in Split (*D* 595).

17. Eusebius dropped his patron Fausta from his two chronicles of Constantine's reign in obedience to Constantine's *damnatio memoriae* of his disgraced wife, whereby all evidence of her existence was officially erased. Compare the Soviet extirpation of un-persons like Trotsky, and the memory-hole in Orwell's *1984*.

18. D. Marshall and D. Manousos: 'Evelyn Waugh Comments on HELENA', *Anno Domini* vol. I, no. 1 (*Fall* 1950), 5–9. Waugh's interviewers suggested *Helena* was not a novel like *Brideshead*, whose 'message was implicit, while in *Helena* you've turned to more explicit statement'. Waugh: 'On the contrary, *Helena* is even less explicit than *Brideshead*. The whole thing is done in anagrams and cyphers' (etc. as above). Last quotation from *NS Interviews, Harriet Waugh* 60.

CHAPTER 11. *MEN AT ARMS*

1. *L* 351, 354, 361, 366, 363–4, 374.
2. Penkirk, an invented name, closely resembles Inverailort Castle, which was requisitioned as a Special Training Centre in May 1940.

Troops arrived to find it in the unprepared state Waugh describes in *MA* 202–3. This and Waugh's transposition of the Bardia raid seem to have escaped critical notice.

3. Plautus' swaggering hero is a soldier with a huge shield and no military achievements who ends his play by being beaten up. His most obvious descendant is the cowardly Braggadochio of Spenser's *Faerie Queene*. Falstaff, Pistol, Parolles and Bottom all have elements of the type.

4. Ariosto's *Orlando Furioso* (1532), a lengthy romance epic, is set against the background of Charlemagne's Christian Paladins defending Europe against the invading pagan Saladins (cf. Waugh's Second World War). Ariosto's episodic narrative, more fantastical than Waugh's, includes combat with fabulous beasts and a trip to the moon.

5. See *Evelyn Waugh and his World*, ed. D. Pryce-Jones (London: Little Brown & Co, 1973), fifth page of illustrations between pp. 160–1. Waugh died of a heart attack on the lavatory – 'symbolising his humour' according to Graham Greene.

6. St Clair-Morford's poignantly puckish photograph bears out Waugh's description. See: http://www.flyingmarines.com/Biographies/1911-1920/St_Clair_Morfordhtm. He is physically unlike Ritchie-Hook, whose name and maimed right hand mark his descent from Captain Hook, the pirate villain of J. M. Barrie's *Peter Pan, or The Boy Who Wouldn't Grow Up* (1904) – an allusion that also helps set the schoolboy tone of this novel.

7. 'Mrs Morford [...] seems to me to lead a peculiar life with the Brigadier. She told us with great relish how, the night before, she had to get up several times to look after a sick child. Each time the Brigadier laid a booby-trap against her return by putting his boots on the top of the door.' (*D* 464, cf. *L* 137).

8. In fact Chamberlain resigned and Churchill took over on 14 May 1940. Book II.8 begins 'On the day that Mr Churchill became Prime Minister, Apthorpe was promoted Captain.' On the next page Apthorpe says his promotion was effective from 1 April, which immediately introduces Guy/Waugh's disenchanted view of Churchill as 'a master of sham-Augustan prose', a Zionist, 'an associate of the press lords' and other traits Waugh deplored.

9. *Hostess*: 'after I saw [Falstaff] fumble with the sheets and play with flowers and smile upon his fingers' ends, I knew there was but one way' (*Henry V* II.iii.15). Apthorpe's funeral is compared to the hugger-mugger 'Burial of Sir John Moore after Corunna' (Charles Wolfe, 1817), and Tennyson's inflated 'Ode on the Death of the Duke of Wellington' (1852).

10. *Memorandum* §11, *D* 495–6.

11. 'Commando Raid on Bardia' (November 1941), *EAR* 263–8.
12. Duff Cooper, Minister of Information, is 'cleverly [...] putting out the surrender of the Channel ports as a great feat of heroism' (*D* 471).
13. *MA* 208, 275, 282, 296.
14. John St John: *To the War with Waugh* (London: The Whittington Press, 1973), 3, presents his enlistment in truly Truslovian terms: a red-tabbed colonel welcomes him with 'You're a lucky fellow! [...] It's not everyone who's chosen for this particular outfit and no wonder! [...]. The task allotted to your outfit will be to raid the enemy's coastline – go in under cover of darkness. Establish a temporary beach-head ... that sort of thing [...] Come back for you 24 hours, maybe 48 hours later ... those of you, that is, who can still make it ...' Comparable Truslovian stylistic markers recur for Guy's exploits at Dakar in *MA* 274 ('It's not much of a show we're going to') and *MA* 293 ('It's only once or twice in a chap's life he gets the chance of a gong [...] You got yours last night and did all right...')
15. See n.6. Further biographical details at http://thebignote.com/2012/03/14/thurlestone-all-saints-church-war-memorial/
16. Acronym for Entertainments National Service Association (popularly, Every Night Something Awful).
17. For this and the following quotations in this paragraph, see *MA* 63, 127, 277. All italics mine.
18. *MA* 259; Stannard II.12.
19. Report from Lieutenant-Colonel Lushington, 18 May 1940, cited in Stannard II.12. Stannard notes that Lushington does not mark Waugh as suitable for specialization or accelerated promotion. Given Waugh's observations on promotion above, the implication may well be that Lushington wanted to keep him as one of his fighting officers, not waste him in barrack duties or behind a desk.
20. News of Guy's captaincy is delayed in the post while he's on the Dakar expedition; as an acting rank it is rescinded after the mission is ended (*MA* 297). As Waugh explained to Laura, his position was 'rather peculiar'. Before Dakar, he had already applied to join the Commandos, so a major took over his captaincy in the R. M. Brigade. He then chose to accompany Colonel Lushington, to whom he was feeling 'deeply devoted', ('my loved Colonel' who 'was very loving to me just then') on the Dakar expedition, with a captain's rank but not duties, a lieutenant's pay, and acting as brigade intelligence officer 'which really means 1st class passenger observer', (*L* 139–40, 13 September 1940). The acting captaincy was rescinded but by November 1940 he was reassuring Laura that 'You need have no misgivings about my prestige ... it is more glorious to be a subaltern [commando] than a captain in the RM Brigade' and

'a great deal more enjoyable' (*L* 145).

21. *MA* 147. Mr Goodall refers to Christ's teaching: 'Are not two sparrows sold for a farthing? And one of them shall not fall on the ground without your Father. But the very hairs of your head are all numbered' (Matthew 10.29–30). Hamlet's version of this text will be repeated in relation to Virginia's death in *US* 261; see p.270. It is one of many significant cross-references uniting the trilogy.

22. *Critical Heritage* 340. The same error as the editor of the *Tablet*'s denunciation of the sex scene between Basil and Prudence in *Black Mischief*. Both scenes are meant to be shoddy; Guy's is also comic. Apthorpe's inopportune phone calls are a reprise from *A Handful of Dust*, where Tony incommodes Brenda in similar sexual circumstances as (we can assume) Adam's calls also interrupt Nina in *Vile Bodies*.

CHAPTER 12. *OFFICERS AND GENTLEMEN*

1. *Happy Warriors* was originally Waugh's working title for the whole novel.

2. One portion of Book I was read on the radio (November 1953), a second appeared in *The London Magazine* while Waugh was still ill in Ceylon. See *L* 419 and R. M. Davis: *Evelyn Waugh, Writer* (Norman, Oklahoma: Pilgrim Books, 1981), 259. Hereafter, Davis: *EW, Writer*. The *Interlude* was trimmed and modified in *Sword of Honour*, and may straddle Waugh's climacteric.

3. Waugh's friends, John Betjeman and the novelist Henry Green, were among them. See Green's *Caught* (1943) for his experiences.

4. *Critical Heritage* 337; *L* 382–3. Next quotation from *L* 414 (9 December 1953). Connolly made three mistakes in the first paragraph of his review, which Waugh politely corrected before agreeing with his substantive criticism.

5. Waugh's blurb reaffirms this: '*Men at Arms* ended with the death of Apthorpe. *Officers and Gentlemen* begins with the placation of his spirit, a ritual preparation for the descent into the nether world of Crete.' Waugh is gesturing towards the trilogy's epic status.

6. *OG* 18. Elpenor in Homer's *Odyssey*, and Palinurus in Virgil's *Aeneid*, two unburied companions in arms, both needed to be laid to rest before the epic quest could be completed. Palinurus was used without irony by Connolly as his authorial *alter ego* in *The Unquiet Grave*, which becomes an overt object of parody later in *OG* and in *Unconditional Surrender*. Waugh's response to classical epic is mock-heroic.

7. Unity Valkyrie Mitford was an ardent follower of Hitler. She shot

herself in the head when war was declared, was brought back to England mentally disabled, and latterly kept out of trouble on the family island of Inch Kenneth, where she died in 1948.

8. See Davis: *EW, Writer*, ch.13, particularly on the expansion of Jumbo's role, and rejected plans for Chatty Corner either 'to be loosed on the Highlanders under Trimmer's command', or to be blown up, or drowned, by the Commandos (264).

9. *MA* 87–8, 155, 276. In the first two references, Guy's Halberdiers are 'immeasurably far from the frontier of Christendom where the great battle had been fought and lost; from those secret forests where the trains were, even then [...] rolling east and west with their doomed loads'. 'Those trains of locked vans still rolling East and West from Poland and the Baltic', coincide with Christmas 1939 and Valentine's Day 1940. They gesture towards the Katyn Massacre, where some 22,000 Polish prisoners captured during the 1939 Soviet invasion of Poland, were massacred in the spring of 1940. The last reference opens out to a broader view of the 'bombs and gas and famine and enemy occupation [...] the lightless concentration camp which all Europe had suddenly become'.

10. John St John: *To the War with Waugh*, 54–5: 'For many of us only a small part of our years in uniform, or no part at all, was spent attacking or defending ourselves in the face of a live enemy. Like the civilians, we followed the course of the war on the radio and in the censored press [...] but we were seldom, if at all, conscious of being the gallant defenders of civilisation. Our preoccupations were more personal [...] The officers' mess of the Halberdiers may offer too narrow, too privileged a viewpoint and the magnitude of Europe's agony only occasionally pervades [Waugh's] pages, yet his observation is meticulous and completely honest. Evelyn described the war as I experienced it.'

11. According to Waugh's letters, at any rate. Roughly equivalent to £20,000 today. On the sea-journey to Egypt he was £850 down in two nights (*L* 149; *D* 493).

12. The Blitz is compared to Turner and Martin (a minor artist); Chatty Corner's lair was more like a Gordon Craig setting for a play by Maeterlink than a Neanderthal cave scrawled with imitation Picassos. In the flight from Crete a dying major upheld by a kneeling sergeant in a dusty sports-car is compared to a death-scene in high opera.

13. See p. 305, n. 17.

14. See D. Gallagher: 'I am Trimmer, you know ... ', *Evelyn Waugh Newsletter Studies* 41 (2), 22–6, and 'Guy Crouchback's Disillusion: Crete, Beevor, and the Soviet Alliance in *Sword of Honour*', in D. Gallagher, A. Pasternak Slater and J. H. Wilson, (eds), '*A Handful of*

Mischief': *New Essays on Evelyn Waugh* (Madison: Fairleigh Dickinson University Press, 2011), 172–219. Hereafter Gallagher: *Trimmer*, and Gallagher: *Disillusion*.

15. For Gallagher's summary argument see *Disillusion*, 172ff; 175–6 for critics' magnifications.
16. *OG* 63, and Ernest Dale, http://waryears.wordpress.com/lochailort-2/ (accessed 3. vi. 2013). For six months in 1942 Dale acted as Lovat's secretary in the Special Training Centre at Inverailort Castle, where Lovat was fieldcraft instructor. The image of Britannia with skirts and staff was familiar for decades on the English penny piece.
17. In the D-Day Normandy Landings (June 1944), Lovat broke army rules by ordering his piper to play him ashore at the head of his unhelmeted, beretted men. Later 12 of them died of head injuries while advancing under enemy fire in the Pegasus bridge area. Lovat's had also been the only Commando wearing berets in the Dieppe Raid in August 1942, for which he was awarded a DSO. Most shocking was his alleged association with the execution of an unknown number of prisoners taken by his Commando at Dieppe. The discovery of bodies – gagged, bound, and shot through the head – triggered an international incident only resolved by the Red Cross. See further Gallagher: '"Liquidated!" How Lord Lovat "Kicked Waugh Out" of the Special Services Brigade and Fantasized About It Afterwards' in Donat Gallagher and Carlos Villar Flor: *In the Picture: The Facts Behind the Fiction in Evelyn Waugh's 'Sword of Honour'* (Amsterdam and New York: Rodopi, 2014), 227–9. Hereafter, *Liquidated!* There may be an allusive nod to the Dieppe episode in the three murdered territorials winning Ivor Claire his MC at Dunkirk.
18. Alexander Waugh points out that *Friseur* (the Scottish pronunciation of 'Fraser') is German for hairdresser; that the Fraser family name was originally 'Frisel' (see Burke's Peerage, 1949 ed. sub Lovat); and that 'Trimmer' obviously refers to 'hairdresser'.
19. See Patey 305, 402 n.29 for this and the next quotation.
20. Joseph Conrad: Preface to *The Nigger of the 'Narcissus'* (1897).
21. An important moment, fully explored in *POMF* 207–8 (see p. 96), and lightly touched in here. Guy 'was in good heart, almost buoyant, as he tramped alone, eased at last of the lead weight of human company' (*OG* 273). For the following episode, see *OG* 274–6.
22. See *L* 431 to Joan Saunders. Waugh needed medical details allowing Guy's recovery to coincide with Germany's invasion of Russia.
23. Gallagher quotes an official report noting of one witness that, 'Like all or most Crete soldiers he found it difficult to distinguish one day from the other.' In his Introduction to Christie Lawrence's *Irregular*

Adventure (London 1948), Waugh described how 'Hunger and exhaustion [...] produced a dream-night condition when people seemed to appear and disappear inconsequently' (*Disillusion* 207, n.8).

24. Gallagher points out that Waugh was unaware, at the time, that the 'stragglers', whose fearful cry of 'take cover' sounded along the roadsides under aerial bombardment, were actually non-combatant personnel from the base camps at defeated Canea. They were already legitimately making their way to the evacuation rendez-vous at Sphakia, as Waugh's reinforcement troops arrived.
25. See Appendix A, *Cretan Chronology in 'Officers and Gentlemen'*, p.278.
26. See Gallagher: *Disillusion*, 202–3.
27. *D* 501, simplified in *OG* 250.
28. *MA* 259; see p.165.
29. *OG* 269–70, *D* 508.
30. *D* 503 (calling Colvin's story of a German attack 'fishy' and 'balls') and *OG* 252–3.
31. *OG* 140, 165, 224–5 and *D* 494, 510, 512: Col. Pedder's 'peculiarities came very near megalomania'. 'We shall never know who killed him. Many of his men had sworn to do so and he was shot in the back by a sniper. He had, however, just led a successful assault and it seems an unlikely occasion for murder.' 'He was half mad but seems to have done well in his final action.'
32. *D* 500, 503, 506, 507: 'A caddish fellow, sacked by Pedder, called Murdoch', who connived at Colvin's forced night-march in excessive retreat, and made his own way to Alexandria.
33. *Macbeth* I.iii.144–5.
34. *Unconditional Surrender* details Ludovic's past as Sir Ralph Bromp-ton's discovery and short-term favourite. The likeliest inference is that Ivor Claire, dismissed as 'a dandy' in its laconic *Synopsis*, was another of Sir Ralph's lovers, leaned on to get Ludovic off Sir Ralph's hands once he had tired of him.
35. *OG* is based on *D* 510 §14; see also 'Bones' Sudeley on *D* 511, 516.
36. See p.291, n.6.

CHAPTER 13. *THE ORDEAL OF GILBERT PINFOLD*

1. *D* 770, Sykes 359.
2. Waugh told Stopp that neither he nor Pinfold 'lost his reason. His reason, like mine, worked incessantly and accurately. The trouble was that all the information he had to work on was fallacious and fantastic.' In the 'novel' Waugh 'reduced and ordered' his material, and added nothing but some fictional minor characters. 'I have been at pains to edit what was said to me, trying to make it light

and printable' (Stopp 219–20).
3. 'Mr Waugh Replies', July 1953, *EAR* 440–3. e.g. G. M. Thomson in the *Evening Standard* 'seems to have studied some file of gossip paragraphs and to have transcribed all the most offensive. He reports that [...] I advocate slavery, that I am sensitive about my low stature. Mr Thomson, alas, is a cipher to me (no doubt he is a fine gangling fellow)[...]'
4. Stannard II.334.
5. *Frankly Speaking*, BBC Home Service, 16 November 1953.
6. William Burges (1827–81), architect, designer, eccentric exponent of the Gothic Revival and Rossetti's contemporary. 'A man not universally recognised but of magisterial status to Mr Pinfold' (*Pinfold* 20). His beautiful Narcissus Washstand (1865–7) is now in the Cecil Higgins Gallery, Bedford; see http://www.cecilhigginsart gallery.org/burges/washstand.htm
7. *Rossetti, His Life and Works* (1928; repr. London: Duckworth, 1975). Ch.VI, 169–79 is summarized here, with direct quotations in italics.
8. *NS Interviews: Gwen*, 451–63. Gwen seems likely to have been the sympathetic Mrs Scarfield in *Pinfold*.
9. Another sign of Gwen's veracity. In reality Miss Margaret Black must have been the delusionary sister of Stephen Black, the BBC interviewer and Waugh's chief supposed persecutor. She appears in no biographical sources, of course, and in *Pinfold* the Black family become the Angels.
10. Waugh had met, and disliked, a Commander Campbell who was a fellow-participant on the radio programme, *The BrainsTrust*, in April 1942 (*D* 520).
11. There is a marked improvement in Waugh's last two letters from Ceylon, when Monroe Wheeler, director of the Museum of Modern Art in New York, takes Waugh on a few days' sightseeing and leaves him safely parked in a hill resort. Responding to Laura's cable urging his return, Waugh says 'it would be civil to stay a day or two after all the trouble the British Council have taken over me' (*L* 420–1). It seems likely that 'Mr Murdoch' was enlisted by the ship's Captain to look after Waugh in Egypt, and the British Council in Ceylon had a part in arranging Wheeler's companionship.
12. Father Caraman, then editor of the Catholic journal, *The Month*. His influential friends were known as the 'caramanserai'.
13. Sykes 361–5; Frances Donaldson: *Portrait of a Country Neighbour* (London 1968), 54–70; *NS Interviews: Caraman*, 116–18.
14. Fellow Commando and author of an experimental war novel, *Captain Smith and Company* (1943); later a successful farmer.
15. *The Letters of Nancy Mitford and Evelyn Waugh*, ed. Charlotte Mosley

(London: Hodder & Stoughton, 1996), 332 (hereafter *Mitford/ Waugh*); Donaldson, op.cit. 62; (*Wu/Stitch* 189). Sykes has further anecdotes to the same effect. 'He was not afflicted by the shame which oppresses those who have temporarily lost mental balance; he was quite uninhibited about it' (Sykes 366).

16. Daphne Fielding, novelist. Waugh said her memoirs were 'marred by discretion and good taste' (*Wu/Stitch* 201).

17. *L* 482. Two years earlier, in November 1954 and soon after Waugh's Pinfold experience, Ann Fleming bought the Queen Anne Press and suggested that Waugh might have 'some small unpublished work of a morbid character that could be illustrated by Francis Bacon', *The Letters of Ann Fleming*, ed. M. Amory (Collins Harvill, 1985), 147. He did not give her the book to publish, but took the idea for the dust-jacket to heart.

18. See *Critical Heritage* 380, 382 for citations from Waugh's blurb. Waugh's *Face to Face* interview, 26 June 1960 repeats what he had already said to Stopp.

19. This distinctive typographical layout trumps the two typefaces of Joyce's 'Aeolus' chapter in *Ulysses*, set in a newspaper office, its narrative and dialogue summarized by mock headlines.

20. Waugh's interview with Elizabeth Jane Howard, *Monitor*, BBC TV, 16 February 1964.

21. 'If I put down a bucket into my own soul's well, sexual department, I draw up [...] Ibsen's and [...] St Aloysius' and Shelley's and Renan's water along with my own. And I am going to do that in my own novel.' Letter to Stanislaus Joyce, 13 November 1906, *Selected Letters of James Joyce*, ed. R. Ellmann (London 1975), 129.

22. Fleming's first five Bond novels were published between 1953 and 1957. His wife Ann was a close friend of Waugh's.

23. D. H. Lawrence: *Lady Chatterley's Lover* (Harmondsworth: Penguin, 1969), ch.18, 296.

24. Caesar's 'boast, 'Veni, vidi, vici' ('I came, I saw, I conquered') is the textbook example of a *tricolon crescens*, three statements rising to a climax. Churchill's 'Never in the field of human conflict was so much owed by so many to so few' is a renowned but clumsy example of the *tricolon diminuens*. Waugh disparaged Churchill's mastery of 'sham-Augustan prose' (see p.000 n.00 above). His own unostentatious trope is lavished on the ludicrous, and is sublimely bathetic.

25. *The Tempest*, III.ii.138–9.

26. Impenitently recounted in *A Little Learning*, 177. Waugh and his friends attributed a taste for canine bestiality to the college Dean, Crutwell, Waugh's much disliked history tutor. They put a stuffed dog in the college quad 'as an allurement for him', and 'used rather often to bark under his windows at night'.

27. *Critical Heritage*, 386–7.
28. J. B. Priestley: 'What was wrong with Pinfold?' (*Critical Heritage* 387–92), ably ridiculed in Waugh's reply, 'Anything Wrong with Priestley?' (*EAR* 527–9). Stopp applies Priestley's diagnostic suggestion of Jung's Shadow and Anima to conclude his analysis of the novel (Stopp 220–34). Stannard (like Stopp) is semi-apologetic about the temptations of this approach: 'Biography should not play at amateur psycho-analysis but it is impossible [...] to avoid some commentary on Waugh's state of mind.' He proposes that Pinfold's drugs 'released a barrage of self-hatred'. The voices 'were not talking "rot"'. 'Ultimately' *Pinfold* is about 'sexual and artistic impotence' (Stannard II.348–9).
29. Shakespeare: 'The devil hath power / T'assume a pleasing shape' (*Hamlet* II.ii.595–6); 'When devils will their blackest sins put on,/ They do suggest at first with heavenly shows' (*Othello* II.iii.340–1); 'Devils soonest tempt resembling spirits of light' (*Love's Labour's Lost* IV.iii.253).
30. First performed in Edinburgh, 1949, and London 1950. The leading Guardian, the Unidentified Guest, turns out to be a psychotherapist who takes on the role of the Psychopomp (the spirit, angel or deity who conveys the dead to the after life) in Eliot's distant classical source, Euripides's *Alcestis*.
31. Waugh removed the double-sided sheet from an edition of Chrisostom's homilies, where the original Greek text in the left-hand column runs parallel to Erasmus's translation on the right. A third text running horizontally across the bottom of each page is titled 'Aniani Interpretatio' (essentially, another translation into Latin). Waugh simply sliced off the top of the page, so that the only complete text running from one page to the next is Anianus's, which begins with the exhortation quoted at the end of this paragraph (my italics).
32. Spark's hallucinations were triggered by Dexedrine, an appetite suppressant she took when impoverished, severely undernourished, and working on a book about T. S. Eliot. One night the words she was reading appeared to form 'anagrams and crosswords'. Like Waugh, she tried to make sense of nonsense, searching for a code to Eliot's work. 'It is difficult to convey how absolutely fascinating that involuntary word-game was.' Spark: *Curriculum Vitae* (London: Constable, 1992), 204. In *A Far Cry from Kensington* (1988, repr. Penguin, 1989), 152–3, Spark gives a brief history of the Box, which Pinfold/Waugh suspected of playing a part in his possession. The novel is set in the fifties and uses the period's fad for the Box as a central plot-device. As in Waugh, it has something of the infernal about it.

CHAPTER 14. TOWARDS *UNCONDITIONAL SURRENDER*

1. 'Why Not War Writers? A Manifesto', *Horizon* IV, 22 (October 1941), 237–8. Signed by A. Calder-Marshall, Cyril Connolly, Arthur Koestler, George Orwell, and others. Waugh's reply, 'Letter: Why Not War Writers?' is in *Horizon* IV, 24 (December 1941), 437–8.
2. *D* 530, 529, cf *Pinfold* 21.
3. See *Liquidated!* 219–52. Lovat's lies concerning Waugh, their uncontested assimilation and magnification by Waugh's biographers are fully documented by Gallagher.
4. On the Dieppe raid see p.305, n.17, and Gallagher: *Liquidated!* 227–9. The cut passage from the *Diaries* runs: 'He [Lovat] gave an interview to Knickerbocker in which by Knickerbocker's account, he claimed to have led the final assault in person (which was actually done by Pettyward who was killed in doing so) and to have murdered his prisoners, choosing four with the most human faces [to be kept captive]. I believe this to be a lie. But he did brilliantly.'
5. 'I regard my posting to the Depot as unprecedented in the history of the Brigade and only explicable on grounds of personal malice' (letter of 19 July 1943, *D* 544). For other Commandos' views, see *Liquidated!* 241.
6. My italics. The letter, dated 30 July 1943, titled 'COPY CON-FIDENTIAL', and addressed to Vice-Admiral the Lord Louis Mountbatten, is now in Alexander Waugh's archive. I am indebted to him and Donat Gallagher for information about it, and access to its text.
7. War Secretary 1935, First Lord of the Admiralty 1937. Resigned after Munich Agreement 1938, Minister of Information 1940, British Ambassador to France 1944.
8. Lovat to M. Davie, the editor of the *Diaries*: 'I do not think [Laycock] had any intention of having Waugh back on his staff where he was the cause of constant trouble' (*D* 545 n.1). Gallagher points out that Laycock's thrice repeated arrangements to have Waugh join him on Husky indicate otherwise. In the same communication to Davie, Lovat claims that Waugh spent the majority of his compassionate leave 'at the bar at White's', another fabrication accepted and even exaggerated by Waugh's later biographers. Gallagher (*Liquidated!* n. 33) cites Lovat's three versions of what happened: his letter to Davie (28 October 1975), his memoir, *March Past* (London 1978), and his interview in Nicholas Shakespeare's *The Waugh Trilogy*, Part II, 'Mayfair and the Jungle', Arena, BBC 2, 19 April 1987, Post-production script, 27–32. Thus Lovat's unreliable recollections date from 32 to 44 years after the events to which they refer. All are after Waugh's death.

9. See Appendix B, *Laycock, Ivor Claire and Mrs Stitch*, p. 279.
10. Letter to Laycock, copied in *D* 544. 'Shimi has alienated the affection of the entire brigade by a series of astoundingly caddish actions', his 'successful and dastardly attack' on Waugh and a fellow officer were all recorded in May and June 1943, as they occurred (*D* 537, 539).
11. 'The Brigadier [...] is leaving in disgrace having quarrelled with everyone. With him the last relic of the spirit of the original brigade seems to be gone'. Morford was sympathetic to Waugh's attempts to gain promotion but warned him that 'I was only suitable to command [a company] in battle' (*D* 519). http://genealogy.kirk patrickaustralian.com/archives/getperson.php?personID=I8504 &tree=TKA adds St Clare-Morford's secondment to India to his record.
12. *Baltimore Evening Sun*, 8 February 1949, 21. See John McGinty and Jeffrey Manley: '"Something Entirely Unique"': Evelyn Waugh's 1948–9 Tours of North America, Part 3, Baltimore', *Evelyn Waugh Studies*, vol. 44 no. 2 (Autumn 2013), 5–6.
13. *L* 197. See Gallagher's authoritative account of Waugh's work in Yugoslavia for an independent local corroboration of Waugh's self-assessment. 'Civil Waugh in Yugoslavia' in Gallagher and Flor: *In the Picture*, pp. 264–5 and n.29.
14. 'Maclean dour, unprincipled, ambitious, probably very wicked; shaved head and devil's ears. I read his reports in one of which he quoted Lawrence of Arabia saying it was a victory to make a province suffer for freedom' (*D* 571); 'Constantius Chlorus of course is Fitzroy Maclean' (*Wu/Stitch* 83).

CHAPTER 15. *UNCONDITIONAL SURRENDER* AND *SWORD OF HONOUR*

1. The Lateran Treaty (1929) created the State of the Vatican City and guaranteed the independent sovereignty of the Holy See. It also regularized relations between the Catholic Church and the Italian State, making Catholicism the national religion taught in all its schools. This resolved the tensions existent since the mid-nineteenth century, when the Papal States resisted incorporation in the newly unified Italy, and 'sulked'.
2. 'And I will restore to you the years that the locust hath eaten, the cankerworm, and the caterpillar, and the palmerworm...' Joel 2.25.
3. *US* 22; *Time and Tide* 24 (November 6, 1943), 912. See Davis: *EW, Writer* 311, n.22. Waugh told his researcher he was particularly

interested in the sword's 'ecclesiastical status. E.g. was it blessed?' How did it come to be displayed in Westminster Abbey? Was it debated in Parliament? 'There should be surviving Canons who have some memory of how the sword came to be exposed there' (*L* 539).

4. *EAR* 206. Ironically, this is also the opening premise of Wallace's speech, officially titled *The Price of Free World Victory*: 'The idea of freedom [...] is derived from the Bible, with its extraordinary emphasis on the dignity of the individual. Democracy is the only true expression of Christianity.' However, the thrust of his speech is a general call to arms in defence of the democratic freedoms won by revolution in America, Russia, and China, couched in a terminology of 'the people's revolution' clearly designed to placate his Soviet ally.

5. *EAR* 206; final quotation in this paragraph from *Frankly Speaking*. See pp. 73–4 and 202.

6. J. H. Wilson (in a personal communication) links this speech to a conversation between Churchill and Fitzroy Maclean in Cairo in December 1943. According to Maclean, Churchill made clear that the Partisans would be intent on establishing a Soviet-style regime with close ties to the USSR, and went on: '"Do you intend to make Jugoslavia your home after the war?" "No, Sir," I replied. "Neither do I," he said. "And, that being so, the less you and I worry about the form of Government they set up, the better. That is for them to decide. What interests us is, which of them is doing more harm to the Germans." I felt convinced that this was the right decision.' Fitzroy Maclean: *Eastern Approaches* (1949; repr. London: Penguin, 1991) 402–3.

7. Waugh added 'though he did not know it' to the 'Compassion' text in *Unconditional Surrender*. He may be referring specifically to the Bleiburg repatriations to Yugoslavia in May 1945, a massacre whose full extent continued to emerge in the decades after the war and even beyond Waugh's death.

8. In *US* Ludovic and Sir Ralph 'were no longer on the old easy terms'. With Ludovic's improved status (decorated for bravery after the fall of Crete), 'he did not look for money, but there were other uses to which their old association could be put'. They meet at Sir Ralph's 'old place of assignation', rooms that were once 'a secret known to barely fifty men' (*US* 34–5).

9. Quotation taken from Stannard II, 89.

10. See *Mitford/Waugh*, indexed under Janetta Woolley.

11. Logan Pearsall Smith (1865–1946) was best known for his aphoristic epigrams and painstaking habits of composition. Like Sir Ralph, he employed a succession of young male secretary-companions,

including the young Connolly, who was influenced by him.

12. 'Like the beat beat beat of the tom-tom / When the jungle shadows fall / [...] /So a voice within me keeps repeating / You you you // Night and day, you are the one / Only you beneath the moon and under the sun ... ' Lyrics by Cole Porter.

13. To his agent, A. D. Peters: 'I don't think the last 1/3 as good as the first 2/3' (*L* 564). Earlier he told Ann Fleming that this sequel to the preceding two volumes 'is quite unintelligible to anyone who doesn't know them by heart. I have to keep dipping into them to find out what I wrote seven or eight years ago' (*L* 548).

14. Keats to J. H. Reynolds, 3 February 1818: 'We hate poetry that has a palpable design on us'.

15. (*Hamlet* V.ii.211–2). For Mr Goodall, see p. 166. He refers to the Biblical text lying behind Hamlet's words.

16. Readers interested in this plot will find it brilliantly reworked in Piers Paul Read's *The Misogynist* (London: Bloomsbury, 2010).

17. The best answer to accusations of Waugh's snobbery comes in the warm family portrait given by Vera Grother, the daughter of a Durham coal-miner, who came straight from convent school in 1945 to look after Waugh's five children, and remained with them for 39 years, and her fellow servant Jean Gabb. On Vera's first arrival at Piers Court she was surprised by the children's 'little sandaled feet, no socks, and their mother in cotton jeans and a man's shirt [...] lovely, beautifully mannered little children with very few personal possessions [...] the first impressions you see were of really I was coming to what I had just left.' Waugh invited her eighty-year-old father, and mother, to visit them, and 'the first thing Mr Waugh did, was take my father up the Bristol Channel to get to know him on a cruiser [...] and Mr Waugh tells me afterwards [...] he was so kind, he said, you realise your father with opportunities would have gone to Oxford like me.' [...] *NS*: 'You were accepted as part of the family? *Vera*: 'Yes, really, to this day we would say that we never ever felt unequal to the family.' (*NS Interviews, Jean Gabb & Vera Grother*, 360–81).

18. *Paradise Lost* II.555–6; *Hamlet* V.ii. 10–11, 211–12, *All's Well that Ends Well*: I.i.203–4.

19. From 'Courtesy', a poem by Hilaire Belloc (1870–1953), a fellow-Catholic author whom Waugh knew well.

20. 'Leaf-catching with Laura' (*D* 410). Eight years later, in a lonely letter from Yugoslavia, he asks her 'Do you remember our catching leaves in the beech avenue at Mells?' (*L* 189) Broome is clearly the Asquiths' home at Mells, a favourite retreat for Waugh.

21. See *A Bitter Trial: Evelyn Waugh and John Carmel Cardinal Heenan on the Liturgical Changes*, ed. Scott M. P. Reid (Home Farm, Curdridge:

The Saint Austin Press, 1996). This excellent compilation brings both sides of Waugh's unpublished correspondence with Cardinal Heenan together with brief extracts from their public pronouncements, Waugh's diaries and his letters. Waugh was profoundly disappointed by Heenan's failure to modify the changes that were ratified in 1965. In 1971 – too late for Waugh – Heenan successfully petitioned Pope Paul VI to permit the celebration of Latin Mass in particular circumstances. It continues to flourish today.

22. *NS Interviews: Harriet Waugh*, 78.
23. *A Bitter Trial*, 52. Final quotation, ibid 66.

APPENDIX B

1. Citations from *The Letters of Ann Fleming*, ed. Mark Amory (London: Collins Harvill, 1985), 155–6 (6–12 July 1955) and *D* 728.
2. Gallagher: *Disillusion*, 202 and 217, n. 182.
3. In Waugh's fiction 'fly', meaning 'lucky', with negative connotations of covert self-interest, first appeared in *Charles Ryder's Schooldays* (begun and abandoned in 1945), where it is unjustly applied to the unpopular O'Malley. See Evelyn Waugh: *The Complete Short Stories*, ed. A. Pasternak Slater (London: Everyman's Library, 1998), 325.
4. Summarized in 'Reckoning', *Disillusion*, 200–02.

Select Bibliography

Waugh's first editions were published by Chapman and Hall, London, unless otherwise specified.

WORKS BY EVELYN WAUGH

A Little Learning, The First Volume of an Autobiography (1964)
Black Mischief (1932)
Brideshead Revisited (Revised Uniform Edition, 1960)
The Complete Short Stories, ed. A. Pasternak Slater (London: Everyman's Library, 1998)
Decline and Fall (1928)
The Diaries of Evelyn Waugh, ed. Michael Davie (London: Weidenfeld & Nicolson, 1980)
The Essays, Articles and Reviews of Evelyn Waugh ed. Donat Gallagher (London: Methuen, 1983)
A Handful of Dust (1934)
Helena (1950)
The Holy Places (London: Queen Anne Press, 1952)
Labels, A Mediterranean Journal (London: Duckworth, 1930)
The Letters of Evelyn Waugh, ed. Mark Amory (London: Weidenfeld & Nicolson, 1980)
The Loved One (1948)
Men At Arms (1952)
Ninety-Two Days (London: Duckworth, 1934)
Officers and Gentlemen (1955)
The Ordeal of Gilbert Pinfold (1957)
Put Out More Flags (1942)
Remote People (London: Duckworth, 1931)
Robbery Under Law, The Mexican Object Question (1939)
Rossetti, His Life and Works (1928, repr. London: Duckworth, 1975)

Scoop: A Novel About Journalists (1938)
Sword of Honour: A Final Version of the Novels: Men At Arms, Officers and Gentlemen, and Unconditional Surrender (1965)
Unconditional Surrender (1961)
Vile Bodies (1930)
Waugh in Abyssinia (London: Longman, Green & Co, 1936)
Work Suspended (1942)

OTHER RELATED WORKS

Cooper, Artemis (ed.), *Mr Wu and Mrs Stitch: The Letters of Evelyn Waugh and Diana Cooper* (London: Hodder and Stoughton, 1991)
Davis, R. M., Doyle, P. A., Gallagher, D., Linck, C. E., Bogaards, W. M., *A Bibliography of Evelyn Waugh* (New York: Whitston, 1986)
Davis, R. M., *A Catalogue of the Evelyn Waugh Collection* (New York: Whitston, 1981)
———, *Evelyn Waugh, Writer* (Norman, Oklahoma: Pilgrim Books, 1981)
Donaldson, Frances, *Portrait of a Country Neighbour* (London: Weidenfeld & Nicolson, 1976)
Gallagher, D. (ed.), 'Memorandum on *Brideshead*' (1947) and 'Memorandum on *Scoop* (1957) in 'Notes on the Film Adaptations of *Brideshead Revisited* and *Scoop*', *Areté* 14 (Summer 2004), 19–29
———, '"I am Trimmer, you know..." Lord Lovat in Evelyn Waugh's *Sword of Honour*', *Evelyn Waugh Newsletter and Studies* 41 (2) (2010), 2–6
———, 'Guy Crouchback's Disillusion: Crete, Beevor and the Soviet Alliance in *Sword of Honour*', in D. Gallagher, A. Pasternak Slater and J. H. Wilson (eds) '*A Handful of Mischief*': *New Essays on Evelyn Waugh* (Madison: Fairleigh Dickinson University Press, 2011), 172–219
Gallagher, D. and Villar Flor, C., *In the Picture: The Facts Behind the Fiction in Evelyn Waugh's 'Sword of Honour'* (Amsterdam and New York: Rodopi, 2014)
Hastings, Selina, *Evelyn Waugh: A Biography* (London: Sinclair-Stevenson, 1994)
Mosley, Charlotte (ed.), *The Letters of Nancy Mitford and Evelyn Waugh* (London: Hodder & Stoughton, 1996)
Patey, D. L., *The Life of Evelyn Waugh: A Critical Biography* (Oxford: Blackwell, 1998)
Shakespeare, Nicholas, Pre-production transcript of twenty-one interviews for Nicholas Shakespeare's 3-part biography, *The Waugh Trilogy*, Arena BBC 2 (1988)
Stannard, Martin (ed.), *Evelyn Waugh: The Critical Heritage* (London: Routledge & Kegan Paul, 1984)

————, *Evelyn Waugh: The Early Years 1903–1939* (London: Dent, 1986)

————, *Evelyn Waugh: No Abiding City 1939–1966* (London: Dent, 1992, repr. Glasgow: HarperCollins, 1993)

Stopp, F. J., *Evelyn Waugh: Portrait of an Artist* (London: Chapman & Hall, 1958)

Sykes, Christopher, *Evelyn Waugh: A Biography* (London: Collins, 1975)

Index

Printed and bound by CPI Group (UK) Ltd, Croydon, CR0 4YY

13/04/2025

14656587-0004